The Olympic Games:

A Social Science Perspective

The Olympic Games:
A Social Science Perspective

Second Edition

Kristine Toohey
Griffith University, Australia

and

A. J. Veal
University of Technology, Sydney, Australia

www.cabi.org

CABI is a trading name of CAB International

CABI Head Office
Nosworthy Way
Wallingford
Oxfordshire OX10 8DE
UK

Tel: +44 (0)1491 832111
Fax: +44 (0)1491 833508
E-mail: cabi@cabi.org
Website: www.cabi.org

CABI North American Office
875 Massachusetts Avenue
7th Floor
Cambridge, MA 02139
USA

Tel: +1 617 395 4056
Fax: +1 617 354 6875
E-mail: cabi-nao@cabi.org

A catalogue record for this book is available from the British Library, London, UK.

Library of Congress Cataloging-in-Publication Data

Toohey, Kristine.
　　The Olympic Games : a social science perspective / Kristine Toohey and A.J.
　　Veal. - 2nd ed.
　　　　p. cm.
　　Includes bibliographical references and index.
　　ISBN 978-0-85199-809-1 (alk. paper)
　　1. Olympics--Social aspects. 2. Olympics--History. I. Veal, Anthony James. II.
　　Title.
　　GV721.5.T64 2007
　　796.48-dc22　　　　　2007025556

ISBN-13:　978 1 84593 346 3 (hardback)
ISBN-13:　978 0 85199 809 1 (paperback)

Printed and bound in the UK by Biddles Ltd, King's Lynn, Norfolk

Contents

List of tables

List of figures

List of abbreviations

AAFLA   Amateur Athletics Federation of Los Angeles (now LA84 Foundation)
ACOG   Atlanta Committee for the Olympic Games
AOC   Australian Olympic Committee
ATHOC   Athens Olympic Committee
BOCOG   Beijing Organising Committee for the Olympic Games
CAS   Court of Arbitration for Sport
COOB'92 Barcelona Olympic Organising Committee
DCMS   Department of Culture, Media and Sport (UK)
EPO   erythropoietin (a human growth hormone)
FIS   Fédération Internationale de Ski
IAAF   International Amateur Athletics Federation
IF   International (Sport) Federation
IOA   International Olympic Academy
IOC   International Olympic Committee
IPC   International Paralympic Committee
LOCOG   London Organising Committee for the Olympic Games
NOC   National Olympic Committee
NPC   National Paralympic Committee
OCA   Olympic Coordination Authority (Sydney)
OCOG   Organising Committee for the Olympic Games
ODA   Olympic Development Authority (London)
OGGI   Olympic Games Global Impact
ONDCP   Office of National Drug Control Policy (USA)
SLOC   Salt Lake Organising Committee
SOBO   Sydney Olympic Broadcasting Organization
SOCOG   Sydney Organising Committee for the Olympic Games
THG   tetrahydrogestrinone (a synthetic steroid)
TOP   The Olympic Programme/Partners
USADA   US Anti-Doping Agency
USOC   United States Olympic Committee
WADA   World Anti-Doping Agency

Preface

The first edition of this book arose as a result of the decision of the International Olympic Committee, in September 1993, to award the Games of the XXVII Olympiad to Sydney, Australia. The announcement prompted us to develop undergraduate and postgraduate courses on the Olympic Games in the School of Leisure, Sport and Tourism at the University of Technology, Sydney (UTS). A considerable amount of research and teaching activity was subsequently developed at UTS, on the Olympic Games generally and on Sydney 2000 specifically. A book seemed a natural progression and it was published in early 2000.

Despite the controversies which enveloped the International Olympic Committee in 1998/99, there is no sign of the Olympic Games fading in terms of their sporting, cultural and economic significance. From their origins in ancient Greece, during their revival at the end of the nineteenth century and through most of their twentieth and twenty-first century existence, the Olympic Games have been more than just another sporting event. There is, consequently, an enormous and varied literature available on the Olympic Games. In the mid-1990s we noted that there was, however, no up-to-date publication which sought to provide a broad, independent, multi-disciplinary account and analysis of the Olympic phenomenon. This book was designed to fill that gap in the literature. It was not possible to provide the definitive analysis of a phenomenon as complex as the Olympic Games in a single, short, book: what we aimed to do was to provide an introduction to the various ways in which the Games have been analysed and to raise issues and provide pointers to further study. The 'social science approach' was not intended to involve a heavily theoretical perspective, but rather to reflect the range of interests which observers with a social scientific outlook had, and continued to have, in the Games.

The second edition of the book updates the first edition in relation to the burgeoning research literature and in relation to Olympic Games and other international sporting events of the last 5–6 years. While the first edition was published in a relatively expensive hardback format, the new edition is being made available as a paperback, to make it affordable for students studying in the growing number of university courses on the Olympic Games. To this end, study questions have been added at the end of most chapters and a supporting website is available at: www.business.uts.edu.au/lst/books.

As part of the process of developing this book we assembled a substantial bibliography on the Olympic Games, much of which is included in the references section of the book. The full bibliography is, however, considerably more extensive and is being continually updated. It is available online at: www.business.uts.edu.au/lst/research/bibliographies.html.

K.T.
A.J.V

Sydney
September 2007

Chapter 1

Introduction: Studying the Olympic Games

> Olympism is a philosophy of life, exalting and combining in a balanced whole the qualities of body, will and mind. Blending sport with culture and education, Olympism seeks to create a way of life based on the joy of effort, the educational value of good example and respect for universal fundamental ethical principles.
>
> – *The Olympic Charter* (IOC, 2004: 9)

> The primary aim of the organisers of sports or Olympic competitions is not sport for its own sake but sport for capitalist profit; or rather, their aim is capitalist profit through sport. – Jean-Marie Brohm (1978: 137)

The phenomenon of the Olympic Games

Every four years, in recent decades, some 10,000 athletes from 200 countries, with a similar number of coaches and officials, as many as 15,000 accredited media representatives and hundreds of thousands of spectators have gathered for more than two weeks to participate in, report on and watch a sporting event which is in turn viewed on television, listened to on radio, read about in the print media and followed on the Internet by billions of people around the world. Each Games has cost enormous sums of money to stage, funded from taxpayers, sponsors and television companies and their advertisers. Sporting records have invariably been broken and national and international heroes created. It is the world's biggest peace-time event: the Summer Olympic Games. These games are followed a couple of weeks later, in the same city, by the Paralympic Games, involving almost 4000 athletes with a variety of disabilities from 136 countries. Two years after each summer Olympic Games the Winter Olympics are held, involving over 2000 athletes from 70 countries and the corresponding Winter Paralympic Games attract almost 500 athletes from 40 countries.

The history of the Olympic Games begins at least 3000 years ago in Ancient Greece. In their ancient form, while they celebrated physical excellence, the Games served a primarily religious purpose. In their modern form, while still ostensibly about physical excellence, they also play a cultural and economic, and often political, role.

The history and global significance of the Games, in sporting, cultural, economic and political terms, therefore justifies their serious consideration as an object of academic enquiry.

The Olympic Games as an object of academic enquiry

The academic literature on both the ancient and the modern Games is massive and growing – an online, English-language, bibliography of mainly academic research on the Games currently runs to some 1800 items (see Veal and Toohey, 2007). A number of research centres has been established around the world, mostly in universities, specifically to foster research on the Olympic phenomenon, including:[1]

- the Olympic Studies Centre at the Olympic Museum in Lausanne, Switzerland;
- the International Centre for Olympic Studies at the University of Western Ontario, Canada;
- the Centre d'Estudis Olímpics at the Universitat Autónoma de Barcelona, Spain;
- the Australian Centre for Olympic Studies at the University of Technology, Sydney, Australia; and
- the Centre for Olympic Studies and Research at Loughborough University, UK.

Across the world, there is now a body of 'Olympic scholars', much of whose work is listed in the bibliography of this book and in the aforementioned online bibliography. Many are listed in the register maintained on the website of the Barcelona centre mentioned above. An academic journal, *Olympika*, is published by the University of Western Ontario centre mentioned above, and many universities offer units of study on the Olympic Games as part of sport management, event management or human movement degrees.

Before embarking on our own review and analysis of the Olympic Games, we examine, in broad terms, the nature and scope of Olympic research and serious commentary to date. This examination is presented under two headings: disciplinary perspectives and paradigms.

Disciplinary perspectives

Most social science disciplines and sub-disciplines have something to offer in the study of the Olympic Games, including history, economics, politics and sociology.

Historians are, not surprisingly, the largest single group of contributors to the research literature on the Olympics. History is, admittedly, generally seen as part of the humanities rather than the social sciences, with which this book is primarily concerned, but historical work on the modern Games is frequently concerned with social issues, such as the changing status of women, issues of race and community politics, and the costs and benefits of the Games, so that sociological and economic dimensions of historical events are often to the fore.

Economic analysis of the Games has become increasingly common with their growing scale and costs. It focuses on such issues as the sources of funding of individual Games and their economic impact on the host city or nation, the funding of the International Olympic Committee (IOC) and the remuneration of athletes.

Politics, political analysis and political debate are never far away from any consideration of the Olympic Games since, while in principle, according to the rhetoric of the International Olympic Committee, athletes who participate in the Games represent just themselves and the 'youth of the world', in practice they represent individual nation states.

As a field of economic enquiry, *political economy* preceded the separate disciplines of economics and political science. As the name implies, political economy covers aspects of both economics and politics and, to some extent, sociology. The works of some of the great social thinkers of the eighteenth and nineteenth century can best be described as political economy. The most notable of these, as far as Olympic Games research is concerned, is Karl Marx. Marx himself died in 1883, so did not write on the modern Olympic Games, but a number of contemporary Marxists or neo-Marxists have done so. These are referred to particularly in Chapter 6.

Sociological perspectives arise from such considerations as the question of gender and racial equity in involvement with the Games, assessing the cultural significance of the Games and the role of the media in shaping and portraying their cultural dimensions. Some of the research and commentary in this area falls into the specialist fields of cultural studies and media studies.

Disciplines provide one way of categorising research on the Olympic Games and they have largely determined the range of topics selected for study, the theoretical frameworks brought to bear on a topic and the research methods used. While much of the research on the Olympic Games has a single disciplinary perspective, particular topics can be seen as multi-disciplinary or inter-disciplinary in nature. For example, examining the issue of drug abuse in the Olympic Games, and in sport generally, involves a range of perspectives, including medical sciences, psychology, sociology, economics and politics. Examining the legacy of the Games in a single host city involves historical, economic, sociological and political analysis (see, for example, Cashman, 2006).

In contrast to most of the existing scholarly publications on the Olympic Games, which have been primarily historical or concerned with a single perspective, such as politics or the media, the aim of this book is to encompass all of these dimensions, at least at an introductory level. We seek to provide an overview of the basic socio-cultural dimensions of the Games from both contemporary and historical perspectives. Because of the breadth of coverage attempted, the book does not deal with any one issue in great depth: it seeks to pose questions, examine issues and provide the reader with information and sources for further reading and study.

Paradigms

Cutting across disciplinary categorisations are *paradigms* or ways of conceptualising and analysing phenomena. We have selected three paradigms which, we believe, between them encompass the bulk of Olympic Games research. They are: a descriptive/pragmatic paradigm; a critical paradigm; and a managerialist paradigm. Each of these is briefly described below.

Descriptive/pragmatic paradigm

Much historical research has been conducted within what we have termed the *descriptive/pragmatic* paradigm. Olympic historians in particular have documented and analysed the ancient and modern Olympic phenomena, with a number of alternative goals and outcomes:

- to fill in gaps in the record, in a purely descriptive way;
- to debunk myths about the Games – in the interest of truth;
- to draw out thematic issues.

Critical paradigm

In research adopting the critical paradigm, analysis of the Games is set within a broader agenda or 'project' which is critical of society from one or more perspectives. The Games and their organisers are then seen as complicit in, hi-jacked by, or the victims of, particular social, economic or political interests or forces. Four types of critical paradigm can be identified as follows.

- *Neo-marxist* – this sees the world, including modern sport and high profile events such as the Olympic Games, as being under the hegemonic control of international capital and business in the interest of the pursuit of profit, to the disadvantage of the mass of people and arguably counter to declared Olympic ideals.
- *Feminist* – sees society, including sport and the Olympic Games, as being dominated and controlled by men in the interests of men and to the disadvantage of women.
- *Environmental* – this paradigm is critical of the materialism of contemporary society and its wasteful and environmentally unsustainable practices; development of infrastructure for the Olympic Games in some host cities has been criticised for not adhering to the 'green' principles declared by the International Olympic Committee.
- *Communitarian* – this sector of Olympic research is concerned with such issues as: the effect of the Games on disadvantaged groups in host cities; the failure of organisers to gain community support when making bids for and planning infrastructure for the Games; the cost to the public purse in hosting the Games; and the elitism which is seen to pervade the Games in general.
- *Ethnic/cultural* – this perspective is critical of the Olympic Movement on grounds of its Eurocentric outlook and European-dominated governance.

Managerialist paradigm

In recent years much research has been commissioned by governments and Olympic Games organising committees to investigate the projected and actual economic impact of the Games and academic researchers in areas such as economics, management and marketing have investigated the Games. Two groups within this paradigm can be identified: evaluative and reformist.

1. *Evaluative* research is generally technical in nature and is dominated by economic impact studies. A common aim is to produce estimates of likely impacts in advance of the Games – sometimes as part of the process of deciding whether to bid to host the Games. Other research in this genre is conducted after

the Games, to establish the extent to which they have met their economic, social, environmental or sporting goals.

2. *Reformist* research is more wide-ranging and is concerned with the governance of the games and such things as the effectiveness and legitimacy of the International Olympic Committee and the scale and organisation of individual Games events.

Of course not all research and commentary can be neatly pigeon-holed under just one paradigm: many have features of two or more. At various points in the book reference is made to these paradigms. Most chapters include references to one or more of the three major paradigms. It is hoped that this will provide a measure of coherence for the reader and assist in making sense of the many diverse contributions to Olympic studies.

Structure of the book

Chapter 2 provides an historical introduction to the original Olympic Games, of Ancient Greece. The Games of the classical era were the source of inspiration for the modern revival of the Games in the late nineteenth century, but the precise nature of those ancient celebrations, which lasted for over a thousand years, is the subject of on-going research, including continuing excavations at the ancient site of Olympia.

Chapter 3 examines the events leading to the modern revival of the Games in Athens in 1896, while noting that this was by no means the first attempt to revive the Olympics. The revival of the Games at this time was not an isolated event, but was associated with enormous changes which had been taking place in sport and indeed in the wider economy and culture during the second half of the nineteenth century.

Chapter 4 presents an overview of the modern Olympics. It focuses particularly on the philosophy and *modus operandi* of the International Olympic Committee, noting the criticisms which this unique body has attracted over the years, many of which were seen to have been vindicated by the scandals which erupted in 1998–1999. The complex worldwide 'Olympic Movement' is examined in this chapter, including: the phenomenon of 'Olympism'; the structure and functioning of the International Olympic Committee; and the roles of National Olympic Committees and International Sport Federations. In addition the Winter Olympics, the Cultural Olympiad, the Paralympic Games and similar international sporting events are examined briefly.

Chapter 5 analyses the issues of politics and nationalism, which permeate the Olympic phenomenon. While sport is widely promoted as being 'beyond politics', the chapter examines six different forms of political intervention in the Games, from international terrorism to local pork-barrelling, illustrating the fact that, far from being 'above politics', sport, and the Olympic Games in particular, are quint-essentially political. They have been used to promote political philosophies and to support sectarian and national political goals. They have themselves been subject to political intrigue, and they have been caught up in many of the major international political events of the last 100 years. The chapter examines the bribery scandals which surrounded the International Olympic Committee in 1989/90, and their aftermath.

Chapter 6 considers the economic and financial dimensions of the Olympics. First the question of 'political economy' is addressed – in particular the questions which increased funding, commercialisation, sponsorship and professionalisation raise about the role of the Games in the wider economic and political world order. As the second quotation at the head of this chapter illustrates, there is no consensus on such issues. Second, the funding of the IOC is examined, noting its transformation from an insignificant and somewhat impoverished organisation up until the 1970s, to the high-profile, relatively wealthy institution we know today. Finally the chapter examines the financing of individual Games and the measurement of their economic impact on host communities.

Chapter 7 reviews the role the media play in funding the Games and in bringing them to the world. The advent of satellite communication has ensured that the role played by the mass communication media has become the single most significant feature which distinguishes the Games of the last three or four decades from those held earlier. It is the billions of dollars generated from television advertising which transformed the Olympic Games in the last quarter of the twentieth century. Millions of sports enthusiasts may feel that they have a close and intimate knowledge of the Olympic Games, but this is entirely based on print and electronic messages filtered by reporters, editors and producers. The chapter therefore addresses the issue of the extent to which the role of the mass media is simply that of passive communicator, and the extent to which media organisations use their editorial and financial power to influence the actual and perceived nature of the Games.

Chapter 8 examines the history of performance-enhancing drug use at the Olympics. The problem of doping at times dominates coverage of international sport, both at the Olympics and elsewhere. Drug scandals have threatened the very future of the Olympic Games. With the IOC occupying a key position in the international 'war against drugs' in sport, the chapter discusses the complex issues which the practice raises and the past, current and future role of the IOC in seeking to eradicate doping from sport.

Chapter 9 examines the history of women's involvement and non-involvement in the Games and considers the equity issues raised by continued discrimination against women in the Olympics. Women played no direct part in the sporting aspects of the ancient Olympic Games, or in the initial celebrations of the modern Games. While women have participated in the Games since 1904, they still account for less than 40 per cent of the participants. The chapter notes that the reasons for the restricted role of women are shrouded in myth, intrigue and backroom politics. It provides a case-study of the experience of one female Olympian who chose to challenge authority.

Chapter 10 examines four recent Summer Olympic Games (Barcelona, Atlanta, Sydney and Athens) as case-studies, and presents a forward look at Beijing 2008 and London 2012. These case-studies demonstrate that, despite certain similarities, each celebration of the Olympic Games is unique, reflecting the social, cultural and physical nature of the host country and city, but also the wider global environment of the time. In addition, the chapter includes, in an appendix, a brief overview of each of the Games of the modern era, with a guide to further reading.

Chapter 11 considers the question of the future of the Games: whether they can survive in their current form and whether current trends in the way they are organised can preserve the proclaimed ideals of the Olympic Movement.

The Olympic Games – more than a sporting event

The Olympic Games are no longer – if they ever were – just a sporting event: they are a cultural, political and economic phenomenon. Particular interests see them as a media event, a tourism attraction, a marketing opportunity, a catalyst for urban development and renewal, a city image creator and booster, a vehicle for 'sport for all' campaigns, an inspiration for youth and a force for peace and international understanding. The message of this book is that the Olympic Games do indeed play all these roles, although not always to the extent or in ways that particular interest groups hope or imagine. In fact, it is arguably these added, mainly non-sporting, roles which make the Olympic Games unique, and their continued survival probably depends on their continuing to play these roles.

The quotation from the *Olympic Charter* which opens this chapter demonstrates a number of features of the Olympic Games which, apart from their scale, makes them unique. Other sporting events do not publish manifestoes like the *Olympic Charter* or promulgate a 'philosophy' or 'way of life', with lofty ideals akin to those of a religion, cult or political movement. Neither do other sporting events involve the degree of pomp and ceremonial that surrounds the celebration of each Olympic Games, although it appears that more and more sports are attempting to emulate these features of the Games. The Olympic Games are very much part of contemporary world culture, but they are hung about with a curious, at times archaic, set of 'trappings' from the nineteenth century and, supposedly, from antiquity. While they officially espouse high ideals and values, they are organised by fallible human beings and are faced with a range of worldly problems and challenges which threaten these values, including accusations of excessive commercialisation, and the problems of prohibited drug use, politicisation and corruption.

Because of their history, both ancient and modern, and their size and international reach, there is a widespread sense of public 'ownership' of the Olympic Games which does not extend to other sporting events. As a result, the Games are subject to a level of scrutiny, analysis and debate which, while it may be common for single 'national games' in individual countries, is unique at the international level. Extravagant sentiments and hyperbole which are never expressed about other sporting events are commonly expressed about the Olympic Games. For example, Sir Roger Bannister, the first man to run a mile in under four minutes, Olympic athlete and later British Minister for Sport, in discussing various reforms for the Games in the 1980s, declared:

> Given a move towards the changes that I have suggested, the Olympic Games should remain one of the great hopes of the world. It is in the deepest interests of the future of the world for them to continue. (Bannister, 1988: 425)

John Lucas, Olympic historian, stated:

> I have abiding faith in the *idea* of a near-perfect Olympic Games as a festival of élite sport, as a peace-filled gathering of the human race in a grand union of the beginning and end of life 'through the endurance of affection, of trust, of friendship, and love'. (Lucas, 1992: 215)

Rod McGeoch, who led Sydney's bid for the 2000 Games, stated:

> The 2000 Olympics will be the greatest peacetime event in Australia's history. It will be something that all Australians will never forget. For many people, it will be the greatest moment of their lives; an event which lives on in their memory. .. Australia is a nation which genuinely does stand for the goals and principles which are the very foundations of the [Olympic] movement. ... It will be one of

the most important moments in Australian history when they light the flame at Sydney Olympic Park. (McGeoch and Korporaal, 1994: 307–8)

Such sentiments perhaps explain the sense of outrage when things go wrong, as they did in 1998–1999, or when Olympic Games organisations are found to be no different from other human organisations. Thus Andrew Jennings, trenchant critic of the IOC and its power and abuse of power, states: 'So you thought the Olympics belonged to the world? Wrong. The Olympic Games are *their* exclusive property' (Jennings, 1996: 12). His initial assumption appears to have been that the Games belonged to 'us' in some way, rather than to a self-selected élite, and somewhat secretive organisation. Such sentiments would not often be expressed about other international sports, such as tennis or motor racing.

All this raises our curiosity as to how this unique phenomenon came about, how its constituent elements fit together and combine to create the modern Olympic Games, and whether the Games can possibly meet the many expectations which various stakeholders have for them. This book seeks to explore these issues and throw light on some of the dilemmas. In a rapidly changing world the currency of any writing on social phenomena is fleeting, and the Olympic Games is no exception. As the second century of the modern Olympic Games unfolds, many changes are happening in the Olympic Movement which will ensure that the present soon becomes the distant past and predictions will become reality or mere flights of fancy.

Further reading

Olympic studies	Warning, *et al.* (2001).
Olympic studies centres	See the list of websites in Appendix 1.
Olympic literature	Veal and Toohey (2007).
Disciplinary approaches	Anthropology: MacAloon (1999); economics: Preuss (2004); history: Booth (2004); social psychology: Guttman (1988a); sociology: Krotee (1981).
Paradigms	In social science: Guba (1990); in sport history: Booth (2005a: 13–20); in leisure studies: Lynch & Veal (2006: 87–106).

Notes

1.   The websites for these centres are listed in Appendix 1.

Questions

There are no discussion questions for this chapter, but later chapters include questions or exercises which, in part, draw on the material on disciplines and paradigms introduced in this chapter.

Chapter 2

The Ancient Olympics and their Relevance to the Modern Games

> During the second great Greek revival, 18th- and 19th-century scholars saw what they wished to see regarding life in Ancient Hellas, including the life of the Olympic competitor. That life, seen through the filter of nearly 15 centuries, was frequently described in terms of honour, patriotism, altruism, non-commercial amateur motive, and above all fervent religious belief. – John Lucas (1992: 2–3)

Introduction

One of the reasons why the modern Olympic Games were revived in Athens in 1896 was their founders' perceptions of certain positive values of sport, which they believed were put into practice by Greek athletes in the Ancient Olympics and which they hoped could be transferred to sport in the late nineteenth century. However, not all their information, and hence ideas, about the Greeks and their athletic festivals was accurate. In reality many of the sports contested in the early modern Games had very little in common with their ancient counterpart, and in recent years the difference has been even more pronounced.

According to Poliakoff (1987), the combination of four features of ancient Greek sport make it different to the sports of most other countries and time periods. First, athletics were taken extremely seriously and high achievement resulted in significant honour and status. Second, it was only winning, rather than participation in a contest, that was valued. Thus, at their sporting major festivals, the Panhellenic Games, it was only the victor who received a prize; there were no rewards for coming second. Third, there were no team sports in Panhellenic Games and, last, while it was difficult for members of the lower classes to compete, there were no specific laws or regulations, such as the amateur code, preventing them from doing so.

Yet, for much of their existence, those who have determined the values, rules and regulations of the modern Olympics have based many of their practices on myths about the purity of the Ancient Games, for example the belief that the Games were not subject to political intervention, commercialism or professionalism and that they were exemplars of peace and equality. It appears that such misconceptions about practices and customs of the ancients were not unique to Olympic revivalists. Hegel, in his celebrated treatise, *Reason in History*, notes that:

> in the turmoil of world affairs no universal principle, no memory of similar conditions in the past can help us – a vague memory has no power against the vitality of the present. Nothing is more shallow in this respect than the oft-repeated appeal to Greek and Roman examples. (Hegel, 1953: 8)

This is not to say that the Ancient Olympics were not without merit. Indeed, they have been acknowledged as one of the strongest unifying forces in the ancient Greek world. Like their modern counterpart there were famous instances and practices which exemplified the sporting code of behaviour of the time, just as there were instances of deviance.

In this chapter we discuss first of all the idea of myth and how it relates to what we know about the Ancient Games. Second, a short history of the Ancient Olympic Games is presented, followed by a discussion, in turn, of: the events which made up the Games programme; political aspects of the history of the Ancient Games; the issue of amateurism and professionalism; the role of women; and the eventual demise of the Games.

Myths about the ancient Olympic Games

People seek to make meaning from their existence. Armstrong (2005) notes that myths are not told for their own sake, rather they instruct us on how we should behave. Myths, according to Cheek and Burch, are:

> .. the grammar and rhetoric of the social order. They not only regularise the flow of information, but also convey feelings. In doing this they serve the function of bringing together a select few, while concurrently setting this group apart from others. (Cheek and Burch, 1976: 86)

Roland Barthes, in his seminal work *Mythologies* (1983), would categorise the hegemony of the modern Games founders' views of the Ancient Olympics as an example of a 'bourgeois norm', in that they assumed that their reality was the correct and natural position and, as a consequence of their power and position, their philosophies initially dominated modern Olympic discourse, whether or not they reflected, or were based on a detailed knowledge of, the recorded history of the Ancient Games.

Myths become regulated by rites, rituals and ceremonies, so it is understandable that such practices have become integral to the modern practices of Olympism. Indeed, mythology is usually inseparable from ritual (Armstrong, 2005). This ritualisation in turn becomes embedded in a set of beliefs associated with the myth, so that a paradigm shift occurs and, as a consequence, the myth becomes an 'inherent aspect of social organisation necessary to the regulation of transactions' (Cheek and Burch, 1976: 182). Consequently, the more a myth becomes a constituent of dominant discourse, the harder it is to challenge. While some Olympic myths have been debunked in the last 100 years, others survive, thrive and, even today, shape hegemonic practice and policy in international, and especially Olympic, sports.

In contemporary culture we often use the term 'myth' to describe something that has not occurred. Armstrong (2005), however, argues that a myth is 'true' if it is effective, rather than if it is factual. This has meant that, as the viewpoints of the founders and later powerbrokers of the modern Games became accepted as 'truth', they then defined what was acceptable and, more importantly, unacceptable within the modern Olympic Movement. As the Games evolved and responded to changes in the twentieth century some of these notions have been challenged and replaced. However, myths have often provided the keystone to the structure and rules of the modern Olympics. Changing these hegemonic practices has at times been a slow and acrimonious process. Indeed, some biases which are still evident and contentious in the contemporary Olympic movement, such as the inequitable participation of women (as athletes and as administrators) have these myths as their philosophical basis. Referring to the commonly acknowledged founder of the modern Games, Baron Pierre de Coubertin, John Lucas states that:

> the core of de Coubertin's philosophy is still a part of Olympic ideology and will probably persist for many years. ... Anyone in today's late 20th century who believes that this kind of thinking has been purged from the minds of people connected with the worldwide Olympic Movement is very much mistaken. (Lucas, 1992: 4)

Hoberman (1986: 1) is less diplomatic about the International Olympic Committee (IOC): 'the Olympic movement does not just overcome its history: it has demonstrated a prodigious ability to forget it'.

A short history of the ancient Olympic Games

While the earliest remaining records of the Olympic Games indicate that they were held as early as 776 BC, and celebrated once every four years, during the second or third full moon after the summer solstice, the beginning of the games is unclear and, as Golden (1998) notes, shrouded in legend. The earliest mention of their foundation is found in the writings of Pindar. He attributed their origin to Heracles who, on his return from victory over King Augeas of Elis, founded the games at the tomb of Pelops (Mouratidis, 1984). Other authors suggest that it was Pelops who was the founder, or Oenomaus, King of Pisa (Golden, 1998). It was not until the 50th Olympiad that there is evidence that the Games honoured Zeus, to whom they are later unquestionably linked (Mouratidis, 1984). Regardless of their beginnings, 'the Greeks located the origin of the Olympic Games squarely in the sphere of the divine; gods and heroes found and compete in them as well as simply receiving worship (Golden, 1998: 14).

At their zenith the Olympic Games lasted for five days, as shown in Table 2.1. They continued to be celebrated until AD 393, when the Roman Emperor, Theodosius I, a Christian, abolished them because of their links to Zeus. This association meant that their rituals and practices were considered pagan and counter to the new Christian religion of the Roman Empire, which at this time encompassed Greek territory.

When the Games are thought to have begun, Greek society was pre-eminent in the Ancient world. Yet, within the area known today as Greece, there was no such thing as a central government, or indeed even a Greek nation. Rather, the region referred to as Ancient Greece was a collection of city states, called *polis*, some of which, at various times, engaged in wars against each other, as well as at other times uniting against common enemies. What united and signified the Greeks was a common

Table 2.1. The Ancient Olympic programme

Day	Time	Event
1	Morning	• swearing-in ceremony • prayers and sacrifices • contest for heralds and trumpeters • boys' wrestling, boxing and running events
	Afternoon	• orations
2	Morning	• chariot and horse races
	Afternoon	• pentathlon
	Night	• funeral rites in honour of Pelops • parade of victors • singing • feast
3	Morning	• procession of competitors and officials • animal sacrifices
	Afternoon	• running races
	Night	• banquet
4	Morning	• wrestling
	Afternoon	• boxing • pankration • hoplite race
5		• crowning of victors • feast and celebration

Adapted from Swaddling (1999: 53).

language and literature, the acceptance of a common ancestry and celebration of sporting festivals. The Olympic Games were the most prestigious of all these sporting festivals. The Athenian orator, Lysias, believed that Heracles founded the Games to promote goodwill and fellowship among the various Greek communities and that the choice of Zeus, as the chief of Greek gods, was similarly motivated, as his following was Hellenic, rather than localised to a specific sub-national region (Mouratidis, 1984). This, of course, also acted to exclude non-Greeks (*barbaroi*) (Golden, 1998). The Games' rise in eminence is closely linked with the ascendancy of Zeus throughout the Greek world.

The two most powerful city states in the ancient Greek world were Athens and Sparta. Yet neither of these important centres hosted one of the four major sporting festivals of the Greeks. These contests, today known as the Panhellenic Games, were held in a four year cycle, which is mirrored in today's Olympic Games. Each of these Panhellenic Games honoured a god, awarded token prizes and was held in a permanent, purpose-built location. They are listed in Table 2.2 in chronological order of their believed starting dates. The Olympic winner received his first award immediately after his event. The winner's name was announced by a herald. One of the judges (*hellanodikai*) then placed a palm tree branch on his hands and red ribbons were tied on his head and hands as a mark of victory. The official award ceremony did not occur until the last day of the Games and was held at the Temple of Zeus. At this, a herald announced the name of the Olympic winner, his father's name and his city. Then, one of the *hellanodikai* placed a sacred olive tree wreath (*kotinos*) on the victor's head. According to Phlegon, a Greek author of the second century AD, the wreath was first instituted at the 752 BC Games, on the advice of the Oracle at Delphi.

Table 2.2. The Panhellenic Games

Games	Location	God honoured	Prize	Frequency
Olympic	Olympia	Zeus	Olive	Every 4 years
Pythian	Delphi	Apollo	Laurel wreath	Every 4 years (3 years after the Olympic Games)
Isthmian	Corinth	Poseidon	Celery	Every 2 years (2nd and 4th year of Olympiads)
Nemean	Nemea	Zeus	Celery, then pine	Every 2 years, as for Isthmian Games

The events

The Olympic Games were the most prestigious of all the festivals. Held in Olympia, (see Figure 2.1) in the Western Peloponnesus, in the city state of Elis, a minor and relatively peaceful *polis*, it is believed that the Games began as a single event, a running race, known as the *stade*. The first known victor, Corobeus of Elis, who won the *stade* race, was a cook. This race, which has obvious links to contemporary use of the word stadium, was the distance of one length of the stadium and finished with the contestants facing the sacred *altis* (altar) as a form of honour to Zeus. All races introduced at later dates finished in the same manner. Thus, even the direction of events was based on religious grounds. Many other aspects and rituals of the games also evolved to honour the Greek gods.

The Olympic Games were originally open only to free born Greek males, who had not been convicted of a crime. Athletes also had to meet other eligibility criteria before being allowed to compete. They were required to swear on slices of boar flesh that they had trained for ten months prior to coming to Olympia and then had to train for one month at Elis under the supervision of the *hellanodikai*. The *hellanodikai* also had an expanded list of functions, some exceeding those of today's Olympic judges. They wore purple robes, had seats on the sidelines (instead of the grass slopes that spectators used) and lived in separate quarters for ten months at Elis. They presented the athletes with their victory wreaths and presided over the final banquet. They also had the power to beat athletes who broke the rules (Golden, 1998).

Although the Ancient Olympics drew crowds of spectators, estimated to be up to 40,000, the facilities were primitive, even by standards of the day. Unlike today's stadia, which are used for many different events, the site at Olympia only saw competitions infrequently; once every four years for the Olympic Games and similarly for the Games of Hera. The latter games were competitions for females, held to honour the goddess Hera, the wife of Zeus. During the intervals between competitions at Olympia, there were only perhaps a few visiting pilgrims and the permanent workers, such as artisans, priests and priestesses, associated with the non-athletic functions of the site. During these extensive breaks, the athletic facilities were, for the most part, deserted and unkempt. One of the first tasks of the Olympic athletes on arrival at the site was to prepare the area for competition. Thus, weeding and other associated chores were expected of competitors. The contrast with today's élite competitors, some of whom no longer even stay in the Olympic Village, but in nearby luxury hotels, is marked. Many of the Greek athletes slept under the stars.

Figure 2.1. Entrance to the Olympic stadium at Olympia

One practical concern during competition was that sanitary conditions were primitive, especially by twentieth century standards, but even in comparison to the Roman stadia, which were in existence in the latter half of the Olympic Games' existence. For example, there were open drains and it was not until the first century AD that the first permanent toilet block for athletes was built at Olympia (Perrottet, 2004). Unlike many other stadia there were few seats at Olympia – hence the word *stadion*, which refers to standing. The majority of spectators sat or stood on the grassy banks which lined the sides of the running track.

Despite their humble beginnings, as the Olympic Games grew in status they became important as a site to demonstrate power and prestige. In a manner similar to some of today's nationalistic and commercial displays of grandeur, the wealthy who attended the Ancient Olympics were sometimes guilty of conspicuous consumption in their attempts to outdo their rivals through their lavish displays of wealth (Swaddling, 1999). In one such example, 'the Syracusan tyrant Dionysius sent several expensive four-horse chariot teams, beautifully decorated tents, and professional actors to recite poetry he himself had written' (Tufts University, 1997a). Another, less prosaic example is offered by Perrottet (2004: 12): 'The squalid tent-city was the scene of a round-the-clock bacchanal where students would squander their inheritances in lavish *symposia* (drinking parties) and prostitutes could make a year's wages in five days'.

During the early Games, however, crowd numbers were relatively small and so, at this point in their history, facilities were in keeping with the nature of the single event. The relative obscurity of the festival changed over time, as did the influence of the event on Greek society. For example, the Greek calendar came to be measured in 'Olympiads'. The term signified four years and was the principle measure of Greek time, although there was disagreement among the Greeks as to when the Olympic year should begin (Golden, 1998). To differentiate Olympiads, each one was named after the winner of the *stade* race, rather than being assigned a numerical symbol as in the modern calendar. Not even the athletes of today are afforded that honour.

The number of events at the Olympic Games increased over time, as shown in Table 2.3. The second event to be added to the Games programme was the two *stade* race, or *dialos*. Athletes began at the *altis* end of the stadium, ran one *stade* away and then turned to finish at the starting line. The Greek historian Philostratis explained the symbolism of this arrangement:

> When the people of Elis had sacrificed, then the ambassadors of the Greeks, whoever happened to be there, were expected to offer a sacrifice. That their approach might not be made without ceremony, runners ran a stade away from the altis as though to invite the Greeks, and back to the same place as though to announce that 'Hellas would be glad to come'. So much then concerning the origins of the two stade race. (Philostratis, 1987: 214)

Table 2.3. Olympic events and their introduction to the Games

Year	No. of games	Events introduced
776 BC	1	Stade
724 BC	14	Diaulos
720 BC	15	Dolichos
708 BC	18	Wrestling and pentathlon
688 BC	23	Boxing
680 BC	25	Chariot race for four horses
648 BC	33	Horse race and pankration
632 BC	37	Stade and wrestling for boys
628 BC	38	Pentathlon for boys (discontinued 628 BC)
616 BC	41	Boxing for boys
520 BC	65	Hoplite race
500 BC	70	Race for mule carts (discontinued 444 BC)
496 BC	71	Race for mares (discontinued 444 BC)
408 BC	93	Chariot race for two horses
396 BC	96	Contest for heralds and trumpeters
384 BC	99	Chariot race for four colts
268 BC	128	Chariot race for two colts
256 BC	131	Colt race
200 BC	145	Pankration for boys

Adapted from Sweet, 1987: 6–7.

Although some details of the events are known or interpreted from writings (such as the above), artefacts and engravings, there are many facets of the Games which are still a mystery. As Golden notes in relation to Ancient Greek sport:

> nothing we read or look or find was produced for our benefit. Whatever we may conclude from the evidence, we may be sure that the Greeks never intended that evidence to be used by us for our purposes. ... Secondly, paradoxically, the evidence is sometimes too close to us. ... Our familiarity with some [athletic] terms and techniques can hinder as well as help. For example, in trying to understand how races began. (Golden, 1998: 47)

One example of the Games which remains unclear is exactly how the foot races were started. The starting lines, which have been excavated, are made of stone, with two parallel grooves running across them (see Figure 2.2). While some scholars believe that there was a starting mechanism, there is no indisputable evidence to determine conclusively how the foot races were started, or indeed how the mechanisms worked. From statues which have been found, for example 'The Runner' (currently in the museum at Olympia), it is believed that runners began from a standing position with their toes in the grooves.

Figure 2.2. Starting grooves in the Olympic stadium at Olympia

The longest foot race, the *dolichos*, was the second known event to be added to the Olympics. Records indicate that it was first held in 720 BC. Scholars believe that it was between 22 to 24 *stades* long (1 *stade* = 192.3 metres) and held entirely in the stadium. Thus, in the Ancient Games, there was no equivalent to the modern marathon event.

An Olympic myth surrounds this, one of the premier events of the modern Games. Even the origin of the legendary Marathon run by Phidippides (a.k.a. Philippedes, Pheidippedes or Phiadiples) is clouded in mythology. According to modern beliefs Phidippides allegedly ran from the plains of Marathon to Athens to announce to the Athenians that their army had defeated the Persians in battle, gave his message and died (Hopkins, 1966). During this battle the Athenians, led by Miltiardes, killed over 6000 Persians while losing only 192 of their own soldiers. Herodotus, the 'father of history', notes this but, like other contemporary accounts, he makes no mention of Phidippides then running to Athens with news of the victory. Instead, he mentions that, before the battle, on behalf of the Athenian army, Phidippides ran to Sparta, a distance of approximately 230 kilometres, in order to seek their assistance in the fight against the Persians. The Spartans' religious practices proscribed their departure until after the full moon and so they declined to assist (Herodotus, 1962). Even this account of Phidippides' run would be regarded suspiciously by modern historians, because of its religious overtones.

> Before they left the city, the generals sent a herald to Sparta: he was Phidippides, an Athenian and moreover, a day-long runner, who made his living in that way. This man, as he himself said and reported to the Athenians, was caught up on the road by Pan. ... This Phidippides, when he was on this errand for the generals and, as he ran, Pan appeared to him, was in Sparta the day after he left the city of the Athenians ... so he delivered the message entrusted to him. (Herodotus, 1962: 105–106)

Herodotus does not mention Phidippides again. Instead, when recording the aftermath of the battle, he describes the Persians' attempts to sail to Athens, attack the city and avenge their defeat. He wrote, 'so they rounded the Cape at Sunium. But the Athenians went as fast as their legs would carry them to the rescue of the city and forestalled the barbarians by getting there first' (Herodotus, 1962: 116).

It is not until the second century AD, in the writings of Lucian of Samosata, that the first mention of Phidippides' alleged run from Marathon to Athens occurs. Lucian refers to the runner as Philippedes in an article, 'A slip of the tongue in salutation', written not as a historical narrative, but rather as an essay dealing with the etymology of the word 'joy'.

> The long-distance runner Philippides is said to have been the first who used this word [rejoice] when he announced the victory to the officials who were sitting in session and were concerned with the outcome of the battle: and with the words 'Rejoice; we have won', he expired with this dying word 'Rejoice'. (Lucian, 1905: 3)

An heroic image of the messenger is at the core of this reference (Sweet, 1987). Thus, the sacrificial aspect of the marathon myth originates in this article (Martin and Gynn, 1979).

Plutarch, another Roman and contemporary of Lucian, also notes a similar event, but his tale describes a run by Euchidas, from Delphi to Plataia in 479 BC (Sweet, 1987). Two other sources from antiquity, Pliny the Elder and Pausanias, both mention Phidippides' run to Sparta, but neither mentions a run to Athens (Martin and Gynn, 1979). Consequently, the legend of Phidippides' run to Athens from Marathon is not found in written sources until 600 years after the event was alleged to have occurred. Given this evidence it is difficult to view Phidippides' run as anything other than a myth, yet a marathon race has been included in all modern Olympic Games and is arguably one of its premier events.

The inclusion of the event in the modern Olympics is credited to Michael Breal, a French contemporary of the modern Games' founder, Pierre de Coubertin, who wrote to him, 'if the Organising Committee of the Olympics would be willing to revive the famous run of the Marathon soldier as part of the programme of the Games I would be willing to offer a prize for this new Marathon race' (Breal, cited in Martin and Gynn, 1979: 5). Also interesting, in the Breal proposal, is the offer of a prize for the victor, a practice contrary to Olympic protocol. Although the Athenian organising committee did not give a special prize for the event, the victor of the 1896 Marathon race, Spyridon Louis, a Greek and the only track and field Olympic victor from his country in the first modern Games, reproduced the practices of his ancient Olympic counterparts in receiving rewards from his victory, if not in terms of contesting such an event. He reputedly received cash and gifts in kind from his grateful government and fellow citizens. Over time, the myth of Phidippides' run from Marathon to Athens has become interwoven into the fabric of the modern Games through the staging of one of the most prestigious events in the Modern Olympics.

Although the marathon has no definite links to the Ancient Olympic Games there are some events held at today's Games which can trace their origins to their ancient counterparts. This occurred because of the growing importance of the Games to Greek society and a consequent diversification of the programme in the sixth century BC. The introduction of pentathlon and wrestling competitions meant that more sporting facilities were needed. The pentathlon consisted of five events: *stade* race; long jump; javelin; discus; and wrestling. During the course of the Ancient Games the long jump and discus were only ever held as part of this contest, while the other components became events in their own right. Like so many other aspects of the Games there is conflicting opinion regarding the order of events for the pentathlon. However, there appears to be consensus on how the winner was chosen. If an athlete won three events then he was crowned the victor. This meant that, theoretically, competition could finish at the conclusion of the third, fourth or fifth event. If there was no absolute winner then a count back system was used to determine the victor.

Exact details of the long jump are sketchy. Records state that one contestant was reported to have jumped 56 feet. Today's world record is only approximately half of this, so it would appear that direct comparisons between the ancient and modern long jump contests would be inappropriate. One reason why results vary may be the fact that the ancient Greek jumpers carried hand weights, called *halteres*, which they jettisoned in mid-flight. This action was designed to increase the distance jumped. Contestants were accompanied by flautists, whose music was deemed to enhance performance through the rhythm of their tunes. Some modern athletes use MP3 players for similar effect during their warm-ups.

The inclusion of the pentathlon and wrestling events heralded the introduction of combative sports into the programme. As with track races, the list of these sports increased as the Games evolved. Later boxing was introduced. Unlike today's boxing there were no weight divisions or rounds. The fights continued until one athlete was declared the winner by the judges, or one competitor indicated that he conceded. This was done by raising an index finger. Spartans, in keeping with their stoic ideals and image of warlike non-compromise, could not compete in these two events lest one of their citizens concede defeat.

The most brutal event at the Ancient Games was arguably the *pankration*. Despite modern notions of the peaceful nature of these Games, winners in this event were also among the most highly rated athletes. A mixture of boxing and wrestling, it was mostly devoid of rules. The only limitations were no eye gouging or biting. Apart from these restrictions it was 'open slather' as, replicating the format of the boxing and wrestling contests, there were neither weight divisions nor rounds.

Figure 2.3. Vase painting of competitors in the Ancient Olympic Games

Events for boys were first held at the Games of 632 BC. To be eligible contestants had to be under 18 as well as qualifying for the standard criteria of citizenship and training.

Not all events had competitions for boys. One event contested only by men was the hoplite race, or race in armour, which was the last running race to be added to the programme. Competitors carried a shield and, at least in the earlier contests, wore a helmet and greaves (leg protectors). The race had obvious connections to military training. Swaddling notes that up to 25 athletes were allowed to enter the event, 'for whom a set of shields was kept in the Temple of Zeus. Presumably this was to ensure that each athlete carried a shield of the same weight' (Swaddling, 1999: 58).

Horse and mule events were not held in the stadium, but in the hippodrome. The site has not been excavated due to extensive flooding, so little is known about the nature of its events. It is estimated that the length of the races was approximately six *stades*.

Chariot races were the first and major horse events at the Games. Chariots had a single axle and were pulled by four or two horses. Charioteers wore a knee length tunic called a *chiton*. Leather thongs were tied around the wrist and chest. Starting procedures for the races were complicated. This was necessitated because all chariots raced the length of the stadium then turned around a single marker. There was a high element of danger in this procedure as chariots were only lightly constructed, usually of wood, and there were many entrants in the races.

History – politics

Another common myth regarding the Ancient Olympics is that a truce was declared throughout the whole of Greece for the duration of the Games and that, becasue of this truce, all wars within Greek territory ceased (Greek Ministry of Culture, 1996). The

IOC and the United Nations both promulgate this belief and use it as part of the justification for a modern Olympic truce, to be declared throughout the world during the Games. However the notion of a complete cessation of hostilities is now disputed. Instead, some scholars claim that, in the spring of every fourth year, heralds (*spondophoroi*) travelled throughout the Greek world proclaiming a truce, in the name of Zeus, only for those spectators and competitors who were travelling to and from the Games. This meant that these travellers had free passage through warring city states (Mandell, 1976a). Golden (1998: 16–17) writes: 'the truce was quite restricted, an armistice (*ekacheiria*), not a period of peace (*eirene*) throughout the Greek world; only open warfare by or against Elis was forbidden. Other wars could (and did) carry on'.

During the zenith of the Ancient Games, in the fifth century BC, the Games remained fairly peaceful. Elis was a small, neutral city state, a lowly position which was orchestrated, to a degree, by the larger city states of Athens and Sparta. The Peloponnesian Wars, however, changed this status, when the Eleans forsook their neutrality and aligned themselves with Athens, banning the common enemy, Sparta, from the Games. According to Swaddling (1999: 99) the Games of 424 BC were held with armed troops present for protection against an attack from the Spartans. Although no skirmishes occurred, such precautions demonstrated that the Olympic truce was no longer held to be inviolate. The city of Syracuse was also banished for the Olympic festival of 480 BC. Later, in 365 BC, 'the Arcadians and Pisatans took over the Altis, and they presided over the 104th Olympiad the next year' (Tufts University, 1997b). During the Games, the Eleans and their allies invaded the sacred site and a pitched battle for control took place (Golden, 1998).When the Eleans finally regained control of Olympia, 'they declared the 104th Games invalid' (Tufts University, 1997b).

Despite these instances of political rivalries, which resulted in violation of the Olympic truce, most acts of violence at Olympia, that had political overtones, occurred later, under the rule of the Romans. By this time Greek interest in the festival had waned and athletes were predominantly professional and known as 'pot hunters' because of the *amphora* (pots) of oil which were often given as prizes to victors. Yet, from the beginning of the modern Games, and for well over 50 years, the idea of professional athletes competing was anathema to the International Olympic Committee.

Amateurism and professionalism

In 416 BC the Athenian Alcibiades complained that the Games were being overtaken by the lower classes. Despite such criticism, free born Greek males who had not committed murder or sacrilege and were registered citizens, were able to enter the Games, no matter what their occupation (Perrottet, 2004). The construction of the concept of amateurism in sport only truly began in the nineteenth century in England, so the fact that there were professionals in the Ancient Olympics was overlooked by the founders of the modern Games in their attempts to stamp the Games with their own élitist values. John Lucas (1992: 5), notes that the term 'amateur athlete' did not even exist in the Greek language. The extent of professionalism in Ancient Greek sport became so strong that, as Coakley comments:

> During the second century BC, these professionals organised athletic guilds similar to the players' associations and unions in today's North American sports. Through these guilds they bargained for athletes' rights and to have a say in the

scheduling of games, travel arrangements, personal amenities, pensions, and old age security in the form of serving as trainers and managers. (Coakley, 1992: 56)

Despite this, the myth of the noble ancient amateur athlete became so interwoven with modern Olympic philosophy that it was cited as a reason to perpetuate the code of amateurism in the Olympics, even when a large number of sports which formed part of the Olympic programme had legitimised professional competitions. Avery Brundage, arguably one of amateurism's most ardent defenders, demonstrating an ignorance of this aspect of Greek history, stated: 'The amateur code, coming to us from antiquity, contributed to and strengthened by the noblest aspirations of great men of each generation, embraces the highest moral laws. No philosophy, no religion, preaches loftier sentiments' (Brundage, in Guttman, 1984: 116).

Coakley (1992: 269) offers an entirely different perspective on why the amateur code was so strictly adhered to, and on its relevance to the modern Games: 'The definition of amateurism used in the Olympic Games worked for many years to the disadvantage of all people who were not white men and members of well-to-do social classes in Western societies'. The citing of amateurism as a practice in Greek athletics is another example of the use of a myth to perpetuate hegemonic twentieth century Olympic practices.

Finding a balance between sport for sport's sake and sport as a means to earn money was problematic for the Ancient Greeks. For example, the increasing nature of professionalism was a vexed issued for some writers. In the fifth century BC one such critic of professionalism in sport was Xenephanes, who believed that prize money in athletics was altering the nature of sport from its true goal, namely, the training of youth. Another criticism levelled at athletes related to the degree of specialisation that was beginning to occur. Some commentators at the time believed that training for a single event had occurred to such a degree that athletes made poor soldiers and also ignored intellectual pursuits, so that they were 'people with limited skills and dull minds' (Coakley, 1992: 56). Some 2000 years later some of the same arguments are still being raised. Some of the competitors in the Ancient Olympics hired personal coaches called *paidotribai*. Often these coaches were former athletes. Perrottet (2004: 31–32) writes that 'the names of the top trainers were bound forever with athletes who won the olive wreath at Olympia, recorded on memorials and repeated in hymns. Coaches joined in all the Olympic ceremonies and had a special section in the Stadium'.

Not all Greeks agreed with Xenephanes and others about the perceived problem of professionalism in sport. Glasser (1978) states that receiving rewards was not in conflict with general Greek ideals of sport during the sixth century BC, citing as an example the Athenian leader Solon who, in about 594 BC, passed a law which granted victors at the Isthmian Games 100 drachma and those at the Olympic Games 500 drachma. It was hoped that these rewards would act as incentives to achieve more victories for Athens.

The practice of city states rewarding their top athletes was not only widespread but enduring. Correspondence from Mark Antony, in 41 BC, grants athletes exemptions from military service, a guarantee of personal safety and other benefits. Other athletes received pensions for life and exemptions from taxes in the third century AD (Glasser, 1978: 48).

Not so acceptable was the practice of athletes changing their political allegiances in order to receive larger rewards. Pausanias, in his *Guide to Greece*, notes:

> Sotades at the ninety-ninth Festival was victorious in the long race and proclaimed a Cretan, as in fact he was. But at the next Festival he made himself an Ephesian, being bribed to do so by the Ephesian people. For this act he was banished by the Cretans. (Pausanias, 1962: 18.6)

There are many parallels between many of the practices cited above (perhaps excluding the sacrifices) and contemporary sport in regard to commercial aspects. Certainly, more similarities exist between these examples and sport at the turn of the twenty-first century than the amateur ideals held and promulgated by the IOC for most of its existence.

Linked to the view of the purity of the amateur athlete is the larger issue of the role of commercialism in the Games of the modern era. Again, the nexus between sport and money, this time in the form of commerce, is believed to degrade the former. Today there is no longer a philosophical argument about whether or not there should be commercialism in the Games, but rather debate is centred on the extent of such commercial involvement and the ramifications for Olympic athletes and officials. As the influence of commercialism in the Games has increased, through sponsorship and television rights, those who favour a less commercial Olympics have harked back to the Ancient Games as being 'pure' sport, exempt from the taint of 'filthy lucre'. But herein lies another Olympic myth, for ancient Olympia, once every few years when the Olympic festival took place, was the scene of commercial activity. The stadium was surrounded by concession stands selling food, drink and souvenirs, and artists, sculptors and poets hawked their wares (Swaddling, 1999). 'Vendors were required to have licenses, and the Elians appointed a commissioner of marketers to impose on-the-spot fines for shoddy merchandise or price gouging' (Perrottet, 2004: 46). An interesting parallel lies between this scene and the 1996 Atlanta Olympics, where commercial excess was one of the strongest points of criticism of the Games by the IOC. Yet, as the above demonstrates, there had been a commercial aspect present to the Olympics long before the Atlanta Games. It appears that the difficulty lies in striking an acceptable balance between sport and commerce.

Like today's athletes, the quest for victory sometimes resulted in instances of cheating by athletes in the Ancient Olympics. Penalties for offenders, when caught, were harsh. Contestants and their trainers could be whipped by the *mastigophorai* (whip bearers) for failing to obey the rules. Additionally, heavy fines were meted out for bribery and, interestingly:

> as a warning to potential offenders money from such fines was used to pay for bronze statues of Zeus (known as *Zanes*, a dialect form of Zeus) which were set up along the terrace wall leading to the entrance of the stadium. ... According to Pausanias, there were sixteen of these in all. (Swaddling, 1999: 39)

The first example of cheating that we know of occurred in 388 BC when the boxer, Eupolus of Thessaly, bribed three opponents to throw their fights against him (Perrottet, 2004).

Women

Pierre de Coubertin believed that the Olympic Games should be the preserve of male athletes, citing Ancient Olympic Games practices to reinforce the discriminatory sporting practices of the late nineteenth century. In the main, de Coubertin was correct in his assertions about the place of women in the Greek world. However, in relation to the Ancient Olympics he was not entirely accurate, so again this practice touches on the realm of myth. Pausanias, in his *Guide to Greece*, interestingly notes that female virgins were not refused admission to the Games and that it was only married women who were forbidden to compete or be spectators at the Games, with the exception of the priestess of Demeter Chamyne whose presence was required (Swaddling, 1999: 40). Others challenge this view. For example, Gardiner (1930) notes that, apart from the priestess, there is no written evidence of any women being present as spectators and there would be little accommodation for their needs at Olympia. Harris (in Mouratidis, 1984) agrees with this viewpoint. Mouratidis (1984) argued that women's exclusion was linked to the warrior elements of the worship of Heracles, whom the Olympic Games honoured: the presence of women was believed to dilute the hero's power.

One married woman, Kallipateira or Pherenike, is recorded to have been admitted to the Games, although the authorities were initially unaware of her sex, as she had disguised herself as a male trainer. Fortuitously, because of previous Olympic boxing victories by her father, brother and son, she did not meet the death punishment (being thrown from a mountain) suggested for such female transgressors, when her identity was discovered.

Records indicate that, despite these restrictions on women as spectators and competitors, there were female winners at the Games. Such inconsistency was possible because, in the horse races, the prizes were awarded to owners rather than the charioteers or jockeys. Interestingly, this occurrence also demonstrates the degree of professionalism present in the Ancient Games, as the charioteers or jockeys were professional athletes. Several women won Olympic victories by this means. The most well known was Kyniska, the daughter of Archidamos, the King of Sparta. To celebrate her victory she erected two statues at Olympia. On one of the statues was the following inscription:

> Sparta's Kings were fathers and brothers of mine,
> But since with my chariot and storming horses I, Kyniska,
> Have won the prize, I place my effigy here
> And proudly proclaim
> That of all Grecian women I first bore the crown. (Swaddling, 1999: 41)

The demise of the Games

The Olympic Games had reached their zenith by the fifth century BC, when belief in the gods' influence on athletic victory was still widely accepted. However, with increased training and specialisation the athletes themselves began to be credited for their sporting successes or failures. Greek society was also changing in other, more direct ways, and when the Romans later incorporated the Greek mainland into their territory, the end of the Ancient Olympic years of glory was signalled. For example, Sulla, a Roman general, sacked Olympia in order to finance his army. He also transferred one Games, those of 80 BC, to Rome. Additionally, some of the Roman Olympic competitors had a different code of conduct, one in antithesis to the modern Games founders' idealised view of the noble Ancient Olympian. For example, the emperor Nero wished to compete at Olympia, so he postponed the Games from AD 65 to AD 67, in order for them to coincide with his schedule. Although he failed to complete his event, the chariot race, he was still proclaimed the winner. The aftermath of this debacle was more in line with the modern Olympic principles of fair play. 'After his death in AD 68, these Games were declared invalid, and Nero's name was expunged from the victor-lists. His successor Galba also insisted that a 250,000 drachma bribe to the judges should be paid back' (Swaddling, 1999: 98).

Although the Ancient Olympics later enjoyed a brief revival under some Roman rulers they failed to regain their former glory and prestige. The Romans copied the games, so that there were at least twenty 'Olympic' Games outside Olympia during the imperial period (Golden, 1998).

Once the Ancient Olympic Games ceased the site at Olympia lay neglected. In the time of the Romans, Sulla sacked the site at Olympia and from this time on its decline continued apace. In AD 267 a tribe from southern Russia, the *Heruli*, invaded Olympia and fortifications were built to protect the sacred temple of Zeus. The games, by this stage, were reduced to a few events, but they continued for over a century, probably until AD 393, when the Emperor Theodosius I abolished all pagan festivals. Later, in AD 426, the Temple of Zeus was destroyed by fire. Swaddling (1999: 100) suggests the fire may have been deliberately lit, a result of an edict of the Roman Emperor Theodosius II, which ordered all pagan temples in the Mediterranean region to be demolished. Nature, too, contributed to the demise of the site; in the fourth century AD, earthquakes and floods covered the area. The site remained virtually undisturbed until 1875 when excavations uncovered the site and the seeds of revival of the Olympic Games were planted.

Conclusion

Despite the many myths about the Ancient Olympics which have influenced the modern Games, there were some similarities. Crowther (2002) describes disturbing similarities in the organisation of both the Ancient and modern Games, through 'home town' decisions, bribery and political pressures. Golden (1998: 4) notes that Greek sport 'was enveloped in a series of hierarchies in which events, festivals, genders, nations and other groups were ranged and ranked no less than individuals'. Today, the modern Olympic Games, like their ancient counterpart, are considered the pinnacle of athletic excellence. They are prized by athletes, spectators, sponsors and the media. However, Coakley details one other resemblance between Ancient Greek sport and its counterpart in the twentieth century which merits a different consideration:

> They reflected and recreated the dominant social structural characteristics and patterns of social relations in the society as a whole. The power and advantages that went along with being wealthy, male and young in Greek society served to shape games and contests that limited the participation of women, older people and those without economic resources. In fact the definitions of excellence used to evaluate performance even reflected the abilities of young males. This meant that the abilities of others were by definition sub-standard ... We can see the same things in organised sport today (Coakley, 1992: 56).

Further reading

On the Salt Lake City scandals and the Ancient Games: Crowther (2002).
The Ancient Games: Golden (1998); Swaddling (1999); Phillips and Pritchard (2003); Perrottet (2004).

Questions

1. Do the Ancient Olympic Games really have any relevance to the Olympic Games of the 21st century?
2. What are some of the main differences, in lifestyle, training and competing, between the athletes of Greek antiquity and the athletes of today?
3. List all the events of the Athens Olympics of 2004 that can be traced back to events contested at the Ancient Olympics. What are the origins of the other events?

Chapter 3

The Revival of the Olympic Games

I saw the necessity for re-establishing the Olympic Games as a supreme consecration of the cult of athletics practiced in the purest spirit of true sport, proudly, joyfully, and loyally. Pierre de Coubertin (1988: 103)

Introduction

Ceremonies and symbolism have been utilised throughout history. Rituals have been used as legitimisers, tools and methods by which credibility, a sense of tradition and, at times, reverence are imparted to an institution. Eventually these rituals become so intertwined with the institution itself that they serve to define its place in society. Examples of cultural institutions which use rituals include religion, the judicial system and government. In sport, the example *par excellence* is the Olympic Movement.

At the Olympic Games ritual is immediately and best exemplified through the Opening Ceremony, the event which receives the greatest media coverage and highest television ratings of any aspect of the Games. However, other facets of the Olympic Movement are also replete with symbolism and ceremony, for example, the medal presentation ceremonies, the lighting of the Olympic torch, International Olympic Committee (IOC) Sessions and meetings of the International Olympic Academy (IOA). In addition to their other, more overt, functions these are all devices which have been manufactured by Olympic administrators who have sought to elevate the Games beyond sport into the realm of festival by stamping the Olympic Movement with religious and mystical overtones.

Underpinning many of the ceremonial aspects of the Olympic Games is the homage paid to the 'founder' of the modern Olympics, Baron Pierre de Coubertin. Official IOC publications often contain sections glorifying de Coubertin's role in reviving the Games and many scholars credit him as the Modern Games' founder (Lucas, 1988a; Durantez Corral, 1994; Kirsty, 1995). But what exactly was de Coubertin's part in reviving the Games? It appears that by examining this question historians have recently discovered more cracks in the columns supporting Olympic ideology. For, although de Coubertin deserves credit for instigating the establishment of the International Olympic Committee (IOC) and was instrumental in the staging of the first modern Olympics, he was, in fact, building on the work of others, including individuals in Greece, Germany, North America and Great Britain, who had already managed to stage 'Olympic' style events, albeit on a small scale. But then, it must be remembered that the first Olympic Games of the modern era were themselves minimal in comparison to today's extravaganzas. Only 311 athletes from just 14 countries attended the first modern Olympic Games in Athens in 1896. Over 11,000 athletes, from 202 nations, competed in the Athens Olympics of 2004. Table 3.1 shows the growth of the modern Summer Games.

Table 3.1. Modern Summer Olympic Games chronology

Olympiad	Year	Host City	Sports	Events	Countries/ NOCs	Competitors
I	1896	Athens	9	43	14	245
II	1900	Paris	17	86	19	1078
III	1904	Saint-Louis	13	96	13	689
IV	1908	London	21	107	22	2 035
V	1912	Stockholm	13	102	28	2 437
VI	1916	Not held	-	-	-	-
VII	1920	Antwerp	21	152	29	2 607
VIII	1924	Paris	17	126	44	2 972
IX	1928	Amsterdam	14	109	46	2 884
X	1932	Los Angeles	14	117	37	1 333
XI	1936	Berlin	19	129	49	3 936
XII	1940	Not held	-	-	-	-
XIII	1944	Not held	-	-	-	-
XIV	1948	London	17	136	59	4092
XV	1952	Helsinki	17	149	69	5429
XVI	1956	Melbourne	16	145	67	3 178
		Stockholm†	1	6	29	159
XVII	1960	Rome	17	150	83	5 313
XVIII	1964	Tokyo	19	163	93	5 133
XIX	1968	Mexico City	18	172	112	5 498
XX	1972	Munich	21	172	121	7 121
XXI	1976	Montreal	21	198	92	6 043
XXII	1980	Moscow	21	203	80	5 283
XXIII	1984	Los Angeles	21	221	140	6 802
XXIV	1988	Seoul	23	237	159	8 473
XXV	1992	Barcelona	25	257	169	9 368
XXVI	1996	Atlanta	26	271	197	10 332
XXVII	2000	Sydney	28	300	199 #	10 651
XXVIII	2004	Athens	28	301	202	11 099

† equestrian events were held in Stockholm because of Australia's quarantine laws. # an additional four athletes, not representing an NOC, also competed. Sources: Miller (2003: 491) and IOC (n.d.).

The interregnum

Even before the Ancient Olympic Games ended, in about AD 393, the new Christian religion had preached to the Western world that the desires of the body were sinful and this sentiment, coupled with emphasis on preparing for the afterlife, was at odds with the widespread practice and celebration of sport, except for military training.

> The spirit of sport however could not be suppressed forever and thus centuries later, the institution of chivalry was grafted onto the code of Christian behaviour. In this way, knighthood, though only to a limited extent, and only when it was expedient, became a revival of the Olympic spirit. (Messinesi, 1976: 41)

While, as indicated in Chapter 2, the Olympic Games site at Olympia lay hidden and forgotten for over a thousand years, numerous revivals of the Olympic Games took place from the seventeenth century. In the nineteenth century archaeologists began to excavate the Olympia site, thus amplifying the public's burgeoning interest in the nascent Olympic Games revivals. The history of the modern Olympic Games' emergence is therefore a story of independent, but interconnected revivals, culminating in the staging of the Athens Olympics of 1896 (Young, 1996).

There are symbolic connections between the first modern Olympic Games and their ancient counterparts, though, in reality, the new celebrations evidenced more concrete associations with medieval chivalry and nineteenth century sport, as practised in England. Admittedly, the practice of the code of chivalry can claim only a slender link to the Games' regeneration. Certainly, the notion of chivalry, exemplified in the fair play ethic, is evident in contemporary Olympic doctrine, yet it was more the result of other determinants, occurring later, that served to strengthen any philosophic bond between chivalry and the Olympics. The first of these was the advent of public games in the sixteenth century, especially in England. These helped to bring sporting events more frequently into the public domain. Concurrently, the study of Greece by Renaissance scholars was beginning to shed some light, or at least present one version of the accomplishments of ancient athletes, by glorifying their philosophies and their achievements.

In England, at the beginning of the seventeenth century, under the reign of James I, Robert Dover received permission to promote the Cotswold Games as the 'Olympick Games' (Gibbs, 1898). Their celebration was enduring. They were held on most Whit-Sundays from 1612 until 1852, in Chipping Camden, Gloucestershire. Their varied sporting and cultural programme included running, equestrian, jumping, wrestling, throwing, fencing and hunting events as well as chess, poetry, dancing and music. The games were discontinued because of the anti-social behaviour of some participants, an occurrence that would appal Olympic idealists. However, due to renewed interest, the festivities were revived in 1980 and are celebrated each June (British Olympic Association, 1998).

In an Olympic context, the Cotswold Games can be seen as an isolated event in the seventeenth century. However, in the nineteenth century, other sporting events with 'Olympic' connections in Europe and North America became numerous, as shown in Table 3.2. These events, held in Greece, England, continental Europe, North America and Germany are discussed in turn below.

Table 3.2. Some Olympic Games revivals

Year	Event	Organisers	Country
1662–1952	Cotswold 'Olympick Games'	Robert Dover	England
1679	'Hampton Court Olympics'	Royal court	England
1790	Proposed Games in Paris		France
1779	Olympic Games, Worlitz		Germany
1819–present	Highland Games		Scotland & overseas
1830s	'Greek Competitions', Poznan	Commercial	Poland
1834, 1836	Scandinavian Olympic Games, Ramlösa	Johann Schartau	Sweden
1844	Montreal 'Olympic Games'	Olympic Club	Canada
1849–1895	Much Wenlock Games – annual	W.P. Brookes	England
1853	Franconi's Hippodrome, New York	Commercial	USA
1859, 1870, 1875, 1888	'Zappas Games', Athens	Evangelios Zappas	Greece
1861	Wellington Games	Shropshire Olympian Soc.	England
1862–67	Liverpool Olympics, annual	Liverpool Athletic Club	England
1866	Olympic Festival, Llandudno	Athletic Society of GB	Wales
1866–68, 1874, 1877, 1883	National Olympiad Assn. Games (London, Birmingham, Wellington, Much Wenlock, Shrewsbury, Hadley)	National Olympiad Assn.	England
1870s	'Olympic Games', Wrzesnia		Poland
1892	Campaign for 'Anglo-Saxon Olympiad'	J.A. Cooper	England
1893	'Ancient Greco-Roman Games'	Olympic Club of San Francisco	USA

From: Redmond (1988); Rühl and Keuser (1997).

Greece

The ideas and ideals of the Ancient Games have been referred to in literature throughout the ages. For example, Shakespeare mentions them in *Henry VI* and *Troilus and Cressida*. Likewise, Milton notes their existence in *Paradise Lost*. Voltaire, Flaubert and Gide also alluded to the Olympics in their works (Mandell, 1976b). Young, in his definitive history of the revival of the Games, *The Modern Olympics: A Struggle for Revival*, notes another, more consequential Olympic and literary connection. 'Our modern Olympic movement – even the Olympic idea - seems to have begun as the glancing thought of a poet. He was a Greek, Panagiotis Soutsos, born in 1806 in Constantinople' (Young, 1996: 17). Soutsos's inspiration for a revival of the Games stemmed from a poetic muse. Later, he put his thoughts into action by writing to the Greek Minister of the Interior, John Kolletis, suggesting that March 25 be declared a national holiday. This was the starting date of the Greek War of Independence, in which Greece gained her freedom from Turkish rule. Soutsos proposed that, on this anniversary, festivities should be held, including a revival of the Ancient Olympics. The Minister believed the proposal had merit and in turn recommended it to the Greek King, Otto. According to Young (1996: 4): 'it is not wholly a coincidence that our own modern Olympic series began – the opening day of Olympiad I, 1896 – on March 25 in Athens'. However, before Kolletis could take any action he was replaced as Minister by the Prime Minister, Rhodartes, who approved only of the idea of marking March 25 as a national holiday (Young, 1996). It appeared that the Greek revival plans were stalemated. However, in 1837, a new direction in Greek domestic policy began the process which eventually led to an Olympic festival on Greek soil.

The King created a 'committee for the encouragement of national industry' to promote and foster commercial interests. One of the committee's proposed outcomes was a three day festival whose purpose would be to highlight Greek products and individuals and also to recreate some of the events contested at the Ancient Olympics (Young, 1996). The individual most credited with establishing these Greek Olympic Festivals is Evangelios Zappas, a wealthy grain merchant. He based his proposal on that of Soutsos and in November 1859 the first of these festivals was held at the Place Louis in Athens (Young, 1996). In addition to a prize of £10, donated by the Much Wenlock Olympian Society of England, victors received wreaths, cash and other prizes from Greek sources (Redmond, 1981). Both Young (1996) and Messinesi (1976) consider these to be the first true games of the modern Olympic tradition. However, in a cautionary note, they also report that they were not considered to be successful by their organisers.

The 1859 games were made possible by the large monetary contribution from Zappas, who also financed further industrial Olympic Games posthumously through his estate. These festivals were held in 1870, 1875, 1888 and 1889, rather than in an Olympian four-year cycle as initially proposed by their benefactor (Young, 1996). The programme expanded during the latter of these games to include swimming, equestrian, shooting and novelty events. Like their English counterparts a class-based approach developed and the last of the Greek festivals was restricted to members of the 'cultured class' (Mandell, 1976a). As in the Olympic-style festivals which were concurrently being held in Victorian England (discussed below), a strict observance of the code of amateurism appeared to be somewhat hypocritical. The games organisers attempted to exclude the lower classes on the basis that their motives for participation were less pure than those who could afford to compete without financial recompense. Yet it could be argued that the awarding of prizes in fact negated this principle.

England

The birth of modern sport is credited to England, dating from the middle of the nineteenth century. Although at this time games and sports were not the prerogative solely of the English, they have been acknowledged as the society that was most influential in developing and moulding them into their current forms (Messinesi, 1976). It was here that many of sports' rules were first codified and their governing bodies formed.

Formative in this evolution of sport were the Greater Public Schools, élite private boarding schools, where team sports were efficiently utilised as agents of a form of social control. As an important component of the curriculum sport was linked with religion in a concerted effort to help mould 'Muscular Christians'. These individuals supposedly exhibited the positive qualities of both sport and religion. Many of the privileged classes who attended these institutions practised and preached this ethic even after they left school, spreading it throughout the British Empire. The notion of Muscular Christianity harked back to the Ancient Greek ideal of a 'sound mind in a sound body', with one major variation: essential to its core was the practice of Christianity, rather than worship of a pantheon of gods. Thus, in many aspects, it was similar to the notion of chivalry, practised in the middle ages.

It was believed that some of the virtues required for sound, masculine, muscular Christian practice could be learnt through participating in team sports. These included qualities such as sportsmanship, leadership, teamwork, the ability to be both a good winner and loser, as well as a work (or practice) ethic. One of the foremost and most famous exponents of this doctrine was Thomas Arnold, headmaster of Rugby School. His message was further spread by two of the most popular books of the day, the novels *Tom Brown's Schooldays* and *Tom Brown at Oxford*, written by Thomas Hughes, an ex-pupil of Arnold. These works chronicled the moral and physical development of a youth, Tom Brown, who exemplified these Muscular Christian traits, achieving success through practising this philosophy and the occasional failure when he strayed from this doctrine, thus learning from moral lessons.

Inherent and central to this model of sport was the notion of 'amateurism', that is, playing the game for intrinsic, rather than extrinsic rewards. Amateurism was a nineteenth century construct, which served many functions in Victorian England, not all of them as noble as the ideals it proclaimed. According to Glasser:

> ... one of the primary and original purposes of amateurism as a category of sports was social distinction, that is, to separate the so-called gentleman amateur from the lower classes of society ... any person who competed for money was not only basically inferior, but also a person of questionable character. (Glasser, 1978: 15–16)

One reason proposed for this distinction and classification was the increasing participation of the middle and lower classes in certain leisure and sporting activities which had previously been the domain and prerogative of the upper class. To further rationalise the distinction between amateur and professional athletes it was considered by the élite (and thus sport's powerbrokers) that the latter, 'whose livelihood depended on his success and achievement', could not be 'imbued with the same disinterested sense of fair play' (Messinesi, 1976: 49). Consequently, character development, as a moral outcome of games, was accepted to be exclusively an outcome of amateur sport, but not its professional equivalent. Definitions of amateurism accentuated the idea that its adherents 'competed solely for the love of sport, or solely for pleasure and physical, mental and social benefit that could be derived from athletics' (Glasser, 1978: 18).

This view of amateurism, formed in England and viewed as being the practise of 'pure sport', together with a misunderstood belief of the practices of the Ancient Games, provided the basis of Olympic rules for approximately the first 75 years of the modern Games' existence, regardless of the reality of under-the-table payments and government subsidies to athletes. Chapter 2 include a more detailed discussion of amateurism in Ancient Greece.

In the nineteenth century the increasing involvement in organized sport by the lower classes was linked to the Industrial Revolution and its associated changes and regulations in work practices. Concomitantly, other leisure activities were being opened to the *hoi polloi*. Some of these pursuits, sponsored by the upper classes, were associated with the concept of *noblesse oblige*, through movements designed to improve the character of the less fortunate to open their eyes through more academic pursuits. Dr William Penny Brookes, of Much Wenlock, a small village in Shropshire, funded one such venture in 1841. The Agricultural Reading Society was formed 'for the promotion and diffusion of useful information. From the society evolved various classes including the Art, Philharmonic and Botany classes and in 1850 Brookes formed the Wenlock Olympian class' (Furbank *et al.*, 1996: 2).

Its first games were held in October of that year and were an amalgam of traditional country games and athletics. For example: tilting, football, quoits and cricket were contested. According to Furbank *et al.* (1996: 3) 'the early Games sometimes included a 'fun' event, once a wheelbarrow race, another year an old women's race for a pound of tea, although it was not usually part of the actual program'. It is important, in the context of Olympic history and philosophy, to note that cash prizes were also awarded to victors in some events.

In 1860, the Olympian class withdrew from the Agricultural Reading Society and became a separate entity. In 1860 the Shropshire Olympics were established which rotated around the county. These were not lone ventures. Other Olympic carnivals were also being organised throughout England during this period. In 1862 John Hulley founded the Liverpudlian Olympics, which were also held during the following two years. In 1865 Brookes and Hulley, together with Ravenstein of the German Gymnastics Club in London, formed the National Olympian Association (NOA). 'The aim was to provide a sports association for amateur athletes. Their first festival, held the following year at the Crystal Palace was a great success and attracted 10,000 spectators' (Redmond, 1981:12). Over 200 athletes entered a variety of events in track and field as well as fencing, wrestling, boxing and gymnastic contests. Gold, silver and bronze medals were awarded to place-getters and a special champion's gold medal presented to the most successful athlete. In response, the Amateur Athletic Association (AAA) was hastily formed by a London élite who were determined that British sport should be under their control and restricted to 'amateurs and gentlemen', in other words athletes from the public schools and the Universities of Oxford and Cambridge. The NOA faced powerful opposition, but by its very existence, forced the AAA to open its doors to men from the lower classes (Furbank *et al.*, 1996).

In an interesting portent for the amateur issue, that was destined to be one of the most divisive issues of the modern Olympic Games in the twentieth century, the question of eligibility proved to be contentious, even in these local contests. When the AAA was formed it marked the first time that the word 'amateur' appeared in the title of a sporting organisation. The association continued to grow in influence in England and in 1866 and 1867 it too organised Olympic festivals, the first in North Wales and the second in Liverpool. It was a three day festival which, like previous Olympic festivals, was popular with spectators (Redmond, 1981). In all, six national 'Olympic Games' were held in England between 1866 and 1883. Despite the public's approval these games ceased, but the Much Wenlock festivals continued and are still being celebrated.

In an effort to improve his Much Wenlock Olympics Dr Brookes began corresponding with like minded individuals who were staging Olympic festivals over-seas. Foremost of these were his Greek contemporaries. Results of this communication were fruitful and, as a result of the links forged between Brookes and the Greek Olympic revivalists, the Greek King donated a prize of a silver urn to the winner of the Much Wenlock pentathlon (Redmond, 1981). In turn Brookes sent a cup to the winners of the Greek 'Olympic Games' organised by Evangelios Zappas and first held in 1859.

Brookes should be also credited with being one of the first to attempt to internationalise his Olympic revivals. In June 1881, 13 years before the Sorbonne Conference, which led to the true emergence of the modern Olympics, a Greek newspaper reported: 'Dr Brookes, this enthusiastic philhellene is endeavouring to organise an International Olympian festival, to be held in Athens' (Furbank *et al.*, 1996: 10). The Greek government rejected his proposal. Another international linkage was ultimately to prove more auspicious.

The Frenchman, Baron Pierre de Coubertin had been charged with organising an International Congress on Physical Education, to be held in his country and, in this capacity, wrote to a number of English newspapers appealing for information which would be of benefit to his planning. His strategy was successful. As a result of his requests, William Penny Brookes replied and subsequently corresponded with the minor French aristocrat who visited him in Much Wenlock, in October, 1890. At this time Brookes was 81 and de Coubertin was only 27. It was here, at the only meeting of the two men, that de Coubertin first heard the suggestion of an international Olympic Games. He wrote in an article for the December issue of *La Revue Athletique*: 'if the Olympic Games that Modern Greece has not yet been able to revive still survives today, it is due, not to a Greek, but to Dr. W. P. Brookes' (in Furbank *et al.*, 1996: 10). After that time de Coubertin gave no further credit to Brookes or Zappas, in his writings regarding the revival of the Games.

At the time of the Sorbonne Conference of 1894, when de Coubertin received support for his plan to revive the Games, William Penny Brookes was too ill to travel. He died in 1896, before the first Modern Games were celebrated. However his place in Olympic history needs to be properly acknowledged, as should the contributions of those other individuals whose national and regional Olympic festivals were precursors to the first international Games. Similarly, Müller writes: 'in 1891 in the magazine *Great Britain*, another Englishman, John Astley Cooper, proposed that a regular "Anglo-Saxon" Olympiad be organized. ... It is possible that de Coubertin was influenced by this idea' (in de Coubertin, 2000: 38).

North America

Beginning in the middle of the nineteenth century, organised sports and games spread from England throughout Europe and North America. Included in the trans-Atlantic sports diaspora was an American version of the Olympic revival movement.

In Montréal, Canada, in 1842, a sporting club called the Olympic Club was formed. This was significant in that it was probably the first time that 'Olympic' featured in the title of a sporting club. In August 1844, the club conducted a two-day 'Montréal Olympic Games'. These games comprised 29 events, including a game of lacrosse between a white team and a first nations team (Redmond, 1981). However, the most popular of the sporting and athletic festivals of that time were the Scottish Highland (Caledonian) Games, which were regularly held throughout the British Empire and other countries, such as the USA, where large numbers of Scots had migrated. The strongest link between the Caledonian Games and the Olympic Games was that each had a track and field programme. They also served a further function in providing a climate conducive to an international Olympic revival, by proving that athletic contests could be popular and enduring, ironically qualities which the early Olympic Games did not necessarily indicate would be their legacy.

The USA was also involved in Olympic-style festivals. In 1853, in New York, a re-enactment of ancient sports in Franconi's Hippodrome included a segment on the Ancient Olympic Games. Its purpose was theatrical rather than competitive and so:

> the Boston Caledonian Games of 1853, the New York Caledonian Games of 1856, or the inaugural sports of the New York Athletic Club in 1868 and its successors had much more in common with other pseudo-Olympics of the nineteenth century than did these 'Olympic Games'. (Redmond, 1981: 14)

De Coubertin himself visited the San Francisco Olympic Club in 1893 (de Coubertin, 2000).

Thus, in North America, as in Europe, during the latter part of the nineteenth century, the foundations were being laid for an interest in a sports festival with an international flavour. One of de Coubertin's greatest allies in his Olympic quest proved to be William Milligan Sloane from Yale University. However, on his 1893 visit to the USA, de Coubertin wrote: 'nowhere did the idea for the Olympic Games meet with the enthusiasm it deserved. My kind friend William Sloane alone was wildly enthusiastic about the project' (de Coubertin, 2000: 317). At the Athens Olympics of 1896 the dominance of the American team was attributed in part to their tradition of athletic carnivals and university sports programmes. However, even this did not mean that the USA accepted the Olympic Games as the world's peak athletic contest. Far from it. As one American spectator commented:

> From the standpoint of modern athletics the contests witnessed by the imposing audience were not remarkable save in one respect, the invincibility of our American champions. No records were broken, in fact our men were not called upon to even equal their own best previous work in their respective lines.
>
> (Holmes, 1984: 61)

France and Germany

In 1779, even before the staging of the American Olympic-style events, an 'Olympic Games' had been instigated in Worlitz, Germany. Predating this, in neighbouring France:

> in 1790 the revolutionary Republican pedagogues of France, Condorcet, Lekanau and Dannou, saw the possibility of a democratic levelling in the revival of the Games. ... Their idea was to hold the 'Olympic Games' in the Paris Champs de Mars. ... to the military exercises were added ... a number of public games revived from the Greeks. (Messinesi, 1976: 52)

Later, in Germany, the 'Turner movement' similarly used sport, specifically a regimented style of gymnastics, to enhance its political agenda. This link between politics and sport in the Olympics proved to be consequential, even in this pre-Games phase. The fitness of the Prussian soldiers was one of the reasons de Coubertin credited Prussia with victory in the Franco-Prussian war of 1870–1871, as discussed below.

The Germans were not the only ones to whom fitness was becoming more important. In central Europe and Scandinavia other gymnastic organisations were formed in the nineteenth century. While these movements had no direct link to the modern Games they were central to the creation of a pro-fitness climate in Europe. By the end of the nineteenth century the world was at a juncture where it was receptive to an international sporting festival which celebrated athletic endeavours imbued with links to the Ancient Greeks. De Coubertin provided the impetus to turn receptivity into reality.

Pierre de Coubertin

Pierre Fredy, Baron de Coubertin (see Figure 3.1), was born in Paris, France on 1 January 1863 and died 74 years later in Geneva, Switzerland, on 2 September 1937. He was educated, as befitted a French aristocrat of his era, in a classical Catholic Jesuit tradition, whereby he learnt about and came to admire many Greek philosophies, writings and practices. Like many of his contemporaries he was also deeply affected and shamed by his country's defeat in the Franco-Prussian War of 1870–1871. He believed that 'the nation had been humiliated by Prussia's ludicrously easy victory over an effeminate, non-sporting, excessively intellectual French population' (Lucas, 1988a: 90). His fervent wish for his country was that it could overcome this deficiency and regain its pre-eminent position in Europe. He believed that sport was the perfect vehicle to achieve this end. As previously mentioned he came to an understanding of the physical and political potential of sport, and specifically the Olympic Games, in no small part, through his meeting with William Penny Brookes (Young, 1996).

His readings of *Tom Brown's School Days* and subsequent trips to England had previously convinced him that Britain's success as a world super power was linked to the sports ethic taught in its élite private schools. De Coubertin believed that if France could emulate this system, then the nation's former glory days could be revived. This patriotic belief was pivotal in his suggestion that the Olympic Games be revived. He first publicly proposed this on 25 November 1892, in Paris in a speech at the Sorbonne at a meeting of the Union de Sports Athletiques (USFSA) (Lucas, 1988a: 92). This suggestion, according to Durántez Corral (1994: 20), 'floundered through general incomprehension, despite the enthusiasm with which the idea was greeted. Two years later, in the same place, the idea was unanimously accepted'.

Nationalistic sentiments were not the only driving ideals behind his proposals. His belief in the purity of sport also extended to a wider, more altruistic perspective, whereby he believed that international understanding could be enhanced through athletic endeavours – of the purely amateur kind. The topic of amateurism was the core of the meeting the USFSA hosted in June 1894, again at the Sorbonne. The main agenda item was the question of amateur athletics, but its most lasting outcome, and part of de Coubertin's strategy was the tenth proposal on the agenda, the formation of an International Olympic Committee (IOC). Apart from the ten members of the organising committee, a total of 78 delegates from eight countries and 37 sports associations attended the eight day conference. Of these, 58 delegates were French and they represented 24 of the sports and clubs (Müller, 1994).

The Congress of the Sorbonne was held in Paris from 16–24 June, and marks the date from which the modern Olympic Games evolved. National rivalries were in evidence even at this nascent stage of the Olympics and threatened to cause the conference's cancellation. In January 1894, de Coubertin had issued invitations to attend the congress to all the athletic clubs in Europe and overseas for which he had

Figure 3.1. Baron Pierre de Coubertin

addresses. The response from both the French and English clubs was excellent, however no one from Holland or Switzerland answered his circular. He had invited no German representatives because of enduring bitterness on the part of the French, a legacy of the Franco-Prussian hostilities. However, in order to give validity to an 'international' congress and because the German Turner organisations were the largest sporting clubs in the world, de Coubertin realised that German representation would be necessary politically, to give the congress legitimacy in the eyes of the sporting world. Consequently, he visited the German Embassy in Paris to obtain the names of German sport officials.

Before any German club could reply to his invitation the French leader of the Union de Sociétiés Gymnastiques declared that if the Turners were represented then the French gymnasts would withdraw. This was to be the first in a century of threatened Olympic boycotts. To circumvent his problem, de Coubertin invited Baron von Rieffenstein, a German residing in London, to the congress in an unofficial capacity. De Coubertin's diplomacy placated the French and the congress proceeded without disruption. Its enduring contribution to the realm of sport was its decision to schedule the first modern Olympic Games in Athens in 1896 (Warning, 1980). Originally de Coubertin had hoped to stage the first games in Paris in 1900, however delegates wanted a speedier outcome and Demetrius Bikelas (also known as Vikelas) suggested Athens in 1896 as a site. London was also suggested, but de Coubertin favoured the Greek capital (Müller, 1994).

At the Sorbonne meeting it was decided that the IOC president would come from the host country and so Bikelas, a Greek, was elected President of the 15-member IOC, and de Coubertin, General Secretary. Bikelas returned to Greece to inform the government of the honour of Athens being chosen as the first site.

This choice of venue was understandable, if unfortunate. Greece was politically and financially unstable. As a result, the modern Olympic Games tradition began, as it was to continue in many instances, in an admixture of political and social conflict. Although the Greek people eagerly welcomed the idea of reviving the Games, the Greek government was not initially so enthusiastic and consequently refused any commitment to them. The Greek Prime Minister, Charios Tricoupis (also written as Trikoupis or Tricupis), decided that Greece could not afford to accept the honour and wrote to de Coubertin to inform him of this fact.

> Greece had undergone a decade of extreme instability from 1869–1879 and continued to be plagued by domestic unrest and turmoil. Frequent elections, short term governments and the pursuit of irredentism characterised the politics of the period. The attempts ... to rekindle rebellion in Crete brought Greece to the point of bankruptcy. ... By 1893 foreign indebtedness was consuming 33% of the national income. Trikoupis reduced foreign interest payments 70% [and] decided in addition, that Greece would have to balance its budget, which left no room for expenses for items such as Coubertin's festivities. (Strenk, 1970: 33)

De Coubertin saw his Olympic dream being threatened, and departed for Greece to forestall the collapse of his plans. Once in Athens he lobbied successfully with Crown Prince Constantine and persuaded him to provide royal support for the staging of the Games. King George backed his son's position and in 1895, in an unrelated move, the Prime Minister, Tricoupis resigned. This removed de Coubertin's main opponent. The preparations for the Games could now proceed, albeit slowly, due to lack of funds. Collections were made in Greece and amongst Greeks living abroad to obtain monies essential for construction of necessary sporting facilities. The most generous benefactor was Georgios (George) Averoff, a wealthy Athenian businessman, who donated 920,000 drachmae in gold for the reconstruction of the Panathenian stadium (see Figure 3.2) to hold the Opening Ceremony and the track and field events (Warning, 1980).

The Greek Royal Family welcomed the success of the preparations. They realised that the Games offered the chance to increase the prestige of the monarchy while concurrently arousing the national consciousness and identity of the Greek population.

The Games opened in Athens on Easter Sunday, 1896, and were so successful that the early struggles, which had threatened cancellation at one point during the preparatory phase, were all but forgotten. The Olympic's political legacy had begun though and Coubertin himself wrote: 'in the case of Greece, the Games will be found to have a double affect, one athletic and the other political. Besides working to solve the centuries old Eastern question the Games helped to increase the personality of the King and the Crown Prince' (Strenk, 1970: 33). De Coubertin also wrote of the focus of the Games: 'in Athens all efforts had been concentrated on the sporting side of the venture in a historical context: there had been no congress, no sign of any moral or educational purpose' (de Coubertin, 1997:51).

It is no exaggeration to acknowledge de Coubertin as the driving force and designer of the modern Olympic Games. He became its second president, serving in this capacity between 1896 and 1925. However, towards the end of his life he became less involved in the Games' administration.

> The last Olympics de Coubertin attended were in Paris in 1924 ... Coubertin never saw, and so failed to appreciate, the extraordinary transformation the Olympics underwent in the '30s when they arrived at truly spectacular proportion and were drawn to the centre of international political, ideological and commercial life. (Hoberman, 1986: 44)

Figure 3.2. Crowds flock to the Olympic Stadium, Athens, 1896

However, despite his withdrawal from IOC leadership and his growing financial difficulties he was not forgotten by at least one prominent political figure. Shortly before his death de Coubertin was nominated for the Nobel Peace Prize. His sponsor was Adolf Hitler, a fact which may have been responsible for the nomination's failure (Kirsty, 1995).

Even though de Coubertin's personal influence waned, his philosophies continued to dominate Olympic philosophy and do so to the present. His ideal of Olympism, a fusion of supposed Ancient Greek practices and nineteenth century British sporting ideas, internationalism and peace, is still widely articulated in official documents and IOC rhetoric. Its understanding and implementation by Olympic administrators, athletes and the public seems to be less universal.

De Coubertin died in Lausanne, Switzerland on 2 September 1937. Although he was buried in Switzerland his heart was taken to Olympia where it was installed in a marble stele near the site of the Ancient Games. It has become the site of many official Olympic ceremonies, continuing the symbolic association that has been fostered with the Ancient Games. As Durántez Corral (1994: 51) notes, he 'created a whole series of emblems and ceremonies which have shaped the Olympic Movement within a terminological paradox, resulting in the formal creation of a secular religion'.

Summary

The developments in sport during the nineteenth century, at both national and international levels, provided the impetus which led to the establishment of the modern Olympic Games, an event based on British sporting ethics and recalling the perceived glories of antiquity. De Coubertin drew on the ideas, philosophies and actions of others to fashion his successful Olympic revival. His drive led to the formation of what was arguably to become the most famous multi-sport festival of the twentieth century. Like all large socially constructed institutions the Olympic Games have been controversial. Since their beginnings the modern Games have been plagued by a plethora of controversies and problems, some arising from the world's contemporary political problems, but others having their origins in the philosophies and practices which were established from the beginning of the modern Games. These issues are the result of the rules and ideals fashioned by the IOC's male élite at the end of the nineteenth century. Problems such as the question of women's participation and amateurism stem from this original modern Olympic philosophy, espoused in the rambling, and at times contradictory, writings of de Coubertin and held to fast by the IOC in the face of a changing world.

The IOC has based many of its rituals on a quasi-historical veneration of de Coubertin. This serves to perpetuate a symbolism replete with an amalgam of religious, physical and moral qualities which form the basis of the philosophy of Olympism. But to understand Olympism does not necessarily equate to an understanding of Olympic history. Many of those involved with the Olympic movement are themselves ignorant of the meanings of Olympism and its potential. As Hoberman states:

> The theatrical qualities of the Games, and the mystical sentiments they inspire, have given rise to a spectacular overestimation of their value to the cohesion of the world community. As a result, Olympic internationalism has been charged with a salvational mission for which it is unsuited. The idea that the Olympic movement has been an important vehicle of moral influence since its inception is an illusion which has thinned for nearly a century. (Hoberman, 1986: 6)

While de Coubertin believed that sport had a moral purpose, he did acknowledge its limitations. He wrote, 'athletics can bring into play both the noblest and the basest passions... they can be chivalrous or corrupt, virile or bestial; finally they can be used to strengthen peace or to prepare for war' (1997: 28).

What Hoberman suggests is that Olympic idealists forget these limitations and expect the impossible. It is unreasonable to hope that a sporting festival can achieve the universal peace that politics has so far failed to accomplish, and it is misguided, or at the very least disingenuous, to promise such a possibility. Horton (1994: 56) takes this point one step further when he suggests that 'today we cling to the ideals of Olympism as philosophical justifications for the continuation of the Games'.

Further reading

On de Coubertin:	De Coubertin (1997)
Other Olympic Revivals:	Furbank *et al.* (1996); Clarke (1997)
The Athens, 1896 Games:	Holmes (1984)
Other revivals:	Redmond (1988); Kidd (2005)

Questions

1. Should the International Olympic Committee give more credit to William Penny Brookes and others who had instigated Olympic revivals before de Coubertin?
2. Why do you think that the Olympic Movement continues to place so much emphasis on de Coubertin's efforts to revive the Games as a central tenet of its history?
3. Do the figures presented in Table 3.1 about the growth of the Olympic Games and their host city locations show any discernible trends? What are they?

Chapter 4

The Modern Olympic Phenomenon

As a contemporary historical phenomenon, the Modern Olympics have no comparison. Although regarded and interpreted in relation to the social order and political structure of our time, the Olympic games elude classification in a traditional pattern. Horst Ueberhorst (1976b: 248)

Introduction

This chapter outlines the major characteristics of the Olympic phenomenon as we know it today. It examines:

- the phenomenon of Olympism;
- the organisational structure of the Olympic Movement;
- the role, composition and functioning of the International Olympic Committee;
- the IOC Commissions;
- symbols and ceremonial;
- the bidding process and selection of host cities;
- hosting the Games;
- the Cultural Programme;
- the Winter Olympics;
- local opposition;
- evaluation and reporting;
- the legacy of the Games; and
- competing and related international sporting events.

The chapter is primarily descriptive, but it also draws attention to unique characteristics and features of the Games and raises questions as to how and why these arose and what functions they continue to play.

The starting point for a number of the topics discussed in this chapter is *The Olympic Charter*, which was first promulgated by the International Olympic Committee in 1908 and has been updated many times since. The Olympic Charter:

- is a 'basic instrument of a constitutional nature';
- sets out the fundamental principles and values of Olympism;
- defines the main reciprocal rights and obligations of Olympic organisations, 'all of which are required to comply with the Olympic Charter'. (IOC, 2004: 9)

Olympism

We begin with the idea of 'Olympism' because of the central role it plays in the terms of reference of the various organisations and individual members of the Olympic Movement, as set out in the *Olympic Charter*. Olympism was conceived by Pierre de Coubertin and is defined in the *Charter* as:

> a philosophy of life, exalting and combining in a balanced whole the qualities of body, will and mind. Blending sport with culture and education, Olympism seeks to create a way of life based on the joy found in effort, the educational value of good example and respect for universal fundamental ethical principles. ... The goal of Olympism is to place everywhere sport at the service of the harmonious development of man, with a view to encouraging the establishment of a peaceful society concerned with the preservation of human dignity. To this effect, the Olympic Movement engages, alone or in cooperation with other organizations and within the limits of its means, in actions to promote peace. (IOC, 2004: 9)

The concept of Olympism has been subject to much comment, both from disciples and critics. The quasi-religious or cult-like, uncritical adherence to the idea is exemplified in the following quotation:

> Olympism is all pervading, it is life and the way that life is lived by one person, a group, or a country and is best shown in international relationships. These principles of living are epitomised in the pageantry, panoply, contest and atmosphere of spectator and athlete alike at the celebration of an Olympic Festival. ... Olympism enables things to happen for good – but one must believe in it, work for it and allow it to be the driving force within every person. It is easy to believe, for a moment: it is much more difficult to believe, to justify one's belief, to be known for it and to be an example of it. ... Many people join in but few lead. Each has to be imbued with the essence of all that is done through study and action – and then, and only then, can Olympism be realised. (Powell, 1994: 81)

Applying such sentiments to a sporting movement makes them appear grandiose and even somewhat pretentious. How can sport provide a 'philosophy of life'? This is a role normally reserved for religion or political ideology. Should these claims be taken seriously? The temptation is to treat them in the same way that the majority of people treat the claims of extremist cults. But a number of commentators have suggested that the founder of Olympism, Pierre de Coubertin, deserves to be taken seriously as a humanistic philosopher.

Da Costa (1998: 189) argues that, while 'from today's point of view the unsystematic writings of de Coubertin are likely to be seen as superficial, intensely diverse and even contradictory', they can be rendered respectable by being viewed in the context of the eighteenth and nineteenth century philosophical tradition of *eclecticism*. This approach was more inductive than the emerging positivist schools of thought of the time and accommodated ideas such as Olympism, which de Coubertin described as a 'state of mind' rather than a 'system'. The key elements of the state of mind were identified as the relationship between physical effort (sport) and 'eurhythmy' (control) and the search for equilibrium, or 'the 'balanced whole' of body, will and mind' (Da Costa, 1998: 196). Da Costa then seeks to bring the philosophy of Olympism up to date by linking it with contemporary notions of pluralism – suggesting that 'pluralistic Olympism' might take on different forms, depending on 'each specific cultural identity'.

Loland (1994) seeks to explore and add philosophical legitimacy to de Coubertin's ideas by exploring them from the perspective of the 'history of ideas', identifying the goals of Olympism, its historical origins and the associated 'unit-ideas' which underpin it. He divides the historical influences on De Coubertin into four:

1. The *French Connection* draws attention to de Coubertin's own upper class upbringing in nineteenth century France and his concerns about France's place in the world, and various influences on his philosophical thinking.
2. The *Anglo-Saxon Connection* involved the influence of English and American sport, as described in Chapter 2.
3. The *Internationalist Connection* involved, in war-torn Europe, a concern for international peace.
4. The Ancient Connection concerned de Coubertin's idealisation of Ancient Greece and its sporting activities.

From this Loland (1994: 36) attempts to identify 'stable elements in terms of four main goals and to link Olympism to one central unit-idea which seems to found the very basis of the ideology'. The four goals are:

1. to educate and cultivate the individual through sport;
2. to cultivate the relation between men [sic] and society;
3. to promote international understanding and peace;
4. to worship human greatness and possibility.

Loland's conclusion is that these four goals represent, essentially, the goals of Western *humanism*. Nevertheless he admits that de Coubertin 'is, of course, not among the strongest representatives of the humanist tradition' (Loland, 1994: 39).

Neither Da Costa or Loland seem to consider the paradox that the unique characteristic of Olympism, its basis in physical activity and sport, are both its strength and weakness. The strength lies in its popular appeal. The weakness lies in the fact that contemporary Western philosophy is essentially cerebral and is disinclined to take seriously a philosophy which celebrates physical prowess. Indeed, it was the physicality of the Ancient Games which is said to have been a reason for, as we have seen in Chapter 2, their eventual prohibition by a Christian Emperor. This is, of course, in contrast to a number of non-Western philosophies which celebrate physical prowess and, albeit often in caricatured form, attract popular followings in the West. This suggests that, in the context of Da Costa's 'pluralist Olympism', this Western-based movement could have, after all, more resonance in the East.

While the contemporary world may be ambivalent about embracing Olympism as a whole 'way of life', there seems little doubt that it is seen as a distinctive way of conducting sport. The moral stance of the Olympic Movement has set it apart from lesser sporting phenomena. One consequence is that, in publicly declaring adherence to a set of lofty ideals, the Olympic Movement lays itself open to criticism whenever it deviates from them – an issue we return to at a number of points in the book.

The Olympic Movement

The Olympic Games are unique in sport, not only in having associated with them a declared philosophy, but also in being recognised as a 'movement'. The *Olympic Movement* is described in the *Olympic Charter* as: 'the concerted, organised, universal and permanent action, carried out under the supreme authority of the IOC, of all individuals and entities who are inspired by the values of Olympism (IOC, 2004: 9).

The Olympic Movement 'encompasses organizations, athletes and other persons who agree to be guided by the Olympic Charter. The criterion for belonging to the Olympic Movement is recognition by the IOC' (2004: 1). Membership of the Olympic Movement therefore comprises:

* the International Olympic Committee (IOC);
* International Sports Federations (IFs);
* National Olympic Committees (NOCs);
* the Organising Committees of the Olympic Games (OCOGs);
* national associations, clubs and persons belonging to the IFs and NOCs, including judges, referees, coaches and the other sports officials and technicians and 'particularly the athletes, whose interests constitute a fundamental element of the Olympic Movement's action';
* other organisations and institutions as recognised by the IOC. (IOC, 2004: 10)

In short, anyone who has played a formal role in organising or participating in the Olympic Games is considered to be part of the Olympic Movement.

The *Charter* also outlines the *goals* of the Olympic Movement, as follows.

> The goal of the Olympic Movement is to contribute to building a peaceful and better world by educating youth through sport practised in accordance with Olympism and its values. (IOC, 2004: 10)

Such sentiments appear to locate the IOC, not just as another sporting body, but as an organisation which transcends sport and links sporting endeavours to such activities as the pursuit of peace and protection of human rights – a role generally associated with the United Nations and its agencies. Indeed, reminiscent of the *Universal Declaration of Human Rights*, the *Olympic Charter* states:

> The practice of sport is a human right. Every individual must have the possibility of practising sport without discrimination of any kind and in the Olympic spirit, which requires mutual understanding with a spirit of friendship, solidarity and fair play. (IOC, 2004: 9)

The idea of 'educating youth through sport' goes right back to de Coubertin and the influence of the British public school tradition on his thinking, as discussed in Chapter 2. While education features in various ways in Olympic events and activities, the élitism of Olympic performance, particularly in the professional era, makes the links with democratic mass education somewhat tenuous.

Olympic organisation

The Olympic Games involve some 36 different sports (29–30 in the Summer Games and seven in the Winter Games). The administration of any one of these sports is complicated, typically involving multi-million dollar budgets and development programmes and systems of competition, promotion and regulation at local, national, regional and world levels. The Olympic Games organisation has to mesh with this complex, world-wide gaggle of sporting organisations to produce major, over-arching sporting events every two years.

The basic structure of the network of international Olympic organisations is summarised in Figure 4.1. At the centre is the International Olympic Committee (IOC), a self-perpetuating body of some 111 members, with virtually absolute power over the Games phenomenon. The various individual sports are represented in the organisational chart by the International Federations (IFs) of individual sports, themselves generally complex organisations, each representing up to 200 national governing bodies. Also represented are the 200 National Olympic Committees (NOCs). With a few exceptions, neither the IFs or the NOCs have direct representation on the IOC – some of their members are also members of the IOC in their own right, but not as representatives of their own country or sport. Formal relationships between the IOC and these bodies are conducted through bi-lateral negotiations and joint meetings.

Figure 4.1. International Organisation of the Olympic Movement

The International Olympic Committee

Origins

The IOC was founded at the 1894 International Athletic Congress convened by Baron Pierre de Coubertin and held at the Sorbonne in Paris. De Coubertin was initially secretary and then president (1896–1925) of the organisation, and for many years the IOC *was*, to all intents and purposes, de Coubertin. Until after about 1908:

there was no working I.O.C. Only after that date, and then very slowly, did Coubertin begin to consult the princes, millionaires, and elderly bureaucrats (who thought much the same as him anyway) whose names he had assembled to give the I.O.C. credibility. (Mandell, 1976a: 170)

Initially based in Paris, the IOC headquarters moved to Lausanne, Switzerland, when de Coubertin moved his residence there in 1918 (Mandell, 1976a: 169, 172), and has remained there ever since. There was some advantage in this location during much of the twentieth century when Switzerland maintained its political neutrality during hot and cold wars.

Mission and roles

The *Olympic Charter* (IOC, 2004: 10) describes the IOC as the 'supreme authority' of the Olympic Movement. It also outlines its *mission* and *roles*, which are summarised in Table 4.1.

Table 4.1. International Olympic Committee mission and roles

Mission: To promote Olympism throughout the world and to lead the Olympic Movement.

Roles: The roles of the IOC relate to:

- *ethics* in sport;
- education of youth through sport;
- encouraging spirit of fair play;
- banning of *violence*;
- encouraging/supporting *sport and sports competitions*;
- ensuring *regular celebration of the Olympic Games*;
- placing sport at the *service of humanity* to *promote peace*;
- the *unity and independence* of the Olympic Movement;
- any form of *discrimination* affecting the Olympic Movement;
- promotion of *women in sport*;
- the fight *against doping* in sport;
- protecting the *health of athletes*;
- opposing political or commercial abuse of sport and athletes;
- the social and *professional future of athletes*;
- sport for all;
- sustainable development in sport;
- a *positive legacy* for host cities and countries;
- blending sport with *culture and education*;
- supporting the *International Olympic Academy (IOA) and other Olympic education.*

Source: IOC (2004: 10)

Thus the organisation of the Olympic Games is just one of the IOC's roles; it also sees itself as promoting a wide range of values and practices related to sport in general and to wider social and political issues. But the organisation is not just concerned with high ideals: it has a business-like, even commercial, approach to its Olympic 'property' – the Olympic 'brand'.

Protecting the Olympic 'brand'

Clause 11 of the *Olympic Charter* states:

> The Olympic Games are the exclusive property of the IOC which owns all rights relating thereto, in particular, and without limitation, the rights relating to their organization, exploitation, broadcasting, recording, representation, reproduction, access and dissemination in any form and by any means or mechanism whatsoever, whether now existing or developed in the future.
>
> (IOC, 2004: 17)

These rights are jealously guarded:

> The Olympic symbol, flag, motto, anthem, identifications (including but not limited to 'Olympic Games' and 'Games of the Olympiad'), designations, emblems, flame and torches, ... shall be collectively or individually referred to as 'Olympic properties'. All rights to any and all Olympic properties, as well as all rights to the use thereof, belong exclusively to the IOC, including but not limited to the use for any profit-making, commercial or advertising purposes.
>
> (IOC, 2004: 17)

Typically, countries which host Olympic Games enact legislation to protect Olympic symbols from unauthorised commercial exploitation. While the marketing and funding potential of the Olympic 'brand' was fully recognised only in the last quarter of the twentieth century, awareness dates from much earlier, as demonstrated by Barney *et al.* (2002: 31–50) in their account of 'Avery Brundage and the Great Bread War', in which an American baker was pursued by the IOC for unauthorised selling of 'Olympic Bread' in the 1930s and 40s.

Funding

The major reason for the concern about the 'ownership' of the Olympic Games and their symbols is financial. The IOC has not always been financially secure but from the 1980s the recognition of the commercial value of the Olympics brand and its exploitation through sponsorship, together with the sale of broadcasting rights, has provided substantial funding for the organisation. The issue of funding of the IOC and the Olympic Games generally are discussed in detail in Chapter 6.

Membership

The original IOC consisted of 14 men selected in the main by de Coubertin. While the membership has since expanded to 111 (see IOC website), it remains a self-perpetuating organisation with a somewhat élitist air (a complete listing of IOC members can be found on the IOC website). It is an 'international non-governmental non-profit organisation'. New members are appointed by the IOC itself for indefinite periods, but are expected to retire at age 70 (or 80 if they were elected before 1999). Of the 111 members:

3. three were elected 30 years ago or more;
4. 15 were elected than 20–29 years ago;
5. 11 have royal or aristocratic titles;
6. 40 have participated in at least one Olympic Games;
7. 25 have won Olympic medals.

IOC members are deemed to be 'representatives of the IOC' in their respective countries, not representatives or delegates of their country to the IOC. They are intended to be independent and, according to the *Charter*, 'may not accept from governments, organizations, or other legal entities or natural persons, any mandate liable to bind them or interfere with the freedom of their action and vote' (IOC, 2004: 28).

The history of the IOC membership is important for an understanding of its current nature and *modus operandi* (Leiper, 1976). At the end of the nineteenth century and during the early years of the twentieth century, given the lack of the sorts of communication technology which are taken for granted today and the slowness and high cost, by modern standards, of international travel, the successful establishment of any sort of international organisation can be seen as a considerable achievement. To have succeeded without any government subvention is even more remarkable. Such an organisation could only have functioned at the time if its members were independently wealthy and had the time to devote to the enterprise. Thus male members of royal, aristocratic and upper class élites from around the Western world dominated the IOC membership. As Dick Pound, IOC member and a former vice-president puts it:

> The International Olympic Committee lived from hand to mouth for the first sixty or seventy years of its existence and the criticism often directed at it – that it was a rich man's club – was entirely true. To be a member meant that you had to be able to pay all your own expenses to attend the meetings and the Olympic Games. (Pound, 2004: 139)

Such individuals would not have readily thought in terms of democratic or participatory processes; neither would they have travelled third class or stayed in two-star hotels. Out of their own pockets, they established an IOC 'style' which was an extension of their own privileged lifestyles, and which has been slow to change. While the membership has widened in recent years, to include, in particular, more former and current Olympic athletes and sport administrators, the traditional type of member is still common and, along with them, the élitist and patrician style.

The president

The IOC president is elected for a period of eight years, renewable. In over 100 years of existence, the organisation has had only eight presidents, including de Coubertin, as shown in Table 4.2. Presidents have tended to be long-serving, just four of them having a combined period of office of 90 years. Presidents have been enormously influential in setting the tone and direction of the IOC during their terms of office. Biographies of their terms in office have been written for most of them (see Further

Reading). In recent years, particularly under the former incumbent Juan Antonio Samaranch, the office has assumed the status of an ambassador or quasi-head of state, with the courtesy title of 'his excellency' often used. Many of the significant changes in the Olympic Games of the last quarter of the twentieth century took place during the 24–year presidency of Juan Antonio Samaranch, who was replaced on his retirement in 2001 by Jacques Rogge (see Fig. 4.2).

Table 4.2. Presidents of the International Olympic Committee.

Dates	Years in office	Name	Country
1894–1896	2	Demetrias Vikélas	Greece
1896–1925	29	Baron Pierre de Coubertin	France
1925–1942	17	Count Henry de Baillet-Latour	Belgium
1942–1952	10	J. Sigfried Edström	Sweden
1952–1972	20	Avery Brundage	USA
1972–1980	8	Lord Killanin	Ireland
1980–2004	24	Juan Antonio Samaranch	Spain
2004–	-	Jacques Rogge	Belgium

Figure 4.2. IOC Presidents: Juan Antonio Samaranch (1980-2004) and Jacques Rogge (2004-)

Organisation

The meetings of the whole IOC, which generally take place once or twice a year, are referred to as 'sessions' and are quite grand affairs in their own right. Cities are eager to host IOC Sessions as 'events' since they will generally be an occasion for meetings of commissions and International Federations and will be involve attendances by delegations from bid cities, as well as a substantial media presence.

The affairs of the IOC are managed by the Executive Board, comprising the President, four Vice-Presidents and ten other members; all are elected by the IOC as a whole by secret ballot at an IOC session. Only the President is a full-time salaried appointment. The Executive Board is supported by a Director General and a headquarters staff of some 200, including the staff of the Olympic Museum.

Critics of the IOC

An organisation with a profile as prominent as that of the IOC inevitably has its critics. As a non-democratic, non-representative international body, it appears some-what anachronistic in the modern world and has therefore been particularly subject to criticism for its undemocratic, oligarchic and secretive nature. The organisation's success in recent decades in securing substantial funding, together with its power to determine the location of the Games, which can bring millions, even billions, of dollars to successful host cities, have led to scrutiny, and criticism, of its operations. Some of this scrutiny has been academic and analytical (e. g. Alexandrakis and Krotee, 1988; Krotee, 1988), while some of it, especially recently, has been more sensational in nature.

Lucas (1992: 117–132) identifies five types of criticism of the Olympic Movement, most of it directed principally at the IOC itself. These are:

- criticisms from a generally left-wing political perspective;
- criticisms of excessive commercialisation;
- 'persistent vexation' against the IOC;
- criticisms of the betrayal of Olympic ideals (particularly the abandonment of amateurism); and
- criticism related to the encouragement of excessive nationalism – the Olympics as 'war without weapons'.

While Lucas notes that the first type of criticism emanates mostly from academic sources (e. g. from Brohm, 1978; Gruneau, 1984; Tomlinson, 1984), the others seem to arise largely in press commentaries.

The most comprehensive critique of the IOC was put forward in the book, *Lords of the Rings*, by journalists Vyv Simson and Andrew Jennings (1992), and in its successors, *New Lords of the Rings* (Jennings, 1996) and *The Great Olympic Swindle* (Jennings, 2000). The tone of these books is indicated by their sub-titles, respectively: *Power, Money and Drugs in the Modern Olympics*; *Olympic Corruption and How to Buy Gold Medals* and *When the World Wanted its Games Back*. Typical of the accusations of Simson and Jennings is the following statement on the first page of the second book:

Allegations that bribes have been paid to win gold medals, sex scandals and positive dope tests covered up and Olympic funds diverted to a campaign for the Nobel Peace Prize all pointed back to the secretive leadership of the IOC ... who own and control the Games. They bank substantial profits and live like royalty while young athletes sweat and make sacrifices just to qualify for their heats.

(Jennings, 1996: 1)

Of IOC members, Jennings stated:

> Some conduct themselves with integrity. Many don't. Some care about sport and its values. Others are more concerned about their wallets. Unfortunately, sports fans know little about them. Individual committee members stay out of the stadium floodlights and conspire to have their disagreements in private.
>
> (Jennings, 1996: 11)

In reflecting on the IOC's commercial and proprietorial approach to the Olympic phenomenon, Jennings stated:

> If the committee hadn't got the rights to this multi-billion dollar exercise in global marketing locked up and ring-fenced by sabre-toothed attorneys, they could kiss good-bye to their first class flights, five-star hotels, police-escorted limos and fawning hostesses. No more mountains of Beluga caviare, creative expenses claims or free seats at the front row everywhere from Wimbledon to the Olympics. (Jennings, 1996: 12)

Among the many negative claims made by Jennings and Simson are (page numbers of second book in brackets):

- information on positive drug tests on athletes at the Los Angeles Games was suppressed (p. 7);
- bribery was involved in the boxing contest in Seoul in 1988 (p. 9);
- a senior international sporting official was a member of the East German secret police (p. 10);
- the IOC manipulated press coverage of its activities (pp. 13–14);
- information on then president Samaranch's links with the former fascist Franco regime in Spain had been suppressed (pp. 15, 18–19, 28–33);
- IOC members gladly accepted excessive gifts from potential host cities, in breach of IOC rules (pp. 17–18);
- Olympic Games events generated controversy and dissent in host communities as well as peace and consensus (pp. 18–27);
- offers of sexual favours have been used to attempt to influence IOC members' votes in selection of host cities (pp. 39–40);
- the IOC has 'sold out' the Games to commercialism (pp. 47–54);
- IOC members are selected on the basis of who will give the President 'least trouble', rather than being the best for the job (p. 56);
- the IOC has become a 'corpulent bureaucracy' (p. 61).

Overall, Jennings and Simson paint a picture of the IOC as a self-indulgent group of people, prone to political machination, susceptible to personal flattery and over-fond of the creature comforts, especially when provided by others, namely potential and actual host cities.

For a number of years Jennings and Simson were almost alone among the world's journalists in their comprehensive condemnation of the IOC and its workings. The 1989/99 revelations and accusations concerning IOC member activities surrounding the selection of host cities for the Games appear to have largely vindicated these lone critics. These events are discussed Chapter 5.

Less sensational critics concentrate on more mundane, but perhaps more fundamental, features of the IOC. For example, Alexandrakis and Krotee (1988) argue that the undemocratic nature of the IOC is outmoded. While virtually all other international sporting bodies operate on a representative basis, the IOC continues to appoint its own members on the basis of undeclared criteria, and to insist that its members are representatives of the IOC in their countries, rather than the other way around. While de Coubertin's initial intention was that every country which took part in the Games would be represented on the IOC, as the number of participating countries has grown to 203, this principle has been abandoned. While it might be accepted that a 203–member Committee would be unwieldy, critics question the criteria used to select members, with its over-emphasis on Europe and such idio-syncracies as longstanding members from the 'mini-states' of Liechtenstein and Monaco and four members from Switzerland. The geographical distribution of membership has changed little in the ten years since Alexandrakis and Krotee analysed it, as shown in Table 4.3.

Table 4.3. Geographical distribution of IOC membership and NOCs

Region	IOC members			NOCs		
	1988*	1998**	2006†	1988*	1998**	2006†
	%	%	%	%	%	%
Europe	42	41	44	18	26	24
Asia	15	16	20	24	21	22
Africa	19	19	15	29	21	26
America	20	18	15	24	24	21
Oceania	4	5	5	5	6	8

Sources: * from IOC (1998a); ** from Alexandrakis and Krotee (1988); † from IOC (n.d.)

Whether the IOC can, or should, survive in its current form is one of the key issues discussed in the final chapter of the book, concerning the future of the Games.

A second major criticism of the IOC is that, in seeking financial independence by means of the sale of television rights and pursuit of sponsorship, the IOC is 'selling out' the Olympic ideal to media and commercial interests. These claims are not discussed further here, but are dealt with in the chapters on finance and economics (Chapter 6) and the media (Chapter 7).

A further criticism of the IOC is that, despite the responsibility it has assumed for the control of doping in Olympic sports, it has not been sufficiently 'tough on drugs'. It is claimed that, for fear of offending major member nations or particular sporting federations, it has been slow to use its moral authority to demand tough penalties on offenders and has put insufficient resources into testing. Again, this issue is discussed fully in the relevant chapter on drugs (Chapter 8).

The Olympic Museum

The Olympic Museum was established in 1993 at a cost of almost $US70 million. The 11,000 square metre building occupies a prime site in Lausanne, overlooking Lake Geneva (see Figure 4.3). The purpose of the museum is to be a 'universal repository of the written, visual and graphic memory of the Olympic games' (IOC, n.d.). In the words of former president Juan Antonio Samaranch, the museum is intended to be a 'global source of information on the impact of the Olympic tradition on art, culture, economy and world peace' (IOC, n.d.). Pierre de Coubertin had declared his intention to establish a museum to house the IOC archives when the IOC moved to Lausanne in 1915, but little was done until Samaranch was elected to the presidency in 1980 and declared the establishment of a museum as a prime goal. Some 84 per cent of the cost was provided by 55 individual, institutional and corporate donors. Among the donors were the TOP partners (see Chapter 6), such as Coca Cola and Panasonic, Olympic Organising Committees, such as Albertville and Barcelona, and numerous other large corporations. Pound and Johnson (1999) draw attention to the opportune timing of some corporate contributions to the museum fund, noting that: 'Japanese companies donated about $20 million to the museum project, fuelling suspicion that corporate interests there bought the 1998 Winter Games for Nagano'. They also claim that NBC, which won the US broadcasting rights for the Games up to 2008, donated $1 million to the museum, but NBC is not listed as a donor on the IOC website.

Figure 4.3. The Olympic Museum, Lausanne

The museum also houses the Centre for Olympic Studies and acts as the publishing arm of the IOC. It attracts some 250,000 visitors a year and, in 1995, won the European Museum of the Year Award.

IOC Commissions

The IOC operates largely through a number of appointed commissions, or committees, as shown in Table 4.4. While ultimate authority rests with the IOC itself, widespread involvement of sporting and media representatives is achieved by means of the

Table 4.4. IOC Commissions

Commission	Functions
Athletes' Commission	Represents the views of athletes to the IOC – composed of retired and active Olympic athletes.
Culture and Olympic Education Commission	Development of links between sport and culture and education, working with NOCs; responsible for International Olympic Academy.
Coordination Commissions for the Olympic Games	Provides the link between the IOC and host city OCOGs, IFs and NOCs.
Ethics Commission	Establishes ethical rules for IOC and Olympic activities, including a 'Code of Ethics' – established in 1999 following corruption allegations.
Finance Commission	Oversees accounting and finance of the IOC.
International Relations	Promote relationships between the Olympic Movement and governments and public authorities.
Juridical Commission	Legal advice to IOC.
Marketing Commission	Advises the IOC on sources of 'financing and revenue' and on marketing.
Medical Commission	Implementation of the Olympic Medical Code re the policing of prohibited drug use (see Chapter 8).
Nominations Commission	Organises the nomination of new IOC members.
Olympic Philately, Numismatic and Memorabilia Commission	Oversees commemorative stamps, coins and other Olympic memorabilia.
Olympic Programme Commission	Reviews the programme of sports, disciplines, events, and no. of athletes, in each Olympic sport.
Olympic Solidarity Commission	Distribution of IOC funds to NOCs, particularly those in less wealthy countries.
Press Commission	Advises on relationships with print media.
Radio and Television Commission	Advises on relationships with radio and television.
Sport and Environment Commission	Concerned with promoting a 'green Games'.
Sport and the Law Commission	The legal framework within which sport operates.
Sport for All Commission	Promotion of general sport participation, adopting the European campaign phrase 'Sport for All'.
TV Rights and New Media Commission	Responsible for the overall IOC strategy for future broadcast rights negotiations.
Women and Sport Commission	Women's involvement in the Olympics.
Olympic Games Study Commission	A special commission to study the 'current scale and cost of staging the Olympic Games'.

Details of the membership of IOC commissions can be found at the IOC website.

commissions, thus maintaining some semblance of participation, if not democracy. Most of the commissions and their terms of reference are self-explanatory. A few merit particular mention.

Culture and Olympic Education Commission

Education appears as a key theme in Olympism and responsibility for its promotion lies with the *Culture and Olympic Education Commission*. The commission is responsible for the promotion of the study of Olympism, primarily through sponsorship of the International Olympic Academy. It also has oversight of the Olympic Games cultural programmes which are discussed separately later in the chapter.

The International Olympic Academy (IOA) was founded at Olympia, the site of the Ancient Olympic Games, in 1961, although the idea had initially been put forward by de Coubertin in 1927. The IOA conducts annual seminars attended by young people from around the world and is complemented by National Olympic Academies in 40 or more countries. As with many Olympic phenomena, the Academy has been subject to much discussion as to its nature and role (Ueberhorst, 1976a; Georgiadis; 1992; Lucas, 1992: 171–82), with one enthusiast even calling for it to be considered the 'Olympic University' (Powell, 1994: 81–95).

Ethics Commission

The *Ethics Commission* was established in March 1999 in the wake of allegations of corruption in the selection of cities to host the Games, particularly in relation to Salt Lake City, but extending to other cities and Olympiads as well. According to the IOC website, the Ethics Commission has three roles:

- It draws up and constantly updates a framework of ethical principles, including especially a Code of Ethics based on the values and principles enshrined in the Olympic Charter. These principles must be respected by the IOC and its members, by the cities wishing to organise the Olympic Games, by the Organising Committees of the Olympic Games (OCOGs), by the National Olympic Committees (NOCs) as well as by the 'participants' in the Olympic Games.
- It plays a monitoring role; as such, it ensures that ethical principles are respected; it conducts investigations into breaches of ethics submitted to it, and, when needed, makes recommendations to the Executive Board.
- It has a mission of prevention and advising the Olympic parties on the application of the ethical principles and rules. (IOC, n.d.)

The Ethics Commission is unusual in having a majority of members from outside of the IOC. The membership of eight includes just three IOC members. The external members have included a former UN Secretary General, a former US Senator, a former President of the French Constitutional Court, a former President of Switzerland and an Olympic athlete.

In view of the serious allegations made against IOC members, the subsequent proving of the allegations and resignations and sackings from the IOC (see Chapter 5), the high-powered Ethics Commission was seen as a key element in the strategy to restore its moral standing in the world. The Code of Ethics reaffirms the 'fundamental principles' of Olympism set out in the *Olympic Charter*, and sets down rules of behaviour in seven areas; A. dignity; B. integrity; C. resources; D. candidatures; E. relations with states; F. confidentiality; and G. implementation (IOC, n.d.).Among the rules included are:

- no soliciting, accepting or offering of any 'concealed remuneration, commission, benefit or service of any nature connected with the organisation of the Olympic Games';
- only gifts of nominal value, in accordance with prevailing local customs, may be given or accepted by the Olympic parties;
- hospitality shown to members and staff of the Olympic parties shall not exceed the standards prevailing in the host country;
- Olympic parties must avoid any conflict of interest between the organisation to which they belong and any other organisation within the Olympic Movement;
- Olympic parties must not be involved with firms or persons whose activity is inconsistent with the principles set out in the *Olympic Charter* and the Code of Ethics;
- Olympic parties shall neither give nor accept instructions to vote or intervene in a given manner within the organs of the IOC;
- income and expenditure of the Olympic parties shall be recorded in their accounts, which must be maintained in accordance with generally accepted accounting principles and   audited.

Environment Commission

The *Environment Commission* is one of the newest, but created with much less controversy. Its creation signals that, together with sport and culture, 'the environment' is to be promoted as a third key value of the Olympic Movement. Guidelines and principles for conducting a 'green Games' are set out in the *Manual on Sport and the Environment* (IOC, 1997). The Sydney 2000 Games were the first to be subject to the new code and, as noted in the case study in Chapter 10, the environmental organisation Greenpeace was involved in devising the numerous measures taken to conduct a 'Green Games' and an organisation, Green Games Watch 2000, was established to monitor the results.

Marketing Commission

Organisations generally see marketing as a relatively expensive function designed to promote the organisation and its products to the market. Marketing has been defined in many ways but, put simply, it can be seen as 'identifying the needs and wants of consumers both now and in the future, and then meeting them' (Horner and Swarbrooke, 2005: 3). Who are the 'consumers' of the Olympic Games? It might be thought that they are the hundreds of thousands of spectators who watch the Games live and the billions who watch them and read about them via the mass communication media. And perhaps the Olympic athletes, actual and aspiring, could be considered 'consumers', although they can also be seen as part of the 'production' side of the 'product'.

The International Olympic Committee, however, sees 'marketing' of the Olympic Games differently. The first item in the Marketing Commission's mandate is to 'review and study possible sources of financing and revenue for the International

Olympic Committee (IOC) and the Olympic Movement' (IOC, n.d.). Thus the selling of broadcasting rights arrangements with sponsors for the use of the Olympic logo can be seen as *marketing* activities, but they also provide the major source of revenue for the IOC and the rest of the Olympic organisation. So, for the IOC, 'marketing' means mainly 'revenue raising'. The 'product' of the Olympic Games is provided free to the consumer. Revenue is generated not from selling the product to the consumers (Games spectators) but by selling the rights to use the product as a vehicle for marketing other products (products sold through television advertising and products sold by Olympic sponsors). Thus, in selling broadcasting rights to television broadcasters, the IOC plays a similar to that of a television film producer selling a series to a television network. But the existence of worldwide sponsorship means that the process has similarities to a blockbuster film with associated merchandise.

The IOC engages in relatively little marketing activity in the traditional sense. In the recent review of the Olympic Programme conducted by the Programme Commission (see below), market research on consumer preferences, in the form of a study of television audiences, was only one of over 30 criteria used to judge whether a sport should be included in the programme. The IOC's first 'global promotion' was developed only recently, in the lead-up to the Sydney 2000 Games; it was entitled *Celebrate Humanity* and involved a series of television advertisements promoting Olympism. Similar promotions have been developed for each of the subsequent Summer and Winter Games. The current promotion, or 'global integrated marketing communications campaign', was announced in April 2007 and aims to 'communicate the key Olympic values of *Excellence, Friendship and Respect* to a youth audience around the world' (IOC, 2007b).

The bulk of the marketing of the Games is done by the Organising Committees of individual Games and sponsors and broadcasters. It is at the local level that the normal revenue stream from selling a product to a consumer is found, in the form of ticket sales to live spectators. But, as shown in Chapter 6, a peculiarity of the Olympics, as a business, is that ticket sales revenue typically constitutes only about 15 per cent of total revenue, and often much less. A further peculiarity of the Olympic marketing environment is that no advertising is permitted within Olympic venues – in the jargon, venues must be 'clean'.

Revenue and sponsorship are discussed in more detail in Chapter 6.

Olympic Programme Commission

The Olympic Programme Commission is responsible for agreeing, with the host city organising committee, the programme of sports to be included in any Olympic Games. The range of sports included in the modern Summer Olympic Games has varied over the years, and continues to change and develop with each Games. Some 35 Olympic and associated International Olympic Sports Federations are recognised by the IOC, as shown in Table 4.5. A further 29 sports and IFs are recognised by the IOC but have not, to date, featured in Olympic programmes.

We have seen, in Chapter 1, that the programme of sports included in the modern Olympic Games has little in common with the programme of the Ancient Games. So how did the modern programme arise? Redmond (1988: 81–82) notes that de Coubertin's experience of various nineteenth century 'pseudo-Olympics', including the Much Wenlock Games and the Highland Games, as discussed in Chapter 3, were key influences on the track and field programme of the first modern Olympic Games in Athens in 1896. Subsequent developments of the programme have reflected the interests of host nations, the IOC's view of the commercial value of certain sports and the lobbying power of various sporting federations.

The latest two sports to be included in the Games, which appeared for the first time at the Sydney 2000 games, illustrate this diversity of motive. The inclusion of Taekwondo can be attributed to the influence of former IOC Executive Board member Un Yong Kim, who was also President of the World Taekwondo Federation. The story behind the inclusion of triathlon, a sport that is only about ten years old, is described by one journalist as follows:

Table 4.5. Olympic Sports

Summer Games programme			Winter Games
Aquatics	Fencing	Shooting	Biathlon
Archery	Football	Table tennis	Bobsleigh
Athletics	Gymnastics	Taekwondo	Curling
Badminton	Handball	Tennis	Ice Hockey
Basketball	Hockey	Triathlon	Luge
Boxing	Judo	Volleyball	Skating
Canoe/kayak	Modern pentathlon	Weightlifting	Skiing
Cycling	Rowing	Wrestling	
Equestrian	Sailing		
Sports recognised by the IOC but not included in the Olympic programme			
Air sports	Dancesport	Netball	Softball**
Bandy	Golf*	Orienteering	Squash*
Baseball**	Karate*	Pelote Basque	Surfing
Billiard sports	Korfball	Polo	Sumo
Boules	Life-saving	Powerboating	Tug-of-War
Bowling	Motorcycle racing	Racquetball	Underwater sports
Bridge	Mountaineering/	Roller sports*	Water skiing
Chess	Climbing	Rugby*	Wushu

Source: IOC website. * = 'recognised' sports included in the 2005 programme review
**= sports deleted from the programme in the 2005 programme review.

According to one version of events, International Olympic Committee President, Juan Antonio Samaranch, was watching television at the 1984 Los Angeles Olympic games when he saw a triathlon and said: 'get that sport into the games'. Mr Samaranch was said to be transfixed by the sight of so many glamorous, fit young athletes swimming, cycling and running at will. They were the embodiment of the Olympic motto – Faster, Higher, Stronger – and they looked fantastic. According to another story, International Triathlon Union president Les McDonald used money inherited after his mother's death to fly around the world promoting the triathlon cause until Olympic delegates agreed that the greatest sporting event in the world could not go on without it. (Evans, 1998: 16–17)

The 26 sports which form the 'summer programme' and the seven sports which form the 'winter programme' are listed in the *Olympic Charter* and a two thirds majority

Table 4.6. Programme Commission criteria for assessing sports

Overview	List of disciplines in latest Summer Games*
	Events*
	No. of days competition*
	Description of events
	Changes proposed for next Games
	Venue requirements
	Quotas (maximum no. of athletes) + proposed changes
History & tradition	Date of establishment of IF
	Olympic Games and/or World Games participated in
	World Championships held
	Other multi-sport games participated in
Universality	No. of member National Federations (NFs)
	No. of Active NFs (i.e. have organised national championships)
	% of NFs in Olympic and/or World Games qualifying events
	% of IFs taking part in IF Continental Championships
	No. of medals awarded*
	No. of NOCs that won medals*
	Continental distribution of medals*
Popularity	Participation of best athletes in Olympic Games
	Ticket sales - % of total available*
	Media accreditation requests at last two World Championships
	Television coverage – hours per day*
	Prime-time TV audience – viewer-hours per day*
	No. of countries broadcasting last two World Championships
	No. of countries paid for TV rights for last two World Champs
	Income from sale of World Champs TV rights
	No. of press articles*
	No. of articles per publication sampled*
	Daily hits on IF website in 2003 and during World Champs
	Visits to sport page of IOC website
	Five major IF sponsors and benefits provided
Image and Environment	Proportions of male, female participation in qualifying events
	Proportions of male, female participation in World Games
	Gender composition of IF Executive board
	Impact of judging on competition results
	Judge/referee system and training/certification
	IF activities to promote the sport
	IF's environmental programme/impact of sport on environment
Athlete welfare	Involvement of athletes in IF decision-making
	No. of out-of-competition drug tests
	Total all tests in 2003–04

Development	Four-year strategic plan
	% of IF revenue from Olympic sources
	% of IF revenue from marketing and broadcasting
	Income from World Champs TV rights
	IF's three main development programmes
	National and continental distribution of finances
Costs	Venue costs at Olympic Games
	Technology requirements at Olympic Games
	Television production costs

Source: Olympic Programme Commission (2005: 11–16). * Information provided for latest Summer Olympics: Athens 2004 (and for some items also Sydney 2000).

is required to add or delete sports from the list. In 2002 the IOC decided to conduct a 'systematic review' of the summer Olympic programme, involving an appraisal of the then 28 sports and five of the 'recognised' sports'. For each sport, data on some 50 criteria, as listed in Table 4.6, were collected from International Federations and IOC sources. These included information on the historical record of involvement with the Games, the geographical spread of membership, the number of countries sending teams to the Olympics and to the sport's world championships, and the extent of television coverage. The report lists 'benchmarks' against which each IF's performance on each criterion is assessed. The results were presented in a substantial report (Olympic Programme Commission, 2005) presented to the IOC session held in Singapore in July 2005. On the basis of the information presented in the report, IOC members voted on which sports should remain in the programme. Baseball and softball were excluded. Squash and karate were nominated to replace the deleted sports, but failed to gain a two thirds majority, so the summer programme, as from London 2012, will include only 26 sports. (Details of the review process are provided on the Programme Commission page of the IOC website.)

This elaborate decision-making process would be seen by most observers as a great advance on the *ad hoc* processes of the past. However, despite the mass of data gathered to inform the decision-making process, the final decisions on inclusion and exclusion of sports was taken using the usual IOC secret ballot process, so it is not clear how the data influenced the decisions. The exercise would have been suitable for application of some sort of formal decision-making procedure, such as 'importance-performance' analysis (Veal, 2002: 110, 220), in which each IF would be scored not only on the basis of its *performance* on each criterion, but also in regard to the *importance* of each criterion.

Olympic Solidarity Commission

The *Olympic Solidarity Commission* plays a key role in maintaining the world-wide reach of the Olympic Games, being responsible for the distribution of IOC funds to NOCs, particularly those in less wealthy countries, thus enabling them to develop Olympic sport and field Olympic teams (Lucas, 1992: 85–94; IOC, 1996b). The assistance takes the form of scholarships for athletes and funding of coaches and NOC management. In the four year period 2005–2008 the budget for this programme is US$110 million (IOC, n.d.).

Olympic Games Study Commission

The *Olympic Games Study Commission* is not an ongoing commission, but a task-force established in 2001, for a limited time, under the chairmanship of Canadian IOC member Dick Pound, to investigate and report on a specific topic: the scale and cost of Olympic Games. It arose from a concern that the increasing scale, complexity and cost of running an Olympic Games would discourage many cities from bidding to host the Games. This is an issue discussed in the final chapter of the book when the future of the Olympic Games is considered. The final report of the commission, the 'Pound Report' (Olympic Games Study Commission, 2003) made numerous recommendations, including:

- the encouragement of the use of existing venues and temporary structures rather than construction of costly permanent new venues;
- passing on of existing know-how concerning the management of the games, through standardised operating procedures and best practice guides;
- closer integration of Paralympic Games and Olympic Games organisation.

Symbols and ceremonial

From the beginning of the revival, at de Coubertin's behest, the organisers of the modern Olympic Games sought to replicate the ceremonial nature and religious aura of the Ancient Olympic Games, by adopting some of their trappings, but also by adding some of their own (Slowinowski, 1991a, 1993; De Moragas *at al.*, 1996). The symbols and ceremonies discussed here are listed in Table 4.7.

The Olympic Symbol

The Olympic Symbol is the familiar five Olympic rings, in blue, yellow, black, green and red, representing 'the union of the five continents and the meeting of athletes from throughout the world at the Olympic Games' (IOC, 2004: 8). Despite some attempts to make the link, there is, in fact, no connection between the symbol and the Ancient Games. It is suggested that, when originally introduced, de Coubertin intended the rings to represent the first five host nations of the modern Games (Greece, France, USA, England, Sweden) – indeed, de Coubertin indicated that the six colours of the symbol (including the white background) included all the colours of these five nations' flags (Van Wynsberghe and Ritchie, 1994). It is even suggested that the original intention was to add new rings for every nation which subsequently hosted a games (Van Wynsberghe and Ritchie, 1994: 125). Regardless of its origins, what is clear today is that the symbol is the most widely recognised 'logo' in the world, with market research conducted in nine countries showing that, even outside of Games periods, around 80 per cent of the general public identify the rings with the Olympic Games, ahead of commercial logos such as those of Shell and McDonald's (Meenaghan, 1997). Clearly such worldwide recognition has enormous potential commercial value.

Table 4.7. Olympic symbols and ceremonies

	Description	Origins
Olympic Symbol	Five intertwined rings, in blue, yellow, black, green and red, and representing the five continents	First used by de Coubertin in 1913 – no link with Ancient Games
Olympic Flag	The five rings on a white background	Created in 1914 and first carried at a games in Antwerp, 1920
Olympic Motto	Citius . Altius . Fortius (faster, higher, stronger)	Created 1886 by Pierre Didon, Dominican priest
Olympic Emblems	The 'logo' designed for each Olympic Games	Created for each Olympic Games. Arguably first apparent at Mexico City, 1968
Olympic Anthem	Greek poem 'Ancient eternal and immortal spirit' set to music by Spyros Samaras	Performed at 1896 games, but adopted in 1958
Olympic Creed	The most important thing in the Olympic Games is not to win but to take part	Attributed to de Coubertin
Olympic Flame, Torch and Relay	Torch lit at Olympia and relayed by runners to the Olympic city to light the cauldron	Flame first lit in Amsterdam, 1928
Olympic Cauldron	Cauldron lit from the torch at the opening ceremony and extinguished at the closing ceremony	Lighting of the flame at Olympia and the relay instigated by Carl Diem for 1936 Berlin Games
Athletes' Oath	Oath spoken at the opening ceremony by one athlete, on behalf of all, to abide by the rues and spirit of the Games	Written by de Coubertin,. First delivered in Antwerp, 1920. Similar oath for officials introduced in Munich, 1972
Medal Ceremonies	Presentation of gold, silver and bronze medals to first, second and third places in each event, preceded by the playing of the winner's national anthem	Medals presented from the beginning, in 1896, but individual podium ceremonies from 1932 (see Barney, 1998)
Olympic Truce	Various initiatives to promote suspension of international hostilities during the Games.	Based on practice in the Ancient Games, to ensure safe passage for participants. Revived 1992
Olympic Order	Highest award of the Olympic movement , awarded for outstanding contributions to the movement	Inaugurated 1975

The Olympic Flag

The Olympic Flag portrays the five rings of the Olympic Symbol on a white background. Created by a Greek, Angelo Bolanki, in 1912 (Krüger, 1996: 101), it was originally presented by Pierre de Coubertin at the Paris Congress of the IOC in 1914 and was first paraded at the Antwerp Games of 1920. It is carried at opening ceremonies and is passed on for safe keeping from one host city to the next during closing ceremonies.

The Olympic Motto

The Olympic Motto is: *Citius • Altius • Fortius*. Created in 1886 by Pierre Didon, a Dominican priest and school teacher, and friend of de Coubertin, it is Latin for faster, higher, stronger. According to the *Olympic Charter*, it 'expresses the aspirations of the Olympic Movement' (IOC, 2004: 18).

Olympic Emblems

Olympic Emblems are designed for each Olympic Games by the host organisation, and incorporate the Olympic Symbol. Such emblems become the logo of the particular Games event. Early modern Olympic Games posters generally incorporate classical references such as olive branches and Greek columns, but a specific design incorporating the contemporary idea of a 'logo' appeared with the Mexico City Games of 1968.

The Olympic Anthem

The Olympic Anthem was introduced in 1958 in Tokyo and is sung at opening and closing ceremonies. The anthem consists of the Greek poem 'Ancient eternal and immortal spirit' set to music by Spyros Samaras. It was performed for the first time at the 1896 Athens Olympic Games, but was not formally adopted until the 55th session of the IOC in Tokyo in 1958.

The Olympic Flame, Torch and Relay

The Olympic Torch and the Olympic Flame are a major feature of the ceremonial of the modern Olympic Games. While flames were lit at the 1928 Amsterdam Games and the 1932 Los Angeles Games, the ceremony as practised today was introduced in the 1936 Berlin Games, at the instigation of Carl Diem, chairman of the Organising Committee for the Berlin Games (Durantez, 1988: 49). Diem instigated the practice of the torch being lit by the sun's rays at Olympia, in a ceremony conducted by classically attired 'priestesses', then being carried in relay procession to the host country.

The lighted torch is carried by a relay of several thousand runners on an extensive international tour prior to the Games, including a nationwide, highly publicised tour in the host country. The torch's journey culminates in its entry into the Olympic Stadium during the opening ceremony. The torch, usually borne by a local Olympic hero or heroine, is then used to light the Olympic Flame – one of the highlights of the occasion. The Olympic Flame burns throughout the Games and is extinguished during the closing ceremony to mark the end of the Games (Slowinowski, 1991b).

While there is no exact parallel in the Ancient Olympic Games, Durantez (1988: 30) points out that torch relay races took place in classical Athens and ceremonies involving lighted torches took place at the Olympic Games, related to the lighting of sacrificial fires in religious ceremonies.

Following the example of Los Angeles, the Torch Relay has now become a money-making aspect of the Games, with a major sponsor usually involved and members of the public being permitted to pay to carry the torch on part of its journey. Ceremonies and local festivals are held in designated host communities along the route. The relay therefore serves a key function in symbolically 'bringing the Games' to many, often remote, parts of the host country (see also Buschman and Lennartz, 1996; Cahill, 1998, 1999a, b).

The Olympic Athletes' Oath

The Olympic Athletes' Oath, introduced in Antwerp in 1920, is recited at the opening ceremony by a single athlete, chosen to represent all participants:

> In the name of all the competitors I promise that we shall take part in the Olympic Games, respecting and abiding by the rules which govern them, in the true spirit of sportsmanship, for the glory of sport and the honour of our teams.

A similar oath is sworn on behalf of the officials taking part in the Games was introduced in Munich in 1972.

The Olympic Creed

The Olympic Creed, attributed to Pierre de Coubertin, states:

> The most important thing in the Olympic Games is not to win but to take part, just as the most important thing in life is not the triumph but the struggle. The essential thing is not to have conquered but to have fought well. (USOC, 1999)

Medal Ceremonies

Medal Ceremonies in the early modern Games were relatively simple affairs. Medals were presented to the athletes by an appropriate dignitary, generally all together at the closing ceremony; flags of victors' countries were raised and national anthems played, but there was no victory podium (Barney, 1998). The latter was first introduced at the Lake Placid and Los Angeles Games of 1932. Barney relates that the idea – and directive – came from the IOC President of the time, Count Baillet-Latour, who had seen a podium used at the first British Empire Games at Hamilton, Ontario, two years earlier. At Hamilton victors had simply been presented to the crowd on a two-level podium – at the Lake Placid and Los Angeles Olympics, however, the current practice of actually awarding medals to athletes standing on the podium was introduced.

While the awarding of medals has not been subject to criticism, the raising of national flags and playing of national anthems has been criticised for stimulating a chauvinistic atmosphere which can be seen as being at variance with the Olympic internationalist ideal, as discussed in Chapter 5.

The Olympic Truce

During the Ancient Olympic Games a truce of up to three months was declared in regard to any hostilities taking place among the Greek states, to enable athletes to pass safely to and from Olympia (Swaddling, 1999: 10–11). The idea of declaring a truce during the modern Games arose in the 1920s, but it was not until 1992 that the IOC secured support for the idea from the United Nations (Roche, 2000: 212–15). Such a truce is duly declared by the UN during the period of Olympic Games. The truce is clearly not universally observed, but certain symbolic acts have taken place under its auspices: for example, the war-torn former Republic of Yugoslavia was able to participate in the 1994 Barcelona Games and, in the Opening Ceremony of the Sydney 2000 Games, the South and North Korean delegations marched together under a single flag (Lambrinidis, 2003; Mascagni, 2003).

The Olympic Order

Mimicking national honours systems, the IOC awards the *Olympic Order* to persons who have 'illustrated the Olympic ideal' and have 'achieved remarkable merit in the sporting world' or have 'rendered outstanding services to the Olympic Movement', either through their own personal achievement or their contribution to the development of sport. Inaugurated in 1975, recipients have included outstanding Olympic athletes and presidents and CEOs of Games organising committees.

The bidding process and host city selection

The organisation of the Olympic Games is complicated by the practice of choosing a new summer and winter site for every Olympiad. This involves a two-year cycle of location selection, with the Winter Games alternating with the Summer Games, each run every four years. Thus for every Games, a long and elaborate bidding process is entered into, in which hopeful city bid committees spend tens of millions of dollars. Host cities are announced seven years in advance of the Games themselves. It has been suggested from time to time that a permanent site should be selected for the Games, thus avoiding the continual site-selection 'circus' – but such a proposition has disadvantages as well as advantages, as discussed in Chapter 11.

Bidding for the Games

Only one city can bid from any one country, so if more than one city expresses an interest, the NOC must conduct an initial selection process before the bid can be prepared. For successful cities, therefore, the whole process of bidding for and staging an Olympic Games takes about a decade. Since few cities are selected on their first bid, successful, and unsuccessful, cities may well be involved in the bidding process

Table 4.8. Bidding for the Games; 1976–2012

Year	Successful city	Unsuccessful bidders
Summer Games		
1976	Montréal	Los Angeles, Moscow
1980	Moscow	Los Angeles
1984	Los Angeles	None
1988	Seoul	Nagoya
1992	Barcelona	Amsterdam, Belgrade, Birmingham, Brisbane, Paris
1996	Atlanta	Athens, Belgrade, Manchester, Melbourne, Toronto
2000	Sydney	Beijing, Berlin, Istanbul, Manchester
2004	Athens	Buenos Aires, Cape Town, Istanbul, Lille, Rio de Janeiro, Rome, San Juan, Seville, Stockholm, St Petersburg
2008	Beijing	Istanbul, Osaka, Paris, Toronto
2010	Vancouver	Pyeong Chang, Salzburg
2012	London	Madrid, Moscow, New York, Paris
Winter Games		
1976	Innsbruck	Denver, Sion, Tampere/Are, Vancouver
1980	Lake Placid	Vancouver-Garibaldi (withdrew before the final vote)
1984	Sarajevo	Saporo, Fallun-Göteborg
1988	Calgary	Falun, Cortina d'Ampezzo
1992	Albertville	Anchorage, Berchtesgaden, Cortina d'Ampezzo, Lillehammer, Falun, Sofia
1994	Lillehammer	Anchorage, Oestersund/Are, Sofia
1998	Nagano	Aoste, Jacca, Oestersund, Salt Lake City
2002	Salt Lake City	Oestersund, Quebec City, Sion
2006	Torino	Helsinki, Klagenfurt, Poprad-Tatry, Sion, Zakopane

for a number of decades. Table 4.8 shows the successful and unsuccessful bidding cities since 1976. It is notable that Los Angeles was the only city to enter a bid for the 1984 Games, following the widely publicised financial problems of the 1976 Montréal Games. The subsequent financial success of the Los Angeles Games resulted in a revival of interest, with as many as ten cities bidding for the 2004 games.

Preparing a bid to host an Olympic Games is a substantial undertaking. Detailed information must be provided on:

I.   Motivation, overall concept and public opinion
II.   Political support
III.   Finance
IV.   Venues and programme
V.   Accommodation (athlete/media villages, hotel accommodation for IOC etc.)
VI.   Transport
VII.   Security
VIII.   General conditions (demographics, environment, climate) and experience in running events. (IOC, 2005a)

The practice in the past was for each city entering the bid process to seek to entice as many IOC members as possible to visit and view the attractions of the city and its proposed Olympic sites, facilities and plans. The revelation that this process involved excessive giving of gifts and other enticements to IOC members and their families, led to the crisis of 1998/99 and subsequent reforms, as discussed in more detail in Chapter 5. As noted above, these practices had been extensively documented before the crisis, and since, in a series of books by journalists Vyv Simpson and Andrew Jennings (Simpson and Jennings,1992; Jennings, 1996, 2000).

Under the current guidelines only members of an appointed Evaluation Commission may visit candidate cities during the bid period. Included in the *Rules of Conduct Applicable to all Cities Wishing to Organise the Olympic Games* are the following:

Article 8: After IOC acceptance of their Candidature File, or any other date set by the IOC, in the final stage of the procedure, the Candidate Cities may promote their candidature among the IOC members, but exclusively by means of sending written documents. The embassies of the countries with Candidate Cities may not invite IOC members to any reception.

Article 9: No gifts may be given to or received by Olympic parties. This prohibition must be respected by the cities and their NOCs as well as by all those acting on behalf of or supporting the candidature. The same principle applies to the cities' relations with third parties, in particular the media, IFs and organisations recognised by the IOC.

Article 11: There will be no visits by IOC members to the cities, nor from the cities to IOC members. If an IOC member must travel to a city for any reason, he or she must inform the IOC Ethics Commission beforehand. The city may not take advantage of this occasion for the promotion of its candidature, nor cover the costs and other expenses linked to such a visit, in particular, travel and accommodation. (IOC, 2005b)

Site selection

The Evaluation Commission prepares published reports on each of the bids for the IOC. At a highly publicised meeting of the IOC – itself a major event for a host city – an exhaustive ballot results in the announcement of the winning city, some seven years before the actual event.

The site selection process is partly technical and partly political. The technical aspects concern the availability of suitable sporting facilities and other infrastructure, such as transport, hotel accommodation and security, and organisational capabilities of the would-be hosts. Political aspects arise at the local and the international level.

Locally, the question arises as to the extent of community support for the bid, and subsequently, if successful, for the Games themselves. Often a bid is initially put together by a consortium of business and sporting interests, with or without input from city, regional or national governments – such loose organisations can be seen as examples of 'urban growth regimes' (Harding, 1994; Burbank *et al.*, 2000). The extent to which a bid has widespread political support can therefore vary. There have been cases where public opposition to a bid has caused it to be aborted, notably Berlin's bid for the 2000 and Toronto's bid for the 1996 Games (see Henderson, 1989; Kidd,

1992a, b; Lenskyj, 1992, 1994). Once a bid has been successful, continued political and community support for the Games is not necessarily guaranteed, as discussed later in this chapter.

International politics inevitably arise in the selection of host cities. The Cold War years saw block voting by Western, Eastern bloc and Third World IOC members, the effects of the long-running South African apartheid issue and boycotts brought about by events such as the Soviet invasion of Afghanistan. And the human rights records of bidding countries continues to be an issue. These political dimensions of the Games are considered in detail in Chapter 5.

Being involved in bidding to host an Olympic Games is an all-consuming process for those centrally involved. So much so that at least two bid CEOs have written books on the experience. Rod McGeoch (1994) has recorded his experience in leading the bid for the Sydney 2000 Games and Mike Lee (2006) has done the same for the London 2012 Games.

Hosting the Games

Once a host city has been selected, the final element of the 'Olympic Family' is established, namely the local Organising Committee for the Olympic Games (OCOG). While financial guarantees for the Games are generally sought and given from city, regional and/or national government, it is the OCOG, in association with the local NOC, which is the body responsible to the IOC for the running of the Games. The extent to which the Games are, in reality, hosted by a *city*, as opposed to a state or national government, varies from case to case – for example, the Moscow Games of 1980 were clearly hosted by the government of the USSR, while the Los Angeles Games were much more clearly hosted by the local OCOG. In the case of the year 2000 Games in Sydney, it was the state government of New South Wales which was the *de facto* host. The OCOG is nevertheless the entity held responsible for the day-to-day operation of the Games.

The IOC enters into a formal contract – the *host city contract* – with the host city and the NOC, the responsibilities subsequently being assumed by the OCOG. The contract makes clear that the IOC retains a high level of control over the Games, while the host organisation takes full responsibility, particularly financial responsibility, for implementation. Thus the Sydney 2000 host contract stated, in clauses 1, 6 and 7:

> 1. *Entrustment of the Organisation of the Games*: The IOC hereby entrusts the organization of the Games to the City and the NOC which undertake, jointly and severally, to fulfil their obligations in full compliance with the provisions of the Olympic Charter and of this Contract, including, without limitation, all matters referred to in the appendices to this Contract.

> 6. *Joint and Several Obligations of the City, the NOC and the OCOG*: The City, the NOC and the OCOG shall be jointly and severally responsible for all commitments entered into by any or all of them concerning the organization and staging of the Games and shall assume, jointly and severally, the entire financial responsibility for the organization of the Games. All agreements entered into between the City and/or the NOC and/or the OCOG relating to or having any effect upon their financial responsibility with respect to the Games, including the manner in which they share any consideration, surplus or loss relating to the Games, shall be submitted to the IOC Executive Board for approval.

7. *Indemnification and Waiver of Claims Against the IOC*: The City, the NOC and the OCOG shall be jointly and severally undertake to indemnify, hold harmless and exempt the IOC, its officers, members, directors, employees. consultants, agents and other representatives, from all payment in respect of any damages, including all costs, resulting from all acts or omissions relating to the games, including, but not limited to, *force majeure*. Furthermore, the City, the NOC and the OCOG shall be jointly and severally waive any claim against the IOC, its officers, members, directors, employees, consultants, agents and other representatives, for any damages, including all costs, resulting from all acts or omissions relating to the Games, including, but not limited to, *force majeure*, as well as any performance, non-performance, violation or termination of this Contract. This indemnification and waiver shall not apply to wilful misconduct or gross negligence by the IOC, its officers, members, directors, employees. consultants, agents and other representatives. (IOC, City of Sydney, AOC, 1993: 2–3)

The contract specified the requirements for running the Games in various appendices to the agreement – in the case of the Sydney 2000 contract, eleven appendices, running to some 350 pages. These provided guidelines for:

- the organisation of meetings, including IOC sessions, and meetings of the IOC Executive Board, IOC commissions, NOCs and IFs and media briefings (Appendix A);
- accreditation to the Games, covering access for athletes, coaches, VIPs, media and Olympic Family (Appendix B);
- transportation for the Olympic Family, including provision, at the OCOG's expense, of individual cars and drivers for IOC members and senior officials, and presidents and secretaries-general of participating NOCs and IFs during the Games (Appendix C);
- the Olympic Village (Appendix D);
- arrangements for the media (Appendix E);
- broadcasting, comprising extensive specification of technical facilities, including numbers and positions of television cameras for different types of venue (Appendix F);
- hotel accommodation for the Olympic Family, estimated to be some 2500 rooms (Appendix G);
- international marketing, relating to IOC international sponsors, including ensuring the availability of 4000 five-star hotel rooms for 'sponsors, suppliers and broadcaster guests and marketing partners' (Appendix H);
- provisions for the IOC Medical Commission (Appendix I);
- provision of insurance cover for the Olympic Family (Appendix J);
- Olympic Protocol, concerning a miscellany of matters, such as design of signage, brochures and medals and ticketing and spectator seating (Appendix K).

The Sydney 2000 contract document provided very detailed guidelines on certain matters, such as accreditation and broadcasting, but was curiously brief on other matters, such as the Cultural Programme (five lines), the Torch Relay (three lines) and drug testing (no specific mention, except for reference to provision of facilities for the Medical Commission).

The seven years between the announcement of a successful bid and the staging of the Games, as well as involving a programme of organisation, construction, marketing and promotion, is also invariably a period of political controversy, cost-blow-outs and embarrassments, uncertainties and set-backs. The organisational 'saga' of each Games is different, although there are some common themes. Some of these differences and commonalities are explored in the case-studies in Chapter 10.

Cultural programme

Each Olympic Games Organising Committee is required by the IOC to organise a cultural programme which, according to the 1995 edition of the *Oympic Charter*, was required to:

> promote harmonious relations, mutual understanding and friendship among the participants and others attending the Olympic Games. (IOC, 1995: 30)

De Coubertin's vision for the modern Olympic Games included a coming together of the arts and sport. This involved not just a cultural programme, but arts competitions, or a 'pentathlon of the Muses' (Bandy, 1988: 166). These were to include architecture, dramatic art, choreography, decoration, literature, music, painting and sculpture – all with a sporting theme. Such competitions were held from the 1912 Stockholm Games through to the 1948 London Games. Their success was, however, mixed: as Bandy (1988: 167) observes, they 'failed to achieve the union of sport and art desired by Coubertin'. So from 1952, the arts have been celebrated at the Games by exhibition and performance only, not by competition.

As Stevenson (1998) points out, despite de Coubertin's aim, the cultural programme has always been subordinate to the sports programme. Since the Barcelona Games in 1992, she notes, host cities have organised cultural programmes which span the four years of the Olympiad, rather than merely being focused on the period of the Games. While offering the potential for greater exposure for the programme, the extended time-period and associated organisational requirements and costs, can also highlight the tendency for the programme to be under-funded, compared with the sports programme. In reviewing the development of the Sydney 2000 programme, Stevenson notes the problem of clashes of interest between official Olympic sponsors and actual and potential sponsors of local arts organisations. The question of sponsorship is considered more fully in Chapter 6. Theatre at the 1984 Los Angeles Games cultural programme has been analysed by Levitt (1990).

The official Cultural Programmes are, however, not the only association of the Olympic Games with the arts. Over the years, the Games have, for example, spawned a considerable amount of music, as documented by Guegold (1996). Opening and closing ceremonies have become increasingly elaborate over the years, and generally seek to portray the history and culture of the host country through music, dance and spectacle. Watched by billions, the television coverage of opening ceremonies have themselves become the focus of research, raising issues as to the extent to which commercial forces undermine the ability of the coverage to convey Olympic ideals of internationalism and participation for its own sake (Larson, 1989; Larson and Rivenburgh, 1991; Rivenburgh, 1991; de Moragas *et al.*, 1996; Gordon and Sibson, 1998).

The Winter Olympics

Krüger (1996: 103) points out that international ice-skating championships first took place in the early 1890s and that the original intention was to include ice sports in the revived Olympic Games. But due to the lack of facilities in Athens, lack of any Greek competitive tradition in the area and, possibly, de Coubertin's ambivalence towards winter sports, they were excluded. Krüger (1996: 104) further relates that winter sports were slow to be introduced because of the tradition of holding the Games in a single city, and few cities were able to host both summer and winter sports. Further, the success of the existing Nordic Games suggested that a winter Olympic Games event was not considered necessary. While ice-skating featured in the 1908 London Games (Onigman, 1976: 227), moves to introduce winter sports into the Stockholm Games of 1912 were unsuccessful, although they were planned for the cancelled 1916 Berlin Games. Ice skating and ice hockey were included in the official programme of the 1920 Antwerp Games (Krüger, 1996: 104), although only as exhibition sports. Finally, in 1921, the IOC agreed that host countries should organise winter sports competitions as well as summer competitions, and the first official Winter Games took place in 1924 in Chamonix, France. Later the IOC decided that if the host of the Summer Games was unable to organise a winter competition, then the Winter Games could be awarded to another country. The results of these decisions was the sequence of Winter Games shown in Table 4.9.

The Winter Games have not always run smoothly. Onigman, in examining the Winter Olympics over the period 1908 to 1980, noted that they had:

> amassed a relatively enviable record of disputes, protests, political posturing, and general confusion ... have been laced with the same kinds of difficulties that have plagued the Summer Games ... difficulties have ranged from 'eligibility interpret-ations, choosing referees for a hockey game and granting visas, to embarrassment about the length of women's skating attire and temper tantrums thrown by temperamental participants. (Onigman, 1976: 226)

More recently, controversy over the environmental impacts of developments for the Winter Games in sensitive Alpine environments (May, 1995; McIntyre, 1995) and over the judging of figure skating (Rosenberg and Lockwood, 2005) have come to the fore.

Local opposition

Not everyone is a supporter of the Olympic Games – in general or in terms of having them in their own city. In Chapters 5 and 6, general critics, from a political and political economy perspective, are noted. Here we examine the phenomenon of opposition in regard to hosting the Olympics in specific cities. In general this opposition reflects the 'communitarian' critical paradigm discussed in Chapter 1. Opposition can begin at the bidding stage, so in the discussion of the bidding process above, it is noted that local political opposition has prevented a number of cities from proceeding with bids. Once a bid has been successful opposition may arise based on a number of factors, including:

Table 4.9. Winter Olympic Games

No.	Year	Location	Country	No. of countries	No. of sports	No. of events	No. of athletes
I	1924	Chamonix	France	16	5	13	294
II	1928	St. Moritz	Switzerland	25	6	13	393
III	1932	Lake Placid	USA	17	5	14	307
IV	1936	Garmich-Partenkirchen	Germany	28	6	17	756
	1940	Not celebrated		-	-	-	-
	1944	Not celebrated		-	-	-	-
V	1948	St. Moritz	Switzerland	28	6	24	713
VI	1952	Oslo	Norway	30	5	22	732
VII	1956	Cortina	Italy	32	5	24	819
VIII	1960	Squaw Valley	USA	30	5	27	648
IX	1964	Innsbruck	Austria	36	7	34	933
X	1968	Grenoble	France	37	7	35	1 293
XI	1972	Sapporo	Japan	35	7	35	1 145
XII	1976	Innsbruck	Austria	37	7	37	1 231
XIII	1980	Lake Placid	USA	38	7	39	1 283
XIV	1984	Sarajevo	Yugoslavia	49	7	40	1 410
XV	1988	Calgary	Canada	57	7	46	1 423
XVI	1992	Albertville	France	64	7	57	1 801
XVII	1994	Lillehammer	Norway	67	7	61	1 737
XVIII	1998	Nagano	Japan	80	7	68	3 000
XIX	2002	Salt Lake City	USA	77	7	78	2 399
XX	2006	Torino	Italy	80	7	84	2 508

Sources: Wallechinsky (1992); IOC (1998a); USOC (1999); Miller (2003).

- disapproval of public expenditure on the Games – because of other, greater needs in the city often allied with a philosophical objection to the 'élitist' nature of the Games – epitomised by the Toronto-based 'Bread not Circuses' move-ment, which also operated in Sydney;
- anticipation of disruption of the city generally and/or of particular groups in particular – notably people whose homes may be displaced by development or who would suffer from increased rents induced by the Games;
- objection to particular developments on environmental and/or social grounds;
- a general anti-growth stance (Burbank *et al.*, 2000)
- concerns about the public's rights to participate in decisions about preparations for the Games (see: Ritchie and Lyons, 1990; Haxton, 1993).

Some opposition groups have put forward an agenda for reform of the way the Games are planned and organised. The 'Bread not Circuses' alliance produced such an agenda covering:

- public participation and democratic accountability;
- financial accountability and costs to the host community;
- social equity – relating to housing/rents/homelessness, cultural equity and civil liberties;
- sexual equity and equal opportunity;
- environmental impacts; and
- employment (summarised in Lenskyj, 2002: 228–31).

A number of the dimensions in the 'Bread not Circuses' list appear in the new evaluation programme, the Olympic Games Global Impact (OGGI), discussed below, which will require them at least to be measured.

Evaluation and reporting

The OCOG is subject to regular review by the appropriate IOC Coordination Commission and, on completion, is required to evaluate its performance in the 'official report' (see Further Reading). The scale and complexity of the Olympic Games is, in part, reflected in the contents of these official reports, which have until recently been published in three volumes of several hundred pages each. For example, the report of the Atlanta Games consisted of three volumes: Volume I deals with planning and organisation; Volume II tells the story of the Games, on a day-by-day basis, from the arrival of the torch in the USA to the closing ceremony, and also examines the post-Games legacy; and Volume III presents the competition results. Volume II runs to 560 pages, with 28 chapters, as listed in Table 4.10.

Table 4.10. Atlanta 1996 Olympic Games official report, Vol. II: chapters

Prologue	15. Marketing
1. Management & Organisation	16. Medical Services
2. Accommodations	17. Olympic Family and Protocol
3. Accreditation	18. Olympic Villages
4. Atlanta Olympic Broadcasting	19. Opening/Closing Ceremonies
5. Centennial Olympic Park	20. Security
6. Communications	21. Sports
7. Construction	22. Staffing of the Games
8. Creative Services	23. Technology
9. Cultural Olympiad	24. Ticket Sales
10. Event and Guest Services	25. Torch Relay
11. External Relations	26. Transportation
12. Financial Services	27. Venue Management
13. Games Services	28. Youth and Education
14. Logistics	

Recently the requirement has been added for a fourth volume to be added. dealing with the Olympic Games Global Impact (OGGI). This requires OCOGs to collect data on 150 indicators for each of 11 years, from two years before the announcement of the winning bid until two years after the Games (IOC, 2004: 14). The indicators are divided into three 'dimensions', environmental, social and economic, and these are further divided into items directly related to the Games, 'event' indicators, and those indirectly related to the games, but related to the host community as a whole, 'context' indicators. Table 4.11 gives an indication of the scope of the indicators. The list of indicators is extensive and many will not be routinely available from official or administrative records, so their compilation will require a significant research effort. The requirement to include this fourth volume was introduced only recently so, at the time of writing, early 2007, no official report has yet appeared with the OGGI indicators. It therefore remains to be seen to what extent OCOGs will be able to collect and present the data. If it can be done well, and on a comparable basis, the exercise will present an extraordinary database for future researchers and games bidders and organisers.

Table 4.11. Examples of Olympic Games Global Impact (OGGI) Indicators

Dimension	Event indicators	Context indicators
Environmental	Developed area of Olympic sites Average journey times between sites	Greenhouse gas emissions Waste and water treatment
Social	Consultation with specific groups TV/radio audiences Drug testing	Participation rates in sport Crime rate Available sports facilities
Economic	Jobs created OCOG revenue and spending	Per capita energy consumption Consumer price index

After it's all over: the legacy of the Games

A major motivation for host cities is the potential *legacy* of the games – what the games will leave behind. Legacies can take a number of forms. Richard Cashman (1999: 183–6) lists a number of these:

- Economic benefits (direct & indirect)
- Built environment (non-sporting, e.g. transport infrastructure)
- Information and education (concerning sport and culture)
- Public life, politics and culture
- Sport
  - Elite performance
  - Mass participation
  - the 'trickle down' effect Financial support
- Built sporting infrastructure
- Sporting symbols, memory, history.

While the question of a legacy features prominently in the local and national campaigns of cities to bid for the Games and in associated bid documents, serious consideration of how to secure and then evaluate legacy outcomes has, until recently, been neglected by the Olympic Movement. In general, therefore, Olympic legacies have been very much part of the 'spin' of bidding for the Games. This is perhaps not surprising, since the organisations responsible for staging the Games are focused on the games themselves, and are disbanded very soon after the event is concluded. And promises made seven or eight years earlier are rarely to the fore in the political agendas of host city governments. However, evidence that the IOC is beginning to take the question of legacy seriously was evidenced by the sponsorship of a major conference of the topic in 2002 (De Moragas *et al.*, 2003) and the development of the Olympic Games Global Impact (OGGI) framework discussed above. Increasing academic interest in legacy issues is shown by numerous contributions to the above IOC conference and the publication of whole books on the legacy of the Barcelona 1992 Games (De Moragas and Botella, 1995) and the Sydney 2000 Games (Cashman, 2006). A report on likely legacies of the London 2012 Games was published in 2004, a year before the games had even been awarded (Vigor *et al.*, 2004)!

Two aspects of legacy are considered briefly here: sports facilities and sports participation. Economic impacts are considered in Chapter 6.

Sporting facilities

The most visible form of legacy is the sporting facilities left behind for the use of the residents of the host city and nation, both for training for and staging of élite sporting events and for community use. Thus, for example, the *London 2012 Candidature File* states:

> Mounting excitement in the seven years leading up to the Games in London will inspire a new generation of youth to greater sporting activity. ... After the Games are over, London will possess some of the finest sports facilities for hosting national and international events. These facilities will enable London to create The London Olympic Institute, a world-class institution for sport, culture and the environment, which will provide facilities and services for elite athletes as well as encouraging participation in sport. By doing so, the UK will build on the sporting momentum of the expected successes coming out of the 2012 Games. (London 2012 Ltd, 2005: 19)

Two lessons can be drawn from Cashman's (2006: 139–66) account of the experience of Sydney Olympic Park. First, the involvement of the private sector in the building of sports facilities means that any of the risk that the facilities might not be profitable in the long term is not borne by governments. Second, planning for 'life after the Olympics' needs to start well before the Games actually take place, since considerable additional investment in ancillary facilities has been required to develop the Sydney Olympic precinct into a viable commercial and residential, as well as sporting, complex. Chalkley and Essex (1999a) note the tendency for the development of Olympic Games infrastructure to be a catalyst for wider urban development projects.

Sport participation

The idea that hosting an Olympic Games will leave a legacy of increased grassroots participation in sport, especially among young people, is of particular note since it reflects a key aim of the modern Olympic revival (see discussion of the 'Olympic Movement' above). An IOC member speaking at the IOC 202 legacy conference stated: 'The Olympic legacy is ... to remain educational rather than élitist, and always to ensure some degree of continuity between base and summit, competitive sports and leisure sport, professionals and amateurs' (Verbruggen, 2003: 21).

The London 2012 bid document claims that the London Games will 'inspire a new generation of youth to greater participation'. This aim is, apparently, not just national, but global; the London 2012 website declares:

> London 2012 Organising Committee for the Olympic Games and Paralympic Games Chair Sebastian Coe has confirmed its vision 'to stage inspirational Games that capture the imagination of young people around the world and leave a lasting legacy'. (London 2012, n.d.)

In the case of Beijing 2008, the anticipated impact has been quantified: 'It is expected that the proportion of the population who participate in sports activities on a regular basis will rise from 34.9% to over 40% because of the Games' (Xu et al., 2003: 425).

The experience of Sydney, however, raises the issue of the extent to which these aims are carried through in practice and the extent to which they are evaluated. The Sydney 2000 Olympics were seen by the Australian Sports Commission as: 'a major opportunity to market sports participation to the Australian public' (Houlihan , 1997: 71), but the design of the major national survey series on sport participation was changed in 2000, so that 'before and after' levels of sports participation could not be accurately measured. Exacerbated by the limitations imposed by this change, analysis of the available data is inconclusive in that some Olympic sports showed increases while others showed a decrease, and non-Olympic sports showed similar patterns of increase and decrease (Veal, 2003). Thus it is not possible to determine whether the Sydney 2000 Games left a positive sports participation legacy.

Competing and related events

In Chapter 3 the various attempts at reviving the Olympic Games are discussed, but following the establishment of the modern Olympic Games in 1896, numerous sporting events have been organised as alternatives to the 'official' Olympic Games or as spin-offs. Some of these events used the Olympic name in the era before the Olympic 'brand' or image was vigorously defended, some have been acknowledged by the IOC, some have been opposed and some simply ignored. The number of international sporting events now runs into hundreds and a number compete with the Games for prestige, world attention and, today, advertising and sponsorship money. Events discussed here are listed in Table 4.12.

The 'interim' Olympic Games, 1906

An unofficial 'interim' Olympic Games event was held in Athens in 1906, a small-scale event, nevertheless with royal patronage, which 'gave a kiss of life to the

Table 4.12. Alternative and competing events

Event	First city/year held	Latest city/year held
The 'interim' Olympics	Athens, 1906	
Workers' Olympics and Spartakiads (Socialist Workers' Sports International)	Prague, 1921	Antwerp, 1937
Women's Olympic Games/ Women's World Games (Fédération Sportive Féminine International)	Paris, 1922	London, 1934
Marxist Olympics	Chicago, 1932	
The Games of the New Emerging Forces (Indonesia)	Jakarta, 1963	
Paralympic Games (International Paralympic Committee)	Rome, 1960; Toronto, 1976	Same years/cities as Olympic Games
Special Olympics Summer (S) and Winter (W) games	Chicago, 1968	2005, Nagano (W); 2002, Shanghai (S)
World Games (International World Games Assoc.)	Santa Clara, 1981	Duisburg, 2005
Gay Games (Federation of Gay Games)	San Francisco, 1982	Sydney, 2002.
Goodwill Games (Turner Network TV/ AOL Time Warner Inc)	Moscow, 1986	Lake Placid, 2000 (W); Brisbane, 2001 (S)
Empire/Commonwealth Games (Commonwealth Games Federation)	Hamilton, Canada, 1930	Melbourne, 2006
Pan-American Games	Buenos Aires, 1951	Santo Domingo, 2003
Asian Games	New Delhi, 1951	Doha, 2006
Specialist		
World Masters Games	Toronto, 1985	Edmonton, 2005
World University Games	Turin, 1959 (S) Chamonix, 1960 (W)	Izmir, Turkey, 2005 (S) Innsbruck, 2005 (W)
World Cup (soccer)	Uruguay, 1930	Germany, 2006

Sources: See Appendix I: List of websites

Olympic movement, helping to sustain it after the disasters of 1900 and 1904' (Gordon, 1994: 42).

Workers' Olympics

Riordan (1984) provides an account of the growth of socialist and communist workers' sporting organisations which developed in the nineteenth and early twentieth century in opposition to the 'bourgeois' sporting organisations considered to be exclusive, chauvinistic and militaristic. Workers' Olympics frequently rivalled the 'bourgeois Olympics' in terms of numbers of participants, countries represented and spectators. The 1936 games were aborted due to the outbreak of the Spanish Civil War (see Chapter 10) and were replaced by an e vent in Antwerp, which attracted 27,000 participants from 17 countries, but which proved to be the last of the W orkers' Olympics. Butler (1992) describes a similar 'Marxist' Olympics held in Chicago in 1932.

The Paralympic Games

The Paralympic Games, held in each Olympiad, immediately following the Summer and Winter Olympic Games, and in the same locations, have their origin in sporting events established for therapeutic and rehabilitation purposes for people with disabilities in the unit for spinal injuries victims in the Stoke-Mandeville Hospital, England, in 1948 (Landry, 1995). W hile independent of the Olympic organisation, the close association of the Paralympic Games with the Olympic Games began in Rome in 1960 (International Paralympic Committee (IPC), n.d.; Steadward, 1996). The Paralympic Games were held in the same city as the Olympic Games from 1988, as shown in Table 4.13. As with the Olympic Games, the number of athletes and countries participating have grown rapidly over the years. Winter Paralympic Games were inaugurated in 1976 and held in the same locations as the Winter Olympics from 1992. Cities bidding for the Olympic Games are also required to host the Paralympic Games and it is increasingly the case that the same venues and staffing are used.

Over the years, links between the Olympic Games and the Paralympic Games have developed. In Sydney 2000 there was considerable integration of the Olympic and Paralympic organising committees, but in Athens 2004 a single organisation ran both events. Some events for athletes with disabilities are held during the Olympic programme. The experience of the Paralympics has raised issues of accessibility of facilities, for athletes and spectators, not only during the Paralympic Games but also during the Olympics and, indeed, all sporting events (Darcy, 2001, 2003).

Special Olympics

The Paralympic Games do not always include athletes with intellectual disabilities. The summer and winter Special Olympics cater for this group. Begun in 1968, they were hosted entirely in US cities until 1993.

World Games

The World Games operate under the patronage of the International Olympic Committee and cater primarily for the 32 sports which are recognised by the IOC but not included in the Olympic programme. The World Games began in 1981 and, as indicated in Table 4.14, involve some 3000 athletes from over 90 countries.

Gay Games

The organisers of the first Gay Games, which took place in 1982 in San Francisco, originally intended the event to be called the Gay Olympic Games, but were prevented from including the word Olympic in their title by court action on the part of the US Olympic Committee. This was despite the fact that, as the Federation of Gay Games (1996) points out, the Olympic title is used by other events, such as the Special Olympics, the Police Olympics, the Nude Olympics, and even the Dog Olympics.

The Gay Games have been held every four years since 1982. They do not impose performance standards on entrants, who represent cities rather than countries. As a result, the number of participants is greater than that of the Olympic Games. In the Amsterdam Gay Games in 1998 some 15,000 participants (42 per cent women) from 68 countries took part in 30 sporting events – and this all on a budget of US$7 million. In Sydney, in 2002, 11,000 participants took part in 31 sports (Federation of Gay Games, n.d.).

Table 4.13. Paralympic Games

Year	Location	Number of countries	Number of athletes
Summer Games			
1952	Stoke Mandeville, UK	2	130
1960	Rome, Italy	23	400
1964	Tokyo, Japan	21	357
1968	Tel Aviv, Israel	29	750
1972	Heidelberg, Germany	43	984
1976	Toronto, Canada	38	1 657
1980	Arnhem, Netherlands	42	1 973
1984	Stoke Mandeville, UK	41	1 100
	& New York, USA	45	1 800
1988	Seoul, Korea	61	3 013
1992	Barcelona, Spain	82	3 021
1996	Atlanta, USA	103	3 195
2000	Sydney, Australia	122	3 843
2004	Athens, Greece	136	3 806
2008	Beijing, China	150*	4 000*
2012	London, UK	150*	4 200*
Winter Games			
1976	Örnsköldsvik, Sweden	17	250+
1980	Geilo, Norway	18	350
1984	Innsbruck, Austria	21	457
1988	Innsbruck, Austria	22	397
1992	Tignes-Albertville, France	24	475
1994	Lillehammer, Norway	31	492
1998	Nagano, Japan	32	571
2002	Salt Lake City, USA	36	416
2006	Torino, Italy	39	477
2010	Vancouver, Canada	45*	650*

Source: Paralympic Games website, www.paralympic.org. * Estimates

Table 4.14. World Games

Year	Location	Number of sports	Number of countries	Number of athletes
1981	Santa Clara, USA	18	n/a	1 265
1985	London, UK	23	n/a	1 550
1989	Karlsruhe, Germany	19	n/a	1 965
1993	The Hague, Netherlands	25	69	2 275
1997	Lahti, Finland	30	78	2 600
2001	Akita, Japan	31	93	3 200
2005	Duisburg	38	89	3 400

Source: World Games website (see Appendix I)

Goodwill Games

Following the American boycott of the 1980 Moscow Olympics and the tit-for-tat Soviet boycott of the 1984 Los Angeles Games, along with ongoing problems with the apartheid regime of South Africa (see Chapter 5) some believed that international political intrigue threatened the future of the Olympic Games. One response came from Ted Turner, of Turner Broadcasting Systems (TBS), later part of AOL-Time Warner, who organised the Goodwill Games, as an event at which primarily American and Soviet athletes could compete. Bypassing the IOC, the first Goodwill Games took place in Moscow in 1986, involving 3000 participants from 80 countries. Although promoted as a peace-making venture, the event was organised as a commercial venture, with athletes in key events being paid cash prizes and Turner expecting to recoup his outlays, and even make a profit, from television revenues. The games were not, however, a television ratings success in the USA and TBS is said to have lost US$25 million on the venture (Senn, 1999: 214). The Goodwill Games were organised on five further occasions, but failed to capture the imagination of the broadcast media or their viewers. And in any case, the Olympic Games rode out the international politically-based problems of the 1980s, thus removing the main *raison d'être* of the Goodwill Games.

The Empire/Commonwealth Games

The idea of organising a sporting festival for members of the then British Empire, was first mooted in 1928, following the Amsterdam Games, when the Empire Sports Federation was formed (Gordon, 1994: 130). With a third of the world's land surface coloured pink on British maps, this seemed entirely appropriate. The first British Empire Games were held in Hamilton, Canada, in 1930, involving six sports and 400 competitors from 11 countries. While modelled on the Olympic Games, they were designed to have a different atmosphere, a policy statement at the time indicating that they would be:

> designed on the Olympic model, both in general construction and its stern definition of the amateur. But the games will be very different – free from both the excessive stimulus and the babel of the international stadium. They should be merrier and less stern, and will substitute the stimulus of novel adventure for the pressure of international rivalry. (Commonwealth Games Federation, 1997)

The Games have been held at four-yearly intervals ever since (with the exception of 1942 and 1946), their name changing to British Empire and Commonwealth Games, to British Commonwealth Games and eventually to Commonwealth Games – the Commonwealth being the loosely formed 'club' of Britain and its former colonies. The latest Commonwealth Games were held in Kuala Lumpur, Malaysia, and involved 6000 athletes from 71 countries (Commonwealth Games Federation, 1997). The common language arising from the experience of colonial rule certainly reduces the 'babel' of the Games and aids communication, and the games are smaller in scale and are well-known for their friendly atmosphere; however, the historical accident of membership of the British Empire results in a peculiar mix of some 71 Commonwealth countries, so that standards in the various sports are variable.

While the Empire Games were inspired by the Olympic Games, Barney (1998) notes that the Empire Games gave something to the Olympics, in the form of the idea of the two-level victory podium used at the Hamilton Games and copied at Lake Placid and Los Angeles two years later.

World University Games

The World University Games, or *Universiade*, are open to full-time students aged between 17 and 28. They began as a summer event in Turin, Italy, in 1959, with 985 participating athletes from 45 countries. This was followed by a winter games in 1960 in Chamonix, France. The summer games now typically attracts some 6000 athletes from over 160 countries and the winter games 1600 athletes from 50 countries (USOC, 1999).

World Masters Games

The World Masters Games aim to 'promote lifelong competition, friendship and understanding between mature sportspeople, regardless of age, gender, race, religion, or sport status'. While Masters Games had been held at local and national level for some years, the first World Masters Games were held in 1985 and have been held subsequently every four years, as shown in Table 4.15. As with a number of these non-Olympic world events, participation is non-exclusionary, so the number of active participants is much greater than for the Olympic Games.

Table 4.15. World Masters Games

Year	City	Country	No. of Sports	No. of Participants	No. of Countries
1985	Toronto	Canada	22	8 305	61
1989	Herning/Aalborg/Aarhus	Denmark	37	5 500	76
1994	Brisbane	Australia	30	23 600	71
1998	Portland	USA	28	11 400	102
2002	Melbourne	Australia	26	24 900	98
2005	Edmonton	Canada	26	21 600	88

Regional Games

Various regions of the world hold their own multi-sport events, including the Pan-American Games, the Asian Games and the Pan-Pacific Games. The Pan-American games, for example, date back to the 1950s and now attract some 5000 athletes from more than 40 countries (USOC, 1999).

Single Sport Events

The only single-sport event which can match the Olympics in the number of countries competing and in terms of size of television audiences, is the soccer World Cup. However, World Championships in individual sports, or groups of sports, such as athletics or swimming, can be as important as the Olympics to athletes involved. The practice of the Olympic Games of involving all member countries in all Games events leads to participant selection procedures which may not result in a competition between the 'best in the world': thus some World Championships are seen to provide a higher level of competition in some events.

A further issue of potential concern to the Olympic Movement is the availability of sponsorship money. There is no guarantee that sponsors will continue indefinitely to see the Olympic Games as the best vehicle for promotional purposes – especially when some competing events can offer a more exclusive arrangement for single corporations.

Conclusions

As the quotation from Horst Ueberhorst, given at the beginning of the chapter, suggests, the Olympic Games are in many ways unique, and therefore defy classification. They are a 100-year-old phenomenon with a 2 500 year history. But, despite their traditional trappings, they are, in their current form, quintessentially a reflection of contemporary social values and economic and political forces. Social theorists are grappling with questions of whether the contemporary world is still 'modern' or has become 'postmodern' and whether it is still 'industrial' or has become 'post-industrial' (Kumar, 1995). The scale, complexity and economic and cultural significance of the Olympic Games place them at the centre of such debates. The following chapters, which deal with issues as diverse as politics, nationalism, economics, feminism, the media and drugs, illustrate this proposition. The broader issues we return to in the final chapter of the book.

Further reading

Official reports	A listing of official reports on Olympic Games from Organising Committees to the IOC can be found in Veal and Toohey (2007) and downloadable copies can be found on the LA84 Foundation website (see Appendix I)
Bidding	McGeogh (1994); Burroughs (1999); Black and Van Der Westhuizen (2004); Booth (2005b); Davé (2006); Lee (2006)
Olympic Charter	Zakus (2005)

Ceremonies	De Moragas *et al.* (1996); Barney (1998)
Cultural programme	Bandy (1988); Stevenson (1998); Good (1999); Stanton (2000); Aso (2002)
Olympic torch & relay	Borgers (1996); Buschman and Lennartz (1996); Cahill (1999a, b)
Presidential biographies	
De Coubertin	MacAloon (1981)
Baillet-Latour	Lennartz, K. (1994–1997a)
Edström	Lennartz, K. (1994–1997b)
Brundage	Guttman (1984)
Killanin	Landry and Yerlès (1994–1997)
Samaranch	Miller (1996)
Winter Games	Goksøyr *et al.* (1996); Krüger (1996); Klausen (1999); Kok (2002/03); Chappelet (2003); Essex & Chalkley (2003)
Alternative Olympics	Kidd (2005)
Paralympic Games	International Paralympic Committee (IPC) (n.d.); Steadward (1996); Hughes (1999); Goggin and Newell (2000)
Workers' Olympics:	Riordan (1984); Butler (1992)
Gay Games	Borrie (1999); Krane and Waldron (2000); Symons (2002); Stevenson *et al.* (2005); Rowe *et al.* (2006)
Legacy	De Moragas & Botella (1995); French & Disher (1997); Chalkley & Essex (1999a); Cashman (1999b, 2006); Ritchie, J. (2000); Kok (2002/03); Essex & Chalkley (2003); De Moragas *et al.* (2003); Brown (2004)

Questions

1. What are the functions of the various symbols and ceremonies associated with the Olympics?
2. How could the IOC be made more democratic?
3. Are the Olympic Games in danger of being overshadowed by single-sport world events?
4. Should the Olympic Cultural Programme be made competitive?

Chapter 5

Politics, Nationalism and the Olympic Movement

> Few enthusiasts of élite sport nowadays believe that it can be separated from politics, though there must be many who wish that it could.
>
> Christopher Hill (1996: 1)

Introduction

From their inception to the present, the Olympic Games have been influenced by politics at individual, organisational, intra-national and international levels. Unlike some other influences on the Games, the intrusion of politics has not been felt merely during the period of the Summer or Winter Games, but is a continuing phenomenon occurring, and at times being at its most potent, between Games. Just as other international sporting events are influenced by competing ideologies, rivalries and policies, it would be naïve and unrealistic to expect the Olympics to be an exception and remain immune to external influences.

Although each Olympic Games is unique, some political problems have spanned several Olympiads. These problems have reflected the international relations issues of the day. On three occasions these have been so divisive that the Games have been cancelled. In terms of examining the nature of the Olympic Movement, Frisby's (2005: 1) comment that 'organizations are best viewed as operating in a wider cultural, economic, and political context characterized by asymmetrical power relations that are historically entrenched', is particularly applicable.

Politics

When examining the role of politics in sport, it is important to understand the nature of the term itself. Definitions of 'politics' vary widely; however, a common theme appears to be the interaction between power and authority. Even the Olympic credo, *Faster, Higher, Stronger*, suggests an ideological embodiment of power. Carter (2002: 405) sees the relationships between sport and power intersecting at all levels of the social world: 'from athletic bodies to social bodies in myriad, complex, intertwined patterns that penetrate and crosscut local specificities'.

The origin of the word *politics*, interestingly, dates back to the period of the Ancient Olympic Games and is derived from the Greek word *polis*, which meant 'city state', the means by which Greek communities were organised. Politics involves both collaboration and conflict. Cultures must strike an acceptable balance between co-operation and competition, both internally and externally, to survive.

Thus, politics is neither self contained nor static. For example, in relation to the latter, Maguire *et al.* (2002) argue that, because of the speeding up of the processes of globalization, in the 21st century, people are now having to cope with greater problems of increasing political and other forms of interdependence than in the past. Globalisation theory argues that global processes, involving media, technology, economics, politics and the rise of trans-national corporations, are transforming the limits of sovereignty and autonomy of nations. As part of this process, Maguire *et al.* envision people's political worlds as possessing multiple identities, loyalties and allegiances. 'What seems to be developing is a series of overlapping global, regional, transnational, national and local political communities that are contoured along multiple overlapping/intersecting socio-spatial networks of power' (Maguire *et al.*, 2002: 18).

This means that social behaviours (interaction between people), such as political behaviour, can be conceptualised as a form of exchange. Exchanges, in this sense, occur in all spheres of social life, be they political, economic or cultural. These exchanges can be further categorised, depending on the extent to which the behaviour of individuals is contingent on the actions of others. Invariably political exchanges involve interaction with others and, as such, imply both processes and outcomes.

Perhaps one of the most succinct ways of describing the political process is 'who gets what, when, where and how'. This is also a simple and aptly descriptive definition. It is certainly applicable to decisions made in regard to the Olympic Movement. In the vein of other social actors, political actors (including nation states, and organisations such as the IOC) pursue multiple goals with limited resources. Thus, the realisation of some goals comes at the expense of others. The rational pursuit of a goal therefore requires that resources be allocated to that goal up to a point at which the marginal benefits equal marginal costs. This 'exchange perspective' of relationships and actions has been used by anthropologists, sociologists, social psychologists and political scientists (for example, Catlin, 1927; Lasswell and Kaplan, 1950; Dahl and Lindblom, 1953; Curry and Wade, 1968; Baldwin, 1998).

The notion of power, ruling or authority also underlies political exchanges. Some scholars theorise politics in terms of a systems or functional approach. For example, Robert Dahl described a political system as 'a persistent pattern of human relation-ships that involves, to a significant extent, control, influence, power or authority' (Dahl, 1984: 10). Political systems have been classified by many scholars since Ancient Olympic times and the work of Aristotle. His famous six-fold classification (determined by whether rulers governed in their own interests or those of the common weal, and by the number of people entitled to rule) is presented in Table 5.1.

A different and also widely accepted categorisation was provided much later, in the 20th century, by Max Weber and was based on political systems with an accepted 'legitimate' rule. Weber theorised that legitimacy was based on three criteria: tradition, exceptional personal qualities and legality. From these criteria an ideal type

Table 5.1. Aristotle's political system classification

Number of citizens entitled to rule	Rulers rule in the interest of all	Rulers rule in the interest of themselves
One	Kingship (monarchy)	Tyranny
Few	Aristocracy	Oligarchy
Many	Polity	Democracy

Source: Dahl (1984: 64)

of authority followed: traditional authority, charismatic authority and legal authority. Weber recognised that political systems may encompass all three kinds of legitimate authority (Dahl, 1984).

Depending on one's viewpoint of the International Olympic Committee, according to Aristotle's taxonomy, the organisation could be classed as either an aristocracy or an oligarchy. By Weber's scheme it possesses rational and legal authority. Whether or not it possesses the third quality depends to a large extent on the incumbent president.

In a more recent assessment of contemporary writers on power, Haugaard (2003) notes that the literature can be divided into two main areas: the first views power coercively (for example, the works of Weber, Dahl, Wrong, Poggi and Mann), while the second views it as an outcome of social order. Haugaard offers a summary of major writers from the second camp and their varied positions on how power is shaped and maintained.

> Power is created by: systems consensus directed towards systems goals (Parsons); trust in system reproduction (Luhmann); self re-inforcing knowledge of rings of reference which define objects (Barnes); the capacity for social action derived from structuration (Giddens); the bias of a system (Bachrach and Baratz); 'false consciousness' (Lukes); an inseparable link between power and knowledge (Foucault); circuits of power that constitute social order (Clegg); and the ability to act in concert through the creation of legitimate polities (Arendt) and; (taking account of the alternative perspective on the creation of power) coercion. (Haugaard, 2003: 88)

Clegg (1989) has conceptualised power in terms of organisational phenomena in a way that is relevant to the Olympic Movement. He would argue that organisations provide a framework of power and without knowledge of this, power, within the Olympics, could not be adequately theorised. Despite such new theories constantly emerging, thus allowing us to examine the contexts of politics in the contemporary sport world, the relationship between sport and politics *per se* is not just a product of contemporary society but has had an ongoing historical association. For example, military training has been closely aligned with physical education throughout history and, as mentioned in Chapter 2, victories at the Ancient Olympic Games were linked to the prestige and favour of the city state.

Olympic Games and politics

According to Espy (1979), the link between modern sport and politics is a strong union for a number of reasons. First, athletes typically represent an organisation which is competing against a similar body. Second, ritual is used to affirm allegiance to that organisation. Third, governments are involved in the preparation of élite athletes and subsidisation of their training and competition. And fourth, because of the institutional nature of sporting governing bodies, there is politics within and between these federations. Because the Olympics have pre-eminence as an inter-national sporting event, one which is watched in all corners of the world, they have become the ideal medium through which to demonstrate political power and causes. Although the rhetoric of the IOC suggests the opposite, the organisational structure and rituals of the Games themselves added to this incentive. When Olympic medal ceremonies play the national anthem and raise the flag of the victor's country, when team sports are organised on national lines and when, at the Opening Ceremony, athletes march into the stadium nation by nation, these practices are overtly creating nationalistic tensions, rivalries and pride.

While investigating the political influences which have impinged on the Games, it is possible to see trends in the types of such intervention. Six categories of political interference appear to dominate the Games. First, internal politics within the nation where the Olympics are being staged have affected the Games. Second, international rivalries, based on either political or ideological disputes, between nations with National Olympic Committees have impinged on the Olympics, as these nations have used the Games as a tool to advance their own agendas. Third, competitors have used the Games as a forum for political demonstrations against their national governments. Fourth, non-participants have used the Games to further their political causes. Fifth, nations with participating NOCs have attempted to equate Olympic success with their social, economic and political superiority (Warning, 1980) and, last, politics within the IOC have impacted on Olympic policy. Each of these forms of political intervention are examined in turn in this chapter.

Internal politics of the host nation

Athens, 1896

Even before the first modern Games were celebrated in 1896 internal political intervention had affected the Olympics. These first Games were awarded to Athens in recognition of Greece's links with the Ancient Olympics. However, the Greek Prime Minister, Charios Trikoupis, decided that his country could not afford the honour and it required the intervention of the Greek Royal Family, specifically Crown Prince Constantine, for the decision to be reversed and for preparations for the Games to continue (Warning, 1980).

As indicated in Chapter 3, the Greek Royal Family welcomed the success of these preparations as they boosted the prestige of the monarchy and Greek national consciousness. De Coubertin himself neatly summed up the political outcomes of the 1896 Olympics: 'In the case of Greece, the Games will be found to have a double effect, one athletic and the other political. Besides working to solve the centuries old Eastern question the Games helped to increase the personality of the King and Crown Prince' (quoted in Strenk, 1970: 34).

Paris, 1900

Paris, home of de Coubertin, was chosen to be the site of the Games of the second Olympiad and, once again, internal politics within the organising country threatened to disrupt the Games. Problems began early in 1897. Some French athletic officials were hostile to the Olympics and deliberately hindered their planning. Accordingly, de Coubertin decided to align the Games with the Universal Paris Exposition of 1900. Regrettably the Exposition's director, Alfred Picart, neither wanted nor welcomed the Olympic addition to his festival (Killanin and Rhodda, 1976).

Picart finally agreed to include the Games in the Exposition and with that de Coubertin began the organisation of the Games. A committee was formed and progress appeared to be made. However, because of growing opposition and lack of co-operation, the committee dissolved itself in April, 1899, just twelve months before the Games were scheduled to begin. Finally, a member of the original organising committee was appointed to the position of director-general of sporting contests at the Exposition by Picart, thus enabling the organisation of the Games to proceed, although arrangements were still in disarray (Warning, 1980).

De Coubertin found it necessary to undertake a European tour to allay the suspicions of a number of countries, disconcerted by the apparent incompetence of the French officials who were issuing a constant stream of rules, regulations and sometimes contradictory memos. In addition, because of the political situation in Europe, he wished to counter German and British fears of demonstrations against their athletes.

Despite all the organisational mismanagement and internal political squabbling, the Games were staged. They ran from 20 May until 28 October, although accounts show they were less than successful. Even de Coubertin was quoted as saying: 'There was much goodwill but the interesting results had nothing Olympic about them. We have made a hash of our work' (Killanin and Rhodda, 1976: 30).

Mexico City, 1968

Perhaps the most devastating example of internal politics of the host nation intervening in the Olympics occurred in Mexico City in 1968. Mexico was chosen to host these Games despite the fact that it was neither a world player in international politics nor an affluent country. In fact, many of its citizens believed that it was wasteful and misguided to outlay such a large amount of money in the name of sport, rather than spending such resources on housing or welfare. Student protests over this issue had become violent in the months preceding the Games, so that three weeks before the Games army tanks were stationed opposite the Olympic stadium and in the road outside the university. Ten days before the Opening Ceremony on 2 October, the most violent demonstration occurred. Ten thousand anti-Olympic protesters gathered in the Square of the Three Cultures. Troops surrounded the square and opened fire on protesters. In the succeeding five hours more than 260 demonstrators were killed and over 1200 injured. The President of Mexico, Diaz Ordaz, called for calm and order as a result of the mayhem and loss of life. There were no further disruptions because of protests and the Games opened on schedule (Warning, 1980).

Munich, 1972

Disruption at the Munich Games of 1972, because of internal German politics, was also an intrusive force. 'Demonstrators wielding iron bars, battled police for three days outside Munich's massive sooty Palace of Justice in what Bavarian officials called a leftist plot to disrupt the Olympics' (Kirshenbaum, 1972: 24). Of course, this paled into insignificance compared with the later terrorist attack at these games, as discussed later in the chapter.

Montréal, 1976

Montréal, four years later, was also the scene of disorganisation, not the least of which was occasioned by the internal politics of the country, especially at the local government level. The main sources of discontent were problems associated with the high cost and construction of facilities needed for the Games (see Fig. 5.1).

When Montréal first began its planning to host the Games in 1969, Mayor Jean Drapeau estimated the costs at US$120 million. However, by 1976 the cost was US$1.6 billion and the deficit alone was one billion dollars. The facts relating to the excessive costs were revealed after the Games, at an official inquiry by the Quebec provincial government, which was initiated to investigate charges of corruption among the official organising committee and officials of Montréal City:

Figure 5.1. Lavish facilities provided for the Montréal Games, 1976

Drapeau ... and Civic Party politicians visualised the Olympics as a chance to improve their political position and popularity in the city. The Games were, in addition, an opportunity for Montréal to host another international event which would help attract further attention and possible foreign investment to Montréal.

Thirdly, the Games would help increase the power of the local French-Canadian ruling elite. Fourthly, local jobs were created for many unemployed French-Canadians. Finally, the Games would express the will of the French-Canadian populace to survive in the face of Anglo-French domination of Canada as a whole. (Strenk, 1970: 27)

There were lengthy hold-ups in building the facilities. Obtaining money from the federal government for construction took much longer than anticipated, putting schedules months behind and necessitating 24–hour workdays at double and triple rates of pay. Contracts were issued without bidding. Drapeau aggravated this situation by volunteering Montréal as the site of the 1974 world bicycling championships. This meant that the Olympic velodrome had to be completed in less than one year instead of the projected three and was, in fact, not completed in time. Because of administrative problems and ineptitude similar facilities were not completed in time for the Olympic Games themselves. The most noticeable of the unfinished facilities was the main Olympic stadium. Protests by Montréal citizens occurred before and during the Games because:

> the city lacked adequate housing, a water filtration plant, and even enough money to pay striking municipal employees. Drapeau countered such criticism with statements such as: 'The future will be the judge. Every time that a man tries to do something that will last beyond his own time, he has troubles. At the time, I'm sure that no one understood the significance of the Eiffel Tower'. (Strenk, 1970: 27)

In spite of all the disruptions, the 1976 Games began as scheduled. Unfortunately they were to become the victim of more political disruptions from other sources.

Opposing the bid: Toronto

It is likely that, as the Games continue to expand in size and scope, more intra-national opposition to them will occur, because of the ever increasing costs of staging such an event. In Canada the group 'Bread not Circuses' became one of the strongest anti-Olympic organisations in the world. It lobbied against Toronto's (unsuccessful) 1996 and 2008 Olympic Games bids and the successful Vancouver bid for the 2010 Winter Games. Members argued that the perceived profits from the event were only short-term 'economic steroids', and any profits did not filter down to those in need. In a 2001 letter to the IOC the group wrote:

> We are writing to you with a simple message: No Olympics in Toronto!
>
> Many promises have been made about the supposed benefits of bringing the Games to our city. We hear about new affordable housing or creating a debt-free Games. There is a long string of deceptions, misleading statements and half-truths underpinning the Toronto Olympic bid. It's time for a reality check.
>
> We've been told that the bidding for the Olympics won't cost the taxpayers a penny. The reality is Toronto's Olympic boosters need an extra $6 million in government support to pay for the Olympic bid.
>
> Polls show that over 84% of Torontonians oppose a public debt for the Olympics. 55% of Canadians oppose spending taxpayers [sic] money to help with the Bid.

We've been told that Toronto is a city that celebrates its multiculturalism and ethno-racial diversity. Yet, the Mayor of Toronto, Mel Lastman has made outrageous racist comments about his trip to Kenya where he was lobbying African IOC delegates. His comments include that he imagined himself 'in a pot of boiling water with all these natives dancing around me'. Toronto's ethno-racial diversity is a mere commodity used to sell the Bid.

The reality is that the Olympics will bring public debt, tenant evictions, the loss of affordable housing stock, short-term jobs, no long-term growth for our City, increased harassment by the police against people of colour and increased violence against women. Rule 40 in your Olympic Charter will impose a great debt on our city. We will be left holding the bag. The Olympics only bring more sports-palaces and benefits for the corporate sponsors. Our public money needs to go to our real priorities – not the priorities of the IOC.

The Coalition will hold the Olympic organisers accountable. Difference between the Olympic-sized promises and the reality of Toronto's day-to-day life means that opposition to the Olympics will grow. Direct actions against the Games will be organised.

It is time to stop playing Games with Toronto. (Bread not Circuses, n.d.)

This form of political intervention has, to a degree, been beyond the scope of the IOC to control. The responsibility for seeking to host an Olympic Games lies with the city and then the National Olympic Committee that applies for and is awarded them by the IOC. If a host has endeavoured to gain international prestige because of building facilities beyond its financial means then 'it appears on the surface' that it must bear the ultimate responsibility for this type of political interference. However, perhaps this is too simplistic a viewpoint. If a city did not project magnificent, state-of-the-art facilities and infrastructure upgrades it is unlikely that it would be awarded the event in the first place. The nature of the bidding process to host an Olympic Games encourages substantial government expenditure, which many nations can ill afford, financially and/or politically. Lack of national support within the host country has the potential to disrupt and even cancel the Games but, as in the case of Mexico City, the results can be more tragic, even involving the loss of life.

The issue of escalating costs of hosting the Olympics is discussed further in Chapter 6.

Opposing political ideologies

Introduction

From the 1894 Sorbonne Congress to the present, and seemingly with no prospect of cessation, nations with opposing political ideologies and domestic and foreign policies have used the Olympic Games as a political lever against their adversaries. The prestige associated with a nation competing at the Olympic Games, and likewise the loss of prestige accredited to an Olympic Games because of boycotts, has been a political weapon applied on many occasions. It is not the ideals of, nor opposition to, the Games themselves that have resulted in this type of discord, but rather the success, prestige and publicity given to the Games hosts and the Olympic Movement which has exacerbated this process.

Even the conception of the modern Olympics was not without political machinations. De Coubertin's initial dream of reviving the Games was linked to his wish for France to gain prestige through sport after its defeat in 1871 in the Franco-Prussian War. As recounted in Chapter 2, he realised the values of the 'Muscular Christianity' ideals practised in English public schools such as Rugby. Discussions with William Penny Brookes, who staged 'Olympyk Games' in Much Wenlock in Shropshire, strengthened de Coubertin's belief that sport was educative and had the potential to physically and mentally enhance an individual. He saw a re-creation of the Ancient Olympics as the medium by which this would occur.

Berlin, 1916

The Olympic Games of 1916 were awarded to Berlin during the Stockholm Games of 1912. The political climate of Europe was tense and this pressure continued to magnify until 1914, when war was declared. The Germans, like their opponents, felt that the war would be short and did not withdraw their offer of, or cease their preparations for, staging the Games. With the continuation of hostilities pressure was exerted by the Allied powers on the IOC and especially on de Coubertin to move the Games either to the USA or Switzerland. De Coubertin resisted such moves until 4 May 1915, when it became known that the German forces had used chlorine gas in the trenches of the eastern front. At this stage the IOC announced that the Games could not be shifted to an alternate site and would be cancelled. Thus, for the first time in the history of the modern Games, international politics had influenced an Olympic Games to the ultimate extent possible, their cancellation.

Berlin, 1936 – the 'Nazi Games'

The Games of the XII Olympiad, held in Berlin some 30 years later, were also besieged by problems stemming from political and ideological differences, initially involving the issue of discrimination against Jews in Germany under the Nazi regime and escalating from that into a question of a massive boycott to express displeasure at the entire Nazi doctrine.

Adolf Hitler assumed power in January 1933, after Berlin had been awarded the 1936 Games. Although originally opposed to the idea of Germany hosting the Games, he quickly perceived that staging the Olympics would provide an unparalleled opportunity to present Nazi propaganda to the entire world. But the question soon became not whether Germany wanted to host the Games but whether the rest of the world wanted them to.

Hitler's domestic political agenda had included the purging of Jews from all positions of power and influence and this included removal of world class athletes from sports clubs and organisations. These athletes were officially declared ineligible for competition within Germany.

In response to this German policy an international boycott of German goods and services was organised, as well as a proposal to move the Games to an alternative site. This movement failed when the IOC reaffirmed its decision to hold the Olympic Games in Berlin at its meeting on 7 June 1933. However, to placate the protesters, its president, Count Baillet-Latour, demanded that the German government guarantee

Figure 5.2. Berlin, 1936: arrival of the Olympic torch, against a backdrop of Nazi flags

to uphold to the letter every IOC rule and regulation and, in addition, pledge in writing that there would be no discrimination against athletes on the grounds of race or religion.

Those lobbying against the Germans hosting the Games now changed their strategy and focused their energies in the direction of organising an Olympic boycott. In 1933 the Amateur Athletic Union (AAU), the principal sports federation in the USA, voted to boycott the Games unless the treatment afforded Jews was improved. It sent its president, Avery Brundage, to visit Germany in order to make a first-hand evaluation of the situation. The Germans accordingly announced that five Jews, including Helen Meyer, Gretel Bergmann and Rudi Ball, had been selected as candidates for the German Olympic team. Brundage was given VIP treatment on his fact-finding mission and, upon his return, he stated that he did not notice any difference between the treatment of Jews and other Germans. In light of this evaluation the USA accepted the IOC invitation to the Games (Warning, 1980).

The following year, 1935, General Charles Sherrill, an American IOC member, visited Germany and was also favourably impressed by the Nazi regime. Upon his return to the USA he stated:

> I went to Germany for the purpose of getting at least one Jew on the Germany Olympic team and I feel that my job is finished. As to obstacles placed in the way of Jewish athletes or any others trying to reach Olympic ability, I would have no more business discussing that in Germany than if the Germans attempted to discuss the Negro situation in the American South or the treatment of the Japanese in California. (quoted in Kass, 1976: 227)

In 1935 Germany adopted the Nuremberg Laws. These contained a definition of German citizenship that excluded those of Jewish or mixed blood. This automatically excluded all Jews from contention for the German Olympic team. Adverse reaction to these laws was world wide. In New York 35,000 people demonstrated in favour of a boycott. The American Federation of Labor supported the boycott, as did the International Workers' Sport Movement. A 'Committee to Oppose the Olympic Games' was formed in Prague. Russia and Spain announced that they would not participate in the Games. The AAU however stood by its previous decision and voted again to send the US team to Germany. Brundage, a believer in the fallacy that sport and politics could and should be kept separate, was quoted as saying:

> frankly, I don't think we have any business meddling in this question. We are a sports group, organised and pledged to promote clean competition and sportsmanship. When we let politics, racial questions, religious or social disputes creep into our actions, we're in for trouble and plenty of it. (quoted in Kass, 1976: 229)

And on another occasion he declared:

> regardless of what country the Olympic Games are held, there will be some group, some religion, or some race that can register a protest because of the action of the government of that country, past or present. (quoted in Kass, 1976: 227)

To compensate for the growing world opposition to their hosting the Olympics the Nazis spared no effort or expense in their preparations, both in regard to the facilities and the vast amount of propaganda issued. These preparations successfully overrode the efforts of those trying to abort the Games and consequently the Games of the XII Olympiad were held as scheduled.

Tokyo, 1940

The IOC awarded the next Games to Tokyo, Japan. This was regarded by many as an important step in IOC policy, as it was the first occasion that the Games were to be held in an Asian country. However, by 1938, the IOC was in some doubt as to the wisdom of its decision because the Sino-Japanese war had begun. When the IOC could not receive assurances from the Japanese Olympic Committee that the Games would be unaffected by the hostilities they withdrew their offer to the city of Tokyo to host the Games and offered them instead to Helsinki, Finland. The Finns accordingly began their preparations, but in May 1940, the IOC President, Baillet-Latour, issued a statement saying that these Games would have to be cancelled because of World War II. Once again international differences caused the cancellation of the Games.

London, 1944, 1948

The Games of the XIII Olympiad, awarded to London and scheduled for 1944, were likewise affected because of the continuation of hostilities. The next Games, those of the XIV Olympiad, once again awarded to London, were the first Olympic Games to be celebrated after a 12 year moratorium.

   The choice of London as the site for the 1948 Games was controversial from the beginning, both internationally and within Great Britain. London was considered by many to be a poor choice because of the damage the city had suffered as a result of

German bombing during the war and strained economic post-war conditions within the country. Also, because of her position as one of the Allied Powers of World War II, giving the Games to this city was seen by some as a positive backing of the Allies by the IOC, a supposedly non-political body.

The Cold War

London 1948

The question of Soviet participation in the Olympic movement was beginning to emerge in the years immediately preceding the 1948 Games. Correspondence between IOC officials, Avery Brundage and IOC President Edstrom indicates their reluctance to grant the USSR the necessary admission to the international sporting federations. Brundage passed on the sentiments of a colleague in his letter:

> My own guess is that the real object of the Russians is to humiliate the West. .. every time they force a Federation to break its own rules in order to let them compete, Russian prestige is increased and Western prestige is decreased. The trouble at the moment ... is that about half the countries don't want to annoy Russia, and any country which is anxious to obtain a World Championship or a World Congress is reluctant to annoy the Eastern bloc'. (quoted in Espy, 1979: 28)

The issue was easily solved when the Soviets failed to form a National Olympic Committee. Under the *Olympic Charter*, this meant that they were ineligible to participate. They did however send observers to the London Games. The question of German and Japanese participation also was not a problem as no National Olympic Committees had existed in either country since the war.

Incidents of international rivalry manifested themselves on numerous occasions before and during the Games. In 1947 several members of the US Olympic Committee suggested that it would be a nice gesture for the USA to feed all the 1948 Olympic athletes. Not everyone shared this sentiment.

> The Soviet magazine *Ogonyk*, interpreting the gesture as provocative, denounced the offer as a 'Pork Trick', made to bring profits to American capitalists on their 'canned pork' and to provide an excuse in case the United States team was defeated. The magazine predicted that the United States track and field and swimming teams would lose and argued that by offering food to European athletes the United States could later claim, if it lost, that the feed had enhanced the physical power of the European athletes. (Espy, 1979: 30)

Another incident at these Olympics, caused by international rivalry, occurred when an Italian reporter accused the British government of barring him from entering the country to cover the Games because he was a communist. The official British reply was that 'after careful interrogation they had determined he was a possible saboteur' (Espy, 1979: 30). Romania withdrew from competition because of the failure of the Olympic Organising Committee to include Russians and East Germans as part of its membership.

Helsinki 1952

The 1952 Games were awarded to Helsinki as compensation for the cancelled 1940 Games which they were to have hosted. These Olympic Games were held at the height of the Cold War and this created problems both before and during the Games. The key issue was the question of recognition of a team from Germany.

Before World War II, Germany had one National Olympic Committee, however, because of the post-war split of the country, committees were formed in both East and West Germany. Subsequently each approached the IOC for recognition. Under IOC regulations only one committee from any country could be recognised as the Olympic representative of that country. Each of the German states had only received recognition from a smattering of countries and neither from the United Nations. Rivalry between the two Germanys was intense. The IOC decided to give provisional recognition to the West German committee, although the Soviet IOC member insisted that, as there were two states, there should be two separate committees. As a final compromise an agreement was drawn up wherein the two sides would attempt to form a single team, and the formation of a German Olympic Committee would be left to the Germans themselves. The East Germans refused to take part in this compromise, and, as a result, no East Germans participated in the Games. Similar to this problem was the question of whether to recognise Communist China or Nationalist China (Warning, 1980).

Since 1936, a tradition had been established whereby an Olympic torch had been ignited in Olympia, Greece, and carried by a relay of runners to the site of a Games, lighting the Olympic Flame which would burn for the duration of the Games (see Chapter 4). The most direct route for the torch bearers to Helsinki would have necessitated travelling through a section of Estonia. Requests were made to the Soviet government to allow passage through this Soviet territory. All requests were refused and consequently the Finnish organisers had to route the runners over the Arctic Circle, through Sweden to Finland and Helsinki via the southern corner of the country, a far more circuitous route. The supposed reasons for the Soviets' actions were that Estonia, which had only been a Soviet territory since 1944, had not been adequately integrated into the Soviet system and consequently was not open for world view (Warning, 1980).

Another established Olympic tradition broken at these Games concerned the Olympic Village, a concept which had been established at Los Angeles during the 1932 Games and continued ever since. The USSR participated in the Olympics for the first time in these Games, and was allowed to set up its own separate encampment for officials and athletes instead of sharing facilities with other countries in the Olympic Village. Originally the Soviets had planned to fly their team from Leningrad each day. They rescinded this decision contingent upon the agreement that the Eastern bloc countries could be housed in a separate Olympic Village. The Finns acceded to this request and converted what was meant to be the women's quarters, at Andinum, for the exclusive use of the athletes from Bulgaria, Czechoslovakia, Hungary, the USSR, Poland, Rumania, and the non-competing People's Republic of China. At first communist athletes maintained a complete isolationist policy, however, as the Games progressed, interaction with Western athletes became more commonplace.

Melbourne 1956

The 1956 Games were awarded to Melbourne, Australia, and were held in a period of great international tension. Two major world political crises had brought the world to the brink of war, one in Hungary and the other around the Suez Canal, the main shipping route between Europe and the Indian Ocean. The Suez region had been historically a troubled area and the year 1956 was no exception. In early October, Egypt seized the Suez Canal from British control. Israel counterattacked, aided by Great Britain and France. The Egyptian attitude towards the Olympic Games in the light of these circumstances was that 'nations guilty of cowardly aggression should be expelled from the Games' (Killanin and Rodda, 1976: 69). When no action was forthcoming from the IOC, Egypt withdrew from the Games in protest. Lebanon joined in the boycott. Avery Brundage, the President of the IOC, commented, 'we are dead against any country using the Games for political purposes, whether right or wrong. The Olympics are competitions between individuals, not nations' (Killanin and Rhodda, 1976: 69).

The Hungarian situation also resulted in an Olympic boycott. Mass unrest in Poland and Hungary developed during October 1956, into the most significant revolt against the regime in Moscow since the defection of Marshall Tito of Yugoslavia. To counteract this, the Soviets sent troops and equipment into Hungary. Yet the revolts continued and, on 25 October, Soviets troops fired on unarmed crowds in Budapest. In spite of this, the dissension continued and, in retaliation, on 4 November, Soviet forces attacked Budapest, crushing all opposition.

When the revolution began, the Hungarian Olympic team was gathered in Budapest for training. They were scheduled to leave for Australia on October 28, in order to have three weeks in Melbourne before the Games to acclimatise. On 23 October many of the athletes marched in the massive demonstrations, and the Hungarian officials fearing reprisals, endeavoured to gather the team together. It took almost two days for the team to assemble.

> Many of the athletes had been involved in the fighting and, as they came to the hotel, many without their baggage they told us how they had manned machine guns and barricades, fought secret police and Soviet troops and helped carry wounded. Our faces were flushed with pride and pleasure as we went to Prague where we were to leave by air for Australia. The Czechs put us up in a boarding school. ... the atmosphere was explosive and only the warning from Czech authorities that we could not cross the border from Hungary kept many from returning. We were told the border was closed. ... Five days after our arrival in Prague our team leader Gyula Hegyi ... who is head of the Nationalist Sports Council called us together and told us emotionally, 'We must go to the Games'. (*Sports Illustrated*, 1956a: 22)

While the athletes were in Prague, seventeen of their coaches, trainers, masseurs and technicians had left Odessa on 8 October, on the Russian ship 'Gruzia' with the Russian team bound for Melbourne. At first, relations were friendly; however, as knowledge of early events in the revolution became known a certain distance developed between the athletes from the two nations. One Hungarian commented to *Sports Illustrated*: 'there was no clash between Hungarians and Russians but this was due to the fact that at no stage of the voyage were we aware of what really happened in Hungary' (*Sports Illustrated*, 1956b: 23). The Soviets had monitored incoming news broadcasts and only filtered through certain information.

The main contingent of Hungarian athletes was not involved in this situation as they flew from Prague to Melbourne. Here the athletes were greeted enthusiastically by hundreds of ex-patriot Hungarians who had settled in the city. These crowds carried armfuls of flowers and the Hungarian flag of green, red and white, from which the communist symbol was conspicuously absent but to which black streamers had been attached.

Like their counterparts on board ship, these Hungarian athletes had been so closely supervised in Prague that no team members knew of the later attacks on Budapest until their arrival in Melbourne. After some indecision the athletes chose to compete in the Games, but not under the flag of what they referred to as 'Red Hungary'. Other nations took more drastic measures. The Dutch Olympic team withdrew in protest and their Olympic Committee donated 100,000 guilders to Hungarian relief. The Spanish team also withdrew rather than compete against the Soviets. The Swiss team withdrew then reconsidered. On attempting to re-enter the Games however, they found that it was too late to reapply (Toohey, 1990a).

For the first recorded time in Olympic history, open fighting between athletes broke out during the competition. It occurred between Hungarian and Soviet athletes and was, in fact, a manifestation of the political situation in Hungary. It took place during a water-polo game between the two countries.

The game was a minute old when Russia's Peter Mchvenieradze hammer-locked a Hungarian player and wound up in the penalty box. With the battle continuing below the water and belt lines, the Hungarians gained a 2–0 lead by half-time. Just after the second half began, a Russian smacked Hungary's Antol Bolvari in the right eye and the ball was all but disregarded as fighting broke out all over the pool. Like barracudas, the contestants flailed at one another underwater, sending up whirlpool proof of titanic struggles beneath.

The closing whistle was still reverberating when the Russian back, Valantine Prokopov, slammed an elbow into the eye of the Hungarian centre, Irwin Zador, opening a deep gash. Zador struggled from the water and into the arms of a teammate, Hungarian born spectators rushed towards the pool for revenge, the Russian team formed a protective knot, and the police quickly stepped in to enforce peace.

Miklos Maryin, youngest of the Hungarian poloists, decided: 'They play their sports just as they conduct their lives, with brutality and disregard for fair play'. But Maryin and his teammates had the consolation of victory: Hungary 4, Russia 0. (*Sports Illustrated*, 1956b: 23)

Sharing the blame

While Olympic procedures intensify existing rivalries between competing nations, it is the media and most especially the participating nations which must also take a share of the blame. The press embellishes stories and, by concentrating on national rivalries, they accentuate and may exacerbate existing political conditions. Indirectly, the media have aided political intervention in the Games because of their extensive coverage of and fascination with the Olympics throughout the world. If there was not such a widespread publicising of the Games then, arguably, governments, groups and individuals would not use the Games as a means of exposure and publicity for their causes.

The responsibility for political interference in the Olympic Games must also rest with the participating nations themselves, for it is the national governments of participating NOCs and their policies which have provided the greatest number of instances of politics within the Olympic Movement. Nations have evidenced this form of interference within the competitions themselves, or beforehand, to cause political embarrassment to others. They have used the Olympic Movement as a form of leverage against nations whose internal policies may be ideologically opposed to theirs. Most notable instances of this type of interference have been those involving the expulsion of South Africa and Rhodesia from the Olympic Movement.

Boycotts – South Africa and Rhodesia

During the 1960s many countries had curtailed their sporting links with South Africa as well as Rhodesia because of their apartheid policies. In 1968 they were formally suspended from the Olympic Movement for a number of reasons, one of which was that apartheid contravened Section 3 of the *Olympic Charter*, which forbids discrimination on the basis of race.

Despite their expulsion from the Olympic Movement, for a period of time South African rugby and cricket teams continued to compete overseas in defiance of a United Nations General Assembly request to all its members to suspend sporting links with the country (United Nations General Assembly, 1968: 22). By 1976, however, South Africa was almost entirely ostracised by sanctioned sporting bodies. Yet not all countries adhered to the UN request, for example a New Zealand rugby team disregarded world opinion and travelled to South Africa to compete against the South Africa team the Springboks.

As a result of this tour, African countries refused to participate in the Montréal Games unless New Zealand was expelled. According to Ludwig (1976: 6), 'the African countries found in the boycott issue, the only area of agreement likely to unite Kenya, Uganda, Zambia and Zaire'.

Under the auspices of the Supreme Council for Sport in Africa (SCSA), the IOC was asked to ban New Zealand. However, the IOC supported New Zealand's participation in the Games, based on the fact that rugby was not an Olympic sport and, as such, the New Zealand Rugby Federation, which sanctioned the tour, had no direct affiliation with the New Zealand Olympic Committee. New Zealand maintained its right to participate in the Games, refusing to withdraw and, as a consequence, 30 African and Middle Eastern countries boycotted the Games (Warning, 1980).

The effects of the boycott have been widely debated. While many of the boycotting nations were small and their athletes had little chance of success, the large number of countries which were united on the issue demonstrated the degree of solidarity regarding the ostracising of South Africa, and the increasing opposition to apartheid.

Boycotts – Moscow and Los Angeles

The notion of the power of a boycott as an efficient and forceful political weapon was again utilised in the following Olympiad. This time it was the USA which was the instigator. Its objective was to embarrass the Soviet Union, the country in whose capital, Moscow, the Games were to be staged.

In December 1979, the Soviet Union invaded Afghanistan. In response, Jimmy Carter, President of the USA, called on the nations of the world to impose sanctions on the USSR and specifically to boycott the forthcoming 1980 Olympic Games. Not all countries immediately rallied to his cause, even close US allies were at first reluctant. For example, the Australian Prime Minister, Malcolm Fraser, stated: 'the Games .. are an international event – not a Russian event – and should be seen in that context' (Australian Parliament, 1980: 29). Carter was, however, not discouraged by the initial lack of support. He continued to lobby US allies and support for his cause slowly increased. Soon three main factions developed: those governments in favour of boycotting the Games; those in favour of competing; and those who were undecided. However, the USA continued to lobby democratic world leaders and support for the US cause slowly increased (Toohey, 2006).

Ironically, while becoming involved in this process, some leaders appeared confused or even hypocritical about their participation in the boycott movement and its relationship to politics. For example, Malcolm Fraser commented: 'the government places a great deal of importance on being able for the future to re-establish the Olympic ideal in a way which will enable the athletes of the world to compete free of partisan politics of one kind or another' (Australian Parliament, 1980: 97).

Developing nations and other countries closely aligned with one or other of the superpowers followed their opposing stands. At national levels there were additional political machinations. Some governments exerted pressure on their NOCs and individual athletes not to attend the Games. The final outcomes of these pressures varied. When the Australian Olympic Federation announced in April that it was sending a team to Moscow, Fraser, who by this time was firmly in the Carter boycott camp, acted in a manner contrary to his previous statements about the separation of sport and state. The government withdrew all its funding for the Australian Olympic team to travel to Moscow. Like some other countries, such as Great Britain, the Australian team's presence at the Games was funded by private contributions. US athletes however, had no such choice, as Carter threatened to revoke the passport of any US athlete who tried to travel to the USSR (Toohey, 2006).

The Soviets did not accept that their invasion of Afghanistan was the genuine motive for the boycott. Instead they argued that its underlying motives were: that the USSR was a socialist country; that President Carter wished to undermine detente and that he needed to salvage his failing popularity as president.

Athletes from 80 NOCs participated at Moscow, compared with 88 at Montréal (1976), 122 at Munich (1972) and 113 at Mexico City (1968). It was the lowest number of nations since the 1956 Games. Some 65 NOCs turned down their invitations to send a delegation. The IOC estimated that between 45 and 50 of these did so because of the boycott.

It was, according to Kanin (1981: 108), 'the most extensive diplomatic effort ever connected with an Olympic celebration and demonstrated unequivocally that nations saw the Olympics as an effective tool to try to influence the foreign policy of nations with opposing political ideologies'. So politicized had the Games become that political journalists nearly outnumbered the sports writers, and many papers carried two different points of view of the event, written from opposing political frameworks (Toohey, 2006).

The following Games, held in Los Angeles in 1984, were subject to these same constraints. This time it was the Eastern bloc countries boycotting in retaliation for the previous Olympics. Officially they cited four main reasons for their non-attendance: the cost of the athletes' stay in the Olympic villages; the US government's failure to accept Olympic identity cards instead of visas; and lack of permission for

Aeroflot to take athletes to Los Angeles and for a Soviet ship to dock in Los Angeles harbour. In reality, the chance to inflict an embarrassment upon their hosts, similar to the one they had experienced, was certainly on their agenda. In all, 140 NOCs sent teams while 17 nations boycotted the Games, including six of the top ten medal winners at Montréal: the USSR, East Germany, Poland, Bulgaria, Cuba and Hungary. The large number of competing NOCs was overstated, as some territories were allowed to participate even though they did not meet *Olympic Charter* requirements (Vinokur, 1988; Hill,1999; Toohey, 2006).

Since this time Olympic boycotts have not assumed the same importance. The Moscow and Los Angeles boycotts were a weapon in the Cold War diplomatic arsenal. In the intervening period there have been many changes to world politics. The US has itself fought in Afghanistan. The USSR has been dismantled and most of the 15 countries that have emerged from the Eastern bloc are no longer communist, and in 1992 began to compete in the Games in their own right. For example, Estonia and Latvia competed for the first time since 1936 and Lithuania sent its first team since 1928. The other ex-Soviet member states participated as a 'unified team'. Its medal winners were, however, honoured under the flags of their own republics (IOC, n.d.).

Because of ongoing disruptions to the Games due to the boycotts (the first of which was at the 1948 Games), the IOC introduced sanctions for NOCs which engage in boycott activity. Currently they read as: 'the withdrawal of a duly entered delegation, team or individual shall, if effected without the consent of the IOC Executive Board, constitute an infringement of the Olympic Charter and shall be subject to an inquiry and may lead to measures or sanctions' (IOC, 2004: 85). This penalty does not necessarily address or penalise those who instigate the boycotts, namely national governments. And it fails to acknowledge the price that NOCs and athletes may have paid in defying their governments' wishes and attending the Games. While the *Olympic Charter* suggests that NOCs should 'preserve their autonomy and resist all pressures of any kind, including but not limited to political, legal, religious or economic pressures which may prevent them from complying with the Olympic Charter' (IOC, 2004: 61), this is simplistic for poorer NOCs, especially those in developing countries.

Some NOCs, for example the United States Olympic Committee and the Australian Olympic Committee, have been successful in accumulating capital, which allows them a degree of independence from their governments; however, even in these countries, Olympic sports and athletes may still be dependent on their governments for funding to maintain training programmes and subsidies. Thus, while such NOCs can distance themselves from governments in terms of receiving funds for a specific Games, they may still be reliant on the same governments to provide grants for Olympic athletes to develop their athletic skills in the period between Games.

The nexus between government and sport exists on many levels and this makes it possible for governments to use the Olympic Games as a tool to punish other governments for their politics and ideologies. Events such as the Soviet invasion of Afghanistan thus become a part of Olympic history even though, on the surface, there are no obvious links.

Nationalism

Introduction

A victory in an Olympic event means, on the most obvious level, that, on a given day, in a particular event, an athlete or team was the best in the competition. Be that as it may, there are multifaceted levels of meanings in such outcomes. One sub-textual message occurs when nations have used Olympic victories in an attempt to substantiate the relative advantages of their social, political and economic ideologies.

There is a fine but discrete line between the use of the Olympics as a political tool to embarrass opponents and the phenomenon of nationalism. The main difference lies in the fact that the former can occur throughout the entire period of an Olympiad, while nationalism generally arises as a result of outstanding Olympic performances, the national medal tally for particular Summer or Winter Olympic Games, or hosting a Games with the purpose of highlighting national superiority. Another difference between the two phenomena lies in the fact that national rivalry is directed at a particular nation or nations, whereas claims of superiority need not necessarily have a particular government as a target.

London, 1908

The London 1908 Games were the first to exhibit national rivalry to an extent that was disruptive to the Olympic Movement. Originally the Games were to have been staged in Rome, however the Italians let it be known that they could not continue their offer and in 1906 London was assigned the Games in their stead.

The major display of national rivalry in these games was between the American team and British participants and officials. This mirrored a general cooling in Anglo-American relations at the time. This rivalry disrupted the staging of the athletic events. An American official, James Sullivan, exemplified the American attitude: 'They [the officials] were unfair to the Americans, they were unfair to every athlete except the British, but their real aim was to beat the Americans. Their conduct was cruel and unsportsmanlike and absolutely unfair' (in Killanin and Rhodda, 1976: 37). The two most blatant examples of cheating occurred in the 400 metres and the marathon. In the former the US victor was disqualified and in the latter officials assisted the drugged and collapsing Italian, Dorando Pietri, across the finish line so that he would beat the fast finishing American, Johnny Hayes. After American protests about the blatant support the Italian received, Hayes was declared the winner (Warning, 1980).

In response to the criticism of partiality and bias in their judging, the British Olympic Council subsequently issued a 64-page publication entitled, *The Olympic Games of 1908: a Reply to Certain Criticisms* (British Olympic Council, 1908) setting out quotations of charges from the Americans on one side and 'dignified' replies from the British on the other. As a result of this publication, athletic relations between the two countries were temporarily broken off. The scandal of biased judging forced the IOC to alter its policy in regard to officials. From these Games onwards judges came from a variety of countries, rather than exclusively from the host nation (Warning, 1980).

The overt displays of rivalry had begun at the Opening Ceremony when the British neglected to display the American flag. During this ceremony the USA replied in kind by refusing to dip their flag to the King and Queen of England on the principle that 'this flag dips to no earthly King' (Warning, 1980: 31). This established a tradition which American teams have upheld ever since.

Berlin, 1936

Perhaps the most overt example of a nation attempting to use the Olympics to illustrate its superiority occurred 28 years later, at the 1936 Olympic Games. At these Olympics the Nazis attempted to demonstrate to the world that their policies had raised Germany from the devastating effects of World War I reparation payments and then the Great Depression, while at the same time highlighting the greatness of the Aryan race. Their attempts at the latter confirmed how this policy can be a double-edged sword.

The fact that Berlin was awarded the Games in 1931 itself had a political underpinning. The decision by the IOC was an attempt to aid Germany in its restoration after its defeat in World War I (Loder, 1997). As noted above, when Adolf Hitler came to power in 1933 he was initially opposed to hosting the Games, however his opposition was transformed to support when he perceived the propaganda potential of sport. Strenk (1970: 28) notes: 'here was a chance to show the world how modern and progressive Germany was ... to demonstrate that Germans were happy and prosperous under the Nazi system, and to divert public attention away from other areas of Nazi policy such as campaigns against the Jews'.

The Germans were thorough in their preparations in order to achieve these aims. For example, the excavations at the site of the Ancient Games, at Olympia in Greece, were reopened by the Germans in 1935 and a special exhibit was arranged. This toured throughout Germany, showing Olympic artefacts and German cultural exhibits.

The Games themselves highlighted German technology, with a number of new types of recording apparatus being introduced, for example, electronic timing, electronic starting pistols, photo-finish equipment, machines to record 'touches' in fencing, the broadcasting of results on television and short wave radio and wire photos (Warning, 1980).

The host city, Berlin, was cleaned up. Special police units patrolled to prevent price gouging. Violence directed against Jews was temporarily curtailed and Nazi propaganda adorned the buildings. In describing his government's policy aims, an assistant to propaganda Minister Josef Goebbels stated:

> It is the aspiration of the Nationalist Socialist regime to bring visitors here in the largest possible number. ... In this we see the effective defence measures against the lying reports about Germany rampart abroad. ... Every German hotelier, taxi driver represents the Nationalist state to the foreigner. Therefore they all have the duty to behave themselves accordingly and not to shame the Fatherland. (quoted in Strenk, 1979: 31)

Although these measures served to create a favourable impression of the German government, their master plan was not entirely successful. The weak link was on the Olympic field of play. Inherent in the German's scheme to demonstrate Aryan superiority was the premise that their representatives' performances would be superior. This would demonstrate that German efficiency in the community and industry was transferable to human achievement in sport. With the spectacular victories by black athletes (whom the Germans derogatorily termed 'auxiliaries'), notably by Jesse Owens, these hopes were negated. The Nazis' plans, while not wasted, did not achieve their desired goals and Hitler's government had to be content with global acceptance of German efficiency, rather than Aryan supremacy.

The Soviet Union

The USSR competed in the Olympics for the first time in 1952, during the Cold War period. Both the Soviets and their political rivals, the USA, perceived Olympic competition in nationalistic terms. Before these Games the Soviet press, especially the newspapers *Pravda* and *Izvestia*, was instrumental in exhorting their athletes to perform at their best so that their performances would reflect well and bring honour to the Communist system. It was during this time that steroid use increased, partly as a result of systemic pressure in Eastern bloc countries and, in retaliatory moves, Western athletes seeking to negate such advantages by also using similar substances.

The athletes thus played an active role in nationalistic rivalries and many believed in the superiority of their nation state. The 1968 Olympics provide another example of this. Wayne Brauman, a USA wrestler, writing in the *New York Times*, accused the Soviet Union and Romanian teams of trying to broker an athletic deal:

> If the United States 158–pounder let the Rumanian pin him then the United States 198–pounder would be allowed to pin his Russian opponent. ... They thought we were crazy when we turned them down ... and after they went on to pin both of us anyway, they thought we were crazier. .. International athletics is a totally political thing .. Avery Brundage might not like to hear anyone say that of all other countries. Most of them resent the United States ... because we're number one in the world. And sports is one area where they can demonstrate their superiority over us. (*New York Times*, 1972)

Seoul, 1988

Twenty years later the Games were still being affected by this form of political point scoring. After Seoul, South Korea, was awarded the 1988 Games, North Korea unsuccessfully demanded that it co-host the event. These demands were rejected. Following this, two fatal bombings were linked to North Korean efforts to disrupt Games preparations. The Japanese Red Army, an active terrorist group, also threatened to disrupt the Games. Revelations throughout 1988, about North Korea's complicity in the bombing of a South Korean airliner in November 1987, possibly served to prevent the country from any further attempts to create disorder at the Games (Toohey, 2006).

Salt Lake City, 2002

This was not the end of the problem of nationalism for the Olympic Movement. Having survived the IOC corruption and bribery imbroglio, discussed later in the chapter (under 'IOC politics'), the 2002 Winter Games competition was rocked by allegations of cheating by officials. The object, supposedly, was to ensure that selected athletes from the two countries involved (France and Russia) would win their events (pair skating and ice dancing pair). Although the Canadian figure skaters, Jamie Sale and David Pelletier, had performed a nearly perfect routine (and were crowd favourites), they were placed second to the Russians, Elena Berezhnaya and Anton Sikharulidze. There was uproar in the stadium and a media outcry over the result. The Canadians were subsequently also awarded a gold medal by the IOC. This was the first time in Olympic history that there were two gold, a bronze, but no silver medals in a skating competition. The Canadian skaters became instant celebrities and were chosen to be their country's flag bearers for the closing ceremony.

After the Games the drama continued. The French judge implicated in the scandal, Marie-Reine Le Gougne, who had earlier admitted that she had been pressured by her national federation into voting for the Russians, then recanted her allegation. She was later banned for three years. The head of the French skating federation, Didier Gailhaguet, also received a three-year ban. The situation became more farcical when Italian police arrested a Russian tycoon, Alimzhan Tokhtakhounov, on charges related to the fixing of the events. It was alleged he was doing so in order to obtain a French visa. He was subsequently charged by the US government but successfully fought extradition from Italy. There were calls from Russia for his release claiming the arrest was 'a sinister conspiracy led by Washington: Americans are trying to smear us once again to show the entire world that Russia is nothing' (Steven, 2002).

American television alleged that Italian police had made wiretap recordings of Tokhtakhounov meeting about the judging. The FBI and Italian police suspected him of other crimes, including drug-dealing, money-laundering and racketeering, as well as trading ex-Soviet weapons to the Middle East. Transcripts suggested that he might have contacted up to six of the skating judges. Police also released transcripts of telephone conversations between Tokhtakhounov and an Olympic female ice dancer's mother. Another transcript documented a conversation in which an unidentified female ice dancer telephoned Mr Tokhtakhounov and said she could not have won her Olympic event without his help (Nii, 2002; Steven, 2002).

There were concerns as to whether ice skating would survive as an Olympic sport because of the scandal. Again, the combination of 'subjective' sports, nationalism and judge tampering had caused embarrassment to the Games. The International Skating Union reacted to this disagreeable possibility by replacing their traditional 6.0 scoring system for a new one, based on points. However, as a result of the changes, the judges' scores are now totally anonymous, so it could be argued that there is more scope for collusion. The new system includes the following changes:

- The judges focus entirely on scoring the quality of each element and the quality of the five Program Components. Their marks will be based on specific criteria for each element and will provide a comprehensive assessment of each skater's skills and performance.
- A judge is not required to compare and score each skater directly in relation to all other skaters. This permits each judge to focus on the quality of (1) each Technical Element performed and (2) the Program Components, and to enter their scores into a touch-screen.
- The computer records the individual scores as entered by the judges, and compiles aggregate scores for each skater to determine the final rankings.
- There will be a panel of twelve judges, of whom nine are drawn at random. The marks of these nine will form the result. Out of these nine judges, the highest and lowest marks are deleted and the average will be taken from the remainder (trimmed mean). (International Skating Union, 2006)

While it could be argued that this particular Salt Lake City scandal was initiated by someone not directly involved in the Games, it was nationalistic interests that allowed the plan to be actioned. The next section details other incidents that have obstructed Games operations and have been initiated and carried out by individuals with no affiliation to the Olympic Movement.

Political demonstrations, terrorism and security at the Games

With the increasing media coverage of the Olympic Games and its subsequent availability to more of the world through the advent of satellite television, the Games have become a vehicle for individuals with no affiliation to the Olympics to draw attention to issues unrelated to the Olympic Movement. Even before extensive television coverage, protesters had disrupted the Olympic Games with the same purpose although, obviously, their audience was smaller. Those who were present at the Opening Ceremony of the 1952 Games in Helsinki were witness to such an event when Barbara Rotbraut-Pleyer, dubbed the 'Peace Angel' by the press, disturbed the proceedings.

> A rather plump lady, partly veiled and wearing what appeared to be a flowing white nightdress, was able to get on the track, complete half a circle of it, and actually ascend to the rostrum and begin a speech with what sounded something like 'Peace'. ... But lack of breath, because of her girth and exertion, and the timely action of one senior Finnish official who did not know she was not part of the official ceremony stopped her at this point. She was removed by the police who later announced that she was a mentally deranged German girl who had come to address 'Humanity'. (Killanin and Rhodda, 1976: 64)

While this appears to be somewhat bizarre, harmless and even rather amusing, other Games incidents have not been so innocent and are based on acts of terrorism.

Definitions of terrorism

The concept of what exactly is terrorism is an issue which itself has been problematic, as the word 'terrorist' is a value laden term. The etymology of the word can be traced back to the Latin *terrere* (to arouse fear), however no single definition of terrorism has gained global acceptance despite more than 100 definitions being proposed to international organisations (Kennelly, 2005). Attempts to gain consensus have 'proven impossible to satisfy fully the demands of either politics or scholarship' (Selth, 1988: xxiii). While some claim that a standardised definition is a necessary prerequisite to combatting it, others believe that an internationally accepted definition of terrorism can never be fully agreed upon, as any categorisation of it is influenced by interpretation, personal perception and exploitation (Ganor, 2003).

Despite the lack of a universally accepted definition, it is generally acknowledged that terrorism: has always been purposeful; is political in its motives; implies violence or threats thereof; is indiscriminate in its choice of targets; and is designed to have consequences beyond its immediate target/s (Freedman, 2003). Although the targets *per se* may not be pre-selected, there is a strategy behind terrorists' actions. The significant intent is politically motivated and it is this intention that distinguishes it from other forms of violence, such as murder or football hooliganism (Whitaker, 2001; Toohey *et al.*, 2003).

While terrorist acts have had a variety of goals, Selth (1988) has classified them into a broad typology with four (not necessarily mutually exclusive) categories:

1. *domestic* (actions against others in the same country);
2. *state* (terror used by authorities to maintain their position within a nation);
3. *international* (terrorism directed at foreign nationals or governments);
4. *state sponsored* (terrorist tactics used by agents of the state, or independent groups to pursue foreign policy aims).

Munich, 1972

One of the most tragic incidents in Olympic history was of the *international* terrorism genre and occurred in 1972, when Palestinian terrorists invaded the Olympic Village:

> Before the Munich Games began, and during their first days, West German authorities were aware of reports which indicated that there would be political demonstrations connected with the Olympics. None of these reports indicated that Israeli athletes would be the target of the demonstrations; however, German authorities had met with an Israeli diplomat to discuss security arrangements for athletes in the Olympic Village. (Warning, 1980: 49)

The Israeli team was housed at Connolly Strasse 31 in the Athletes' Village. These premises also housed athletes from Uruguay and Hong Kong. On 5 September, Palestinian terrorists, belonging to a group called Black September, infiltrated the village and took ten Israelis hostage in their quarters. In the initial raid an Israeli wrestling coach was killed. For the next two days the ten hostages, who included both athletes and officials, were held captive while the terrorists and German officials negotiated terms for their release. The Black September group demanded the release of over 200 political prisoners held by the Israelis. Additionally, they sought safe passage for themselves and their hostages to an airport of their choice in the Middle East (Warning, 1980).

In keeping with her country's determination not to negotiate with hostages, the Israeli Prime Minister, Golda Meir, announced that Israel would not accede to any of the terrorists' demands. Similarly, Avery Brundage, President of the IOC, declared that the IOC was opposed to the forcible removal of Olympic athletes from the Olympic Village. The Egyptian President, Anwar Sadat, was notified of the attack and implored to intervene. He announced that the Egyptian government knew nothing of the attack and had no intention of becoming involved.

Meanwhile, the West German government decided to implement a plan to free the hostages on German soil. Consequently, the terrorists and hostages were allowed to leave the Olympic Village and proceed to Furstenfeldbrock Airfield, where an attempt was made to free the hostages. When the Palestinians realised that they had been ambushed they detonated hand grenades which they threw into the helicopters containing the hostages. All of the Israelis died in the melée (Groussard, 1975). In all 17 people were killed as a result of the attack.

As a result of the deaths, teams from four nations (Egypt, Israel, Algeria and the Philippines) withdrew, as well as individuals from the Dutch and Norwegian contingents. The Israeli Government called for the cancellation of the Games, however the IOC decided against this course of action, based on the argument that the Games would, in the future, then be more susceptible to further violence (Warning, 1980). The IOC instead decided to cancel all competition on 7 September, and a memorial service for the dead athletes and officials was held. When addressing the service, IOC President Avery Brundage stated:

> Sadly in this imperfect world, the greater and more important the Olympic Games become the more they are open to commercial, political and now criminal pressure. The Games of the Twentieth Olympiad have been subject to two savage attacks. First we lose the Rhodesian battle against naked political blackmail ... We have only the strength of a great ideal. I am sure the that public will agree that we cannot allow a handful of terrorists to destroy this nucleus of international cooperation and goodwill we have in the Olympic Movement – the Games must go on and we must continue our efforts to keep them clean, pure and honest and try to extend the sportsmanship of the athletic field into other areas. (quoted in Guttman, 1984: 254)

This statement was considered by many to be inappropriate, because the question of Rhodesia's participation was a separate issue and the linking of the two problems was seen to be, at the very least, undiplomatic. The following day Brundage issued an apology 'regretting any misunderstanding of words' and the Games continued, one day behind schedule (Kirshenbaum, 1972: 26).

In 2006, Mohammad Oudeh (known previously as Abu Dauod), one of the planners of the attack, reflected on its effects. He commented: 'Before Munich, we were simply terrorists. After Munich, at least people started asking "Who are these terrorists? What do they want?" Before Munich, nobody had the slightest idea about Palestine' (Karam, 2006: 19).

Another, less violent and less well known protest at the Munich Games was undertaken by Irish demonstrators wishing to draw world attention to their protests against British rule in Northern Ireland. The protesters rode bicycles into the British road cycling team during competition.

Montréal, 1976

The following Games in Montréal in 1976 were also not immune from political demonstrations, despite tight security measures adopted in the aftermath of the Munich massacre. Security was said to be so extensive that 'the Olympic Village might well have been a prison camp' (McIntosh, 1984: 26). However, in the venues, a group of Ukrainian immigrants was still able to use the Games as a platform to demonstrate for an independent Ukrainian Olympic team, instead of its then status as part of the Soviet team. These demonstrations were non-violent. The protesters attended many events and waved Ukrainian flags, chanted political slogans and burnt a Soviet flag, which they had removed from an Olympic flagpole (Takac, 1976).

Barcelona, 1992

In 1992, the Basque separatist group Euzkadi Ta Askatasuna (ETA) attempted to interrupt the Barcelona Olympic Games Opening Ceremony by bombing electricity pylons and disrupting electricity supplies. In another attempt to create disorder for the same Games a Marxist group, known as Grupo de Resistencia Antifascista Primo October (GRAPO), planted three bombs on a gas pipeline outside Barcelona. The explosion ruptured the pipeline, caused a fire, and stopped gas supplies reaching northeast Spain. However, while both attacks caused inconvenience, they were unsuccessful in gaining widespread media attention (Kennelly, 2005: 3). The following Games in Atlanta in 1996 evidenced a new form of terrorism, again using bombs, however, this time, the blast was specifically directed at spectators.

Atlanta, 1996

Several bomb threats were received by the Atlanta Organising Committee for the Olympic Games (ACOG) before and during the Games. Before the Games the spectre of violence had been raised when a Georgia-based militia group's headquarters had been raided, after reports that the group intended to disrupt the Games (Hinds, 1996). Pipe bombs were discovered and seized in the raid.

The attack occurred in Olympic Centennial Park, a recreation area created especially for the Games, where athletes and the public could meet and enjoy and consume activities and products designed by Olympic sponsors such as Coca Cola and Swatch. The bomb, hidden in a knapsack, exploded early in the morning of Saturday, 27 July. Fragments of the bomb were thrown as far as 80 metres from the site of the explosion. One woman was killed by the blast, a reporter died from a heart attack directly attributable to the bomb and another 110 people were injured. After the bombing a telephone conference between the Atlanta Committee for the Olympic Games (ACOG), the White House and Georgia state officials was held (Hinds, 1996). As in 1972, the authorities decided that cancelling the Games would equate with a victory to terrorism. US President, Bill Clinton, declared, 'We cannot let terrorism win' (Hewitt, 1996: 11) and Francois Carrard, the IOC Director General, echoed Avery Brundage's 1972 comment when he announced 'the Games must go on' (Magnay and Hinds, 1996: 7). As a mark of respect for those killed or injured in the blast all Olympic flags were lowered to half mast and there was a minute's silence at all Olympic venues (Loder, 1997). The Olympic competitions continued, but Centennial Park was closed for three days and when it reopened, on 30 July, security measures to enter the precinct were far more stringent. The official report of the Atlanta Games gave the incident only a relatively brief mention and put a spin on the outcome that could be considered to be somewhat insensitive to the victims:

> this tragedy brought together in a universal appeal to continue the Olympic Games in the spirit in which they were started. ... The 40,000 people who participated in the park's emotional reopening demonstrated their unwavering support of the celebration of the Olympic Games. (Watkins, 1997: 87)

Further adding to the incident's dismal saga was the search for the culprit. It was flawed and described as 'circus-like' (CNN, 1996). Richard Jewell, the security guard who found the bomb shortly before it exploded, was the first publicly named suspect. Although he was subsequently cleared, it took authorities five years to finally catch the bomber, Eric Rudolph, a US citizen. For much of that time he had eluded law enforcement agencies by hiding in the Appalachian Mountains. In 2005 he was sentenced to life in prison for the attack. He claimed his motivation was that he opposed abortion and wanted to embarrass the government for its stand on the issue (Cooper, 2005; see also Chapter 10 case study).

Increasing security – Sydney, 2000

As a result of these acts of terrorism and the threats of other politically motivated violence at other Olympic Games, for example in Seoul in 1988, Olympic security measures have become increasingly sophisticated. As the 1996 bombing was directed towards the largest contingent of Olympic stakeholders present at a Games – the spectators – the job of securing the Olympic Games has became increasingly complex. This is demonstrated by the principles underlying security planning at the Sydney 2000 Olympic Games. They were to:

• protect the integrity of international entry and accreditation processes to ensure they were consistent with security and Australia's existing policies;
• ensure all accredited persons were subjected to appropriate background checks;
• restrict sensitive areas to accredited persons;
• sanitise all Olympic venues and sites for the presence of explosive devices after 'lockdown' of the venue by SOCOG, and re-sanitise as required on the basis of specific risk;
• impose random, but carefully targeted, screening procedures using metal detectors and searches of hand-carried items, under the supervision of NSW Police officers, for all spectators entering Olympic venues and sites;
• apply more thorough checking procedures of all people and items entering higher risk areas such as the Olympic Village;
• apply strict and consistent zone controls within each venue and site, aimed primarily at the protection of the Olympic Family and VIPs, and impose strict and consistent controls on the entry of vehicles and commercial materials into all Olympic venues and sites. (Toohey, 2001: 150)

As part of the 2000 security preparations, an Olympic Intelligence Centre, with strong links to the Australian Security Intelligence Organisation (ASIO), was created within the organising committee (Toohey, 2001). Although security threats to the Games were considered to be slight, precautions were taken to prevent the four potential sources of attack that had been identified: 'state agents of terror, formalized terrorist groups, loosely affiliated extremists and lone militants'. Islamic extremists, especially groups associated with Osama bin Laden, were listed as one of the loosely affiliated extremists threats (Terrorism Research Centre, 2000: 1).

In 2000, New Zealand police foiled a suspected plot to target Sydney's Lucas Heights Nuclear Reactor during the Sydney Olympic Games (*New Zealand Herald*, 2000). During an investigation into people smuggling, Auckland police raided a house and found evidence suggesting the existence of the scheme. At the time it was thought possible that the leader of Al Qaeda, Osama bin Laden, was associated with the plot. In another episode in May 2000, a man, whose home near the Olympic site was discovered packed with explosives, was arrested (Kennelly, 2005).

Post-9/11

Following the 11 September, 2001 (9/11) attacks in the USA, the Olympic Games have been seen to have greater than ever 'terrorism capital', because of their media diffusion and symbolic representation. In the aftermath of the bombings there were calls for a re-evaluation of security procedures for the 2002 Salt Lake City Winter Olympic Games (Diaz, 2001). This was a clear indication that Olympic organisers were now more concerned for the safety of spectators, athletes and officials, and venues. A press statement released by the White House, entitled *Preparing for the World: Homeland Security and Winter Olympics* (White House, 2002), outlined the approach to security as 'highly visible equals highly secure'. In particular, air security was tightened. There was a 45–mile restricted airspace around the city and the areas above venues became no-fly zones. Salt Lake City International airport was closed to commercial traffic during the opening and closing ceremonies and all baggage going through the airport was screened for explosives. Vehicles were prohibited within 300 feet of venues and other selected buildings (Kennelly, 2005: 18). In addition, the Salt Lake City Organising Committee acquired 15,000 anti-anthrax tablets (Snider, 2002) and the state of Utah commissioned the design and implementation of health monitoring systems and biometric systems, such as retinal identification and facial recognition to identify accredited athletes and officials and manage incidents of bio-terrorism (Gesterland *et al.*, 2003; Tsui *et al.*, 2003; Whisenant, 2003).

The tightening of security attributable to September 11 resulted in an estimated additional US$70 million spending on security, bringing the Salt Lake City security budget to around US$500 million (Kennelly, 2005: 19). Sixty different federal, state and local agencies and over 15,000 personnel were involved in the security operations during the Games, including 10,000 national guardsmen,

The perceived risk of terrorism has been cited as a reason for low spectator numbers at the 2004 Athens Olympics, and it influenced the experiences of those who attended (Toohey and Taylor, 2005). Before the Games there were many media reports of the possibility of terrorist attacks. Some analysts claimed that the Greek government had been downplaying the risks involved despite the fact that Greece had passed anti-terrorism legislation, bringing it up to date with other members of the European Union (Hope, 2001; Kennelly, 2005: 19). Other criticism claimed that the government had initially been loathe to accept outside help. However, closer to the event, Greece accepted security planning, training and intelligence assistance from the first ever international Olympic security advisory group. This unit included members from Great Britain, Germany, the USA, Spain, France, Australia and Israel (Kennelly: 2005: 20).

Despite these precautions, it was rumoured that the US team would withdraw if the perceived threat of terrorism was too high (Dahlberg, 2004). In the face of the criticism of security arrangements, Athens Mayor Dora Bakoyianni, countered by protesting that: 'we are paying the price for September 11' (Lui, Vlahou and Robert, 2004: 22).

The Games security force included tens of thousands of trained personnel, fighter jets, airborne surveillance, Patriot, Stinger and Hawk missiles, off-shore and port security, and assistance from the North Atlantic Treaty Organisation (NATO) (Kennelly, 2005: 20). Athens 2004 was the most guarded Olympic Games in history and the 'biggest – most expensive – peace time security operation ever' with security allegedly costing in the vicinity of an unprecedented three quarters of a billion US dollars (Wilson, 2004). One of the new cost items was for insurance. In the past, events like the Olympic Games were not insured for acts of terrorism. However, post 9/11, the IOC sought insurance for cancellation of the Games (Trott and Jenkins, 2003; BBC Sport, 2004; Wilson, 2004).

Despite the pre-Games concerns about safety, there were no major terrorism incidents. The most tragic security-related episode occurred when a security guard, who was playing 'Russian roulette' while on duty, killed himself.

The issue of terrorism at the Games appears to be one which is not going to disappear. While the Olympic Games are pre-eminent in the sporting world they will continue to be a target for terrorists. As Atkinson and Young suggest:

> while sports may seemingly share few conceptual links with acts of terrorism... we cannot ignore how sports events may become targets ... or the contexts of terrorism.... For many reasons, individual terrorists or terrorist organizations might find suitable targets in athletes participating in games, spectators attending the events, or selected corporate sponsors of sports contests. (Atkinson and Young, 2002: 54)

The above comments of the Munich terrorist suggest this is the case.

Olympic athletes and politics: Mexico City, 1968

Athletes too have used the Olympics as a forum of protest. Just as terrorists see the Olympics as the medium to advertise their causes, athletes have also seen this potential to reach large audiences and simultaneously embarrass their government.

The first such example of this form of intervention occurred at the 1968 Mexico Olympics and involved US athletes. Initially, this demonstration began in support of South Africa's expulsion from the Olympic Movement, however, even when this issue was resolved to the protesters' satisfaction, their demonstrations continued. Their cause shifted to highlight the inferior treatment of black athletes in the USA.

It was in July 1967, at the first National Conference on Black Power, held at Newark, New Jersey, that a boycott of black athletes at the Mexico Games was first proposed, in conjunction with a boycott of professional boxing to protest against the World Boxing Association stripping Mohammad Ali of his title. By November the proposed boycott was gaining momentum. It was led by Harry Edwards, a sociology professor at San José State College, California and endorsed by Martin Luther King (Warning, 1980).

The protesters released a set of demands which would have to be met before their boycott would be lifted. Included in this was the demand that Avery Brundage resign as President of the IOC because of his racist beliefs, and that a black member be appointed to the United States Olympic Committee. Brundage replied in his characteristically blunt manner that if the black Americans boycotted the Olympics they would not be missed (Lapchick, 1975).

The assassination of Martin Luther King in April 1968 added to the resolve of the protesters and increased their ranks, however a vote of black athletes at the Olympic trials indicated that only about 50 per cent were against competing. An official boycott was called off and a decision made to stage a protest at the Games instead (Lapchick, 1975).

The first sign of trouble at the Games occurred when Tommy Smith, a 200 metres sprinter, said that if he won his event he did not want Avery Brundage to present him with a medal. In their heats of the 200 metres Smith and fellow American, John Carlos, wore black knee-length socks instead of their uniform issue, as a sign of their protest.

On 15 October Smith and Carlos finished first and third respectively in the final of this event. During the medal ceremony Smith wore a black glove on his right hand and a black scarf around his neck and Carlos a black glove on his left hand and beads around his neck. Both wore civil rights badges, as did Peter Norman, the Australian sprinter who won the silver medal (Gordon, 1994: 281). While the US anthem was played Smith and Carlos raised their gloved hands and refused to look at their flag being raised (see Fig. 5.3). As a result of this demonstration the IOC applied pressure on the USOC and the two athletes were expelled from the US team (Warning, 1980). Despite IOC warnings, further demonstrations occurred by US athletes and, although not as powerful as the Smith and Carlos incident, enabled protesters to feel that their demonstrations were successful in gaining the attention of the world press for their cause. Similar protests by blacks at the Munich Games resulted in the expulsion of a further two athletes, Vince Mathews and Wayne Collet. However, the press attention was focused on a more tragic protest at these Games, which resulted in the death of 11 Israeli athletes.

Figure 5.3. Black Power salute, Mexico City, 1968

Political demonstrations, terrorism and security: conclusion

Because the Olympics have pre-eminence as an international sporting event and festival, they have become the ideal medium for appropriation by nations, groups and individuals and thereby to demonstrate and exploit their political power and causes. The overtly political organisational structure and rituals of the Games themselves exacerbate the event's political construction. They draw upon and provide symbolic capital to various interest groups, despite the fact that the rhetoric and philosophy of the IOC suggest the opposite and portray the movement in terms of its potential as a mechanism for achieving world peace, reconciliation and concord.

IOC politics

Introduction

Since before the 1894 Sorbonne Conference, when political decisions were made regarding whether or not to invite a German representative, politics have been an overt and, more commonly, covert facet of the internal workings of the IOC.

The Olympic Movement has been rated by some political analysts as a very successful organisation (Hoberman, 1986). Aligned to this perception is its increasing popularity with the general public throughout the world and concomitant attractiveness to a variety of political interests that wish to harness the passions it creates (Houlihan, 1994). Ironically, the IOC has fostered such manipulation because it 'has continually seen the Olympic Games as a sporting event with a philosophy that placed the Olympics above such mundane preoccupations as politics' (Leiper, 1981: 105). In other words it has created a political agenda while maintaining its aloofness from such quotidian affairs. Houlihan (1994: 111) suggests that this has had negative repercussions for the movement because 'such inherently contradictory practices are obviously difficult to sustain while not enabling other organisations to exploit their ambiguities. ... The Olympics therefore provide a conveniently adaptable context for the furthering of interests'.

The structure of the IOC was discussed in Chapter 4. It is structured as a self-electing, self-regulating association and, until 1981, it consisted entirely of men. Even today its power élite is still selected primarily from Westernised nations. Its executive has usually been selected from among individuals who are professionally powerful, wealthy or members of the nobility, or who meet a combination of these three criteria. Sitting at the top of the Olympic power structure is the IOC President, whose influence in the world of sports is supreme.

Juan Antonio Samaranch

Juan Antonio Samaranch, IOC president from 1980 to 2004, had to deal with a plethora of political issues through which, until late 1998, he invariably adroitly manoeuvred the organisation to a position of greater status. The most consequential of these efforts was the period of rapid transformation of the IOC in financial terms. When Avery Brundage retired as IOC President in 1972 the organisation had borrowed money against its forthcoming Munich television rights income in order to remain operational. The term of Lord Killanin's presidency, from 1972 to 1980, saw IOC assets grow to US$5 million (Miller, 1996). Because of the substantial increases in the value of television rights since that time and the successful TOP strategy, as discussed in Chapter 6, even these figures seem insignificant when compared to current IOC assets.

Juan Antonio Samaranch was born in Barcelona on 17 July 1920. His first Olympic role came in 1954, when he was appointed to the Spanish Olympic Committee. In 1965, he was proposed for IOC membership at its session in Madrid; however, as five new members had already been accepted at this session, a decision as to his status was deferred (Pound, 1994). The wait was relatively short. The following year, at the 56th IOC Session, in Rome, he was appointed as an IOC member. Interestingly, in light of his subsequent presidential rulings on IOC membership tenure, the result of this delay made him subject to the determination that members who were appointed post-1995 were required to retire at the age of 72. In a less than open manner, the ruling was later changed, allowing him to remain at the helm until after the 2000 Games (Pound, 1994).

In 1974 Samaranch was appointed as a Vice-President and when, three years later, he was appointed Spanish Ambassador to the Soviet Union in Moscow, he was perfectly placed to campaign for the up-coming election for the IOC presidency. His lobbying was successful and, during the IOC Session held in Moscow in conjunction with the Games, he was elected its seventh president (Miller, 1996).

Decisions on the awarding of IOC membership have often been the result of political manoeuvring. One of the IOC's fiercest critics, Andrew Jennings, documents in his book, *The New Lords of the Rings*, how both Samaranch and Brundage adopted a dictatorial style of leadership. He comments: 'Brundage dominated the Olympic Committee; he selected new members, arbitrarily took the big decisions and devolved little power' (Jennings, 1996: 32). Of IOC President Samaranch he says: 'Samaranch selects new members who won't cause him trouble. He nominates and the committee rubber stamps' (Jennings, 1996: 56). In terms of the politics of gender he adds, 'it's an Olympic family dominated by men; ninety three per cent of it, average age sixty three ... Women were excluded until 1981' (Jennings, 1996: 67). This issue is discussed in more detail in Chapter 9.

The 1998 corruption scandal

Politics surrounding IOC membership was brought to the fore in 1998. The year was in many ways a watershed year for international sport in a number of areas. It was rocked by a number of scandals, including the drug use revelations in the *Tour de France*, the Pakistani and Australian cricket bribery allegations and positive drug tests for high profile athletes, including Irish Olympic medal-winning swimmer Michelle de Bruin (Smith), tennis player Peter Korda and the Chinese national swimming team. The Olympic Games added, in no small measure, to this year of scandal. Indeed, as a result of allegations of involvement in bribery and corruption by its own members, the IOC faced one of the most serious crises in its history. Samaranch himself admitted to the gravity of the situation when he acknowledged that, 'the system is not working ... we have to change the system' (in Korporaal and Evans, 1999: 3).

The crisis erupted in November 1998, when a Salt Lake City television station broke a story alleging that the city's Bid Committee had paid for an IOC member's daughter to attend the American University in Washington DC (Evans, 1999). Following this revelation, in December 1998, the Swiss IOC member, Marc Hodler, announced publicly that he believed that there was 'massive corruption' in the IOC, that there were up to 25 corrupt IOC members whose votes could be bought and, reflecting the claims of Simpson and Jennings made five years earlier (1992, Jennings, 1996), that every Games for the last ten years had been tainted by such bribery (IOC, 1999b; Stevens and Stewart, 1999).

Initially Hodler was considered to be a 'whistle blower', with an axe to grind, and he received no support from his fellow IOC members. Hodler was, however, 'a very senior member of the IOC, the author ... of the so-called "Hodler Rules" designed to limit the expenses incurred by candidate cities, as well as the President of the

International Skiing Federation (FIS) for almost 50 years' (IOC, 1999b: 4). 'Whistle blowing' from such a source could not easily be ignored. As a result of the growing press attacks on its credibility the IOC felt obliged to investigate the claims, establishing an *ad hoc* Commission of Inquiry under the chairmanship of IOC Vice-President, Dick Pound of Canada. This was initially concerned only with Salt Lake City, but later widened its scope to include bidding for all Olympic Games since 1996. Meanwhile, the Salt Lake Organising Committee (SLOC) established a Board of Ethics to investigate the claims, reporting in February 1999 (Board of Ethics, 1999), the United States Olympic Committee (USOC) also established an inquiry, which reported in early March 1999 (Special Bid Oversight Commission, 1999), the FBI began investigations to determine whether criminal acts had taken place, and the US Senate began holding hearings on the matter (Riley, 1999).

The IOC Commission sought information from SLOC, USOC, NOCs, all cities involved in Games bids since 1996 and IOC members against whom accusations of improper behaviour had been made. It produced two reports, in January and March 1999 (IOC, 1999b, c). In relation to the Salt Lake City bid, it investigated claims of payments totalling more than US$400,000 (IOC, 1999b, 1999c; Lusetich 1999).

Typical of the accusations involving IOC members and the Salt Lake Bid Committee (SLBC) were:

- payments to support members' children while at university or working in USA;
- payments of tens of thousands of dollars for travel and hotel costs of members and their families to holiday in Utah and for 'side-trips' to the 1995 'Superbowl' in Florida and 'stop-offs' in Paris;
- payment of medical costs for members on trips to Salt Lake City;
- direct cash payments, later claimed to have been passed on to NOCs or other sporting organisations in members' home countries;
- cash payments for consultancy services;
- provision of gifts valued at well above the IOC limit of US$250;
- request for favours for relatives and/or colleagues, such as places in universities.

The accused members defended themselves by claiming, among other things: that they were unaware of the payments in question, especially when they involved relatives; that they had been led to believe that the payments were from private individuals or companies, not from the SLBC itself; that SLBC representatives had persuaded them to accept gifts and favours against their own wishes; or that various of the trips at issue were not made during the period of Salt Lake City's candidature. Commentators have also pointed out that a number of the accused members were from developing countries where practices which would be seen as corrupt in Western culture are seen as quite acceptable – indeed, the commission itself, in reflecting on the practice of gift-giving, declared:

> When passing judgement on what has been characterized as 'improper gift giving', one cannot overlook the fact that gifts viewed as 'improper' in some parts of the world are looked upon with a totally different perception in many others. ... Although such behaviour may create the appearance of misconduct and potential conflicts of interest (and for this reason must be strictly regulated), gift giving should not reflexively be labelled a 'flourishing culture of improper gifts'. In many societies, these exchanges are viewed as an honourable tradition and are not corrupt'. (IOC, 1999b: 11)

The Commission adjudicated on 19 IOC members, recommending that seven be 'excluded from the IOC', ten be warned about their behaviour (ranging from 'warning' to 'serious warning' to 'most serious warning') and two be exonerated. Ultimately there were four resignations, six expulsions and ten official warnings (see Appendix 4.1 of IOC, 1999b).

At the same time, the Commission was critical of a number of the practices of the Salt Lake City Bid Committee and USOC. The Commission's report therefore fully vindicated Hodler and a number of the external IOC critics. In addition to adjudications on individual members, it made three recommendations to the IOC:

1. that changes be made to the bidding process, beginning with the 2006 Winter Games;
2. that limitations be placed on members' travel to bid cities; and
3. that an *Ethics Commission* be established.

The first and third of these recommendations were acted on immediately: the Ethics Commission was established in April 1999 (see Chapter 4); and bidding procedures were reviewed by the newly established 80-member *IOC 2000 Commission*.

The timing of the bribery revelations hampered the efforts of the 2000 and 2002 Games organisers in seeking sponsorship. And existing sponsors, at world and national levels, expressed concern and indicated that sponsorship funds might no longer be forthcoming if the IOC failed to 'clean up its act'. For example, General Motors Holden, one of the Sydney 2000 Olympics major sponsors, acknowledged that the present situation had undermined its support. Its public relations manager noted, 'We obviously are a bit disturbed ... It is difficult for a sponsor in the current environment to maximise its association with the Games as long as these revelations keep coming to the surface' (quoted in Evans, 1999). One of the most influential of Olympic sponsors, McDonald's Restaurants, has consistently sought, through sport sponsorship, to promote a public image of itself as a wholesome corporate citizen. It could not therefore afford to be aligned with a partner which did not have an appropriately wholesome image. Thus, the head of marketing of the McDonald's German subsidiary said, 'If the corruption suspicions are confirmed, McDonald's will ask itself if sponsorship of the games still has a place in the group's image' (Hans Munichhausen, quoted in Korporaal and Evans, 1999: 3). TOP member John Hancock's withdrawal of a multi-million dollar Olympic theme advertising campaign on NBC (the US Olympic broadcaster) was an indirect message to the IOC. Later, five of the TOP sponsors called for Samaranch to step down as IOC President.

Ironically, therefore, the IOC's very success in raising sponsorship to lessen its dependence on television networks increased its vulnerability, given the increase in the number of influential stakeholders who had a vested interest in how the IOC conducted its business. There is a sense of the wheel coming full circle and a degree of irony when commercial interests, long associated, as discussed in Chapter 6, with the debasement of Olympic values, now seek to purify the Olympic Movement. But some would see a degree of hypocrisy in such calls for moral purity from the business sector which uses quite similar practices to do business on a regular basis.

What reforms resulted to ensure that such practices do not recur? According to the IOC these were:

• Procedure for electing candidate cities for 2006 amended and visits by IOC members to candidate cities abolished.

- 15 active Olympic athletes, elected to the IOC by their peers at the Olympic Games.
- Creation of a Nominations Commission for IOC membership.
- Mandate of IOC Members to last eight years, renewable through re-election.
- IOC to have a maximum of 115 members.
- Presidential mandate limited to eight years, renewable once for four years.
- 15 members to come from IFs, 15 from the NOCs and 70 other as individual members.
- Age limit lowered to 70.
- Creation of the IOC Ethics Commission.
- Creation of the World Anti-Doping Agency.
- Greater financial transparency through the publication of financial reports on the sources and use of the Olympic Movement's income.
- IOC Session opened to the media for the first time. (IOC website)

But longer term reform would involve a reconstitution of the IOC itself, to bring it in line with other modern international organisations. This would involve some sort of democratic, representational membership. The results of such a move would be to make the IOC more clearly accountable to the Olympic Movement and the sporting community as a whole, as discussed in Chapter 11.

The 1998 scandal occurred during the Presidency of Juan Antonio Samaranch. On 16 July 2001 at the 112th IOC Session in Moscow, Jacques Rogge was elected as the eighth IOC President. Rogge adopted a zero tolerance policy on corruption within the Olympic Movement and has announced that, while he finds it 'painful' to expel a colleague, he believes that the Olympic Movement is more important than the individual (IOC, 2005e). Unfortunately he is still experiencing pain. The latest IOC members to be expelled were Russian Ivan Slavkov and Korean Un Yong Kim. The former's fall from grace occurred following allegations made by BBC journalists from the *Panorama* programme who were investigating corrupt practices linked to the selection of the host city for the 2012 Olympic Games (awarded to London). Kim was imprisoned in 2004 in Korea for embezzlement and corruption. It was alleged that he embezzled several billion Korean won, for personal use, from (amongst others) the World Taekwondo Federation, the Kukkiwon and the General Association of International Sports Federations. Threatened with expulsion from the IOC, he resigned in May 2005 (*Dawn*, 2005).

Conclusion

From their inception to the present, the modern Olympic Games have been influenced by politics at both intra-national and international levels. Just as other international sporting events organised similarly along national lines (such as the Commonwealth Games and the Soccer World Cup) are influenced by the ideologies, rivalries and policies of competing nations, and become political currency, it would be unrealistic to expect the Olympics to be an exception to this exchange. Yet, we still hear that hackneyed and illusory phrase 'politics should be kept out of the Olympics', ironically often voiced by politicians. According to Clarke and Clarke:

> This is a proposition which assumes that politics and sport are two clearly separated fields of life. ... But to describe politics in this way is to leave out a different level of political relations. These relations lie outside the formal arena

of party politics, and operate in the maintenance of social patterns of power, domination and subordination throughout the whole of society. It is this aspect of politics that is involved in 'managing' a society composed of divided and conflicting classes and groups. It is... a level of political activity that stresses the importance of ideology, particularly, in the role of presenting a divided society as if it was an harmonious unity. (Clarke and Clarke, 1982: 62)

The IOC states that, 'the goal of Olympism is to place sport at the service of the harmonious development of man, with a view to promoting a peaceful society concerned with the preservation of human dignity' (IOC, 2004: 9). This mission, itself a hotly contested claim, can be literally and figuratively hijacked by Olympic protocol itself, which is highly ritualistic and replete with political symbolism and overtones. When, during the Olympic medal ceremonies, national anthems are played and the flags of the victors' countries are raised, when team sports are organised on national lines and, during the Opening Ceremony athletes march into the stadium nation by nation, these practices are overtly creating nationalistic tensions, self-regard and rivalries. Such discords do not dissolve at the perimeters of the Olympic venues. Indeed, it is often events outside the Games' control and jurisdiction and the media's subsequent interpretation and mediation of them that precipitate and serve to incite the Olympics' political tensions:

Athletes (and sometimes spectators) are the living, breathing representatives of national or racial characteristics. ... sporting competition is invested with, and helps to keep in circulation, a whole repertoire of national and racial mythologies – myths of 'their' strangeness, difference, peculiarity, which help to reinforce the present resentments, hostilities and conflicts of their own experiences – experiences which lie outside sport. (Clarke and Clarke 1982: 66)

There is prestige associated with hosting an Olympic Games. The Nazis capitalised on this, and, in recent Olympiads, nations hosting the Games have endeavoured to stage ever more spectacular festivals, with more grandiose facilities, than the preceding Olympics. Today it is prohibitive to all but the most wealthy developed countries to host the Games for, although the Olympic Games is awarded to a city rather than a country, it is generally impossible for any city to bear the financial burden without assistance from national or regional governments. The 1968 Mexico City Games demonstrated that many of the developing country's citizens thought that such a high level of expenditure on a sporting event was unwarranted, while the citizens of Montréal were faced with large tax increases because of their city government's insistence upon using the Olympics as a showcase for the city.

On a more positive, but nevertheless nationalistic note, Australia's international reputation was enhanced by the success of the 2000 Summer Olympic Games; at least the country itself believed it to be so. The success of the Games provided a platform for the nation to present itself to the world as innovative, capable and technologically sophisticated. Phillip Knightly (2000), writing in the *Sydney Morning Herald* noted: 'staging the Games was an opportunity to ... show the world the face of new Australia – a modern, prosperous, independent, confident and, above all multicultural country looking to its future. Australia, consciously or not, seized this chance'. The Australian Prime Minister, John Howard, wrote in the *Australian* newspaper in October 2000:

I do not think there is another country that can look to the future with such optimism, or that faces such an array of opportunities. ... We should recommit ourselves to ensuring that the Australian spirit on display during the Olympics is not only maintained during our second centenary of Federation, but is extended so that we can also achieve our full potential as a nation. (Howard, 2000)

The nation's press and politicians, even those who had been critical of the Games organisers in the years leading up to 2000, sustained and glorified this self-aggrandisement (Cashman *et al.*, 2002).

There are few indications that there will be any diminution in political intrusions into the Games. Various proposals have been put forward in an attempt to minimise political interference by reducing their political significance, including the idea of establishing a permanent site for the Games, as discussed in Chapter 11, or splitting the Games into a series of smaller-scale world championships. However, the effect of implementing such proposals would be to diminish the overall significance of the Games – a price which the Olympic Movement is unlikely to be prepared to pay.

Further reading

Olympic politics generally	Houlihan (1994, 2005); Hill (1996); Senn (1999)
The 1936 Olympics	Mandell (1971, 1978, 1987); Rippon (2006); Walters (2006); Graham (1986, 1989)
The Munich Games	Brasher (1972); Groussard (1975); Czula (1978); Mandell (1991)
The 1998/99 crisis	Jennings and Sambrook (2000)
Samaranch	Pound (2004: 229ff)
Security	CNN (1996); Atkinson and Young (2002, 2005); Johnson (2005)

Questions

1. What reforms, if any, could be implemented to improve IOC governance?
2. What are President Jacques Rogge's greatest achievements in his role as IOC President? What are his greatest failures?
3. What measures should the Olympic Movement take to protect itself from terrorist attacks?

Chapter 6

The Economics and Financing of the Games

The staging of a hallmark event can provide a significant boost to the economy of a city or region in which it is held. Such an event can generate substantial expenditure within both the public and private sectors of the economy and the impact of this expenditure is distributed widely throughout the economy. Unfortunately, hallmark events can also generate significant economic costs that often get forgotten in the euphoria surrounding an event. A common legacy of many past events has been a huge debt and a great deal of under-utilised infrastructure. Roberts and McLeod (1989: 242)

Introduction

In cities and countries which host the Olympic Games, the question of their cost, particularly to the public purse, arguably attracts as much attention from the media, governments and the public as the sporting aspects of the event. This is perhaps not surprising, since the sheer scale of the modern Games generally results, with few exceptions, in significant government involvement and considerable government expense, raising inevitable questions about the appropriate use of public funds. This poses intrinsically economic questions about the costs and benefits of such exepnditure. The increasing scale of the Olympic Games has called for increasing levels of funding and the IOC and hosts of individual Olympic Games events have turned not only to governments but increasingly to the commercial sector for resources. These trends have naturally attracted the attention of economists, but also of sociologists, as discussed below, and historians (e.g. Barney *et al.*, 2002). In this chapter three related economic dimensions of the Olympic Games are considered, namely the *political economy* of the Games, their *financing* and their *economic impact*.

- *Political economy*, as discussed in Chapter 1, involves both economic and political concerns: it addresses questions about the role of the Olympic Games in national and international economic and political systems.

- *Finance* is concerned more narrowly with the question of money and concerns both the funding of the Olympic Movement as a whole and the financing of individual Olympic Games events.
- *Economic impact* is concerned with the effects of the Olympic Games on the host community, in terms of incomes and job creation.

Political economy

The main contributions to discussion of the political economy of the Olympic Games have come from Marxist and neo-Marxist writers, notably Jean-Marie Brohm (1978) and Richard Gruneau (1984). In Chapter 1 this is classified as one of the *critical* paradigms used in theorising the Olympic phenomenon. *Marxism* sees the basic dynamic in capitalist society, or Western market economies, as arising from the clash of interests between the capitalist (bourgeois) class, which owns the 'means of production', and the working class (proletariat), which owns nothing but its labour power, which it must sell to the capitalists to live. Marx argued that, as capitalism developed, opportunities for profitable investment of capital would become increasingly scarce, so capitalists would continually seek out new areas for investment and would seek to reduce the wages paid to workers in order to maintain profitability and growth. Since such a situation is clearly unstable, Marx predicted that the system would inevitably fall apart, as a result of increasingly severe crises, such as depression and wars, or as a result of violent revolution on the part of the workers, or a combination of the two. In the first half of the twentieth century, in the face of wars and depressions, Marx's predictions seemed increasingly plausible, but as the second half of the century unfolded, they seemed less plausible.

Where do the Olympic Games fit into such scenarios? To answer this we should consider the later development of Marxist ideas referred to as *neo-Marxism*. Neo-Marxism, while retaining Marx's basic analysis, modifies the basic ideas in order to explain why capitalism has managed to survive so long, despite its contradictions and periodic crises. Neo-Marxist analyses depict the commercialisation of sport as one example of the opportunities which have been exploited to prolong the life of the capitalist system. In its search for investment opportunities, international capital has 'discovered sport', including the Olympic Games.

With the collapse of the Marxist communist regimes of Eastern Europe and the Soviet Union in the late 1980s, and with the increasing market orientation of remaining Marxist regimes, such as China and Vietnam, Western, largely academic, Marxist thought has experienced a crisis of its own, since capitalism and the market system seems increasingly triumphant around the world. Thus the Marxist and neo-Marxist analysis of sport and other phenomena seems less relevant today. Nevertheless a considerable amount of writing on the Olympic Games over the last two or three decades has been imbued with Marxist and neo-Marxist ideas, and the critique offers a perspective which is largely absent from other writing, so it is appropriate that it be considered here. Canadian sociologist Rick Gruneau's writing on the Games is typical of this genre. His paper on 'Commercialism and the modern Olympics' (Gruneau, 1984) presents a sequence of observations and arguments related to: commercialisation; amateurism; nationalism; élitism; resistance; and the role of the state.

Commercialisation

Gruneau notes, with obvious displeasure, that the 1984 Los Angeles Games, which was being planned at the time he was writing, received substantial sponsorship funds from major US companies, such as McDonald's, Coca Cola, Mars and Budweiser. He observes that the companies involved used sponsorship of the Games to project an image of public-spiritedness and wholesomeness through association with the positive images of youth and sports and notes that 'many people' objected to 'such obvious commercialism'. But, he argues, this is nothing new:

> the Los Angeles Games are in no way a significant departure from practices established in earlier Olympics. Rather, I believe the 1984 Games are best understood as a more fully developed expression of the incorporation of sporting practice into the ever-expanding marketplace of international capitalism. (Gruneau, 1984: 2)

Elaborating on this historical perspective, Gruneau first observes that, by the end of the nineteenth century, when the Olympics were being revived, industrialisation and urbanisation in Britain and other Western nations had created a market for spectator sports, which could be exploited by business interests. This was exemplified by the Games of the early part of the twentieth century, which were associated with trade fairs, designed to promote capitalist trade and commerce (the Paris Universal Exhibition in 1900, the St Louis World Fair in 1904 and the Anglo-French Exhibition in London in 1908). The notion that the Olympic Games represented the ideal of sport for its own sake, untarnished by commercialism, was already, according to Gruneau, a doubtful proposition.

Amateurism

The association of sport with commercialisation was, however, taking place alongside the creation by the British middle and upper classes of the idea of *amateurism* in sport. Gruneau sees amateurism as an expression of class supremacy and an effort to keep the working class in its place, but he does not remark on the paradox of parts of the bourgeoisie apparently developing ways of commercially exploiting sport while another part of the same class was simultaneously instituting the decidedly non-commercial phenomenon of amateurism, except to say, in passing: '*Amateurism notwithstanding*, sporting competition became clearly drawn into the universal market during the latter half of the nineteenth century' (Gruneau, 1984: 4, emphasis added).

Later in the paper, however, Gruneau recognises the 'lingering anti-professional traditions of amateurism' as part of the 'resistance to sport's absorption into capitalism's universal market' (p. 12). So amateurism, oddly, plays two contradictory roles in Gruneau's neo-Marxist critique: it is both a reinforcer of class division (in support of capital) and a form of resistance against the power of capital. Further paradox is added to the discussion when other critical writers discuss the recent *removal* of amateurism from the Olympic ideal – here the rise of the professional athlete is seen as further evidence of the encroachment of capitalism into the field of sport rather than a defeat of a class-based institution (see, for example, Lawrence, 1986: 212).

Nationalism

As, in the course of the twentieth century, the Games increased in scale and prestige, Gruneau notes, they came to be recognised as a means for nationalistic promotion and were used to boost the fortunes of whichever regime or economic system held sway in the host city or country at the time. Thus the Los Angeles Games of 1932 projected the 'American Dream' of prosperity based on free-enterprise, while the Berlin Olympics of 1936 sought to promote Nazism. Further, the Games of the post-Second World War era became a pawn in the cold war political and economic rivalries between East and West. Eventually, Gruneau observes, by the 1960s the Olympic Games were: 'increasingly intertwined with a powerful international bloc of financial, travel, retail, and media interests; potential profits were tied to the growing size and visibility of the Games' (Gruneau, 1984: 8–9).

Élitism

The Los Angeles Games are seen by Gruneau as the culmination of the process of commercialisation and commodification of the Olympics and, while this involves exposure to the masses through the media, Gruneau sees the Games as essentially élitist, rather than democratic:

> What kind of sport is the Los Angeles Olympic Organizing Committee and its corporate sponsors supporting? ... My answer is that it is a highly specialised, élite sport that is being supported here, and not a form of recreational sport for the broadest possible number of participants. Furthermore, the presence of the great corporations is a statement in itself: such sponsorship signifies the omni-presence of corporate capital in our lives, even to the extent of dominating our games. Throughout this century sport has become progressively more commodified – to the point where, at its highest levels, it now stands before us as a simple division of the entertainment and light consumer-goods industries. (Gruneau, 1984: 12)

Resistance

Gruneau then introduces the neo-Marxist idea of 'resistance' – the notion that the working classes and other oppressed groups under capitalism engage in various forms of opposition to the oppressive, controlling forces of capital. In the case of the Olympic Games, however, resistance has most frequently taken the form of protests against public expenditure, thus contributing to the process of Games events becoming increasingly dependent on private, commercial funding. Such 'resistance' to the onslaught of capital would therefore seem somewhat counter-productive on the part of the protesters:

> there has been a considerable degree of resistance to sport's absorption into capitalism's universal market. Not only the lingering anti-professional traditions of amateurism, but also community and trade union groups have objected to the excesses and spending priorities of the Olympic circus. In the late 1970s considerable popular resistance focused on the use of public revenues to build elaborate facilities and to offset Olympic deficits. Yet the result of this resistance

was to clear the way for the 'Hamburger Olympics' [Los Angeles] and another stage in the commodification of international sport. (Gruneau, 1984: 13)

Gruneau advocates resistance as an agenda for the left of politics:

> Yet this situation is far from immutable. People dissatisfied with the messages embodied in the 'Hamburger Olympics' can still struggle to relocate sport on the welfare rather than the accumulation side of modern state policy. But for there to be a popular mobilisation – in trade unions, community groups and political parties – in support of a non-market sporting practice, such a practice must be seen to be a legitimate concern for the left. (Gruneau, 1984: 15)

The idea of resistance to the Olympics is pursued further by Lenskyj (2004).

The state

Gruneau then notes a further paradox: the role of the state in sport. On the one hand the state generally appears to provide non-market, subsidised, welfare-orientated sports services, including providing support for the non-commercial ideals of the Olympics. This can be seen as anti-commercial or anti-capital. But, on the other hand, the state can be seen to be *supporting* capital (or the 'accumulation' of capital) by promoting a commercialised Games, by underwriting any deficits which may arise and by generating business for private firms – for example in the form of contracts for the building of stadia. And ultimately, in a capitalist economy, the state is itself dependent on a thriving commercial sector for its tax income. Ultimately, he sees the state as part of the:

> growing bloc of shared interests in high-performance sport, complete with elaborate centralised facilities, state and commercial sponsorship, and a complex infrastructure of sports scientists, coaches, technical personnel and bureaucrats. ... Sports policies in most capitalist countries ... are so tied into the bloc of vested interests supporting the Olympic movement that they cannot be easily opposed. (Gruneau, 1984: 14–15)

Thus it can be seen that the Olympic Games touches on most of the concerns of Marxism and neo-Marxism – class conflict, commodification, global market power, the role of the state and the question of resistance and the struggle of the masses against the powerful forces of capital.

Other sociologists have also addressed these issues from a critical stance, including Nixon (1988) and Lawrence (1986), who also focus on issues arising from the Los Angeles Games, Whitson (1998), who brings the discussion up to date in focusing on the concept of globalisation and gender issues, and Tomlinson (2005), who discusses the roles of corporate sponsors. While not developed in a theoretical way, and not within a neo-Marxist framework, the critique of the Games by Simson and Jennings (1992; Jennings, 1996), referred to in earlier chapters, is also concerned, in part, with political economy. Basically, the Simson and Jennings thesis is that the personal pursuit of money and power by those involved with the organisation of the Games, has resulted in the Games being transformed from a traditional non-profit phenomenon into an international marketing, money-making, enterprise. To the extent that certain IOC processes, such as the selection of cities to host the Games, are shown to be tainted by corruption, as a number of highly publicised events would indicate, this would add strength to the arguments of critics of whatever ideological persuasion.

The literature on the political economy of sport, and the Olympic Games in particular, has focused primarily on the West, but it should also be noted that sport and the Olympics can be seen as having played an important part in sustaining the communist regimes of Eastern Europe and the Soviet Union and continues to play such a role among those few that remain, such as China, Vietnam, North Korea and Cuba. While the role of sport under these regimes may be viewed as serving primarily political and nationalistic goals, as discussed in Chapter 5, there is also an economic dimension, in that communism or socialism represents a type of *economic* system as well as a political ideology. Thus the success of athletes from the 'second world' was intended, along with the success of such efforts as space and nuclear programmes, to demonstrate the superiority of the communist economic system. However, as with these non-sport endeavours, there is evidence to suggest that success was achieved only at inordinate financial expense, which probably distorted the very economic system it was intended to celebrate (Riordan, 1993: 51–2).

Financing the Olympic Movement

As we have seen (Chapter 4), the Olympic Movement comprises a large, worldwide, multi-faceted network of organisations, with the International Olympic Committee (IOC) at its heart. The IOC is not a government or United Nations organisation – so how is it funded? In the early days of Baron de Coubertin, as noted in Chapter 4, IOC members were wealthy men (they were all *men* until recent times), who paid their own way and provided for the minimal requirements of the organisation largely out of their own ample pockets. For many years the IOC was therefore run by wealthy people but was itself a relatively poor organisation, with no assured independent source of income.

Two things changed this situation dramatically. The first was the growth and popularity of the coverage of the Games on television and the subsequent growth in the value of the broadcasting rights. The second was the advent of sponsorship, in the form of The Olympic Programme. These are discussed in turn below.

Broadcasting rights

As indicated in Table 6.1, the value of the broadcasting rights for the Olympic Games has grown rapidly from around a million (US) dollars for the Rome 1960 Games, to some US$1700 million for the Beijing 2008 Games. Even making allowances for inflation, as shown in Table 6.1, the growth has been dramatic, showing a 150-fold increase since 1960. The fees for the Winter Games are less than half those for the Summer Games, but the rate of growth has been equally dramatic. The key factor in this pattern of growth was the advent of satellite broadcasting, which enabled television signals to be beamed instantly around the world. Prior to the 1970s, pictures could only be broadcast internationally by means of relatively costly and slow physical transport of film and video-tape.

Table 6.1. Value of Olympic broadcasting rights

Summer Games	Year	Value, US$ millions		Winter Games	Year	Value, US$ millions	
		*Current prices**	*2006 prices***			*Current prices**	*2006 prices***
Rome	1960	1	11	Squaw Valley	1960		
Tokyo	1964	2	21	Innsbruck	1964		
Mexico City	1968	10	93	Grenoble	1968		
Munich	1972	18	141	Sapporo	1972		
Montreal	1976	35	172	Innsbruck	1976		
Moscow	1980	89	296	Lake Placid	1980	21	70
Los Angeles	1984	287	669	Sarajevo	1984	103	240
Seoul	1988	403	704	Calgary	1988	325	567
Barcelona	1992	636	898	Albertville	1992	292	412
Atlanta	1996	898	1 146	Lillehammer	1994	353	486
Sydney	2000	1 332	1 616	Nagano	1998	513	640
Athens	2004	1 493	1 574	Salt Lake	2002	736	818
Beijing***	2008	1 706	1 706	Torino	2006	833	833

Source: Brunet, 1995 and IOC website. * at time of the Games. **using Australian Consumer Price Index. *** estimates at 2006 prices.

The broadcasting rights for the Olympic Games are owned by the IOC, not the local Games organisers. Only a portion of the proceeds from the sale of the rights to a particular Games event – usually about half – is passed to the local organising committee. The rest is distributed to NOCs, via the Olympic Solidarity programme or retained by the IOC.

Clearly the Olympic Movement is significantly dependent on income from broadcasting rights and, since as much as 80 per cent of the revenue derives from the USA (Slater, 1998: 56), it is particularly dependent on the American television networks. The issue of the possible direct effects of this dependency is not discussed further here, since the media are discussed in detail in Chapter 7. The broadcasting companies which pay these large sums are mostly commercial organisations which must generate audiences which will in turn attract advertisers, to recoup their outlays and produce a profit. In fact, the picture is more complex than this. Olympic broadcasters do not always make a profit from their investment. As Christopher Hill has put it:

the sums paid for television rights in the Olympics are not always rationally determined. Indeed, paying huge sums for them has always been seen by television companies as a loss leader, and [quoting Klatell and Marcus] 'the networks have allowed the Olympics to become so emotional an issue, so much a matter of pride and self-importance, that they no longer measure it by any reasonable business standard normally applied to programming decisions. (Hill, 1996: 78)

There is, however, no sign of this source of funding drying up. Television companies continue to compete to pay increasingly large sums of money for the Olympic broadcasting rights, even signing contracts for several Olympiads in advance.

The Olympic Programme/Partners (TOP)

The Olympic Programme (TOP) was established in 1985 and its name was later changed to The Olympic Partners programme. TOP was devised by International Sports and Leisure (ISL), a marketing and management company jointly owned by the sports clothing manufacturer Adidas and a Japanese advertising agency, Dentsu. The connection with Adidas is considered highly significant by Olympic historians, such as Hill (1995: 80–89), Jennings (1996: 47–54) and Barney *et al.*, 2002: 153–80), because of the involvement of Horst Dassler, the owner of the company. Dassler developed his influence in the Olympic Movement and other national and international sporting organisations through generous sponsorship deals, and used his position to promote Adidas products to the sporting community. As early as the 1968 Olympic Games, it is claimed that 83 per cent of medal winners used Adidas shoes and equipment (Hill, 1995: 88).

TOP operates by selling to sponsors worldwide rights to use the Olympic logo in their advertising and promotion for the period of an Olympiad, covering one summer and one Winter Olympic Games, although, as with broadcasting rights, many commit to a number of Olympiads in advance. Sponsorship rights relate to specific product categories, such as soft drinks, computers or credit cards. TOP revenues have risen from US$96 million in the 1985–88 quadrennium to over US$800 million in 2005–08, as shown in Table 6.2. The partners for the 2005–2008 period are listed in Table 6.3 Part of the partners' support is generally provided 'in kind' – that is, in the form of goods and services rather than cash. For example, Omega provides the electronic timing system for the Games and Visa provides the ticket payment system.

Because the commercial presence of the companies varies from country to country, and because NOCs may have existing national sponsorship deals with other companies which may conflict with TOP companies' expectation of exclusivity, negotiations take place with each NOC concerning how the system will operate in their countries and what proportion of the TOP funds each NOC will receive. Proceeds are divided between the NOCs (20 per cent of the total), the summer and Winter Games (70 per cent) and the IOC (10 per cent) (IOC, n.d.; Hill, 1995: 84).

Table 6.2. The Olympic Partners programme, 1985–2008

Quadrennium	Games	No. of Partners	Revenue, US$ million
1985–88	Calgary/Seoul	9	96
1989–92	Albertville/Barcelona	12	172
1993–96	Lillehammer/Atlanta	10	279
1997–2000	Nagano/Sydney	11	579
2001–04	Salt Lake/Athens	11	663
2005–08	Torino/Beijing	11	866

Source: IOC (2006a)

Table 6.3. The Olympic Partners programme members, 2005– 2008

Company	Category
Atos Origin	Information Technology
Coca Cola	Non-alcoholic beverages
General Electric	Energy, healthcare, transportation, infrastructure products & services
Johnson & Johnson	Health-care products
Kodak	Film/photographics and imaging
Lenovo	Computer equipment
Manulife	Life insurance/annuities
McDonald's	Retail food services
Omega	Timing, scoring and venue results services
Panasonic	Audio, TV, video equipment
Samsung	Wireless communication equipment
Visa	Consumer payments systems (Credit cards etc.)

The exceptional feature of Olympic sponsorship, including TOP and local sponsorship of individual Games events, is that the initial sponsorship payment delivers very little by way of direct exposure for the sponsoring companies. In order to capitalise on their initial payment, TOP companies must spend substantial additional sums of money to bring their association with the Games to the public attention. While, as John Crompton (1996) points out, this is often the case in sports sponsorship it is particularly apparent in the Olympic Games since there are no 'naming rights' for the Games as there are for many other sporting events and, as noted above, no advertising is permitted within Olympic venues. In joining the TOP programme companies are purchasing a world-wide license and the cost of 'taking the message to the world' can be substantial. Including the Olympic logo on such things as packaging, letterheads and existing advertisements is a marginal cost but, in most cases, specific advertising and promotional campaigns and sponsorship deals are developed so that the link between the company's name, sporting success and the 'spirit' of the Games is made clear to the consumer and potential consumer over the four years of the Olympiad.

'Selling out'

At the beginning of the chapter we noted the criticism by Gruneau and others of the 'selling out' of the Olympics to commercialisation. While the extent of such selling out is debatable, the extent of the dependency of the IOC and the Olympic Movement on the world of commerce is beyond dispute: the list of TOP companies reads like a 'who's who' of international capitalism. Virtually all other non-profit global organisations depend for their funding on non-commercial sources, such as public subscriptions and/or contributions from governments, although this does not, of course, protect them from outside influences. There have been times in the past when it has seemed that the Olympic Games would become wholly dependent on governments for funding; at other times broadcasting fees have become dominant. The TOP scheme has enabled the IOC to avoid these situations. The accompanying air of commercialisation is, nevertheless, distasteful to many. John Lucas, writing in 1992, was of the opinion that the commercialisation of the Olympic Games was a temporary phenomenon. He wrote:

> The Olympic Movement, especially the IOC, is bedazzled by its newfound avenues of financial opportunity and will continue exploring them for some years to come. By the millennial year 2000, the IOC will have accumulated in properties, investments, credits, and cash sufficient billions of dollars so that it can 'ease off'. It will pull back appreciably from this financial focus and be able at last to devote nearly all of its vast power, influence, and new wealth to educational and altruistic efforts at an even higher level and through a more universal presence than are now possible. (Lucas, 1992: 80)

Clearly Lucas was mistaken, or at least somewhat premature, in his predictions: indeed, the drive for income from commercial sources continues apace. Witness the example of the Atlanta Games in 1996: as a result of the Atlanta Committee for the Olympic Games (ACOG) having to raise funds primarily from private sources, commercialism at the Games was rampant and widely criticised.

The quest for commercial funds is related in part to the growing scale and costs of running the events, an issue which was recognised in the report of the Olympic Games Study Commission presented to the 115th IOC Session held in Prague during July 2003. The report recommended ways of decreasing the size, cost and complexity of organising the Olympic Games in five main areas: the Games' format; venues and facilities; management; the number of accredited persons; and service levels. However, the report conveniently shifted some of the responsibility for the mushrooming overheads away from the IOC when it noted that:

> the enormous increases in Olympic revenues in the past couple of decades, derived principally from the leadership of the IOC, appear to have allowed Games organizers to relax, to some degree, their efforts to control costs, because the revenues to support higher expenditure have been available to them. Also, many stakeholders have become increasingly demanding and have put a great deal of pressure on Games organizers to provide ever bigger facilities and better services, without proper IOC control and approval. (Olympic Games Study Commission, 2003: 13)

The Olympic Games are ultimately dependent for their success on public support and the goodwill of governments, but the unique achievement of the IOC and the Olympic movement – sellout or no sellout – is to manage to juggle the demands of 'Olympism', international capitalism, the media, governments and popular support to achieve a degree of financial independence.

Financial relationships

Before examining the funding of individual Games events, it is worthwhile noting the complex financial relationships between the worldwide Olympic Movement and the IOC, the International Federations, the National Olympic Committees and organisers of individual Olympic Games events. The major sources of funds, broadcasting rights and TOP, are controlled by the IOC, albeit with the majority of the income being passed on to the other organisations in the system. This is represented diagram-matically in Figure 6.1. Perhaps the most important feature of this system to note is that, ultimately, all the resources come from the public who follow the Games through the media and purchase the, mostly non-sporting, goods and services of sponsors and advertisers.

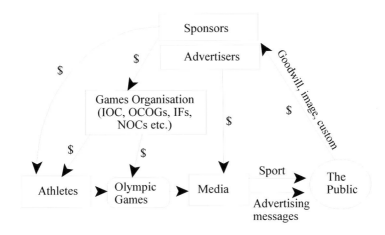

Figure 6.1. Commercial financial structure of the Games

Funding individual Olympic Games

Just to assemble a bid for an Olympic Games costs many millions of dollars. Included in the bid document presented to the IOC must be a detailed budget on just how the event is to be financed (IOC, n.d.). In general it is considered that the difference between the revenue and costs of an Olympic Games will be negative – that is, the Games will cost the host money, rather than make a profit. However, following a detailed analysis of the Olympic Games budgets since 1972, Holger Preuss (2004: 277) concludes that every Summer Games since 1972 has produced a surplus. In this section we consider the nature of the costs and revenues of a typical Olympic Games event.

Games costs

What does it cost to run an Olympic Games? Table 6.4 sets out the expenditures of the organising committees for summer Olympic Games since 1972, as calculated by Holger Preuss. The data exclude investment items (discussed below) and have been converted to US dollars at year 2000 prices. It can be seen that the real costs of organising the games have risen at least fourfold since the 1980s.

The main cost headings for a typical individual Games event are as listed in Table 6.5. The most complex item is the building of new infrastructure or the refurbishment and/or adaptation of existing infrastructure. This is discussed further below.

Table 6.4. Summer Olympic Games Organising Committee expenditure

Games	Year	Expenditure, US$ millions, at year 2000 prices
Munich	1972	656
Montréal	1976	476
Moscow	1980	na
Los Angeles	1984	531
Seoul	1988	664
Barcelona	1992	1793
Atlanta	1996	1346
Sydney	2000	2434
Athens	2004	2404

Source: Preuss (2004: 277). na = not available

Table 6.5. Individual Olympic Games – cost headings

1. Preparing the bid
2. Building new or refurbishing/adapting existing:
    - sport venues
    - infrastructure (e.g. transport facilities)
    - athletes'/officials' village
    - facilities for the media
3. Training and equipping volunteers
4. Staffing and servicing the Organising Committee
5. Organising the Torch Relay
6. Support for athletes' and officials' travel
7. Hosting athletes and team officials (during the Games)
8. Hosting the Olympic Family (IOC, IFs, NOCs, etc.) (before and during the Games)
9. Security
10. Cultural Programme

Investment in infrastructure

Key decisions must be made early on in the process as to what new sporting facilities and other items of infrastructure to construct in the host city. The question then arises as to what to include and what to exclude from the 'Olympic Budget'. For example, a host city may choose to refurbish its airport to coincide with the opening of the Olympic Games – it may even be seen as necessary to do this to be awarded the Games. But the refurbished airport will be enjoyed for many years after the Games are over – so to what extent should this be seen as an *Olympic* cost? Such infrastructure items are often substantial and can be the most controversial aspect of the Olympic hosting process. In Barcelona the provincial Catalan government incurred costs of US$1.25 billion on sporting facilities, health centres, urban development and improvement, and transport and cultural facilities (Brunet, 1993: 59). In the case of the Sydney 2000 Games the New South Wales government spent a total of US$1.9 billion on venues, land reclamation, transport infrastructure and government support services, such as transport and security (Audit Office of New South Wales, 2002: 6–7). But these figures are dwarfed by planned investment in venues and infrastructure for the Beijing 2008 Olympic Games, which is projected to cost US$33.7 billion (Lin, 2003).

Although Olympic Games are awarded to host cities seven years before they are due to take place, this may not provide enough time to process decisions about large projects through the normal political and environmental planning processes and then develop them. Thus 'fast tracking' often takes place; decision-making processes are short-circuited and extra costs loaded onto contracts to ensure completion on time – this was said to be a feature of the Athens 2004 Games. Such additional costs could, arguably, be apportioned to the Olympic Games budget. In other cases, it has been argued, notably in Sydney, that Olympic projects and Olympic-related construction projects disrupt the government's normal capital programme, with transport, schools and hospital investment deferred because of Olympic expenditure. In Sydney's case it has been argued that costs were therefore borne by other public services in terms of delays in the provision of capital facilities (Searle, 2003); although difficult to quantify, these are costs which could arguably be charged to the Olympic Games budget.

The arguments concerning apportionment of investment costs can also be raised in relation to sporting venues, since they also will continue to be used for other sporting events and by local citizens long after the Olympic Games are over. Thus the overall capital costs of sporting infrastructure investments should ideally be excluded when estimating the cost of running an Olympic Games event.

The involvement of the private sector in the provision of sporting facilities illustrates the point that total venue construction costs should not be attributed to the Games event. A private builder and operator of a stadium clearly considers the flow of income and expenditure over the lifetime of the facility; the initial capital cost is an investment, which must produce a return to the investor over the life of the facility. Table 6.6 gives hypothetical examples of how a company investing in a $500 million stadium might view the investment over perhaps a 30 year lifetime for the stadium, with three scenarios, depending on the level of government subsidy. It indicates that a considerable operating surplus would need to be generated each week or year over the life of the facility to justify the investment. Logically the 'Olympic budget' should carry only that proportion of the costs of the stadium which relates to the Olympic Games, in the form of a rent for the use of the facility for the period of the Games. This would be more than the actual four weeks of the Olympic Games and Paralympic Games, because of the time it takes to prepare and decommission a venue for the Games, but to include the total construction costs is clearly inappropriate.

Montréal

The above discussion is particularly relevant to the case of the 1976 Montréal Games, which are invariably referred to as the worst example of Olympic budgetary excess (e.g. Iton, 1978, 1988; Wright, 1978). The assertion that the city accumulated 'colossal debts to be paid by the citizens ... for decades to come' (Tomlinson, 2005: 184) has become something of a cliché in Olympic commentary. It is generally

Table 6.6. Hypothetical economics of constructing and operating a stadium

	Alternative scenarios		
	Zero subsidy	$200m capital grant	$25m annual operating subsidy
	$ million		
a. Construction costs	500	500	500
b. Government capital subsidy	0	200	0
c. Government annual operating subsidy	0	0	25
d. Required annual return (10% of a-b)	50	30	50
e. Annual depreciation (10% of a)	50	50	50
f. Annual operating surplus required (d+e-c)	100	80	75
g. Required weekly operating surplus (f/52)	1.9	1.5	1.4

Source: Hypothetical

accepted that, as a result of the Montréal experience, few cities were willing to bid for subsequent Games – in fact, Los Angeles was the only bidder for the 1984 Games. But, as economist Holger Preuss (2004: 277) shows, when long-term investment items are excluded, the Montréal published deficit of US$2192 million is transformed into a surplus of US$641 million. Individuals buying a house invariably take out a loan, or mortgage, which may take up to 25 years to repay; similarly businesses fund capital expenditure with loans which may take years to repay as the investment produces a stream of income. While many Western governments have been averse to incurring debt in recent years, governments and government agencies, such as transport and utility corporations, have traditionally funded capital investment through loans repaid over a number of years, during the life of the investment. Why the loans taken out to fund the Montréal Games facilities and related items of infrastructure, which are still in use, have been viewed so differently by so many commentators is difficult to understand.

Athletes' and officials' villages

Financial calculations come into play in relation to the construction of the athletes' and officials' villages. A residential complex for some 15,000 people, if newly constructed for the Olympic Games, is clearly expected to have an 'after-Games' life. In the case of the Atlanta Games, the accommodation was destined to house university students (Kittell, 1997a). In the case of Barcelona and Sydney the accommodation was destined for the private sector (Kittell, 1997b; Nello, 1997). This approach means that the developers can expect to recoup their capital outlay quite quickly, as the housing units are sold after the Games. In the case of Sydney, it was felt that the local housing market would not be able to cope with some 5000 townhouses and apartments at one time, so a proportion of the housing consisted of demountable, moveable temporary buildings, which were readily sold to firms such as holiday camp operators after the Games. A large proportion of the residential suburb of which the athletes' village formed the core, was therefore developed at a later date when the market was seen to be able to absorb the stock.

Other costs

Other costs which might be considered include:

- *Security*: The various public services, such as police, ambulance and other emergency services, which a host city must lay on to cope with additional visitor numbers can be substantial. In addition, the presence of numerous high profile visitors and the worldwide media focus raise security issues which require contingency plans involving armed forces and other security services.
- *Team preparation*: Almost 200 NOCs send teams to the Games, ranging in size from a handful to hundreds of athletes and officials. While it may be difficult to disentangle Olympic-related expenditure from the costs of sport generally, it is likely that the worldwide aggregate costs of preparing these 200 teams and 10,000 athletes for the Games, dwarf the costs borne by the Games host organisers. Admittedly, the host nation is in a unique situation and is likely to be particularly keen to perform well 'at home', but Hogan and Norton (2000) estimate that about US$700 million was spent by Australian governments and sporting bodies on athlete preparation in the lead-up to the Sydney 2000 Olympic Games, and that each gold medal won by Australia could therefore be said to have cost US$28 million and all medals US$6 million each. The IOC contributes to the costs of NOCs, so it could be argued that the games do cover a portion of these costs.
- *Sponsor costs*: To capitalise on their sponsorship investment, sponsors generally need to spend many more millions of dollars on advertising, promotions and hospitality, as discussed above. Of course they expect to recover such expenditure through enhanced sales and profits. Some economic impact studies have made estimates of the expenditure of Games sponsors over and above their payments to the IOC or the organising committee this is not an exact science and not all the expenditure takes place in the host city.

Games income

Table 6.7 lists the main sources of income for Games events and Figure 6.2 shows the pattern of income sources for the Summer Games, from 1972 to 2004 (except Moscow, 1980).

Table 6.7. Individual Olympic Games: income headings

- Broadcasting fees (via IOC)
- World sponsorship – TOP funds (via IOC)
- Local sponsorship
- Ticket sales
- Lottery
- Sale of merchandise/coins/stamps
- Government subsidy/donations

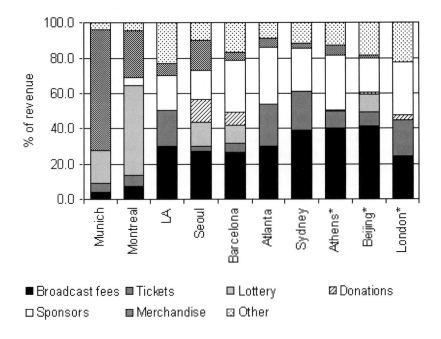

Figure 6.2. Summer Olympic Games: sources of income, 1972– 2012
Data source: based on Preuss (2004: 97) and Table 10.16 . * from bid documents

Broadcasting fees

The largest single item, accounting for 40 per cent of income is the share of broadcasting fees which accrues to the host city. We have already seen that the IOC has become proportionately less dependent on television for its income, particularly with the advent of sponsorship, in the form of TOP. In the case of individual Games, however, the degree of financial dependence on television fees varies. The implications of this for individual Games events are discussed in Chapter 7.

Sponsorship

Sponsorship is the second most significant source of income at around 30 per cent. Global sponsorship under the TOP scheme is discussed above. Local sponsorship is also significant and arrangements generally follow the format of TOP sponsorship deals: sponsors are offered 'exclusive' sponsorship rights in certain categories. Categories already covered by TOP agreements cannot be duplicated locally, but it can be seen from Table 6.2 that a number of categories remain for local sponsorship, including such areas as banking, air transport, land transport, television coverage, clothing, training and telecommunications. As with TOP sponsors, local sponsors often provide support 'in kind' as well as in cash.

A number of corporations continue to support The Olympic Programme (TOP) over several Olympiads, suggesting that Olympic sponsorship is viewed as cost-effective. Research conducted after the Barcelona 1992 Olympics indicated that the American public recognised official sponsors and viewed the connection with the Olympics as positive association (Stipp and Schiavone, 1996). However, survey research following the Atlanta 1996 Games indicated confusion among consumers in relation to official sponsors and 'ambush' marketers – those who engage in sport-related advertising around the time of the Olympic Games in the hope of associating themselves with the Games in consumers' minds (Sandler and Shani, 1989, 1993 and see Chapter 7). A recent view on prospective sponsorship of the Beijing Games notes that many of the, largely Western, sponsors are 'directly involved in high-calorie foods or low physical activity', such as television-viewing and motorised transport, so that, if they are successful in selling more product to the Chinese, the net effect on the health of the Chinese could be negative (Dickson and Schofield, 2005).

Ticket sales

Income from the sale of tickets varies considerably. It would appear that in more affluent host countries (USA, Australia) ticket sales account for about 20 per cent of income, but in less affluent countries ticket prices are pitched at a lower level and therefore produce 10 per cent or less of income.

Merchandising – coins, stamps and licensing

Coins and stamps made a large contribution in Munich and Montréal, but have been less significant in recent Games. Licensing covers mainly the sale of souvenirs.

Lotteries

Special lotteries have been significant contributors in four of the Olympic Games listed. However, while Sydney did not have a special lottery, it should be noted that the New South Wales government derives a substantial annual income from its own lotteries and from casinos and gaming machines, so instituting a special Olympic lottery would probably have attracted money away from existing lotteries and therefore cost the state money.

Donations

Donations by private individuals, corporations and some municipalities were a significant source of income in the case of Seoul, Barcelona and Athens.

Other income

For a number of Games, the major component of the 'other' category is contributions from national and provincial governments. Financial contributions of governments in recent Games nevertheless vary quite markedly, from zero in the case of Los Angeles to some 25 per cent of the total in the case of Seoul.

Volunteers

As Holger Preuss points out (2004: 182), a key aspect of the resourcing of an Olympic Games event is volunteer labour but since, by definition, such labour is provided free of charge, it does not appear in listings of Games revenue. The ability to generate volunteer support is a major feature of cities' bids for the Games, indicating enthusiasm for the Games on the part of the host public as well as offering substantial cost savings. Typically, at the time of the Games, several tens of thousands of volunteers will be involved, in marshalling, providing advice to the public and assisting with numerous, often menial, but necessary tasks. Having to cover these activities with paid staff would have a significant negative impact on organising committees' budgets.

Economic impact

One of the main reasons why cities and nations and their governments bid to host the Olympic Games is the promise of positive *economic impact*. That is, it is anticipated that the Games will bring increased incomes and jobs to the host city, region and country. For many individuals and organisations involved in promoting the idea of hosting the Games in their city or country this is, in fact, their primary motive. Just how significant are these impacts? The economic evaluation of sporting events is a complex process which has itself spawned a small academic and consultancy industry (see Further Reading section).

   Economic impact is different from the financial assessment of income and expenditure discussed above: it is not concerned with profit and loss of the event itself, but with the effect of the event on jobs and incomes in the general local, regional or national economy. So even a loss-making event can have a significant economic impact. Economic impact is also different from cost-benefit analysis, which seeks to take into account *all* effects of an event, even those which do not formally appear in any financial balance sheet. Cost-benefit analysis is discussed briefly at the end of the chapter.

   Assessing the economic impact of an event such as the Olympic Games involves four steps:

1.   identifying all the expenditure items which are attributable to the event, that is, expenditure which would not have taken place without the event;
2.   measuring these expenditure items in money terms;
3.   estimating the *direct* and *indirect* impact of these expenditure items on local, regional and/or national incomes;
4.   converting aggregate expenditure into an estimate of jobs.

These steps are discussed in turn below. They are discussed in general terms only. Actual examples of economic impact studies in action are presented in the case-studies in Chapter 10.

Identifying expenditure items

Identifying relevant expenditure items is not as straightforward as it might seem. For example, expenditure by the Organising Committee which is funded from international television fees or sponsorship is clearly additional expenditure which would not have taken place without the Games. But expenditure which is funded from ticket sales to local residents or sponsorship by local corporations is not 'additional expenditure' because it is likely that if the local ticket buyers or sponsors had not bought tickets to or sponsored the Olympic Games, they would have spent their money locally in some other way – there is no gain to the local economy from these sources as a result of the Games being held in the city.

The exercise is complicated by the issue of the choice of *geographical area* to be studied, that is, whether the focus is the city, the region/province or the whole country. For example, if the national government gives a special grant for the Games to the Organising Committee, this is 'extra' income for the host city or region, but it is not extra income for the *country*, since it can be assumed that if the national government had not given the grant for the Games, it would have spent the money in the country some other way.

Table 6.8 lists the items which are typically included as relevant expenditure items in a national level economic impact study of an event such as the Olympic Games. *Direct expenditure* items arise directly from the event. *Induced expenditure* items arise indirectly – for example, additional tourism may arise as a result of the exposure the host country or city receives in the media as a result of the Games. A related *induced* item is the additional international events, particularly sporting events, which are invariably attracted to a city as a result of hosting the Games. These events are attracted because of the 'glamour' associated with an 'Olympic city', but primarily as a result of the availability of high standard sport competition venues.

Table 6.8. Economic impact expenditure items – national level study

Direct expenditure

1. Expenditure financed from fees for international broadcasting rights
2. Expenditure financed from international sponsorship income (inc. TOP)
3. Expenditure of international broadcasters in host country
4. Expenditure of foreign athletes and officials in host country
5. Expenditure of international spectators to the Games
6. Expenditure of international sponsoring organisations (over and above sponsorship fee)

Induced expenditure

7. Expenditure by foreign tourists drawn to host country as a result of heightened profile
8. Expenditure arising from additional international 'spin-off' events (e.g. sport, congresses) which take place as a result of the Games

Measuring expenditure

How are data on these expenditure items collected? Table 6.9 gives an indication of typical data sources which can be used. Some items are relatively easy to ascertain – for example the first two items, on television and sponsor income, should be available from the Games Organising Committee. Other items usually require some sort of research study, possibly involving surveys of relevant organisations and individuals or use of data from tourist authorities on tourist expenditure patterns during the period affected by the Games.

Table 6.9. Data sources for expenditure items

Item	Data source
1. International broadcasting rights fees	Organising Committee/IOC
2. International sponsorship income	Organising Committee/IOC
3. Expenditure of international broadcasters	Study 1*
4. Expenditure of foreign athletes/officials	Study 2*
5. Expenditure of international spectators	Study 3*
6. Expenditure of international sponsors	Study 4*
7. Expenditure by additional foreign tourists	Tourism Commission
8. Expenditure from 'spin-off' events	Tourism Commission

* specific research projects

Multiplier effects

When a visitor or construction company spends money in a city the impact on the local economy does not stop there. The recipients of this expenditure – for example hotels or restaurants or construction workers – spend the money they receive. Part of this expenditure goes to local businesses, such as shops and service providers, which in turn pay wages to their staff and buy supplies, again partly from other local businesses. The initial expenditure therefore circulates in the economy, creating additional personal and business income. The process does not go on for ever because expenditure 'leaks' out of the system, in the form of savings, taxes and expenditure paid to organisations outside the study area. The overall effect can, however, be measured by economists, and is known as the 'multiplier' effect. Thus, for example, a 'multiplier' of 1.9 indicates that an initial £1 million expenditure would result in total direct and indirect expenditure of £1.9 million.

Two alternative methods are used to measure multiplier effects. The first involves using survey evidence on the pattern of distribution of individuals' expenditure (with local/non-local suppliers, taxes, savings, etc.) and organisations' expenditure (on wages, investment, local/non-local suppliers, taxes, dividend payments, etc.) and following the initial expenditure through a number of 'rounds' (see Veal, 2002: 203–6).

An alternative is to use a complete macro-economic model of the city or regional economy, similar to those used by national governments. Such models trace the flows of expenditure between the various sectors of the economy and provide estimates of the effect on personal incomes, tax income, jobs and gross domestic product (see Fletcher, 1989). Macro-economic models used are of two main kinds: input-output (I-O) models and computable general equilibrium (CGE) models (Kasimati, 2003; Blake: 2005: 4–13). Input-output models resemble a large spreadsheet with columns representing industries or industry sectors, including the labour sector, and rows representing products. In studies of the Olympic Games, the games are introduced as a separate 'industry'. The CGE modelling approach incorporates input-output components, but also introduces considerations such as the effects of demand shifts on prices, labour costs and the currency exchange rate and the effects of these in turn on other industries.

Estimation of jobs

Estimates of levels of expenditure can be converted into an estimate of 'jobs created', by dividing the total by a suitable wage or salary level. For example, if an average gross wage/salary of about £20,000 is assumed, the £1.9 million expenditure given in the example above would convert to 95 one-year jobs. Since much of the indirect expenditure is scattered in small amounts around many organisations in the host economy, not every pound of expenditure works to create specific jobs. In some cases it may result in payment of overtime for full-time workers, new part-time jobs or increased hours for existing part-time workers or increased profits for companies and their owners. Given the nature of a sporting event such as the Olympic Games, the jobs created are likely to be short-term. Construction jobs may last a year or two, as would jobs with the Organising Committee, and some of the jobs created in the tourism industry would last as long as the positive effects on tourism lasted, while many jobs would be just for a few months, or even days, at the time of the event. But in some cases, the effect of a burst of economic activity generated by a major sporting event can have the effect of 'kick-starting' the local economy, so that the effect is self-sustaining and has a continuing impact after the event is over. It is believed that this was experienced to some extent in the case of the Barcelona Games of 1992 (Brunet, 1993).

Collection of data for an economic impact study, as discussed above, is an exacting and relatively expensive task. In view of these difficulties, Baade and Matheson (2002) pursued a different approach based on comparison of employment growth rates in cities which did and did not host the Olympics. They developed a model relating change in employment in 50 US cities for 1984, the year of the Los Angeles Games, and 1996, the year of the Atlanta Games. The model included change in employment as the 'dependent variable' and a number of 'independent variables', such as the size of the city population, per capita income, wage rates and state and local taxes, and a 'dummy' variable for the city hosting the Olympics. The resultant model enabled them to draw conclusions concerning the number of jobs created by the Olympics in the Olympic year. A similar approach was taken by Hotchkiss *et al.* (2003) in relation to Atlanta 1996.

A further approach adopted by some economists has been to examine local stock market reactions to Olympic announcements, on the grounds that the collective knowledge of stock market operators might provide a realistic assessment of the value of anticipated Olympic impacts. However, the results of studies of the effect of the announcement of successful bids for the Olympics have been mixed. In the case of Sydney 2000 there was no effect on the stock exchange as a whole, although there were positive impacts on specific New South Wales-based companies (Berman *et al.*, 2000). In the case of Athens 2004 there was an overall positive effect, but none in the case of Torino (Milano stock exchange) (Veraros *et al.*, 2004). A study of the effect of Olympic sponsorship announcements showed no effect on the stock market rating of sponsoring companies in a study of Atlanta 1996 (Miyazaki and Morgan, 2001).

Economic impact studies

Measurement of economic outcomes is, as we have seen, a complex undertaking and therefore can be costly to implement. Since they involve research utilising social survey data, the results are often far from certain and are open to challenge and debate. Table 6.10 lists examples of economic impact studies for recent summer Olympic Games. We have already noted the work of Preuss (2004: 9) which demonstrates that comparing financial data from one Olympic Games to another is fraught with difficulty. The data in Table 6.10 are therefore to be viewed very cautiously.

Table 6.10. Examples of economic impact studies

Games/year	Author(s)/reference	National Impact, US$ '000s	Jobs impact '000s	Time period, yrs
Los Angeles 1984	Economics Research Asstes (1984)	2 300	73.3	11
	Baade & Matheson (2002)	-	5.0	
Seoul 1988	Kim (1988)	2 550	336	8
Barcelona 1992	Brunet (1993, 1995)	24 862	296.6	6
Atlanta 1996	Humphreys & Plummer (1995) + Glisson (1996)	5 141*	77.0*	7 315
	Baade & Matheson (2002)	-	42.4*	
	Hotchkiss, *et al.* (2003)	-	+ 17%§	
Sydney 2000	KPMG Peat Marwick (1993)	7 300	156.2	13
	NSW Treasury/CRE (1997)	6 400	197.6	12
	Madden/Arthur Andersen (2002)	6 500	63.6	12
Athens 2004	Balfousia-Savva *et al.* **	11 000	300.4	1 111
	Papanikos**	15 900	445.0	
Vancouver 2010	InterVISTAS (2002), Ministry of Competition, Science & Enterprise (2002)	3 563†	100.0†	20
London 2012	Blake (2005), PriceWaterhouse Coopers (2005)	3 777	8.1	12

* State of Georgia. ** Studies in Greek, brief results reported in English via Kasimati (2003), Table 3. † 'Medium' estimate. § jobs impact in nearby compared with more distant counties.

The second two Sydney studies and the London study used the CGE model discussed above, so provide more conservative estimates than standard input-output methods.

The Barcelona and Athens studies seem out of line with the others, which show a steady increase over the last 20 years, but the value of infrastructure investments in Barcelona was three times as high as that in Seoul and 18 times as high as that in Los Angeles, and accounted for a large proportion of the economic impact (Brunet, 1995: 16–17). Similarly, the non-sport infrastructure investments associated with Athens

2004 were very costly. Such investments should, however, only be counted as 'economic impact' if they were funded from sources outside the study area which would not have been available in the absence of the Olympics.

Economic impacts are also considered in relation to the case studies in Chapter 10.

Cost-benefit analysis

Cost-benefit analysis is a more complex process than economic impact analysis: it seeks to assess, and if possible measure in money terms, all the impacts of an event, not just the obviously economic effects. Examples of additional *negative* effects which cost-benefit analysis might seek to measure include noise disturbance to residents, traffic congestion and accidents and increased accommodation costs.

Examples of additional *positive* effects are environmental enhancements in the host city, city image boosting, possible increased sport participation (and hence health benefits) among the population and general community enjoyment of the event.

Each of these items poses challenges to the researcher and involves significant data collection costs. For example, measurement of the effects of traffic congestion would involve either detailed monitoring of traffic volumes and speeds before and during the event or surveys of residents to discover the effects of the event on their travel times. Total time lost due to traffic delays and congestion could then be valued using some sort of valuation of time (e.g. the average wage rate) and costs of vehicle fuel. The cost of traffic accidents is routinely assessed by transport organisations, in terms of medical costs and pain and suffering (valued by using sums arrived at in typical court awards).

The 'general community enjoyment' of the event should be particularly noted. Economists call this the 'psychic' value of the event. We are often told that the host city, and even the host country, experiences a 'party atmosphere' during the Olympic Games and that a general boost to the overall sense of well-being is experienced as a result of successfully hosting the Games. Thus even those not directly involved, as spectators, athletes, workers or volunteers, may obtain some benefit from the Games. Economists have devised ways of discovering how much this psychic value is worth to people in monetary terms – sometimes simply by asking people in a survey. Such a survey was carried out in connection with the London 2012 Games even before they had been awarded, and it was found that London households were willing to pay, on average, £22 a year for ten years in order to host the games, while the corresponding figure for non-London households was £12 (PriceWaterhouseCoopers, 2005: 12). This implies that the UK population place a value of £3.2 billion on hosting the Games. In one example of such an assessment carried out after the running of an Adelaide Formula One Grand Prix, it was found that the psychic value of the event to the population of Adelaide far outweighed all the costs of staging the event (Burns *et al.*, 1986).

Economic impact – the future

There can be no doubt that financial and economic considerations lie as close to the heart of the Olympic phenomenon as do sporting values. Since the 1980s cities and nations have vied with one another to host the Games largely because of their hoped-for economic effects. It is the money generated from television rights and sponsorship which transformed the Games over the last half of the twentieth century, from an event dominated by the amateur ideal and government and voluntary funding to the professional and commercially orientated phenomenon of today. Much of the controversy surrounding the Olympic Games arises from financial and economic factors. Even apparently non-economic issues, such as the problems caused by the use of prohibited drugs, have strong economic or financial dimensions, brought about by the professionalisation of sport.

Table 6.10 shows that, since the mid-1990s, studies of the projected economic impact of the Olympic Games have increasingly been conducted in advance of the Games and even as part of the bid-preparation process. Post-Games evaluations remain important because they are based on 'real', as opposed to estimated effects. In general, the growing number of studies should be having a long-term effect on the quality of decision-making. Such studies are taken into account by bidding cities and now provide a basis for making plausible, as opposed to hopeful, assumptions about likely patterns of income and expenditure.

Further Reading

* *Political economy of sport*: Nauright and Schimmel (2005)
* *History of commercialisation of the Games*: Barney *et al.* (2002)
* *Neo-Marxist political economy of the Olympics*: Brohm (1978); Gruneau (1983, 1984, 1999); Gruneau and Cantelon (1988); Tomlinson (2005)
* *Economics/Economic impact of the Olympic Games*: see Brain and Manolakos (1991); Preuss (2000, 2004); and see Table 6.10
* *Economic impact of sporting events generally*: Burns *et al.* (1986); Syme *et al.* (1989); Hall (1994)
* *Economic impact vs cost-benefit analysis*: Veal (2002: 185–210).
* *Olympic villages*: De Moragas *et al.* (1997).
* *Olympic Games legacy*: De Moragas *et al.* (2003); Cashman (2006).

Questions

1. In the chapter, six topics are discussed under the heading of the 'political economy' of the Olympic Games. Name three of these topics and the critique offered by commentators such as Gruneau.
2. What is the 'TOP' programme and how does it work?
3. Why is precise costing of an Olympic Games difficult?
4. What issues arise in deciding whether an Olympic Games has been profitable for a host city/country?
5. What are the key factors which need to be taken into account in assessing the economic impact of an Olympic Games?

Chapter 7

The Olympics and the Mass Media

Whatever else the Olympic Games have been, they are now the ultimate media festival. Garry Whannel (1984: 30)

Introduction

If you weren't convinced of the above quotation and thought the Olympic Games were just a sports event, the following might persuade you. At the 2005 American television Emmy Awards the prize for 'Outstanding directing for a Variety/Music/ Comedy' was awarded to Bucky Gunts. The programme he won the award for was *The Games of the XXVIII Olympiad*. This result was neither an aberration for entering the programme in that particular category nor his first win for Olympic coverage. In 2002 he had shared the same award with Ron de Moraes and Kenny Ortega for their contribution to *Opening Ceremony Salt Lake 2002 Olympic Winter Games*. This view, that the most suitable category for entering Olympic broadcasting in the Emmys includes the genres of music and comedy, raises the question – what are the purposes and outcomes of Olympic broadcasting and what theories can help explain how it affects our understandings of the Games?

'The press is traditionally viewed as having four principal functions: to inform (the news function), to persuade (the advertising function), to entertain (the features function), and to pass on the cultural heritage (the educational function)' (Slater, 1998: 51). Through these purposes, and because of their global reach, the media are active in defining and shaping contemporary cultures. However, in fulfilling these functions they are neither unbiased nor without other agendas. As one way to explain this, the *propaganda model* of media, presented in the book *Manufacturing Consent* (Herman and Chomsky, 1988), asserts that, as part of their influence, the media echo, maintain and propagate the viewpoints of those who have power, specifically government and business élites. 'The media serve this purpose in many ways: through selection of topics, distribution of concerns, framing of issues, filtering of information, emphasis and tone, and by keeping debate within the bounds of acceptable premises' (Toohey and Taylor, 2006). The propaganda model is based on the premise that, in

Western capitalist societies, the dominant media are firmly embedded in the market system and thus mass media discourse is 'shaped by ownership and profit orientation'.

By their selection of what is worth reading, hearing and seeing, owners, editors and journalists involved in the media perform a gate-keeping function. They do not have to suppress information totally to achieve this, instead, after they choose which material to publish or broadcast. They then add their interpretation to it. Thus, Herman and Chomsky posited that the media frame news and allow debate only within the confines of selected perspectives. Similarly, the media may omit many important stories through a system designed to sift out material that falls outside what is considered to be acceptable socio/political boundaries. Five filters of the dissemination of information presented in the propaganda model are:

1. The size, concentrated ownership, and profit motives and orientation of the dominant mass media oligopolies.
2. Advertising as the primary source of income.
3. Reliance on information provided by government, business and 'experts', funded and approved by primary sources and agents of power.
4. 'Flak' as a means of disciplining the media.
5. 'Anti-communism' as a control mechanism.

The last filter is a reflection of the period when the propaganda model was developed during the Cold War. A more current reading of the fifth filter now is acknowledged to be the identification of an 'evil empire' or dictator (Toohey and Taylor, 2006).

The third filter asserts that, when there is dissension to the hegemonic viewpoint of the media, it is:

> managed and contained and the public is not provided with a full view. ... Views incompatible with the interests of corporate and government élites are attributed to special interest groups. ... A supply of experts is 'bought' in to add legitimacy to media messages that serve élite interests. (Lenskyj, 1997: 3)

As an example of this, the Australian Centre for Independent Journalism, in writing about the role of the media in Sydney during its bid for the 2000 Games, observed that journalists who were critical of the Bid Committee were labelled as being unpatriotic, inaccurate or even eccentric (Australian Centre for Independent Journalism, 1993).

Richard Gruneau has examined the theme of cultural/sporting and media hegemony, specifically in the context of the relationship between the institutions of sport and the media, coming to conclusions about its hegemonic role. He states:

> Television's elaboration and selection of preferred emphases and meanings, its favoured narratives, its 'management' of contradictory themes and values (e.g., between unbridled individual success and obligations to team, nation or community), can all be seen as part of a complex process through which *some* understandings of sport, the body, consumer culture and the pursuit of excellence are naturalized while others are marginalised, downgraded, or ignored. (Gruneau, 1989: 7.28)

The propaganda model thus has currency when examining the hegemonic relationships between the media and the Olympic Movement. While a variety of government and commercial élites interests are best served through the perpetuation of the Olympic Games' current elevated status in the sporting world, none of these has greater cause for self-interest in maintaining the *status quo* than the International Olympic Committee (IOC). Thus, the fact that for journalists to have access to Olympic venues they must be accredited by the Olympic authorities also adds credence to the propaganda model. Another example of the model's utility occurred in 1992, when then IOC President, Juan Antonio Samaranch, took the Olympic Movement's most public critic, British journalist, Andrew Jennings, to court over charges of libel and scandal to suppress publication of an anti-Olympic book. Interestingly, it is not only the IOC that Jennings has criticised: the world of football has also been under his investigative lens (Jennings, 2006). Perhaps this is why he is also the only journalist banned from attending FIFA matches.

This chapter examines the multi-faceted relationship between the Olympics and the mass media from the viewpoint of Herman and Chomsky's propaganda model, with one basic difference. While, in 1988, they argued, with legitimacy, that community radio and television rather than mainstream media sources were the key to effecting positive change to allow dissenting media viewpoints to be heard, by 1998 the changing nature of information technology meant that the Internet had now usurped this function. It now has the ability to be the most potent vehicle by which dissent about current Olympic policies and practices can be aired without élite censorship, although there are still limitations to 'complete freedom of the press'.

The relationship between the Olympics and the mass media

The connection between the Olympic Games and mass media has long been of interest to academics. According to John Slater (1998: 49) 'While the mass media and the Olympic Games both needed each other in the early years, the media held the upper hand… the relationship only recently has evolved into one in which the Olympic Movement has become the dominant partner'. Slater divides the development of the relationship into four distinct phases:

- pre-television (1894–1932);
- television, before satellites (1936–1964);
- satellite television before the Internet (1968–1988);
- era of Olympic dominance (1992 onwards).

He notes two important factors relevant to the transition between phases: that progression to the next stage is related to technical innovations and that the length of time between phases is diminishing.

Despite the strengthening relationship, in 1956 Avery Brundage, president of the IOC, is quoted as saying: 'the IOC has managed without TV for sixty years and, believe me, we are going to manage for another sixty' (quoted in Lyberg, 1996: 350). Since this time, and counter to Brundage's prediction, the Olympic Games have now become a global spectacle because of television. Technological advances in the mass media have enabled the Games to become more accessible to audiences throughout the globe: the cumulative number of television viewers for the 2004 Athens Games was estimated to have been in excess of 40 billion (Wilson, 2004).

The growth of the television audience, as shown in Table 7.1, has resulted in both positive and negative outcomes for the Olympic Movement. It has enabled substantial amounts of funding to be channelled to the IOC and, in turn, to Olympic sports, NOCs

Table 7.1. Growth of television coverage of the Olympics

Summer Games			Winter Games		
		No. of countries			*No. of countries*
Year	*City*	*with coverage*	*Year*	*City*	*with coverage*
1936	Berlin	11			
1948	London	11			
1952	Helsinki	22			
1956	Melbourne	1	1956	Cortina	22
1960	Rome	21	1960	Squaw Valley	27
1964	Tokyo	40	1964	Innsbruck	30
1968	Mexico City	n/a	1968	Grenoble	32
1972	Munich	98	1972	Sapporo	41
1976	Montréal	124	1976	Innsbruck	38
1980	Moscow	111	1980	Lake Placid	40
1984	Los Angeles	156	1984	Sarajevo	100
1988	Seoul	160	1988	Calgary	64
1992	Barcelona	193	1992	Albertville	86
1996	Atlanta	214	1994	Lillehammer	120
2000	Sydney	220	1998	Nagano	160
2004	Athens	220	2002	Salt Lake City	160
			2006	Turin	160

Source: IOC, 1998c: 32; 2006a

and Olympic Solidarity. It has allowed viewers throughout the world to share in the pageantry of the opening and closing ceremonies and the victories and achievements of outstanding athletes. It has, in many ways, been responsible for the growth of sponsorship for Olympic athletes and teams and thus, indirectly, for the positive accomplishments which have resulted from this. On a less favourable note, it is also accountable for many of the problems and excesses that have ensued as a result of the accompanying increase in commercialism.

The negative consequences of the alliance between television and the Olympic Movement have caused some critics to question the influence of television networks, especially those from the USA, in applying pressure to schedule some Olympic events at a time which will boost their viewing audiences, rather than at a time most suitable for athletes or live audiences. For example, the swimming finals at the 2008 Beijing Games have been scheduled for the mornings, rather than the usual evenings, in order to accommodate the needs of the US television broadcaster, NBC. On a more global scale, the growth of the Olympic Games, as a consequence of the expanded television audience, has led to concerns about gigantism of the Olympic Movement. Likewise, over-commercialisation is accepted as a by-product of the Games' success and is linked to television's ability to reach a world audience.

While critics perceive these to be problems, the IOC and the broadcast industry appear to be content with their alliance, at least outwardly. Its benefits flow to both partners. Nevertheless, it is important to analyse the ramifications of television on the Games, not only in terms of the impact on the Olympic Movement itself, but also because of the implications for the ultimate consumer, the viewing audience.

There is no single universal Olympic broadcast seen and heard by all of the world's viewers and the mediated views are different to what spectators in Olympic venues experience. Not all Olympic events, and indeed not all Olympic sports, are shown by each broadcaster, thus limiting television viewers' choices. Not only is content restricted in this manner, it is further altered, especially in larger events, by directors segmenting or fragmenting sports coverage. Verbal commentary further interprets and modifies the Olympic experience for the home viewer, while slow-motion replays distort the sense of time. Camera angles can provide unique visual images that spectators viewing the event live do not have the opportunity to witness. The underwater cameras at the swimming, those at the top of the diving platform and those in the bull's eye of the archery targets, all direct the viewer's attention in a manner distinctive to television. Linked to this, it is interesting to note the pattern that has emerged at recent Games of many athletes themselves watching and immediately reliving their victories on the giant screens at the stadium. There is no question that the visual and auditory images received live in the Olympic venues and the experiences of those watching in the living room are very different.

The majority of the world's Olympic audience see, via the medium of television, a mediated Games, enhanced, compacted, interpreted, interrupted and replaced with a distortion of time and space, often complete with the signage and advertising that is banned from Olympic venues (courtesy of the advertisement breaks). While the 'clean stadium' approach at all Olympic venues has enabled the IOC to claim that it has set limits on its policies regarding commercialism, it is interesting to note how television has allowed, not so much a bending of this rule, but clever uses of it.

After his 200 metre victory at the Atlanta Games, Michael Johnson was seen proudly giving television interviews adjacent to the official timing equipment. The Swatch company, the Olympic Partner (TOP) sponsors in the 'time keeping' category, received worldwide publicity when their label was clearly visible right beside Johnson's head. Athletic shoe and apparel companies likewise appear to benefit immensely from television exposure. Remaining with Michael Johnson as the example, Nike, which was not an official Olympic sponsor, received a substantial return on its investment in the manufacture of Johnson's signature 'golden' shoes, through the publicity they received in the media both before and after his 1996 Olympic victories. Of course, expectations of media coverage can be a two-edged sword, especially for TOP sponsors. Reebok was the official sports shoe of the 1996 Games, yet was outsmarted by ambush marketer Nike's clever choice of sponsored athletes, whose successes, personalities and images made them both crowd pleasers and televisual. Olympic ambush marketing is directed at television audiences as much, if not more, than at spectators. In terms of the propaganda model, the banning of ambush marketing provides evidence of the power of commercial élites.

A classic example of this occurred during the Sydney 2000 Olympics. In the lead-up to the Games, the *Sydney 2000 Games (Indicia and Images) Protection Act 1996* was introduced to prohibit unauthorised use of the Olympic rings and images for commercial purposes. While the act was seen to effectively control ambush marketing more successfully than had occurred in Atlanta, it still did not prevent all instances. The Chinese liquor brand 'Wu Liang Ye' was neither an official sponsor of the Games nor of the Chinese Olympic team, however it reportedly dispatched 'cheer squads' and gave out Chinese flags (which also included the brand's name and/or logo) to Chinese spectators at events where Chinese athletes were successful, such as the women's volleyball. The Olympic officials charged with preventing ambush marketing did not read Chinese and assumed that the flags were simply to support the Chinese athletes, rather than to promote a product. So the flags were not confiscated. When the television cameras panned to crowd scenes showing the supportive spectators cheering on their successful athletes and waving the flags, the company received free advertising targeted specifically to influence the Chinese audience watching the Games on television back in China (Allens Arthur Robinson, 2000).

The nature of Olympic television broadcasts

Olympic broadcasts are different to most other sportscasts, understandably so because of the extended length of the Olympic Games in comparison to most sports events. It is much harder to maintain viewer interest consistently over a 16 or 17 day period than for, say, a single three hour event. A direct result of this need to retain audiences throughout the Games has been the evolution of a new Olympic sub-genre of sports-casting, one which has emerged in the networks' effort to build a larger share of the sports audience market, beyond the traditional sport demographic of the 18–35 male. For example, the American broadcaster, NBC, deliberately tailored its 1996 broadcast to cater more for a female audience. Dick Ebersol, President of NBC Sports and Chairman and Chief Executive Officer, NBC Olympics Unit, when describing the network's previous telecasts of the Seoul and Barcelona Games, commented: 'every minute we showed boxing we lost a minimum of 25 per cent of the audience. The Olympics are driven by female-appeal sports, and we lost all the women' (Hruska, 1996: 8). (For a discussion of the nature of Olympic broadcasts of female athletes see Chapter 9.)

In order to cater for this previously under-acknowledged and under-appreciated viewing audience for its Atlanta coverage NBC 'used its muscle to alter the schedule so events that appeal to women will extend throughout the Games' 17 days' (Hruska, 1996: 9). Consequently, the swimming programme was extended by an extra day and the gymnastics programme was similarly extended by two days, with an additional closing 'Champions Gala', based on the figure skating exhibition, which had been a successful feature of the Winter Games. To further attract the female demographic NBC devised a strategy of presenting the Olympics as a 'story', rather than sport. Ebersol explained 'You lose this special audience if you treat the Olympics as a normal, results driven sporting event on TV' (Hruska 1996: 9).

Yet, it could legitimately be argued that the heart of the Games broadcasts should be the presentation of sport. After all, the Olympics are, in reality, a series of sporting events. The deliberate manipulation by television to alter this has in many ways detracted from the essence of the sport experience for the television viewer. As a result, the viewer has a television package wherein the host city, targeted athletes and celebrities with no Olympic connections, become featured actors in an Olympic story, which at times has all the makings of a soap opera. They receive star billing for short segments, of approximately 2–5 minutes, which focus on their history, past triumphs or adversities, their Olympic dreams and aspirations. Sometimes a very long bow needs to be drawn to even establish a relationship between some of the celebrities and the Games. This additional coverage allows an unsophisticated form of plot development to occur, whereby there may be multiple story lines, ones that at times have overshadowed the sports competition. Indeed, while these vignettes are being broadcast over the airwaves, Olympic sports themselves are being conducted, and obviously these are not receiving air-time. As Whannel (1998: 23) notes: 'the media narrativises the events of sport, transforming them into stories with stars and characters; heroes and villains'.

This additional, 'human-interest' material allows Olympic sport to merge with other genres of television programming so that Games coverage becomes at various times; 'infotainment', drama, current affairs, news and even, as previously mentioned, a soap opera. Meadow proposes three hypotheses to explain why Olympic broadcasts have mutated from purely sporting programmes into these other formats, designed to target the widest possible audience. The first hypothesis suggests that, as 'the Olympics replaced so much of the ordinary broadcasts, the conventions of all other programmes were included under the Olympic broadcast umbrella' (Meadow, 1989: 6–7). His next two hypotheses relate to the expectations of the viewing audience. Meadow maintains that the public desires the style of Olympic broadcasts to mirror its regular diet of programmes. Broadcasters have conformed to these wishes, by providing a mode of delivery that ends in a climax. Meadow lastly suggests that Olympic television is designed to appeal to the nationalistic biases of the audience, by presenting home-grown athletes as superior to their foreign opponents. This third proposition fits well in terms of the propaganda model.

Whatever the networks' intent, it is commonplace that, during prime-time sport viewing, television broadcasts often become a *potpourri* of segmented highlights. As one Australian television producer, Bob Kemp, of Channel 10, commented:

> the Americans used the policy that they need to change their perspective of what they're looking at, at least every four or five minutes because they think that's the attention span of their average viewer. I give the average viewer audience more credit than that – in Australia anyway. (quoted in Goldlust, 1987: 99)

Ironically, in the subsequent Olympics, the Ten Network offered Australians a format similar to the one being criticised. The average length of a segment during the whole of their 1988 Olympic broadcast was less than six minutes (Toohey, 1997).

Many of the Olympic glamour sports do not receive regular television coverage, apart from 16 days every four years, when the summer or Winter Games are broadcast. Ken Sutcliffe, one of Australia's most respected sports commentators, noted 'the Olympics by and large are minority sports well packaged and they're successful because they provide the combination of character, courage, fashion, speed and danger' (Sutcliffe, 1995: 23).

Another appeal of Olympic broadcasts as television programming, as suggested by Meadow (1989) above, is their nationalistic focus. Olympic networks can, to a large degree, individualise their coverage to suit their audiences' perceived needs, by choosing which feed they take from the host broadcaster (for example swimming or gymnastics). Thus, the choice of sports and events that British viewers are presented with may be very different to the coverage shown in Japan. Networks tailor and may even supplement the host broadcasts by providing their own footage to suit their potential audience and to target their nation's most popular athletes. This individuality is seen as critical to a ratings success, and the ability to do this is one of the main reasons that networks bid for Olympic broadcast rights.

Despite ratings successes, networks have been accused of taking their nationalistic focus to jingoistic excess and concentrating almost exclusively on their own nation's athletes, while ignoring heroic performances of foreigners. Both the 1996 NBC American and the 2000 Australian Network 7 coverage was heavily criticised for this. Many of the international press were unimpressed with NBC's 1996 coverage, as the network concentrated on American competitors, ignoring some events in which there were remarkable performances by non-American athletes. For example, the 1500 metres swimming freestyle, in which Australian Kieren Perkins won a second consecutive gold medal but there were no US place-getters, was not broadcast by NBC. Critics considered this domestic focus to be a self-indulgent exercise in national self-aggrandisement.

Commentators may also play an active role in this nationalistic and even at times xenophobic process, as it is often their commentary that provides or accentuates the political focus of the broadcast, while casting aspersions on their national rivals. For example, the Chinese female swimmers were the objects of intense media scrutiny in Atlanta because of their suspected drug use, as was the Irish champion Michelle Smith. While neither the Chinese swimmers nor Smith returned positive samples during the Games, the media suspicions, especially in the case of Smith, detracted from their achievements and provided a forum for disgruntled athletes to voice their opinions, since this time the actions of those under the microscope vindicated the suspicion of their accusers. Nevertheless, the fact remains that these accused athletes passed the IOC drug testing procedures during the Games. This, in turn, reflected poorly on the IOC's doping tests and policy.

Thus, while the television medium has the potential to truly internationalise the Olympics, in line with the *Olympic Charter*, this potential is restricted by networks' tendency to focus primarily on what they consider to be the glamour events and also on their own country's athletes. Consequently, some Olympic sports and champion athletes do not receive due media recognition. Concurrently, the Olympic message becomes modified, subsumed or altered in exchange for national prestige.

While networks may believe they are providing their audience with the format, focus and a nationalistic perspective that their viewers want, this is not always the case. Australia's Network 10 kept a tally of viewer complaints regarding their broadcast of the 1988 Olympics. 'Too much concentration on Australian athletes was the third highest complaint, yet not enough focus on Australian athletes also featured high on the list at number four' (Toohey, 1990b).

The Olympic networks need to be in tune with their viewers' requirements because of the huge financial outlay they expend to secure broadcast rights. Table 7.2 illustrates the escalating costs of securing television rights since 1960.

Profit is, however, not the only motive for networks to secure the broadcast rights. On occasion they are motivated more by network prestige than sound business decisions, although many networks do recoup their outlays through advertising revenue. Advertising income is related to their audience share (the higher the share, the more the network can charge for advertisements). Australia's Network 7 historically achieves about 60 per cent of the commercial audience share during the 17 days of the Olympics. This in turn, means that it can ask higher than normal prices from advertisers. However, in many countries, the non-Olympic network, which historically filled programming with 'also runs' during the Games period, are now adopting a more aggressive attitude to gaining back market share during this time period. For example, in 2006, in the USA, NBC's 17 nights of prime-time winter Olympics coverage did not win the February ratings in the key 'adults 18–49' demographic. Both ABC, based on the strength of its Superbowl coverage and its strategy of scheduling first-run programming against the Olympics, and Fox, based on the drawing power of *American Idol*, finished ahead of NBC.

This was not an unmitigated disaster for the NBC network, as the prime-time advertising revenue accounted for only 45 per cent of its US$900 million total advertising revenue for the Games. Even though the prime-time Olympic coverage was out-rated in the 18–49 demographic by ABC and Fox, the Olympics were still

Table 7.2. Television rights holders and fees – USA, Europe and Australia

		USA		Europe		Australia	
Year	City	Co.	Fee, US$ m.	Co.	Fee, US$ m.	Co.	Fee, US$ m.
1960	Rome	CBS	0.4	EBU	0.7	ATVP	na
1964	Tokyo	NBC	1.5	EBU	na	ATVP	na
1968	Mexico City	ABC	4.5	EBU	1	ATVP	na
1972	Munich	ABC	7.5	EBU	2	ATVP	na
1976	Montreal	ABC	25	EBU	6	ATVP	na
1980	Moscow	NBC	72	EBU	7	Ch. 7	1.4
1984	Los Angeles	ABC	226	EBU	22	Ch. 10	10.6
1988	Seoul	NBC	300	EBU	30	Ch. 10	7.4
1992	Barcelona	NBC	401	EBU	95	Ch. 7	34
1996	Atlanta	NBC	456	EBU	247	Ch. 7	30
2000	Sydney	NBC	705	EBU	350	Ch. 7	45
2004	Athens	NBC	793.5	EBU	394	Ch. 7	50

Source: Sydney Olympic Broadcasting Organisation, 1998: 20; IOC, 2006a: 53.
na = not available. EBU = European Broadcasting Union. ATVP = Australian TV Pool. NB for total broadcasting fees at constant prices see Table 6.1.

watched by more than 200 million people across all the NBC networks. The Games earned a profit for the network of between US$60 million and US$70 million (Consoli, 2006).

A study that monitored the effectiveness of advertising during the Olympic telecast provided some joy to those companies who paid the US$700,000 to NBC for their prime time spots. These prices were far less than ABC's Superbowl prices, where the 30-second commercial spots cost some US$2.5 million.

> The study showed that, on average, ads in the Olympics generated 17 percent higher brand recall, 35 percent higher message recall, and 36 percent higher likeability than ads in the average prime-time show. Heavy Olympic advertisers like McDonald's, Coca-Cola and Target saw their ads attract significantly higher brand and message recall during the Games telecasts. (Consoli, 2006)

Currently, the cost of broadcasting the Games means that networks need to invest in this market research to understand how they can best exploit their outlay. The environment in the early days of Olympic broadcasting was much simpler.

History of Olympic television coverage

Early days: 1936–56

Television cameras first captured Olympic images at the 1936 Berlin Games, when a closed circuit television system broadcast Olympic events within the Berlin city vicinity to an audience estimated at more than 162,000. It was at the next Games, not celebrated until 1948 because of the Second World War, that a financial return for broadcasts was first arranged. The BBC agreed to pay 1000 guineas to the organising committee to show events on television. 'Reports at the time indicated that the BBC later pleaded desperate poverty, but, as they were all gentlemen, when the BBC paid up the organisers never cashed the cheque' (IOC, 1998b: 25). Nevertheless, the fundamental principle of seeking broadcast rights fees was established.

At the 1952 Helsinki Games the American television network, NBC, sought to obtain exclusive coverage of the Olympics, however because of strong opposition within the broadcasting community this did not eventuate and all networks received free and equal access (Wenn, 1993).

The first live broadcast of a winter Olympics occurred at the 1956 Cortina Games. There was an interesting sidelight to this media milestone when the final torch bearer tripped over a television cable, placed on the ice surface of the Olympic stadium. He dropped and temporarily extinguished the Olympic flame. This new technology obviously still had some minor hiccups (IOC, 1998b).

On a more serious note, the Melbourne Olympics of 1956 provided a turning point in the relationship between the IOC and the media. Some members of the IOC had already recognised the potential financial windfall that television rights could provide. However, there was debate within the organisation on whether such an initiative was in keeping with the Olympic ethos, because of the possible taint of commercialism. The IOC President, Avery Brundage, an apostle of the amateur ethos, was sceptical of becoming involved with marketing television rights; however, other Olympic officials took a more pragmatic approach.

The 1956 Melbourne Organising Committee had begun discussions with NBC in 1954, regarding potential television rights; however the US network was not particularly interested. Australia's location meant that broadcasting to its American audience would not be easy and there would be a large time lag between the events and their coverage. This era was before the advent of satellite television, so all footage would have to be flown (rather than beamed as it is now) to the USA. Following NBC's rejection a tentative agreement for exclusive film rights was reached with a London firm, Associated Rediffusion. As with the previous Olympics this proposal caused controversy.

The television networks argued that the Games were a news event, rather than entertainment (unlike the recent Emmy awards categorisation) and, as such, should be available free of charge to all broadcasters. They requested nine minutes of free coverage every day (Wenn, 1993). This was not acceptable to the Melbourne Organising Committee, which argued in turn that such an understanding would be detrimental to the potential sale of an official Olympic film. Negotiations between the television networks and the Organising Committee broke down and, as a result, the networks boycotted the Games. Consequently, there was only limited television coverage of the Melbourne Games overseas.

IOC involvement, 1958 – present

In learning from these events, the IOC took a more proactive stance before the next Games and formalised its broadcasting procedures. In 1958, Rule 49 of the *Olympic Charter* was altered to allow the television rights to be negotiated by each organising committee. At this time the IOC did not receive the resultant revenue; however, perhaps this new approach was precipitated by the fact that it was not until the 1960s that the IOC had begun to accurately realise the economic potential of television. The first sign of this growth occurred in 1960, when broadcast rights of the Rome Olympics were sold to the American ABC group for US$4 million.

Despite the realisation of the potential pot of gold to be gained from television, not everyone in the IOC executive was in favour of wholeheartedly embracing this new source of revenue. Some even saw it as a potential millstone. During the 1960s, the IOC President, Avery Brundage, became increasingly less enthralled with the lobbying of the IFs and organising committees (OCOGs) to increase their share of the potential windfall. Consequently, in an effort to satisfy all partners, in 1966, the IOC devised a new television revenue sharing formula, known as the 'Rome Formula' (Wenn, 1995).

This revised allocation of money to the IFs and OCOGs did not satisfy their demands. Be that as it may, on this point, as with so many others, Brundage refused to negotiate. Wenn (1995) argues that he adopted a non-conciliatory approach for two reasons: he believed that the sporting bodies might expend the money in a way that might be to the detriment of the IOC and also that future OCOGs would need this large cash infusion in order to stage the Games effectively.

Brundage's strategy was, however, flawed. In a move to circumvent the 'Rome Formula' ruling, OCOGs began to negotiate separate 'technical services' contracts with television networks to increase their share of revenue. In 1969, the Munich Organising Committee led the way when it signed a tentative contract for US$13.5 million with ABC for the US television rights. Only US$7.5 million of this was designated as a rights payment. The rest was allocated to the OCOG as recompense for its technical services, such as installations and facilities (Wenn, 1995).

Bitter negotiations between Willi Daume, the Munich Organising Committee's President, and the IOC Finance Committee, resulted in a compromise which greatly reduced Munich's portion of the money. Yet another media precedent had been set and, accordingly, this practice of separate media contracts continued. For example, for the 1996 Games, the Atlanta Organising Committee signed a technical services contract of US$5 million with the European Broadcasting Union in addition to the broadcast rights agreement (De Moragas *et al.*, 1995: 21).

Technological advances

The escalation of the television revenue rights for the Olympic Games is, in many ways, directly related to advances in broadcast technology which have enabled the Olympic Games to be seen by more of the world's population. For example, in 1960 the Olympics were able to be televised live to 18 European cities and shown hours later in Japan and North America (IOC, 1998a).

Some key improvements which have been critical to increasing the Olympic television audience include the advent of satellite broadcasts (first used in the Olympics in 1964) and the introduction of colour television, initially used in Olympic broadcasts in 1972. Other, smaller, but nevertheless important technological advances, which have enhanced the appeal of Games broadcasts, include slow motion replays and small cameras (cams) placed in key positions at events. Also, in 1972, it was decided that no final was to overlap another, giving broadcasters the opportunity to broadcast live all medals being won if they so chose (IOC, 1998a).

These television advances, in turn, led to increased commercialisation in the Olympic Games and a concomitant diminution in the belief in the sanctity of the amateur ethos that had dominated the philosophical platform of the Games since their revival. Stephen Wenn argues that there were three main causes for the advent of the interdependence between the commodification of the Games and Avery Brundage's failure to control the Olympics to maintain his idealised amateur version of the Olympics:

> First, international athletes who discovered that sports equipment manufacturers were willing to supply them with funds for services rendered (with the display of their brand name equipment to a worldwide service). ... Second, Brundage's colleagues ... coveted commercial television revenue. They believed that the money would assist the IOC in executing its mandate to spread the Olympic message throughout the world. ... Third, Brundage had few options in his quest to temper the financial ambitions of the IFs, NOCs and representatives of the Organising Committees. ... It was predictable that the Organizing Committees would attempt to maximize their share of the income. (Wenn, 1995: 14).

Following Brundage's resignation and Lord Killanin's election as President of the IOC in 1972, the organisation became increasingly reliant on television revenue. In 1974, when the IOC received 98 per cent of its income from television it formed a Television Subcommittee, to which it appointed representatives from the media. This has evolved to become the Radio and Television Commission which currently has 12 of its 20 members drawn from the ranks of the media.

Record audiences

In 1984, for the Los Angeles Olympics, 156 nations acquired the broadcast rights, resulting in an estimated 2.5 billion viewers worldwide. The continuing technological progression of the medium resulted in the introduction of the 'super slo-mo' and the multilateral picture during these Games (IOC, 1998a).

Television audience interest in the Games has continued to increase since its modest 1936 debut. During the 1992 Barcelona Games the major broadcasters were showing about 17 hours of Olympic coverage per day. It was estimated that the typical viewer watched the Games an average of 11 times (IOC, 1998a).

The 1998 Nagano Winter Olympics set a new record for the number of countries televising the Games and the cumulative global audience equalled Lillehammer's 10.7 billion viewers, despite the time zone differences for the advantageous markets of Europe and North America. The most significant increase in audience numbers understandably was in the Asia-Pacific region, where there were smaller time differences. For example, in Australia, the cumulative audience increased by 90 per cent, to an estimated 40 million viewers (IOC, 1998b).

As a result of increases in the revenue needed to secure broadcasting rights some television networks, realising that they do not have the financial resources to bid alone, have formed alliances or unions to secure Olympic coverage. Other, smaller networks which do not have the funds to bid, do not even bother to try. This tends to limit the field of Olympic television networks to the larger, more traditional broadcast companies and continues and strengthens the hegemonic Olympic broadcasts suggested in Herman and Chomsky's propaganda model.

When networks from smaller or poorer regions are successful in gaining television rights to the Games they are often subject to financial and human resource limitations. These affect the means, if any, by which they can customise their broadcasts to suit their particular audience. They may not be able to afford to supplement the host feed, or indeed even be able to send personnel to cover the Games, once again resulting in a mainstream homogenised broadcast.

While these and other constraints are a direct consequence of IOC policy there is also a concurrent realisation within the Olympic Movement that its continued success is dependent on its ability to reach the widest possible audience. Consequently, for the Sydney 2000 Games, the IOC chose the European Broadcasting Union (EBU) as the European rights holder, despite the fact that Rupert Murdoch's Sky Channel had bid at a higher price. The rationale for the decision was that the EBU could reach a larger audience, as Sky Channel is a subscription network, while the EBU is a free to air broadcaster.

Similarly, to increase interest in the Winter Games in parts of the world that do not traditionally compete, or have the resources to bid for broadcasts, the IOC reached an agreement with Canal France International (CFI) to broadcast the 2006 Turin Winter Olympic Games in up to 40 sub-Saharan African countries. The viewers saw a daily broadcast (including a daily highlights package, the Closing Ceremony, an end-of-Games highlights programme and the IOC's global promotional campaign, *Celebrate Humanity*), tailor-made for the region and available to broadcasters free of rights. The Torino Olympic Broadcasting Organisation (TOBO) produced the programming and provided English commentary, while CFI provided French commentary and the distribution of the signal. While these are encouraging examples of the IOC's willingness to follow its dictum of reaching the widest possible audience, it is fair to say that commercial interests still rule.

A new trend has developed in the television rights bidding. Networks are now adopting a strategy of offering to purchase the rights for a package of future Olympic Games, without even knowing where all of these Games will be held. Leading this new strategy has been the US broadcaster NBC, which in August 1995, contracted to pay US$1.25 billion for the US rights to the 2000 Summer Games in Sydney and the 2002 Winter Games in Salt Lake City. NBC renegotiated this contract only three months later when it offered US$3.55 billion for these Games plus the Summer Games of 2004 and 2008 and the Winter Games of 2006, a total of five Olympics. In 2003 it secured the contracts for the 2010 and 2012 Games for US$2.2 billion (US$820 million for the 2010 Winter Games and US$1.181 billion for the 2012 Olympics). Additionally, General Electric (which owns NBC) will also pay between US$160–200 million to join the TOP programme for two Olympiads.

The Athens 2004 Olympic Games set further record levels for dedicated coverage and global audience. Details of broadcasting organisations and rights fees are shown in Table 7.3. More than 300 television channels provided 35,000 hours of dedicated Olympic Games coverage (a 27 per cent increase over Sydney 2000) over 17 days. It delivered images to an unduplicated audience of 3.9 billion people (beating the previous record of 3.6 billion viewers for the 2000 Sydney Olympics) in 220 countries and territories. There was an increase in live and prime-time Olympic coverage and a substantial increase in around-the-clock coverage in key markets. Athens Olympic Broadcasting (AOB), the host broadcaster, provided feed of 3800 hours of sport and ceremony images to Olympic broadcast partners in high definition for the first time in Olympic Games broadcasting history (IOC, 2004c; Wilson, 2004).

Host broadcasters

The task of broadcasting the Games has become far more complex since television began its Olympic association. Until 1988, the Olympic broadcaster from the host country reached an agreement with the IOC to provide coverage to all the international rights holders (De Moragas *et al.*, 1995: 21). The Seoul Olympics began

Table 7.3. Athens 2004 Olympic broadcast partners and rights fees

Country	Network	Broadcaster Rights Fee, US$ millions
United States	NBC	793
Canada	CBC	37
Latin America	OTI	17
Puerto Rico	WKAQ	1
Caribbean	CBU	0.3
Asia-Pacific	ABU	15
Japan	AOJC	155
Arab States	ASBU	5
Chinese Taipei	CTAP	4
Korea	AOKP	15
Europe	EBU	394
Australia	Seven	51
New Zealand	TVNZ	3
Africa	URTNA	N/A
South Africa	SABC	9
Supersport International	SSI	3
Total		1 503

Source: IOC 2006 Marketing Fact File

a new phase when a purpose-formed television and radio organisation, linked to the OCOG, assumed the role of host broadcaster. The latest phase, which mirrors the IOC's general 'transfer of know-how' philosophy, links a local provider with an ongoing IOC related company, Olympic Broadcasting Services (OBS). The latter is a Swiss company created by the IOC, specifically to fulfil the host broadcaster/OBO function for the Olympic Games and maintain an Olympic archival service for the rights holders.

The following figures provide some idea of the scale of organisation currently needed to broadcast an Olympic Games. In 2004 the Athens Olympic Broadcasting Organisation:

- provided 35,000 hours of live television;
- provided coverage of all 300 Olympic events;
- utilised more than 1000 cameras and 450 video-tape machines;
- employed 3700 personnel;
- worked with more than 12,000 accredited broadcast personnel.

In 2006 the Turin Olympic Broadcasting Organisation, 2006:

- provided more than 900 hours of live television coverage of Olympic events;
- provided coverage of all Olympic winter events;
- utilised more than 400 cameras and 150 video-tape machines;
- worked with more than 80 Rights Holding Broadcast Organisations.

On 6 September 2004, the Beijing Olympic Broadcasting Company (BOB) was established to broadcast the 2008 Games. It is a Sino-foreign joint venture funded by the Beijing Organising Committee for the Olympic Games (BOCOG) and Olympic Broadcasting Services (OBS). It will perform the role of Olympic Broadcasting Organization (OBO) for both the Beijing Olympic and Paralympic Games. BOB will provide international television and radio (ITVR) signals for the broadcasters across the world. It will plan, design, install, construct and operate the International Broadcast Centre (IBC) and the necessary broadcast facilities in other venues, and provide related services for the rights-holding broadcasters during the Beijing Games.

The number of media personnel covering the Olympics has grown in correlation with the increasing importance of television as the most effective medium to disseminate the Games to the world. From Barcelona onwards the total number of accredited press at the Games has exceeded the number of athletes. De Moragas *et al.* (1995: 39) see this growth of media personnel as a result of: 'the continued development of the media industry worldwide; the increased technical complexity (and thus personnel needed) to broadcast the Games; the desire of broadcasters to customise the output of their distinct audience needs; and, of course, the allure for any professional of being where the action is'.

Other major players in the broadcast of the Games include the National Olympic Committees (NOCs) and the International Sports Federations (IFs). At times these two groups have acted on behalf of athletes when broadcasters have sought to initiate changes at the Games that would be advantageous to their broadcasts and perhaps not as beneficial to the athletes. For example, networks believed that the sport of fencing would be more televisual if face masks were redesigned and the traditional white outfits were changed to colour. In Seoul, US broadcasters had requested that the timing of events be altered to capitalise on their prime time audience (De Moragas *et al.*, 1995). These requests highlight the pressures brought to bear by an interest group, whose presence is not essential for the staging of the Games, but vital to its pre-eminence in the world of sport and necessary for the economic survival of the Olympic Movement in its current form.

While television has become the most widespread medium by which people access Olympic Games information and results, other forms of communications technology are playing an increasingly important role. Currently, at the forefront of this diversification is the Internet.

The Internet

Official sites

When this chapter was written, in 2006, there were approximately 134,000,000 Olympic-related pages on the World Wide Web (twice that of 1998), and this number will keep growing.

In the twenty-first century, a crucial component of every major sporting event is its 'official' public website. This website has multiple roles and functions, including:

- an online shop for tickets and merchandise;
- a guide to the event;
- a directory for services such as transport;
- a description of the rules of the competition;

- a guide to the biographies of athletes; and
- a source of news.

From a pre-event beginning of several hundreds of pages of static text, it develops into a site with thousands of pages and real time updates during the event. Potentially, after the event, an archive of the site becomes a component of the legacy of the event and a valuable reference source for information and historical research (Halbwirth *et al.*, 2005).

Beginning with its first website in 1995, the IOC has increased and leveraged its understanding of the Internet's communication potential (IOC, 1999:1). In the world of sport, the IOC was a relatively early adopter of the Internet as a communications tool. Also in 1995, the Organizing Committee of the Olympic Games in Atlanta (ACOG) established the first individual Olympic Games website. It included data from the press guide, public information materials, competition schedules and graphics, for example, virtual tours of venues. From March 1996, the site also enabled users to purchase tickets online. This medium accounted for approximately 12 per cent of all ticket sales. While, in its early days, the site received only about 10,000 hits per day, this number had grown to 400,000 by 1996. During the 16 days of the Games, the site attracted approximately 200 million visitors, a record for that period of time. The majority of users (60 per cent) were domestic (USA) (ACOG, 1998: 106). The Atlanta Games site was designed and programmed against a tight deadline and was a bold attempt to utilize the 'new' communication channel (De Moragas Spa, 2001).

The Nagano 1998 Winter Olympic Games site was launched in November 1996 as the first official site for a winter Olympic Games. This site was tested and developed with a far more complex and permanent infrastructure than Atlanta's (Dantzig, 2002). It included a 'Kids Plaza', specifically designed for younger users, with Olympic graphics, text and games and a 'volunteer corner', 'which functioned as a forum for volunteers to exchange ideas and suggestions with each other and organizers' (Nagano Olympic Organizing Committee, 1999: 112). In total the site received 766 million hits, with 635 million of these coming during the Games (7–22 February 1998; Nagano Olympic Organizing Committee, 1999). The Nagano site was designed to accommodate cross-reference searches, with news and photos being organised on the basis of countries and athletes, as well as sports and events. The site broke two Guinness records; 'The Most Popular Internet Event Ever Recorded' and 'The Most Hits on an Internet Site in One Minute' (Dantzig, 2002). However, regardless of being labelled a technical success, with 100 per cent availability, the user-friendliness of the Nagano site could still be questioned, as the website totalled 48,493 pages of content (De Moragas Spa, 2001).

These beginnings meant that the groundwork was laid for the Sydney 2000 Olympic Games Internet site to push boundaries of Internet sites for multi-sport events even further, or, to use an Olympic metaphor, 'faster, higher, stronger'. For the IOC's technology sponsor, IBM, the Sydney 2000 website was also an expedient way to showcase its expertise in hosting high volume websites, after technology glitches had damaged its reputation at the Atlanta Games. The Sydney 2000 Games were IBM's last as a major sponsor, as its sponsorship association with the IOC ceased after these Games (Halbwirth *et al.*, 2005).

The Sydney 2000 website handled (at that time) unprecedented traffic and even today the statistics are impressive. It was not until a year later, with the events of 11 September, 2001, that the CNN website received similar levels of Internet usage. According to an IBM press release in 2000, the Sydney 2000 site received:

11.3 billion hits, a 1,700 percent increase over the Nagano Games official site in 1998. More than 8.7 million unique visitors accounted for 230 million web page views from September 13 when competition began until the closing ceremony on October 1. The majority of visitors, 62 per cent, were from countries outside the United States. (IBM, 2000)

The 2002 Salt Lake City Olympic Committee (SLOC) website, which was partnered with the NBC site, also broke new Olympic records. SLOC was the first organising committee in Olympic history to offer instant updates, with scores, images and articles through its website. The site also achieved other objectives. SLOC realised that the Internet could serve as both an operations tool and a media property. Many of the organisation's functional areas integrated SLOC's website into their operations. (Salt Lake City Olympic Committee, 2002: 252). During the Games (8–24 February), the site received 353 million unique page views. Each day some two million unique visitors logged on for real-time results, news and graphics (Salt Lake City Olympic Committee, 2002: 253).

The Athens 2004 Olympic Games website was launched in December 2003. Again the site was integrated, with live result feeds generated by the Games results system, ensuring that it was the quickest media location for access to results (within minutes of the completion of events). The site had more than 100,000 Web pages in each of its three languages (English, French and Greek), with 9000 distinct information channels for segmented audiences, more than 21,000 pieces of news, 3800 event results (contained on more than 8000 pages), 40,000 athlete biographies, more than 7500 photographs, and 45,000 static files (images and pdf files of venues etc). Users from the USA visited the site the most, followed by those from Australia, Canada, France, the United Kingdom and the host country, Greece (Vignette, 2004).

The IOC has been concerned for some time about the increasing convergence between television and the Internet and any subsequent effects that an increasing net presence might have on its broadcast rights (which are limited by geo-political region, while the Internet is not). In the late 1990s this fear reached its peak. With television rights bringing in almost half the Games operating revenue, the IOC feared the Internet could undermine its whole economic structure (Moore, 1998). As a result moving pictures were not permitted to be shown on the Internet for the 2000 Games. Michael Payne, the IOC's Marketing Manager, acknowledged that, while the Internet was a threat to its television revenue. it had potential to be an important revenue generator. He noted: 'it's a great asset for promotion. ... and there are revenue-generating aspects of it down the road' (*Sydney Morning Herald*, 1988).

The same prohibitions were still in place for the 2002 Salt Lake City Games. The IOC felt the public power of the Internet, however, when the controversy in the pairs figure skating resulted in a flood of email to its site. Additionally, many unofficial discussion forums and chat rooms were dominated by debates about the incident and its aftermath. The reactions of these posts, disseminated over the Internet, played a significant role in the IOC's move to review the judges' decision (Canton, 2006).

Thus, realising the growing power of the Internet, the IOC offered Internet licences to broadcasters who had the television rights for the 2004 Athens Games. The BBC and other European broadcasters offered simulcast coverage, while NBC offered video recap clips.

Since then, the IOC has further embraced the Internet even further, including . greater availability for its use by Olympians. Athletes in Turin had Internet access throughout their Village residences. Also, a custom network was implemented, so that broadcasters will have instant access to information via touch screens.

In 2005, Internet video streaming and wireless rights had formed part of the negotiations for Olympic broadcast rights for the Beijing (2008) and Vancouver 2010 Games. This raises an issue which the IOC may have not yet fully grasped. As the broadcast rights licences for Beijing and Vancouver were negotiated in 2005, by the time of the Vancouver Games broadcasters will be bound to a licence agreement that is five years old. In terms of the Internet, five years is an eternity (Canton, 2006). For example, in the five years since the Turin licence was negotiated, wireless video and podcasting have greatly altered the Internet field.

Internet newsgroups

As well as providing Olympic results and information, as evidenced by the 2002 figure skating controversy, the net provides another, more interactive format. Discussion, interest and news groups permit subscribers to communicate with other fans on sports-related topics. One such newsgroup is *www.rec.sport.olympics*, which caters for those interested in the Olympic Games. A study by Toohey and Warning in 1998 specifically analysed its content over the month of July, 1996, the month in which the Atlanta Games began. For the period of analysis all postings were recorded. The most prolific thread (i.e. series of correspondences) was one which began from a posting that expressed an opinion that the Chinese contingent was being treated unfairly by the media, especially regarding the underlying assumption of their use of drugs: *'Then why are Chinese athletics* [sic] *continuously being ridiculed, being hound* [sic] *after. I will tell you why. It is racially motivated hate to cause distraction and frustration and you know how damaging that can be for top rank athletics* [sic]*'*. This thread contained 347 postings, representing approximately 1.3 per cent of all the *rec.sport.olympics* postings during the period. The thread was then chosen for an in-depth analysis to identify and trace the discussion that this topic generated.

'Posters' with opposing viewpoints were often dismissed and vilified by 'flaming' (abusive criticism of the previous poster's comments), often with a personal attack on the poster's character. For example: *'Oh, you just pulled this one out of your ass? I understand. Typical'* (19: 26); and *' ... You could have snipped your own. In any case, yours is the sort of nonsensical excuse with which cheaters face themselves in the mirror in the first place'* (Toohey and Warning, 1998: 10). The thread developed into a series of sub-topics all related to the original posting. These threads and their relative weights are listed in Table 7.4.

Newsgroups make this type of behaviour expedient, as correspondents are physically separated. Also, posters can remain anonymous by adopting pseudonyms and concealing their actual Internet addresses. The level of controversy of the topic being discussed is also related to the incidence of flaming. Interestingly, the percentage of flames in this study was significantly higher than the results of a content analyses of two fitness-related newsgroups (Toohey and Warning, 1998).

There were few, if any, examples of posters changing their original positions regarding the Chinese swimmers on the basis of arguments presented by other correspondents. The ethical, philosophical and national divides that were evident at the beginning of the survey period intensified over the month studied, despite the chance to communicate and exchange ideas.

Table 7.4. The development of the thread

	Postings	
Topic	No.	%
Professionalism	15	4.3
Performance	15	4.3
Racism	46	13.3
Media	55	15.9
Gymnastics	16	4.6
Politics	13	3.7
Table tennis	10	2.9
Drugs	101	29.1
Drugs in swimming	32	9.2
Netiquette	33	9.5
Other	11	3.2
Total	347	100

Source: Toohey and Warning, 1998

The dynamics displayed by the posters on *rec.sport.olympics* epitomises the passion that the Olympic Games evoke in many people. It also reflects the inevitability that the nexus between politics (which underpinned many of the posters' viewpoints) and the Games are enduring, with little likelihood of diminishing. It may be that the Internet actually exacerbates such political discord, rather than mollifying it. As the net becomes increasingly a part of the Olympic media, then this possibility will amplify and be beyond the influence of the existing media moguls. The term 'Olympic flame' has now taken on a whole new meaning.

With the ever increasing media coverage of the Olympic Games and its availability to more of the world's population, first through the advent of satellite television and now more interactively through the Internet and in the future through third generation mobile technology, the Games have become a potent mechanism for individuals with no affiliation to the Olympics whatsoever to draw attention to issues which may also be essentially unrelated to the Olympic Movement, but vital to themselves.

Rec.sport.olympics is beyond the control of the IOC, however the effects of this and similar discussion groups may have a significant impact on the Olympics in the future, as was evidenced through the Salt Lake City experience. The final word on the possibility on constructive international dialogue through *rec.sport.olympics* comes from one of the participants who conducted his own survey of the thread:

After reading postings, there is a survey of the quality of the discussions I made:
1) 'Everybody is a racist to everybody';
2) 'I am not living in a racist country';
3) 'Doping is OK because others have done it';
4) 'It is not doping because it is not in the rules';
5) 'I am a fidel citizen, so the others are wrong';
6) 'You are a fidel citizen so you are wrong';
7) 'My country's human rights report card is better than yours';
8) 'My father is stronger than yours';
9) etc...[sic]   (Toohey and Warning, 1998: 12).

Radio

While radio has played a significant role in the development of twentieth century sport generally, its influence on the Olympic Games has been far less consequential than television.

> The four year intervals of the Olympiad did not coincide with radio's great technical improvements. Radio and the Olympic Games did not synchronize. When radio broadcasting had finally achieved a technical level at which it could provide live accounts of the Games, television was already making its appearance. (Beezley, cited in McCoy, 1997: 20)

Radio began its public broadcasts on a notable scale in the early 1920s, so that the 1924 Paris Games were the first Olympics for which large scale radio broadcasts were technically feasible. Despite this, these Games and also the following Olympics, held in Amsterdam in 1928, received scant radio coverage in the major English-speaking countries. Possible explanations for this lack of interest could be that, at this time, it would have been difficult to broadcast live outside the host country, as there were no international regulations or conformity regarding the allocation of wavelengths to radio stations. Additionally, trans-oceanic transmissions were yet to be perfected (McCoy, 1997).

The next Olympics, the 1932 Los Angeles Games, theoretically opened a window of opportunity for radio broadcasters to reach the large and influential American audience. Yet, even as this window opened, it was promptly snapped shut and the shutters boarded by Games organisers and their influential film-producing neighbours in Hollywood. Both of these powerful groups believed that radio broadcasts of sporting events were counterproductive to their most profitable revenue source – the spectators. They argued that radio had the potential to keep their paying customers at home, glued to their crystal sets, rather than placing their 'bums on seats' either at Olympic events or at the movie houses. Consequently, the radio coverage of these Games was limited to short summaries of results, broadcast late at night, after the prime-time programmes. The notion of seeking sponsorship and air time advertising during Olympic broadcasts was obviously not the economic force that it became by the end of the twentieth century.

The 1936 Berlin Olympic Games provided a greatly improved radio service.

> With renowned German efficiency, technicians created an elaborate short wave system which reached 40 countries during the Games. However the German Olympic Organizing Committee also issued guidelines for radio commentators and newspaper journalists, *General Rules and Regulations for the Printed Press and Radio*, which directed announcers and reporters to restrict their comments to Olympic events and travel appreciation, with no mention of the political, and especially religious issues in Germany. (McCoy, 1997: 23)

Ironically, at these Games, as Olympic radio coverage was reaching its zenith, its ultimate media competitor, television, was launching its Olympic association. World politics, in the form of the Second World War, was also destined to play a pivotal role in radio's decline as the broadcast medium of choice for the Olympic Games. During the hiatus between these and the next Games, not celebrated until 1948, commercial and government television broadcasts had begun in many countries. None the less, radio still provided the major source of media coverage in London in 1948, when the host broadcaster, the BBC, provided commentary in 40 languages. While this was an improved service it was not always appreciated. For example, Australians were disappointed in the British broadcaster's lack of coverage of their nation's athletes. Consequently they sent their own commentator to the next Games, in Helsinki in 1952.

These Games, and those following, in Melbourne in 1956, flagged the last two Games where radio coverage outperformed its visual rival. Since this time, while there has been a radio presence at the Games, it has become a poor cousin to television. 'The pageantry, spectacle and athletic contests make the Olympics a visual event – ideal for the age of television. The timing of technological advances and world hostilities meant that radio never quite became the medium of the Olympic Games' (McCoy, 1997: 25).

Film

To date there have been over 100 motion pictures made about the Olympic Games in a number of genres, the most popular form being the documentary.

There is no known extant film of the 1896 Athens Games; however, since that time, there have been visual recordings taken at each Games. The first feature length film about the Olympic Games was based on the 1924 Paris Summer Games and was produced by the Rapid Film Company.

Leni Reifenstahl's account of the 1936 Berlin Olympics, *Olympia*, commissioned by the Nazi government, is considered by many to be the most consequential sporting film ever made. The final version, 225 minutes long, was divided into two parts; the *Festival of the Nations* and the *Festival of Beauty*. While this film's purpose was to highlight Nazi efficiency and Aryan supremacy at the Games, it has also been recognised and revered as an 'art' film and, remarkably, this appeal has endured to the present. For its time it was also inventive in its techniques.

> Riefenstahl used more than 150 borrowed military troops to shoot 1.4 million feet of film. She also introduced a number of innovative cinematographic notions to highlight the dramatic impact of her work. She mounted cameras on rails to follow the sprints, placed them on horses to cover the equestrian events and installed them in tethered balloons in an attempt to shoot overhead views. To film swimming and diving events, photographers would jump into the water with a camera to follow the action in a attempt to shoot overhead views. To film swimming and diving events, photographers would jump into the water with a camera to follow the action. (Crawford, 1996: 406)

Other Olympic documentaries, while not as consequential, have also received a degree of critical acclaim. Director Kon Ichiwaka's *Tokyo Olympiad*, David Wolper's *Visions of 8* (based on the 1972 Munich Games) and Bud Greenspan's *16 Days of Glory* series stand out as making significant contributions to the popular acceptance of such 'infotainment' style films.

Less successful in the public arena have been the majority of those feature movies which use the Olympics as a theme in their storyline. Arguably, the one great exception to this was the 1992 Academy Award winner, *Chariots of Fire*. Set in Cambridge University, England and later at the 1924 Paris Olympic Games. It follows the fortunes of two British athletes, one Jewish (Harold Abrahams) and one a Scottish Congregationalist (Eric Liddell). The film 'to a great extent recreated the flavour and substance of the lifestyles, the ethos of Cambridge, the aristocratic administration of British Track and Field and the events of the 1924 Olympics' (Crawford, 1996: 406). It also highlighted religious and racial relationships with sport, the Olympic Games and the classed-based English society of that period.

The majority of these feature films of the Olympics have been neither commercial or critical successes. There is a certain irony to this, considering the successes of television broadcasts of the Games which have deliberately deviated from pure sports coverage to create a storyline. This formula, of transforming the Olympics from a sporting event to a story, complete with actors, has been highly workable on the small screen. Yet films which base their storylines around the Olympic Games and its sporting aspects appear, literally and figuratively, to 'lose the plot'.

In what is reminiscent of a reversion to the early days of films as the visual medium used to record the images of the Games and then being shown to a paying audience, a new variation on this approach was used to record the 1998 Nagano Winter Games. The IOC licensed a production of a 70mm-IMAX or Large Format Film, which premiered in November, 1998. With the working title of *Olympic Glory* the film was co-produced by EMC Films and Frank Marshall and Kathleen Kennedy, two Hollywood producers whose past film credits include *E.T.*, *Jurassic Park* and *The Color Purple*. It was directed by Keith Merrill, an Oscar winning documentary maker. The script was written by the Australian author, Tom Keneally (IOC, 1998b).

In 1995 the IOC established the Olympic Television Archive Bureau (OTAB) to manage and market its film, television and newsreel Archive, provide rapid fulfilment of Olympic footage clips, as well as administer related licensing procedures. The Archive, managed by Trans World International (TWI), now has over 20,000 hours of film, television and newsreel material dating back to the turn of the twentieth century, with additional material added regularly. Through OTAB, over 100 hours of Olympic Programming, under the title, 'The Olympic Series', is available. The series includes both Summer and Winter Olympic Games, chronicling athletic achievements, as well as human interest aspects.

Olympic-related novels

The Olympic Games, ancient and modern, have also provided a theme for novelists. A number of novels have been published, including:

- *The Games*, by Hughe Atkinson (London: Cassell, 1967)
- *Rainbow Six,* by Tom Clancy (New York: G.P. Putnam Sons, 1988)
- *Five Ring Circus*, by Jon Cleary (London: HarperColllins, 1998)
- *The Games*, by Peter deVries (Newtown, NSW: Zaresky Press, 2002)
- *Games*, by Frances Edmonds (London: Orion, 1997)
- *Olympiad: An Historical Novel*, by Tom Holt (London: Abacus, 2001)
- *Goldengirl*, by Peter Lovesey (New York: Severn House, 2002 – first published 1977 under the pseudonym Peter Lear)
- *The Bomber*, by Liza Marklund (New York: Simon and Schuster, 2003)
- *Not for Glory, Not for Gold,* by Keith Miles (London: Century, 1986
- *Five Ring Circus,* by Joel Rubenstein (Australia: Kirby Books, 2000)

Conclusion

Historically, television rights have provided the IOC with a large percentage of its revenue and have been primarily responsible for the growth of the Olympic Movement. Although recently this percentage has diminished (from 95 per cent in 1980 to under 50 per cent currently), the absolute amount received by the IOC from this source has increased greatly. Agreements totalling more than US$10 billion have been arranged between the IOC and television broadcasters for the time period 1984 until 2008. From 2004, Olympic Organising Committees have received a smaller share of these profits, down from 60 per cent to 49 per cent.

In terms of analysing the effect of Olympic broadcasts, perhaps broadcast content is neither the most fruitful nor indeed the most appropriate source to tap when trying to decode Olympic media meanings. It is important to acknowledge that audiences are not entirely passive. It may be that it is their input, influenced by cues external to the Olympics, that provides the conclusive, multi-faceted and ultimate meanings to Olympic messages.

Like many other aspects of the Games its media relationships have room to improve, to search for democratisation, equality and the values the Olympics espouses. While 'faster, higher, stronger' may apply to the strength of transmission signals emanating from the venues, the messages these signals convey have, at times, malfunctioned in terms of their synchronicity with the ethos of the Games.

Further reading

The Olympics and television	De Moragas *et al.* (1995); Rivenburgh (2004)
IOC media guidelines for Athens	http://multimedia.olympic.org/pdf/en_report_612.pdf
Sport and the media generally	Bernstein and Blain (2003)
Sporting websites	Halbwirth *et al.* (2005)
Film	Crawford (1996); Fuller (1996)
Radio	McCoy (1997)

Questions

1. Should the International Olympic Committee change its Internet broadcasting rules to allow greater access to the Games? How will this impact on revenue?
2. Should the IOC stipulate that broadcasters give equal time to male and female athletes on television broadcasts? Why or why not?
3. What do you think makes a good Olympic television broadcast? Is it the sport, the achievement of your national athletes, or other factors?

Chapter 8

Doping and the Olympics

> Doping is cheating. Doping is akin to death. Death physiologically by profoundly altering, sometimes irreversibly, normal processes through unjustified manipulations. Death physically, as certain tragic cases in recent years have shown. But also death spiritually and intellectually, by agreeing to cheat and conceal one's capabilities, by recognising one's incapacity or unwillingness to accept one's self, or to transcend one's limits. And finally death morally, by excluding oneself de facto from the rules of conduct required by all human society. Juan Antonio Samaranch (n.d.)

Introduction

The issue of doping in sport is more than a question of whether drugs are harmful, it is ultimately an ethical one, as the use of drugs involves seeking an unfair advantage over rivals. This contravenes the philosophy of Olympism and, as such, has special resonance for Olympic authorities. Despite its currency as one of the greatest issues facing élite sport, and as a problem that erodes the honesty of sport, it is not a new phenomenon.

There is written evidence that athletes have ingested performance-enhancing substances since the time of the Ancient Greeks. While these may not have been illegal, unnatural, or outside the spirit of contest, the aim was to improve chances of victory. Wrestlers were known to have eaten ten pounds of meat per day in the belief that it would increase their strength. Long-distance runners of the same era credited sesame seeds with the ability to increase their endurance (Goldman and Klatz, 1992). Human competitors were not the only ones to receive such boosts. Olympic horse trainers administered 'hydromel', a mixture of oats, honey and water, to their animals in an effort to increase their staying power. Over 2000 years later athletes are still seeking substance-assisted advantages over their rivals. In a survey of American athletes who were questioned on whether they would take a performance-enhancing substance if it allowed them to win all competitions they entered for five years but then kill them, over 50 per cent said they would take the drug (Parisotto, 2006).

In 1865, Dutch canal swimmers were reported to be using performance-enhancing drugs. In the next decade so too were six day cyclists. Their coaches were giving them a mixture of heroin and cocaine. The first reported death of a cyclist from doping was recorded in 1886, when Arthur Linton died from an overdose of the stimulant trimethyl (Parisotto, 2006). 'Drug taking in sports cropped up repeatedly through the end of the nineteenth century. ... the Belgians were said to be taking sugar tablets soaked in ether, the French to be taking caffeine tablets, the British to be breathing oxygen and taking cocaine, heroin, strychnine and brandy' (Goldman and Klatz, 1992: 30).

Since then an increasing array of concoctions has been trialled by athletes with varying success. While some of these potions, for example the mixture of brandy and strychnine, may have been of questionable performance-enhancing value, especially when compared to their detrimental physiological effects, their psychological benefits may have resulted in improved performances.

According to Rofe and Ordway (1998: 1–2): 'the alteration of the athlete's diet to attain peak fitness remains an essential part of their routine....At some point in history, however, society decided that a line had to be drawn between those substances that were "fair" and those that gave the athlete an "unfair" advantage'. Thus, in 1928 the International Amateur Athletic Federation (IAAF) became the first international sport federation (IF) to ban the use of doping (use of a stimulating substance). In 1966 the UCI (cycling) and FIFA (football) were among the first IFs to introduce drug tests in their world championships. Most other IFs introduced drug testing by the 1970s.

In 1967 the International Olympic Committee (IOC) constituted its Medical Commission and set up its first list of prohibited substances. The first Olympic drug tests were carried out in 1968 at the Olympic Winter Games in Grenoble and the Summer Games in Mexico City.

Since that time, the problem of cheating through doping has not been ignored, although the efforts of sports authorities have been criticised. One of the reasons why it has been difficult to contain the problem is explained by Robin Parisotto, a former employee of the Australian Institute of Sport, who observes that:

> over the last 50 years, we have witnessed nothing short of a revolution in cheating and doping methodology. The nexus between sport, big business and government has become so confused and the interpretations of the Olympic ideals so twisted that countries have resorted to extraordinary measures, taking matters into their own hands, going so far as creating and implementing sophisticated drugs programs for dubious political gain. (Parisotto, 2006: 13)

Today, many people believe that some performance-enhancing substances used in sport are undetectable using the testing methods chosen by authorities. Writers such as Andrew Jennings and Parisotto are critical of the IOC, which has not always used the latest testing methods available. Drug testers are invariably in a 'catch up' situation. There is a lag between the introduction of a new drug and the development of tests to detect it. With the commercial and political pressures on athletes to succeed, the pressures on talented sportsmen and women to take drugs which will give them a competitive edge are not currently being dismissed as inconsequential. In the period leading up to, until the conclusion of, the Athens 2004 Olympic Games, 3000 drug tests were conducted. Twenty-three athletes tested positive to banned substances. This is the largest number for any Olympic Games to date. Does this mean that illegal drug use is increasing or that the testing was conducted in a time frame where the methods of detection were adequate for all the drugs being used?

Whatever the reason for the high number of positive results, cheating by doping goes against the core of Olympic philosophy of Olympism. Since the leaders of the Olympic Movement espouse this philosophy and condemn doping in sport, they need to be, and be seen to be, continuously proactive in working with scientists and drug testing authorities, in their attempts to eradicate drug use. The Olympic Movement is inexorably linked to the problem of drug use in sport, because of the national prestige and financial success that comes from an Olympic victory. It follows that it should be part of the solution, but the reluctance of the Olympic Movement to embrace all means at its disposal to catch drug cheats has been part of the reason for much of the recent criticism directed at it.

This chapter deals with a general overview of the issue of doping and the Olympic Movement. The first sections give some further background into some of the drugs that have been used in sport. This is followed by an examination of some of the ethical implications of drug use. Later sections provide a history of doping. Finally, possible future scenarios are discussed.

Some modern performance-enhancing substances

Anabolic steroids

Anabolic steroids were originally developed in the 1930s to assist cancer patients and the victims of starvation and for hormonal disorders and repair of muscle tissue. They are derived from the male hormone testosterone. Laura and White (1991) suggest that the Nazis may have been the first to pioneer their non-medical use, when they were issued to soldiers during World War II in order to make them more aggressive and also to facilitate their recuperation after injury. After the introduction of drug testing at the Olympics, the use of steroids by athletes increased, as they were initially more difficult to detect than amphetamines. Since 1974 the IOC has tested their presence by gas chromatography. Currently, there are more than 100 different types of anabolic steroids. They may have a number of negative side effects, which have been widely documented. These include liver cancer and other liver ailments. For males there may be a reduction in testicular size, decrease in sperm production, and loss of libido. Women may be masculinised by the drug in a number of ways, including an increase in facial hair, lowering of the voice and enlargement of the clitoris.

Anabolic steroids can be taken orally, injected intramuscularly, or rubbed on the skin as a gel or cream. They may be taken in patterns called cycling, that is, taking multiple doses over a specific period of time, stopping for a period, and restarting. Users may combine several different types of steroids. This is known as stacking. Pyramiding occurs when users slowly escalate their steroid use by increasing the number of drugs used at one time and/or the dose and frequency of one or more steroids. They reach a peak amount at mid-cycle and gradually taper the dose toward the end of the cycle (ONDCP, 2005: 1).

When the IOC Medical Commission had the lead role in policing doping in the Games it specified a testosterone ratio in urine of greater than 6:1 as an offence under its ruling (Bilder n.d.), unless there was proof that a larger ratio was the result of a physiological or pathological condition. In 1999 the American runner Dennis Reynolds used this as a defence for his positive result. He claimed that he had sex four times the night before his sample was taken and drunk four bottles of beer, resulting in a natural increase in his hormone levels.

Human growth hormone

Human growth hormone (hGH) was originally designed and developed to combat dwarfism and other growth deficiencies in children. Derived from the urine of pregnant women, the drug stimulates muscular development by facilitating the production of the male hormone, testosterone (Laura and White, 1991). While the increased testosterone levels can increase an adult's size (by elongating the long bones) and strength it may have a number of debilitating side-effects, such as 'diabetes, hepatitis, and acromegaly, a disorder of the pituitary associated with enlarged hands and feet, thickened lips and tongue, and facial distortions, including a jutting lower jaw' (Laura and White, 1991: 8).

As athletes use hGH to increase their size and strength, its consumption is primarily located in sports and events which require these attributes, for example, track and field. Interestingly, because of its source, when male users are drug tested they will return a positive result for pregnancy. As hGH occurs naturally in the body, it is hard to distinguish between what is produced naturally and what is an administered dose. 'It is almost impossible to set a blood level of hGH that would be considered unnaturally high and indicative of doping, because levels of naturally-occurring hGH can vary by more than 100-fold in response to factors such as nutritional state, sleep and exercise' (Fordyce, 2003: 1). Athletes at the 2004 Athens Games were the first to have their blood collected for hGH testing.

Drug cheats are always trying to stay one step ahead of the testers. To date, many of them have been quite successful, switching to a new substance once a test has been developed to combat the use of a particular drug. For example, once the IOC had developed a test to detect steroids then some athletes began injecting testosterone (Laura and White, 1991).

Blood doping

Another performance-enhancing option, developed in the 1970s, was blood doping. This technique involves blood being extracted from an athlete, preserved by freezing and then injected back into the athlete before competition, thus increasing the athlete's oxygen capacity by up to 20 per cent (Laura and White, 1991).

While it has never been proven definitively, it was widely rumoured that Lasse Viren, winner of the 5,000 metres and 10,000 metres at the 1976 Montréal Olympic Games, utilised this technique, as did the 1984 US cycling team. More recently there have been accusations that winter Olympians have been using this procedure.

Blood doping was officially banned in 1985 and a test developed to detect its use. However, as a result of this ability to detect blood doping, a new substance, a recombinant human growth hormone, erythropoietin (EPO), was introduced to the drug users' arsenal.

Erythropoietin

Erythropoietin, known as EPO, is a recombinant human protein that dramatically increases aerobic capacity. A naturally occurring hormone, it achieves its effects by stimulating the production of red blood cells that transport oxygen around the body. Thus it serves a similar function to blood doping.

In its natural form it is a colourless hormone produced by the kidneys which stimulates bone marrow to produce new red blood cells (Vamakaris, 1997). When it first became available in 1988 its intended clientele were kidney patients and individuals suffering from chronic anaemia. Artificial EPO was developed to assist these individuals to obtain normal EPO levels.

The drug emerged in the late 1980s and has 'caused as many deaths as all the steroids and stimulants' (Parisotto, 2006: 23). These deaths occurred because EPO thickens the blood, which can result in a stroke or heart attack. Until 2000 it was thought that use of the drug was undetectable. EPO is believed to be widely used in sport and to give a significant advantage to athletes in endurance sports, such as road cycling, cross-country skiing and distance running. 'With one injection, or a series of injections, an automatic improvement in the stimulation of oxygen rich blood cells is generated. It replaces weeks of altitude training and makes blood doping seem cumbersome' (Vamakaris, 1997: 36).

EPO was included in the IOC's list of prohibited substances in 1990; however the fight against EPO was long hampered by the lack of a reliable testing method. The nearest to a reliable and valid test to detect its use was achieved by measuring an athlete's haematocrit levels.

In 1997 blood testing was introduced into professional cycling to combat the growing catastrophe of cyclists' deaths caused by the use of EPO. These tests were not definitive in proving that an athlete has taken EPO, however, athletes who registered a haematocrit haemoglobin level higher than 50 per cent for men and 47 for women were suspended in the interests of their health. This was regarded as a 'health test' rather than a 'drug test'. Athletes 'were suspended for two weeks or until such time that they could show their blood levels were back below the limits. This wasn't a penalty. ... It did nothing to stop the cheats' (Parisotto, 2006: 42). The challenge for the testers was to be able to distinguish the artificial addition from an athlete's natural production of the hormone. The IOC allowed the International Ski Federation to conduct these tests during the Nagano Olympics. A breakthrough occurred when an EPO detection test, based on a combination of blood and urine analysis, was first implemented at the Sydney Olympic Games in 2000.

Bromantan

Five athletes tested positive for this substance at the 1996 Atlanta Games, however the results were overturned by the Court of Arbitration for Sport 'because the drug was too new; there was insufficient data, scientific knowledge, and scientific literature available to enforce the ban' (Kammerer, 2001: 15). It was originally used by the Soviet Army as a stimulant and for its thermoprotective effects. Similar to Mesocarb, it is a psychostimulant. Its properties are similar to amphetamines and thus designed to increase mental and/or physical performances of users (*Africa News*, 1996a).

Tetrahydrogestrinone

The latest drug to cause a scandal in sport is tetrahydrogestrinone, also known as THG, or 'the clear', because athletes had thought it undetectable. It is a synthetically produced steroid, closely related to a previously banned substance, gestrinone. In 2003 a test was developed to detect its use and many élite athletes, unaware of the breakthrough, were caught in the testers' net. However, while sports authorities were hailing their victory there were critics who questioned both THG's performance-enhancing qualities and the authorities' haste in punishing athletes for its use (Rasmussen, 2005). This raises further questions regarding the ethics of using and testing for performance-enhancing substances.

Arguments for and against drug use

Doping contravenes the ethics of both sport and medical science. Doping consists of: the administration of substances belonging to the prohibited classes of pharmacological agents; and/or the use of various prohibited methods (IOC, 1996a: 4).

The word 'doping' is a derivative of the Dutch word 'dop'. It first appeared in an English dictionary in 1889, where it was described as a narcotic opium mixture used in horse racing (Goldman and Klatz, 1992). By the 1930s doping was included in a number of dictionaries. More disturbing than this literary spread of the word, was its literal use in sport. The problem was so great in sport in the first three decades of the twentieth century that, at the 1933 German Swimming Federation annual general meeting, Dr Otto Reissner stated: 'we all know that sporting competitions are often more a matter of doping than training. It is highly regrettable that those who are in charge of supervising sport seem to lack the energy to campaign against this evil' (quoted in Reiterer, 2000: 73).

There are cogent arguments both for and against drug use in sport. Their adherents can present each case eloquently and often quite rationally, so it is primarily an individual's own value system that will decide whether or not performance-enhancing drugs should be allowed in sport. It is a question that athletes today have to answer, although in the past some Eastern bloc athletes and others had little say or, indeed, knowledge about the drugs they were given by their own coaches, officials and team doctors. This systemic doping is still a current dilemma. In the 1990s it was acknowledged that various Chinese swimmers were given steroids routinely by their coaches. Some of these discredited Chinese coaches had previously been employed in East Germany before moving to China when the East German sport system was dismantled as a result of German reunification

In the twenty-first century, the biggest doping scandal to date centred on America and the BALCO laboratory. This latest incident, discussed later in the chapter, demonstrates that it is naïve to assume that the high profile communist bloc athletes caught up in such scandals are the only athletes doped with the connivance of sport authorities, despite media interpretations of drug-free sporting environments in Western nations (Magdalinski, 1998).

Unfortunately, there are also opportunities for athletes to taint their opponents' victories by insinuating that they are using performance-enhancing substances, even with no concrete proof on which to base their allegations. The Irish swimmer Michelle (Smith) de Bruin was one such athlete whose victories at the Atlanta Games were tarnished by such denouncements even before the end of the Games' swimming programme. In this case however it appears that her detractors' suspicions may have been correct, as she was later banned from competition for tainting a urine sample with alcohol.

The case for legalising drug use

There is not universal accord that doping in sport should be outlawed. Those who argue that Olympic athletes should be able to use drugs to enhance their performances cite the following reasons.

1. Drug taking could be monitored by doctors, so that athletes would not be taking excessive amounts of drugs. This might prevent many of the deaths or adverse side effects suffered by drug takers who have followed a 'more is better' policy. Additionally, doctors could instruct athletes regarding which drugs should never be taken and the black market trading in inferior quality drugs could be eliminated.
2. It would create a level playing field in drug use. If all athletes had access to drugs then the Olympics would become a fairer competition. This is not to say that drug taking would be mandatory, but rather, it would become a matter of open choice instead of a clandestine practice, widespread as it is. The unknown edge given to today's drug cheats would thus be eliminated, or at least acknowledged. Current practice suggests that athletes' drug use is higher in counties where doping is systemic or in the richer nations where athletes can more readily afford to pay for the drugs.
3. Sporting records would continue to be broken as performance-enhancing substances were further refined. This would create greater excitement for spectators and continue to make sport a lucrative market for television audiences.
4. If safe drugs were permitted, then there would be pressure to develop safer drugs and the drugs would become safer.
5. The goal of catching all cheaters is unattainable (Savulescu *et al.*, 2004).

As noted previously, there is a lag between the introduction of a new drug, its listing as a banned substance and the development of tests to catch those using it. Despite technological, testing and educational advances, either instances of doping in sport are continuing to increase (which would add to the validity of the arguments above), or, conversely, more cheats are being caught (which would add to the credibility of the arguments below).

The case against legalisation of drug use

Those who argue against the practice of doping do so primarily for the following reasons, mostly related to the issue of 'harm' to the users, other athletes, sport and society (Schneider and Butcher, 2001).

1. The use of performance-enhancing drugs is contrary to the essence of sport and the philosophy of the Olympics, which places its emphasis on fair and equal competition.
2. If doping was accepted then some athletes would still seek to gain an unfair advantage by adopting a 'more is better' policy. Checking whether or not agreed levels of drug usage were being adhered to would be difficult to monitor.
3. Some countries may be unable to afford the ever escalating price of sophisticated drugs. Thus, wealthier nations would be more likely to be able to participate in sanctioned doping programmes.

4. Some athletes are coerced into using drugs or given them without their knowledge. This is completely unprincipled, is dehumanising and potentially damaging to athletes, both physiologically and psychologically. Out of season drug testing can uncover these practices and prevent them becoming more widespread.
5. The medical profession still does not know the long term affects of many drugs. Even if drug use was monitored athletes might still suffer deleterious effects from their use.

History of drug use in the Olympics

Introduction

Athletes have been seeking a competitive advantage over their rivals in many ways since sporting competition began. Ancient sources recount many instances of cheating, in a variety of forms. Ancient Greek writers, when discussing their sporting contests, noted that equipment was tampered with, Olympic judges were bribed and some athletes consumed mushrooms as psychogenic aids. Thus, drug use in sport is not a twentieth-century phenomenon. It is however, now more scientifically advanced and more diverse in its forms than in ancient times.

Goldman and Klatz (1992: 30) point out that drug use 'has been documented in all of the sports in which weight, speed, nerves and endurance are factors'. The first serious case of doping in the Olympics was recorded in 1904, when the American marathon runner, Thomas Hicks, collapsed after ingesting a mixture of brandy and strychnine, the drug of choice for endurance athletes of that era. Alcohol, in a variety of forms, combined with strychnine, was at that time the most common sports cocktail. Other drugs widely used to improve athletic accomplishment included caffeine, heroin and cocaine, until the last became available only by prescription. In the 1920s adrenaline was being used by athletes. Oxygen was also being employed for performance enhancement. It was rumoured that the Japanese swimmers used it during the 1932 Olympics (Reiterer, 2000). During the 1930s amphetamines became the most common performance enhancer. Other techniques also involved 'gland grafting'. This involved 'inserting slices of animal glands into male patients as well as injecting extracts of animal testicles into them to promote virility and fitness' (Reiterer, 2000: 73).

The 1950s

The 1950s, in the era of the Cold War, saw the introduction of perhaps the most devastating drug known to Olympic sport. In the Soviet Union, in an effort to facilitate increases in the strength and power of their athletes, officials and medical personnel gave many of them injections of testosterone. This appeared to give the doped athletes an advantage and the Soviet Olympic medal tallies increased. To combat this unwelcome competition, the US weightlifting team physician, John Zeigler, introduced a medical countermeasure, developed in collaboration with the chemical company, CIBA. Thus began the steroid era, specifically, through the use of Dianabol, which, for the next three decades, became the steroid of choice for the Western world (Reiterer, 2000).

In the same period a number of athletes collapsed at the Games, as a direct result of their drug use. In the 1952 Oslo Winter Olympics, several speed skaters overdosed on amphetamines and needed medical attention.

The 1960s

At the 1960 Rome Olympic Games, Knud Jensen, a Danish cyclist, achieved notoriety when he became the first Olympic athlete to die of a drug overdose during competition.

As doping became more scientific and more widely practised and its negative effects became more widely acknowledged, greater pressure began to mount against its use in sport. In 1963, the Council of Europe established a Committee on Drugs; however, its success was minimal, as it failed even to reach consensus as to what constituted 'doping'. This problem of semantics has resurfaced over the years.

The televised death of cyclist Tommy Smith in the 1967 Tour de France, as a result of an amphetamine overdose, spurred the IOC into action. An IOC committee reached consensus on a definition of doping and drew up a list of banned substances and the IOC Medical Commission was established. The 1968 Mexico City Games marked the beginning of drug testing in the Games.

The 1970s

It was not until 1974 that the IOC declared steroid use illegal. Since that time drug use and drug testing at the Olympic Games have been controversial aspects of the Games. Suggestions that the IOC and/or some OCOGs suppressed positive results have been rife, especially in relation to the 1980 and 1984 Games (Jennings, 1996: 111, 291).

While the IOC's fight against stimulants and steroids was producing some positive outcomes, a new front in the anti-doping war appeared. Blood doping, the removal and subsequent re-infusion of an athlete's blood in order to increase levels of oxygen-carrying haemoglobin, began in earnest in the 1970s. But it was not until 1986 that the IOC banned blood doping as a method.

The 1980s

At the 1980 Moscow Games, no athletes tested positive, a drop of 11 from the Montréal Games and 11 less than the following Games, held in Los Angeles. At these Games there was the suggestion that there were many more positive results, but the list of potential offenders was allegedly stolen from the hotel room safe of the Head of the IOC Medical Commission, Prince Alexandre de Merode (*Africa News*, 1996b).

The most infamous case of drug use at the Olympics occurred at the 1988 Seoul Games when the 100 metres champion, Ben Johnson, of Canada, became the 39th athlete to be disqualified from Olympic competition since testing began in 1968, when he tested positive to stanozolol, an anabolic steroid (see Fig. 8.1). His ignominious exit from Seoul, broadcast live throughout the world, was not an image that the IOC, or Johnson's sponsors, wanted to replicate. Yet, a point was made. The IOC was prepared to expel one of the most famous of its athletes. On this occasion there was no cover up. However, what has subsequently occurred in relation to drug use with the

Figure 8.1. Ben Johnson wins the 100 metres at the Seoul, 1988 Olympics, ahead of Carl Lewis and Lynford Christie

other athletes in the 100 metres event who were not caught and thus, by implication, 'clean' at the time, suggests that he may not have been the only runner in the race who was doping

The 1990s

Since this time an ever expanding cornucopia of drugs used by athletes has been discovered. The low number of positive results in the 1996 Atlanta Games (only five – the same number as in the 1992 Barcelona Games) led some to the conclusion that, far from drug use being curtailed, 'competitors who want to cheat their way to glory are becoming more and more sophisticated about what drugs they take and when' (*Africa News*, 1996b).

2002–2006

The Sydney 2000 Olympic Games saw two innovations in drug testing. Out-of-competition testing was carried out in the two weeks before the Games and blood and urine tests for the drug erythropoietin (EPO) were introduced. While only 300 EPO tests were carried out, it was thought that the possibility of an athlete being caught by the new tests may have been a deterrent. Interestingly, for the first time since the 1948 Olympic Games, there were no world records broken in the track and field events. No athletes tested positive to EPO; however, scientists at the Australian Institute of Sport, using a more sophisticated test on the samples after the Games, found that seven athletes tested positive by this new method. During the Games, using the normal urine tests, four athletes tested positive to steroids, and four for using masking agents (Parisotto, 2006).

The 2004 Athens Olympic Games were marred for the host nation, Greece, by a drugs scandal, even before they had begun. Kosta Kederis, the 2000 men's 200-metre gold medal winner (and rumoured to be the choice for the final torch bearer) and his training partner, Ekaterini Thanou, the Olympic silver medallist in the women's 100 metre in Sydney, claimed to have been unable to report for a drug test because they had been involved in a motorcycle accident. It was the third time in two months that they had failed to report to the testers. The saga of whether or not there really was an accident continued for almost a week and threatened to overshadow media reporting of sport at the Games. There were accusations of their guilt and counter-claims of their innocence. Finally, the two athletes withdrew from the Games. Their controversial coach, Christos Tzekos, also withdrew but was unrepentant about the incident, claiming: 'I don't feel I have made any mistakes'. A government spokesman, Thodoris Roussopoulos, took an opposing viewpoint. He noted: 'it creates a bad image of the country, not only locally but on a world scale' (*Age*, 2004). This was not the end of the saga. The IOC referred the athletes to the IAAF for sanctioning. They were given a two year ban. However, the Greek Athletic Federation (Segas) acquitted them of any wrongdoing. The IAAF then appealed against this decision to the Court of Arbitration for Sport (CAS). A decision was expected to be made in June 2006, almost two years after the alleged offence occurred. Kenteris and Thanou also faced eight criminal charges in regard to the alleged motorbike accident.

At the 2006 Torino Winter Games a road accident was again linked to a drug scandal. This time, an Austrian coach, Walter Mayer, who had been banned from the Olympics for previous infringements at the 2002 Salt Lake City Games, crashed his car into a police roadblock, while trying to avoid Italian authorities. The chase followed a raid of the Austrian biathlon and cross-country team's accommodation. It was alleged that in the raid a number of items with possible doping related uses, such as blood analysis equipment, syringes and asthma medication, were seized (Magnay, 2006). The Austrian team protested against the manner of the raid, which occurred the night before the team competed in the cross-country relay and subsequently finished in last place.

Incidents such as these are only a small example of the doping stories of the Games. They bring no glory to the athletes involved and damage the integrity of the Olympic Movement. In order to counter this, the IOC must continue the work that it has recently initiated with the leading drug-testing agencies and authorities, such as World Anti-Doping Agency (WADA), that its pre-eminent position dictates. It needs to 'put its money where its mouth is' to fund scientific research at appropriate levels to develop ever more sophisticated testing and educational programmes. The actions of the past, however, make the accusations of IOC detractors, such as Andrew Jennings, who claim that the IOC does not want to clean up an epidemic that affects many of its stars, sound credible. Jennings (2000: 291–2) argues that the IOC's inactivity is motivated primarily by financial concerns and pressure placed on it by the International Federations. He argues that sponsorship deals would be curtailed if the public realised how many of their heroes' performances were drug enhanced. If this is indeed the case then the ideals of Olympism, so proudly espoused by the IOC, are being compromised by those individuals who should be living examples of its potential.

The IOC Medical Commission

For many years it was medical commissions of individual sport organisations which were responsible for the fight against doping. In 1967 the IOC and the International Cycling Union became the first sports organisations to establish such commissions (British Olympic Association, n.d.: 1). The commission's tasks have varied over time. Its initial brief of establishing an anti-doping programme, was rapidly expanded to encompass the following three fundamental principles:

- protection of the health of athletes;
- respect for both medical and sport ethics;
- equality for all competing athletes.

Since the creation of WADA, the scope of the IOC Medical Commission has again changed. In addition to the fight against doping, which remains one of its main tasks, both as the representative of the IOC in WADA committees and during the Olympic Games, the IOC Medical Commission's current mission is to address all of the main medical issues which may occur in sports (IOC, 2006b). This is evidenced in the 2004 edition of the *Olympic Charter*, which states that the Medical Commission's terms of reference include the following:

7.1.1 to implement the World Anti-Doping Code and all other IOC Anti-Doping Rules, in particular upon the occasion of the Olympic Games;
7.1.2 to elaborate guidelines relating to the medical care and health of the athletes.
7.2 Members of the Medical Commission shall not act in any medical capacity whatsoever for the delegation of an NOC at the Olympic Games nor participate in the discussions relating to non-compliance with the World Anti-Doping Code by members of their respective NOC's delegations.

(IOC, 2004: 51)

The World Anti-Doping Agency (WADA)

In 1963, France became the first country to enact anti-doping legislation. Other countries followed, but early international cooperation was limited. It was not until the 1980s that cooperation between international sports authorities and various governmental agencies occurred at any meaningful level.

In 1998, because of the drug problems associated with the Tour de France, there was a reappraisal of the role of public authorities in anti-doping affairs. Before this there were conflicting definitions, policies and sanctions, depending on the sport's governing body and location of the offence. This resulted in confusion and penalties that were often disputed or overruled in civil courts.

The scandal in cycling highlighted the need for an international body, which could set unified anti-doping standards and coordinate the efforts of sport, government and NGOs to eradicate doping in sport. As a result of growing pressure to act, the IOC convened the World Conference on Doping in Sport, in Lausanne in February 1999. The conference produced the 'Lausanne Declaration on Doping in Sport', which called for the creation of an independent international anti-doping agency. Subsequently, the World Anti-Doping Agency (WADA) was established in November 1999, to promote and coordinate the fight against doping in sport internationally.

WADA was set up as a foundation under the initiative of the IOC, with the support and participation of intergovernmental organisations, governments, public authorities, and other public and private bodies. It consisted of equal representatives from the Olympic Movement and public authorities. In 2001 WADA's Foundation Board voted to move its headquarters from Lausanne to Montréal. The Montréal headquarters were inaugurated in April 2002.

One of its most important achievements, to date, has been the drafting, acceptance and adoption of a uniform set of anti-doping rules: the *World Anti-Doping Code* (WADA, 2003). This provides the framework for anti-doping policies, rules and regulations within sport organisations and public authorities. The Code has been developed over several years, under the direction of a WADA project group, and in collaboration with a number of stakeholders.

In March 2003, the second World Conference on Doping in Sport, held in Copenhagen, was attended by about 1200 delegates representing: 80 governments; the IOC; the IPC; all Olympic IFs, NOCs and NPCs; athletes; national anti-doping agencies; and international agencies. The delegates unanimously agreed to adopt the Code as the basis for the fight against doping in sport. This has become known as The Copenhagen Resolution. The Code entered into force on 1 January 2004. In 2004, WADA established or renewed agreements with 26 of the 28 Summer Games IFs, and all seven Winter Games IFs.

In 2004 WADA conducted 2327 out-of-competition doping controls in 62 countries on athletes from 118 nations. This resulted in 19 adverse analytical findings and 4 refusals. An additional 169 samples were collected by WADA as part of the WADA/IOC/ATHOC task force, which coordinated sample collection prior to and during the 2004 Athens Olympic Games. As mentioned previously 23 athletes tested positive to these tests (WADA, n.d.). Table 8.1 provides the statistics for WADA out-of-competition tests carried out during 2004.

Categories of IOC prohibited substances

The list of IOC banned substances is forever changing (WADA, nd). As chemists invent newer, more powerful, performance-enhancing drugs, these are added to the total. Sometimes a substance is removed from the list. At the time of the 2006 Torino Winter Olympic Games the following categories of substances and methods were prohibited:

Categories of prohibited substances
   S1. Anabolic agents
   S2. Hormones and related substances
   S3. Beta-2 agonists except salbutamol, formoterol, salmeterol and terbutaline
   S4. Agents with anti-oestrogenic activity
   S5. Diuretics and other Masking agents

Categories of prohibited methods
   M1. Enhancement of oxygen transfer
   M2. Chemical and physical manipulation
   M3. Gene doping.

A complete list of prohibited substances is provided by the World Anti-Doping Agency in its 'Prohibited List' (WADA, nd), which is updated on a regular basis. A

Table 8.1. WADA Out-of-competition tests carried out during 2004

Sport	IF	Urine Tests	Blood Tests	EPO Analysis
Aquatics	FINA	203	9	45
Archery	FITA	15	-	-
Athletics	IAAF	124	10	59
Badminton	IBF	16	-	-
Baseball	IBAF	15	-	-
Basketball	FIBA	32	-	2
Biathlon	IBU	92	25	23
Bobsleigh/Tobogganing	FIBT	66	-	-
Boxing	AIBA	55	-	-
Canoe	ICF	68	2	1
Curling	WCF	12		
Cycling	UCI	128	5	93
Equestrian	FEI	13	-	-
Fencing	FIE	15	-	-
Field Hockey	FIH	30	-	-
Football	FIFA	*	*	0
Gymnastics	FIG	46	-	-
Handball	IHF	30	-	-
Ice Hockey	IIHF	25	-	-
Ice Skating	ISU	82	26	-
Intern'l Paralympic Cttee	IPC	51	25	6
Judo	IJF	30	-	-
Korfball	IKF	6	-	-
Luge	FIL	16	-	-
Orienteering	IOF	12	-	-
Pentathlon	UIPM	23	-	17
Rowing	FISA	161	20	49
Rugby	IRB	80	-	-
Sailing	ISAF	30	-	-
Shooting	ISSF	14	-	-
Skiing	FIS	28	-	22
Softball	ISF	17	-	-
Table Tennis	ITTF	15	-	-
Taekwondo	WTF	27	-	-
Tennis	ITF	8	-	-
Triathlon	ITU	79	-	35
Volleyball	FIVB	*	*	*
Weightlifting	IWF	133	5	-
Wrestling	FILA	51	-	-
Total		1848	127	352

*Agreement not signed. Source: World Anti-Doping Agency: www.wada-ama.org/rtecontent/
document/2004_stats.pdf

substance and/or method is included on the WADA Prohibited List if it meets two of the following three criteria:

1. It has the potential to enhance or enhances sport performance;
2. It represents a potential or actual health risk;
3. It is contrary to the spirit of sport (ASC, 2006).

Athletes' obligations and doping control

All athletes who currently compete in the Olympics are subject to the IOC Eligibility code, which states:

> To be eligible for participation in the Olympic Games, a competitor, coach, trainer or other team official must comply with the Olympic Charter as well as with the rules of the IF concerned as approved by the IOC, and the competitor, coach, trainer or other team official must be entered by his NOC. The above-noted persons must notably:
> - respect the spirit of fair play and non-violence, and behave accordingly; and
> - respect and comply in all aspects with the World Anti-Doping Code.
>
> (IOC, 2004: 80)

The IOC is responsible for doping control during the period of the Olympic Games, and is entitled to delegate all or part of its responsibility to one or several other organisations, such as WADA. During the period of the Games all participating athletes are subject to doping controls initiated by the IOC. Tests may occur at any time or place, with no advance notice. Testing can be done on blood and urine. The IOC, in consultation with the OCOG and the relevant IFs, determines the number of tests to be performed at each Games. After an event, usually the top five placed finishers or all three medallists, plus athletes randomly selected by the IOC Medical Commission, are required to undergo drug testing. The doping control samples are analysed only in WADA-accredited laboratories or as otherwise approved by WADA.

In the period 1968 to 1992, only urine samples were taken. This changed at the 1994 Lillehammer Winter Olympics, when athletes in the Nordic ski events were also required to submit to blood tests (IOC, 1996a).

Gas chromatography, in combination with mass spectronomy (GS/MS), has become the most common method of analysing urine samples. One procedure 'not involving GS/MS is for the corticoids, where high performance, liquid chromatography (HPLC) is used in conjunction with a mass spectrometer and particle beam interface. HPLC is also used as part of the testing procedure for diuretics' (Bilder, n.d.: 3).

The majority of the tests conducted for testing of drugs used by athletes during the Olympics are not quantitative: if any traces of the drug are found in both urine samples, the athlete is considered to be guilty (Bilder, n.d.). An exception to this is the tests for testosterone (which is a naturally occurring hormone). For this test, it is the level of the substance, present in the athlete's urine, which determines whether or not the athlete is deemed to have doped. Tables 8.2 and 8.3 provide an overview of the doping tests carried out at the Olympic Games since 1968.

Table 8.2. Doping tests at the Summer Olympic Games, 1968–2004

Year	Place	Number of tests	Number of positive cases recorded
1968	Mexico City	667	1
1972	Munich	2079	1
1976	Montréal	786	11
1980	Moscow	645	0
1984	Los Angeles	1507	12
1988	Seoul	1598	10
1992	Barcelona	1848	5
1996	Atlanta	1923	2
2000	Sydney	2359	11
2004	Athens	3667	26*

*At the Athens Games, the cases recorded covered not only positive doping tests, but also violations of the anti-doping rules, such as non-arrival within the set deadline for the test, or providing a urine sample that did not conform to the established procedures. Source: IOC website.

Table 8.3. Doping tests: Winter Olympic Games, 1968–2006

Year	Place	Number of tests	Number of positive cases recorded
1968	Grenoble	86	0
1972	Sapporo	211	1
1976	Innsbruck	39	2
1980	Lake Placid	440	0
1984	Sarajevo	424	1
1988	Calgary	492	1
1992	Albertville	522	0
1994	Lillehammer	529	0
1998	Nagano	621	0
2002	Salt Lake City	700	7
2006	Torino	1219	1

Source: IOC (2007c)

Anti-doping procedures for Turin, 2006

The testing period for athletes competing in the 2006 Turin Winter Games began on 31 January 2005 and concluded on 26 February 2006. Athletes could be tested inside the Olympic Village, inside or outside Olympic venues, or indeed anywhere in the world. All selected athletes received notification informing them that they had been selected for a doping control test, because: they had been ranked in the top five places; their name had been pulled out of a draw; or their name was on the testing pool list.

This notification was given by an identified doping control officer. Following its receipt, the athlete had up one hour to go to the doping control station (or other designated place). During this time, the athlete had to remain under the constant supervision of the doping control agent (IOC, 2005d, 2007a).

Upon arrival athletes were required to provide identification, either by using their accreditation card if at an Olympic venue or, if outside an Olympic venue, then by other means.

Athletes then chose a batch of bottles from a group offered to them in which to place their samples. Urine samples were taken under the constant watch of doping control agents of the same sex as the athlete being tested. Then, still under the authority of the doping control officer, the athlete separated the sample into two bottles, A and B, which were then sealed, either by the athlete or, on request, by the doping control officer. The blood sample was taken following the same procedures. At the time of pre-competition tests, blood was taken either at the polyclinic of the Olympic Village or at another approved location outside Olympic venues. During the period of the Games, blood sampling was done either the same day (if competition ended before 6.30 p.m.) or the day after (if the competition finished after 6.30 p.m.) an athlete competed (IOC, 2005d).

Athletes were also required to complete a doping control form, indicating any medicines they had taken in the previous three days. This form was signed by the athlete, the person accompanying them, the doping control officer, and, if applicable, any other person whose presence was authorised during the test. The sealed bottles containing the samples were then transported to an accredited laboratory, where they were analysed in accordance with procedures conforming to the international standards for laboratories as set out by WADA (IOC, 2005d).

If the laboratory found an abnormal test result, it alerted the IOC Medical Commission chairman or his designate. The IOC Medical Commission chairman or designate then compared the code reported by the laboratory with that of the doping control form, thus for the first time allowing the athlete to be identified with his or her sample. Next, they checked whether or not the athlete had a Therapeutic Use Exemption (TUE) or an Abbreviated Therapeutic Use Exemption (ATUE). If the athlete under investigation did not have this clearance then the Medical Commission Chairman concluded that there was a positive result and forwarded this finding to the IOC president who immediately appointed a Disciplinary Commission (IOC, 2005d).

The athlete and the chef de mission from the athlete's National Olympic Committee (NOC), were notified and summoned to attend a hearing of the Disciplinary Commission. They were given the option of being accompanied by up to three people of their choice. The Disciplinary Commission also invited the relevant International Federation (IF) and a WADA independent observer to attend. It could also request the opinion of experts. The Disciplinary Commission informed the athlete of the alleged anti-doping rule violation and provided all the documentation from the laboratory. The possibility of having their B sample examined was then offered to the athletes. If they chose this option, they were informed of the date and time and place that the examination would be performed. This second test occurred in the presence of the athletes or a person of their choice. However, the Disciplinary Commission proceeded with the athlete's hearing, independent of the examination of the B sample. Following the hearing, either the Disciplinary Commission, or the IOC Executive Board, made a decision regarding the offence. This decision was immediately forwarded to the athlete and his/her NOC by the IOC. No communication was made to any third party before the athlete was informed. If the athlete did not agree with the IOC's ruling he or she had the right to appeal against the decision to the Court of Arbitration for Sport (CAS), which set up an *ad hoc* division during the period of the Olympic Games (IOC, 2005d). A violation of the anti-doping rules resulted in disqualification of the athlete's results obtained in the event for which the doping control was carried out, as well as possibly their other events, including forfeiture of any medals, points and prizes won.

The IOC President announced at the conclusion of these Games: 'Athletes, it is to protect you that the International Olympic Committee fights untiringly against doping. I promise that we shall continue to fight for a pure and healthy sport' (Rogge, 2006). The next section details past episodes from the Games, which demonstrate how important this fight is for the integrity of the Olympic Movement. They also indicate how ineffectual the authorities have been.

Episodes in sport, the Olympics and drug use

Four episodes which have been significant in the story of drug use and abuse in sport and the Olympics are briefly outlined below. They relate to East Germany, Chinese athletes, the 1998 Tour de France, and the BALCO Laboratory scandal.

East Germany and drug use

In the 1960s, the relatively small country of East Germany – the German Democratic Republic (GDR) – began experimenting with the use of drugs, especially the androgenic-anabolic steroid, oral-Turinabol, to enhance sporting performances at a systemic level. The Politburo of the Socialist Unity Party (SED) had authorised the programme (State Planning Theme 14.25). Its aim was to improve the GDR teams' sporting performances and through this the country's international prestige. Inherent in the search for prestige was the desire to demonstrate the superiority of their communist system of government over that of their democratic West German rivals (Geitner, 1997; Ungerleider, 2001). 'In the three decades when ... *State Planning Theme 14.25* was in effect, more than ten thousand unsuspecting young athletes were given massive doses of performance-enhancing anabolic steroids' (Ungerleider, 2001: 1).

The steroids were used extensively with female athletes, especially in events where strength and power was required. The swimming team, aided by such drugs, achieved a supremacy over their rivals, previously unheard of in that sport. It was at the 1972 Olympic Games, ironically held in Munich, in West Germany, that the East German women first dominated the Olympic programme. One year later, in 1973, at the first World Athletics Championship, East German women won ten of the 14 events, setting eight world records in the process.

At the Montréal Olympics of 1976, their mastery of the women's swimming competition continued, winning 11 of 13 events. However, the first rumblings about drug use were beginning to surface. As with later cases, the accusers themselves faced counter-charges of being poor losers. Most prominent in the accusations was the American, Shirley Babashoff, who won four silver medals (Jeffrey, 1997).

The East German women continued their reign in the pool. Between 1976 and the opening of the Berlin wall in 1989, they won 28 Olympic gold medals. Confirmation that drugs had been administered to athletes was established after the reunification of Germany when the records of the Ministry for State Security secret police, the STASI, were uncovered. These files indicated that over 2000 athletes, some as young as 14, were systematically and scientifically monitored, so that they passed drug testing during competition. The STASI controlled the whole process euphemistically terming it 'supporting means' (Geitner, 1997). Their programme apparently began as early as

1971 and their involvement was thorough, extending throughout the production, development, testing and doping phases at the Institute of Research into Physical Culture and Sport (Barnes, 1997).

One of the affected athletes, Renate Vogel, described her medical regime as follows:

> The blue pills started after the 1972 Olympics in Munich. ... In the 1973 season we began to get injections also. We were given two injections per week when we were in training camp. No one was sure which shots were the steroids because we were also pumped full of vitamins B, C and D. In the beginning I didn't really think anything of it. You know, when you are around other athletes like yourself, you don't notice the difference in body size. There were very few people on the team who thought about it or really cared. They were of the opinion that the main thing was to swim quickly, and it didn't matter how. I started to notice the effect of the steroids when my clothes didn't fit any more. This was the beginning of 1973. In retrospect I can see that I had really broad shoulders. I went from a size 40 to 44 or larger. My period hardly ever came. (Barnes, 1997: 138)

Another athlete, the shot putter, Andrea Kreiger, was so affected by the male hormones she was given that she decided to have a sex change.

Those athletes who refused to take drugs were punished by exclusion from teams and loss of their special athlete privileges. Perhaps, in retrospect, these athletes were the lucky ones, as many of their counterparts were given extremely high doses of steroids, which later translated into health problems (Barnes, 1997). Some of the East German coaches who were involved in the doping process have been prosecuted. However it is unlikely that all those involved will be caught, and, for those athletes who died, or who are permanently affected by steroids, their punishment will not bring back their health. The political greed of the East German authorities and their wish to triumph over their rivals resulted in one of the most devastating episodes in Olympic history.

Chinese athletes and drug use

At the 1988 Olympic Games the Chinese women's swimming team won three medals. During the next few years they continued to improve dramatically, so that, at the 1994 World Championships in Rome their women won 12 of the 16 events.

Following the revelations of the East German doping programme, a number of coaches from Australia and the USA expressed concerns that the Chinese were achieving their success, with the aid of doping by six East German scientists who had moved to China after the German unification.

The year before, in August 1993, many believed that Chinese authorities, eager to secure the 2000 Olympics for Beijing, had kept their swimmers away from the Pan Pacific Swimming Championships because of the possibility of positive drug tests and subsequent backlash against Beijing's bid.

Chinese female track and field athletes had also been breaking some records, in keeping with their swimming countrywomen. In August, their athletes had won six of nine possible medals at the World Championships held in Rome. More world records were broken at the Chinese national championships, held in Beijing. The athletes' coach, Ma Jungren, denied that his athletes were cheats, insisting that it was scientific methods, endurance training (including running a marathon every day and a unique, but unpalatable diet that included 'rare worms, caterpillar fungus, dog meat and tortoise blood' (Barnes, 1997: 59).

Despite these significant improvements, IOC President, Juan Antonio Samaranch, supported the Chinese, declaring that Chinese sport was 'clean' (Jennings, 1996: 232). Stringer, believed that the reasons for his support were clear. 'Samaranch was widely known to have favoured Beijing's bid for the 2000 Games – not the least because Chinese support was influential in delivering a block of votes vital in maintaining his own power base within the IOC' (Stringer, 1995: 27).

Events were to prove Samaranch's faith in the Chinese misplaced. During the 1994 Asian Games, held in Hiroshima, members of the Chinese team was surprised when they were unexpectedly tested on arrival. The resulting positive tests for five women and six men (seven of them for steroid use) confirmed the suspicions of many in the swimming world.

As a consequence of these results the other Pan Pacific swimming nations did not invite the Chinese to their 1995 championships, held in Atlanta (Jeffrey, 1997). Chinese sports authorities, concerned about their credibility, issued a statement denying that doping was systematic. World swimming authorities seemed loathe to pursue the matter, insisting there was no proof of state-sponsored doping, despite the fact that Chinese athletes had tested positive twenty times since 1991 (*Sydney Morning Herald*, 1998). The IOC issued a statement that read: 'the IOC is very pleased to note the clear and very firm position expressed by China's sporting authorities. ... They have clearly informed the IOC of their intentions to seek out and sanction the true culprits' (Stringer, 1995:27).

No Chinese athletes tested positive at the 1996 Atlanta Games, despite the rumours about their drug usage. Their performances were, however, below expectations, and it appeared that their claims to have cleaned up their own house were founded. However, 18 months later, at the 1998 Swimming World Champion-ships in Perth, Australia the problem resurfaced, when, in a furore matched only by Ben Johnson's 1998 bust, four Chinese swimmers tested positive to the banned diuretic, triamterene. The substance is believed to be used by athletes to flush the body of anabolic steroids. In an unexpected move swimming's ruling body, FINA, had ordered that all competitors in the championships be tested on their arrival in Perth, days before the event began. This was a move identical to the one that had caught the Chinese swimmers in 1994. Earlier, before the Chinese even arrived in Perth, another controversy erupted when one of their swimmers, *en route* to the championships, had been apprehended by customs agents at Sydney with a large supply of human growth hormone in her suitcase.

These two episodes added credence to the assertion by some that the Chinese doping problem was not confined to individuals. Both hGH and steroids, it was argued, were beyond the means of poor athletes (Moore and Magnay, 1998). IOC President Samaranch now appeared to have turned his back on the Chinese, stating that it would be difficult for China to win selection for staging the 2008 Games: 'They have the right to pursue a bid, but it is up to the IOC members to decide what is acceptable. I think that they would be in trouble. I think it's very clear many would not be in favour' (*Advertiser*, 1998). Again, he was mistaken in his assessment, as Beijing was awarded the 2008 Games.

Once more the Chinese authorities denied any involvement in the drug taking by their athletes. Shi Tianshu, the leader of the Chinese delegation at the world championships deflected responsibility to the swimmers claiming: 'it is individuals, definitely individuals' (*Advertiser*, 1998). As the four swimmers caught for diuretic use all came from the same Shanghai club it seemed that this claim was, at the very least, ill informed.

Despite worldwide condemnation of the Chinese and calls for their expulsion from the championships, FINA took no further action, claiming that it was not in their power to do so. While under its rules it could expel a team if it recorded four tests for steroids in 12 months, the athletes had, in fact, tested positive only for a diuretic. This was a technicality, as the purpose of the diuretic was clearly to flush steroids from the body. Sydney's Olympic Organising Committee (SOCOG) put a positive spin on the Perth scandal, contending that the 2000 Games would be cleaner as a result of the drug takers being detected (Jeffrey, 1997). Others took a different perspective, noting that drug taking in sport was a worldwide phenomenon, not limited to China and that, in order to prevent its further acceptance, the Chinese should be expelled from the 2000 Olympic Games. It was noted that Russian swimmers had also tested positive for steroids in December 1997.

Their opponents claimed that such a position lacked credibility for, as Jeffrey (1997) pointed out, 28 of the 58 swimmers caught for drug taking since testing was introduced were Chinese and all of these were in the previous decade. Her view, which is hard to counter, was that systematic doping had far more significant consequences than isolated instances.

The 1988 Tour de France and implications for the Olympic Movement

The 1998 Tour de France became known colloquially in journalistic circles as the Tour de Farce because of the revelations of widespread use of EPO by the cyclists. As the race progressed and more competitors and even whole teams were disqualified it became apparent that the use of performance-enhancing substances was widely accepted within this particular sport. Public reaction ranged from indifference to censure. From the size and behaviour of the crowds that lined the route, even as the scandal progressed, it was evident that many spectators were more interested in seeing the race than investigating or questioning the ethical implications of doping by athletes.

The press was not as forgiving and many journalists called for an overhaul of the existing light sanctions for offenders and the ethos that allowed and contributed to the scandal. Others, of course, took the opposite view. As a result, the topic of drug use in sport received a high profile in the media and many expert opinions and commentaries were sought. One such example was the viewpoint of the IOC President, Juan Antonio Samaranch. In an interview with the Madrid newspaper *El Mundo* in July 1998 he was quoted as saying:

> Doping is any product which, first damages the health of the sportsman and, second, artificially increases his performance. If it produces only this second condition, for me that's not doping. If it produces the first it is. ... The current list of [banned] products must be drastically reduced. Anything that doesn't act against the athlete's health, for me that's not doping. (Samaranch, quoted by Blair, 1998)

In the same article Samaranch was also quoted as suggesting that the IOC needed to reduce its list of banned substances. This position appeared to be going against the hardline stance that the IOC had claimed it was taking against drug use in sport. Samaranch's   interview   was   greeted   with   astonishment   from   many   sports administrators. In Australia, site of the 2000 Games, the Federal Minister for Sport, Andrew Thompson, in typically Australian fashion, announced that he was 'gobsmacked' by the apparent change in direction from sport's most powerful administrator.

The previous year, when Ross Rebagliata, the winner of the snow board giant slalom event at the Nagano Olympics, had tested positive for marijuana (a result he maintained was the result of passive smoking at a party in Whistler, Canada), Samaranch had formed a working group within the IOC to formulate a policy on the drug. This move was greeted with derision in some quarters. 'Many wondered why. Samaranch hadn't minded when positive tests on big track stars had been suppressed' (Jennings and Sambrook, 2000: 111). As a result of the backlash against Samaranch's ill-advised statement he later declared that he would seek a ban on all soft/recreational drugs (Blair, 1998).

As a result of the media approbation regarding Samaranch's statements, and a subsequent clarification of his statements to appease the growing chorus of adverse public and governmental reaction to his comments, the IOC President called for a world conference on doping in sport. The conference was held in Lausanne, in February 1999, and was attended by over 600 delegates.

The conference had four themes: 1. protecting the athletes; 2. legal and political aspects; 3. prevention, ethics, education and communication; and 4. financial considerations (Evans, 1999). It was hoped that the delegates would vote to ensure that sanctions for drug cheats would be applied uniformly by all international sporting federations. This outcome did not, however, eventuate due to the combined power of the sports of cycling, tennis and soccer, which sought and received exemptions from a compulsory two year minimum ban as penalty for first time doping offenders.

The conference voted that the final decision on sanctions applied to offenders was to be the prerogative of each international sporting federation (IF). This determination was not acceptable to some delegates. The British Sport Minister, Tony Banks, speaking on behalf of the European Union nations, declared that they had rejected the sanctions plan. 'It is both minimalist and permissive and it undermines the proposed two year ban' (Magnay and Korporaal, 1999). The IOC adopted a different perspective to the outcome, defending the varied sanctions on legal grounds, by arguing that this approach would result in fewer legal challenges by athletes in civil courts.

The IOC had recently come under increasing pressure from a number of the more powerful IFs to accede to their differing agendas on a number of issues. The IFs were also calling for the IOC to hand over a larger percentage of profits from television and sponsorship income. The threat underlying their demands was the withdrawal of their sports from the Games, thus decreasing the Olympics' attraction to the media. This particular instance of three IFs gaining their objective provides a powerful example of the growing influence of the IFs and the relative weakening of the IOC's authority.

The other setback for the IOC during the conference occurred when government and sporting delegates voted that the new world wide anti-doping authority would not be managed exclusively by the IOC (Stevens, 1999). The conference resolutions were passed by a show of applause, rather than a customary show of hands and were published in the IOC's *Highlights of the Week's Olympic News* as the 'Lausanne Declaration on Doping in Sport'. In this document the conference outcomes were listed as follows:

* Educational and preventative campaigns will be intensified, focusing on youth and athletes and their entourage ...

- The Olympic Movement's Anti-Doping Code is accepted as the basis for the fight against doping ...
- The minimum required sanction for major doping substances or prohibited methods shall be a suspension of the athlete from all competition for a period of two years, for a first offence. However, based on specific, exceptional circumstances to be evaluated in the first instance by the competent IF bodies, there may be a provision for a possible modification of the two year sanction ...
- An independent International Anti-Doping Agency shall be established so as to fully operational for the Games of the XXVII Olympiad. ... The Olympic Movement commits to allocate a capital of US $25 million to the Agency. ...
- The IOC, the IFs and the NOCs will maintain their respective ... responsibility to apply doping rules in accordance with their own procedures. ... Consequently, decisions handed down in the first instance will be under the exclusive responsibility of the IFs, the NOCs or, during the Olympic Games, the IOC ...
- The collaboration in the fight against doping between sports organisations and public authorities shall be reinforced. (IOC, 1999a: 1–2)

However, as described earlier in the chapter, the conference led to the establishment of WADA and was a vital step in controlling a problem which threatened to fracture, not only Olympic sport, but élite sport across the world, however, this was not the last doping saga.

The BALCO Laboratory scandal

As seen from the cycling fiasco, the problem of large scale and systemic doping in sport has not been limited to athletes from socialist countries nor only instigated by governments. The first large scale doping scandal of the twenty-first century emanated from the USA and involved a commercial enterprise. Personnel from the Bay Area Laboratory Cooperative (BALCO), owned by Victor Conte, and located near San Francisco, had been supplying a large number of athletes with a performance-enhancing substance, known colloquially as 'the clear'. In 2003, the press was alerted to the fact that some high profile American and international athletes had been using 'the clear', so named because it was, at that point, undetectable by existing gas chromatography tests. Soon after, the University of California, Los Angeles (UCLA) tested a used syringe of the drug, sent to it by the US Anti-Doping Agency (USADA), which had, in turn, received it from a leading track coach, Trevor Graham. The UCLA scientists determined that the substance found in the syringe was a previously unknown designer steroid and named it tetrahydrogestrinone (THG). The US sporting authorities now realised that a new doping epidemic had been unleashed. It could not be ignored and, fortuitously, at this point, athletes did not realise that the drug could be detected. As a result, when samples were taken from athletes at the 2003 US Track and Field Championships, 350 of the athletes tested positive to THG (Rasmussen, 2005).

Not only were sporting authorities involved, US law enforcement were also drawn into the hunt and investigated those involved in dealing THG. After criminal investigations, Victor Conte and others associated with the BALCO laboratory and/or the distribution of the drug were indicted. After a trial, those indicted were either sentenced to jail or given probationary sentences. The USADA also suspended a number of athletes who had used the drug, such as Kelli White, Chryste Gaines and Alvin Harrison. In the aftermath of the raids and through court testimony, a number of other athletes, such as Marion Jones, came under suspicion for using the drug. Indeed, Victor Conte claimed, in his court testimony, to have injected Jones. The USDA also rewrote its drug code to 'replace its "beyond a reasonable doubt" standard … with a "comfortable satisfaction of hearing body" standard' (Magnay, 2004).

Later, under this new ruling, Michelle Collins became the first athlete to receive a doping ban without testing positive to or admitting use of a banned substance, when she agreed to drop an appeal to the Court of Arbitration for Sport (CAS) against a suspension of a ban for use of EPO and THG. As part of this arrangement her suspension from competition was reduced from eight to four years. Sprinter, Tim Montgomery, who had not followed this compromise route, continued his appeal to the CAS against his two year ban imposed by USADA for use of THG, similarly without failing a drug test. Montgomery lost his case. Dick Pound, President of WADA was jubilant with this new development in prosecuting drug cheats. He was explicit in his views when he used a vampire metaphor (apt if referring to blood doping) to illustrate his stand. 'Finally a stake has been driven through the heart of the preposterous argument that you have to have a doping infraction by producing an analytical positive doping test' (AOC, 2005: 2).

However, not everyone shares Pound's enthusiasm for the new approach in the fight to eliminate doping in sport. Kristian Rasmussen, in an article entitled 'The quest for the imaginary evil: a critique of anti-doping' (Rasmussen, 2005), notes that, when these initial bans were introduced, there was no scientific proof that THG was a performance-enhancing substance. He questions whether the handling of athletes suspected of its use meant that they were denied natural justice and that, in this case, sporting authorities were guilty of a moral panic.

The future

Sometimes life does imitate art. In 1979, the film *Golden Girl* (directed by Joseph Sargent), while a box office failure and arguably not a critical success, demonstrated how the possible future of the Olympic Games could be influenced by genetic programming. An artistic connection with this same imagined future of Olympic competition was further demonstrated at the 2004 Athens Games, when the unravelling of DNA was a feature of the Games opening ceremony.

While it is impossible to predict accurately what doping methods future athletes will be using, there is already concern that the next wave of performance enhancement will be as a result of genetic manipulation. Genetic engineering has already produced the 'Schwarzenegger' mice at the University of Pennsylvania and similar mice in California at the Salk Institute (one known as 'Lance' after Lance Armstrong). A joint American and South Korean team of scientists has also engineered mice to run twice as far as normal. As Parisotto notes:

> It won't just be the athletes who'll be different. Bigger, stronger, faster and taller sportspeople will have consequences for sports infrastructure, sports equipment and sporting rules and policies. What we now regard as middle- and long-distance races may one day become sprints. Power and field sports will need to modify equipment with heavier javelins or discuses, or build larger stadiums, so that the throwing implements don't end up in the crowd. Pitches, courts, and fields would need to get bigger, goals smaller and nets and hoops higher. More umpires will be needed, unless they too get doped up, in order to keep pace with the athletes. (Parisotto, 2006: 218)

Repoxygen, a gene therapy, which has not been produced commercially, is supposedly already being used in sport to gain an unfair advantage (Slot, 2006). These new methods of performance enhancement, which are not yet safe for humans (despite the interest in them shown by some athletes), will also provide a challenge for WADA, which is already funding research into developing tests to detect their use.

Summary

Athletes have been seeking a competitive advantage over their rivals in a number of ways, both legal and illegal, since sport began. Ancient sources recount many instances of cheating, in a variety of forms. For example, the Greeks note that equipment was tampered with and judges bribed at the Ancient Olympic Games. Other athletes ingested potions in order to better their performances. Thus, drug use should not be thought of as a malaise only of twentieth and twenty-first century sport. It is, however, undoubtedly more scientifically advanced and more diverse in its forms than it was in ancient times.

It is both gullible and arrogant to suppose that drug use by athletes only occurs in countries other than one's own. For example, in Australia, which is one of the world leaders in drug testing in sport, positive results are still being recorded on a regular basis, as evidenced in Table 8.4.

Thus, the current use of drugs to enhance performance in the Olympic Games should not be seen as an isolated problem, and one that does not concern athletes from one's own country, no matter where one lives. Of course, because of the consequences of success in today's sport, seeking an advantage over their competition is what athletes require in order to secure and maintain sponsorship, fame and prize money. But this is not the only cause. Drug use in sport is also symptomatic of a larger problem of drug use in the world of today, where we are conditioned to use drugs as the most expedient prophylactic solutions for many conditions, rather than seeking to analyse the root cause of individual medical or social problems. Also, sadly, 'neither athletes nor coaches put much faith in the ability of drug tests to catch cheats' (Leonard, 2001: 227).

Although legislation and banning of offenders has the potential to lessen the problem of drug use in the Olympic Games, it is only a partial solution. A more complete approach also involves the use of more educative initiatives. WADA and many other sport organisations have undertaken this as part of their brief. There is an array of programmes to educate and assist athletes. Ignorance of the effects and illegality of doping is not an excuse that athletes can use. Part of the learning process of all those involved with sport is clearly to recognise the linkages between drug use in society and drug use in the Olympic Games. The latter is a product of the former.

However, there are aspects other than the ethical one to consider, and this compounds the problem for sport. Haugen (cited in Savulescu *et al.*, 2004: 666) 'investigated the suggestion that athletes face a kind of prisoner's dilemma regarding drugs. His game theoretic model shows that, unless the likelihood of athletes being caught doping was raised to unrealistically high levels, or the payoff for winning were reduced to unrealistically low levels, athletes could all be predicted to cheat'. Given the current situation, the issue of doping in sport appears to be here to stay.

Table 8.4. Australian Sport Drug Agency drug testing result trends: 1989–2004

Year	Total tests	Positive/ refusal		% positive	
		Australia	Inter-national	Australia	Total
1989/90	1 272	54	0	4.3	4.3
1990/91	2 656	76	13	2.9	3.4
1991/92	2 444	40	0	1.6	1.6
1992/93	2 877	52	1	1.8	1.8
1993/94	2 802	38	0	1.4	1.4
1994/95	3 108	33	0	1.1	1.1
1995/96	3 296	34	0	1.0	1.0
1996/97	3 499	35	4	1.0	1.1
1997/98	4 313	36	0	0.8	0.8
1998/99	4 801	43	0	0.9	0.9
1999/00	5 745	34	6	0.6	0.7
2000/01	6 194	25	0	0.4	0.4
2001/02	6 869	25	5	0.4	0.4
2002/03	6 263	34	3	0.5	0.6
2003/04	6 615	23	1	0.4	0.4
Total	62 754	582	33	0.9	1.0

Source: www.asda.org.au/media/statistics.htm

Further reading

List of prohibited substances	WADA (nd).
Doping and the Olympics	Hoberman (2001, 2005)
Drugs in sport generally	Wilson & Derse (2001); Mottram (2003); Parisotto (2006); ONDCP (2005)
East Germany	Ungerleider (2001)

Questions

1. If everyone in an Olympic event is doping, then is it a 'level playing field'?
2. What is your position on doping in sport? On what grounds do you justify it?
3. Should all the record breaking performances of athletes who have been found guilty of doping be expunged from the record books, rather than just in the event in which they were found to have cheated? Should their medals be presented to lower place getters in previous events who tested clean?

Chapter 9

Women and the Olympic Games

> Unattractive girls are comparatively good sports. Pretty girls are not. The ugly ducklings, having taken to sport as an escape and to compensate for whatever it is they lack, sex appeal, charm, ready-made beauty, they usually are too grateful to be up there in the championship flight to resent losing so much. ... There is no girl living who can manage to look anything but awful during the process of some strenuous game. ... If there is anything aesthetically more depressing than the fatigue-distorted face of a girl runner at the finish line, I have never seen it. ... No matter how good they are, they can never be good enough, quite, to matter. Paul Gallico (1940: 242–244)

Women and sport

Societies institute, fashion and perpetuate behaviours and expectations that inform and constrain us in most facets of our lives. In sport, as in many other activities, one of the key differences between the acceptance of male and female participation relates to societal perceptions of gender and its subsequent determination of appropriate roles and behaviours based on these expectations. Dimensions of gender are culturally constructed disparities between males and females that are grounded in the praxis of power and associated with concepts of 'femininity' and 'masculinity'. Thus, gender is central to the socio-cultural examination of attitudes to, and behaviours in, sport, including the Olympic Games.

Orthodox stereotypes of male athletes stress their possession and application of strength, muscularity, aggression and power. These are characteristics which accentuate their masculinity. On the other hand, the athletic female is often faced with the expectations of conforming to society's definition of what constitutes 'womanly', and thus more passive, behaviour. Consequently, some of the physical and psychological attributes which contribute to a female athlete's sporting success may conflict with society's sanctioned notions of femininity. If a woman wants to achieve excellence in a sport which involves strength and the development of a muscular body, or participate in a traditionally male sport, she may risk exclusion from society's definition of 'normal'. Censure may be evidenced in various forms, for example labels questioning her sexuality.

The backlash against women who do not conform to idealised feminine images is, of course, not confined to sporting arenas: it is found across many other walks of life. While, in Western societies in recent years, some of the barriers to equality have been partially eroded, they have not disappeared entirely. In other societies, various forms of discrimination between the sexes also exist. Sometimes their perceived disparity causes criticism in the West, such has occurred recently with regard to practices in some Islamic countries.

In other non-Western societies, such as China, in some instances, the place of women in some facets of life may appear to be more 'equal' than in the West and sporting success can be used to promote nationalism. However, this does not imply there is complete equality in life. In terms of Olympic sport, however, Dong Jinxia (2005: 542) notes that 'Olympic victories have put Chinese women centre stage. Successful sportswomen have become heroines of the nation and won enormous social esteem and prestige'.

Historically though, in most societies, sport has been the embodiment of hegemonic masculinity (Connell, 1995: 77), an avenue by which males can demonstrate their superiority over females. To participate in sport is often an empowering experience for males, but it has often been less so for females. This is not to say that sport has been universally positive for males and disadvantageous for females. Indeed, writers such as Michael Messner and Donald Sabo (1990) assert that sport can also be problematic for those males who participate in sports which fall outside the bounds of its traditional masculine persona, while other researchers, for example Karla Henderson (1994), note that sport can be a site of resistance for women.

Generally, however, females have had fewer opportunities than males to develop positive selfhood through physical activity. This is even further accentuated for females of certain social and cultural backgrounds where the dichotomy between masculinity and femininity is greatest and participation by women in many sports is considered to be inappropriate. The sport gender divide may be even further perpetuated by poverty or women's traditional roles in relation to their family and domestic duties, which may leave them little time to pursue sport for leisure purposes.

Gendered differences in sport are not confined to the field but are also evident in administration, coaching and management. Males dominate all of these realms. In the late twentieth century, the works of McKay (1992), Cameron (1995), Theberge (1988, 1991), Bryson (1987, 1990) and Hall *et al.* (1990), amongst others, highlighted the comparatively small number of women in leadership positions in sports administration and coaching. This has not changed significantly so far in the twenty-first century. The male domination of sports participation, management, administration and decision-making has put women in a position of continually having to justify and fight for their right to equal access to facilities, funds, programmes and leadership opportunities.

Many of our gender-biased assumptions about women and sport are reinforced on a daily basis through various channels of media. In print and television, women's sport coverage receives significantly less attention. Murray Phillips (1997) found that in the Australian press: women receive significantly less coverage than men; female sport is less likely to make the front or back pages of the newspaper; and is more likely to appear in mid-week issues. The Amateur Athletic Foundation of Los Angeles (AAFLA - now LA84 Foundation) has conducted four studies on gender in televised sport in the USA. The latest of these was published in 2005 (AAFLA, 2005). Anita DeFrantz, president of the foundation, IOC member and former IOC Vice-President, noted in her foreword to the report that:

'the continued paucity of women's stories occurs against the backdrop of significant growth of girls' and women's sports nationally and internationally, a development that is simply ignored by television sports news. The wilful neglect of women's sports is an abdication of journalistic responsibility and has the effect of diminishing the significance of women's sport, while hindering its further growth. (DeFrantz, 2005: 3).

The consequences of these attitudes are discussed in greater detail later in this chapter.

Research

The major focus of many studies on gender and sport has been on notions of difference or 'otherness' between males and females, the debate often centring on whether these dissimilarities are biologically determined or socially constructed. This philosophy of disparity has allowed its proponents to ground their arguments against equality in a conviction of women's inferiority. This gender positioning has then been employed to justify the maintenance of male domination of sporting spaces and places.

It is because of the relative strength and speed of most males compared to most females that sense definitions of women in sport are often gauged in terms of their otherness or 'lower' standards than males. 'The salient point of this socially constructed ... differentiation is that through these historical definitions women are perceived not only as "other than" but as "less than" men' (Kane and Parks, 1992: 50). However, other writers (e.g. Anne Hall, 1996) caution against the application of gender roles as the foundation for the analysis of women's sport because such arguments nullify the influences of other powerful determinants, such as ethnicity, class and age.

Other research on gender issues in sport has examined sport's ideological and systemic inequities. For example, works by Lois Bryson (1987), Brian Stoddart (1994) and Jim McKay (1991) have highlighted discriminatory practices which prevent many females from attaining equal access and equity on the sporting field. Bryson has suggested that popular sports for boys and men have constructed and reconstructed male dominance by equating maleness with skills and attributes prized in our society, such as aggressiveness, power and strength.

In more recent years, however, much of the research in gender and sport has moved beyond considerations of relative opportunities and participation to a deliberation on the cultural meanings and significance that we attach to participation in physical activity. This research is seeking to examine the power of sport in the construct of ideology (Theberge, 1991). Sport has been accepted to be a particularly dynamic site for the construction and affirmation of gender identity; however it is now also contended to be a site where gender expectations may become contested.

The search for gender equality at the Olympics is based on a liberal feminist perspective. Its defining characteristic has been predicated on examining and analysing discrimination, socialisation, equality of opportunity, and the rights of women. It is considered to be an optimistic approach to gender issues, with links to liberal democratic principles. This theoretical basis has been applied to and driven much of the academic analysis of gendered sport since the 1960s. Sheila Scraton (1992: 7) notes that 'women have developed theoretical frameworks around their practice, claiming that theory can inform practice just as practice must be the cornerstone of theory'.

However, these theoretical underpinnings have allowed scholars to push the barriers of inquiry beyond thinking only in terms of women's Olympic participation rates and associated issues into a broader understanding of gender relations in society. Many studies question the male domination of sport, its institutional bases, values and practices, and call for a re-evaluation of sport to better cater for all its constituents (Kew, 1997).

What is disturbing, however, is research which continues to demonstrate how unequal conditions and their underlying values still exist in the Olympic Games. It seems that, while some advances have been made, academics and social critics are still having to demonstrate, through the use of statistical studies, as well as through qualitative studies which tell more in-depth stories of female athletes and administrators, that there is still a long way to go before Olympic and other international sporting bodies can claim that they offer a 'level playing field' for all.

Women in the Olympic Games

As discussed in Chapter 2, women's participation in the Ancient Olympics, as either athletes or spectators was, at the least, highly restricted. This limitation served to function as part of the rationale for their early exclusion and suppression in the modern Games. However, it was the prevailing mores of the era that were the primary motivation for their early invisibility in the modern Games and this remains the case in regard to current inequities.

According to Jennifer Hargreaves, the story of women's participation in the modern Olympics is one of 'struggle and diversity – power and control were fought over, not just between men and women, but between different groups of women' (Hargreaves, 1994: 10). Hargreaves argues, however, that it is over-simplistic to generalise about all the historical factors influencing women's Olympic participation as a number of the barriers to equal participation are culturally, economically and politically specific. Throughout the era of women's participation in the Olympics, it is evident that, as with other sporting events, the Games have become sites where society's values, meanings and ideologies can be disputed.

At the genesis of the modern Olympics, at the end of the nineteenth century, power relations based on gender were expressed through athletes' participation rights, and in the Olympic arena as in many other facets of life, women came off second best. The founder of the modern Olympic Games, Pierre de Coubertin, wrote much about his views of women and sport. In 1912, in a letter regarding the Stockholm Games he wrote:

> As for the Modern Pentathlon I am personally opposed to the admittance of ladies as competitors in the Olympic Games. But as they are this time admitted as tennis players, swimmers etc. I do not see on what grounds we should stand to refuse them in the Pentathlon. However I repeat that I greatly regret the fact. (de Coubertin, 2000: 447)

Further, in relation to women's overall participation in these same Games he noted:

> It is not in keeping with my concept of the Olympic Games, in which I believe we have tried, and must continue to try, to put the following expression into practice: the solemn and periodic exaltation of male athleticism, based on internationalism,

by means of fairness, in an artistic setting, with the applause of women as a reward. (de Coubertin, 2000: 713)

His views, which were certainly neither unique, nor out of step with many of his contemporaries, did not undergo a major transformation during his lifetime. For example, even in 1928, he gave a speech in Lausanne, in which he stated:

In many countries today, it is the girl who corrupts the boy. ... Can the young women I have mentioned before ... acquire a moral sense through sports, too? I do not believe so. Physical education, athletic physical culture, yes. That is excellent for young girls, for women. But the ruggedness of male exertion, the basis of athletic education when prudently but resolutely applied, is much dreaded when it comes to the female. That ruggedness is achieved physically only when nerves are stretched beyond their normal capacity, and morally only when the most precious feminine characteristics are nullified. (de Coubertin, 2000: 188)

Even after World War I, when the openings created for women in the workplace were reflected in greater freedom in many spheres of their lives, such perceptions of the masculinising effects of sport still remained dominant and acted as a deterrent to equality of access and opportunity (Birrell and Cole, 1994). The modesty, dignity and morality, of female athletes were policed by both sexes, but remained the responsibility of women. This too had an effect on determining which Olympic sports were deemed seemly for women and defined the behavioural and dress standards for female athletes who chose, or were allowed, to participate. It is interesting to note that the long-standing role of the chaperone for female Olympic athletes did not have a male equivalent.

Jennifer Hargreaves (1994) has identified three phases of women's participation in the modern Olympic Games:

1. *1896–1928*: was marked by the exclusion of women and efforts on the part of some of them to resist this dismissal.
2. *1928–1952*: was a time of consolidation and struggles for women in the Olympics, where their events were confined to those that met the criteria of acceptability.
3. *1952 – the present*: the period of challenge to masculine hegemony. This span was triggered by the entry of the Soviet bloc into the Games and the resulting influence of their political medal agenda, wherein it was immaterial to their national governments whether their nation's medals were won by male or female athletes.

The pattern of women's participation in the Games is summarised in Tables 9.1 and 9.2.

Introduction of women's sports to the Olympic programme

Although Pierre de Coubertin had opposed women's participation in his plans for the revival of the Games, this exclusivity was short-lived. At the shambolic 1900 Paris Olympic Games, Charlotte Cooper became the first female modern Olympic victor, when she won the ladies singles in tennis, beating Helene Prevost of France, 6–1,

Table 9.1. Women's participation in the Summer Olympic Games

Year	City	No. of Sports for women	No. of Events for women	No. of NOCs sending female athletes	Participants	
					Female	Total
1896	Athens	0	0	0	0	311
1900	Paris	2	3	5	19	1330
1904	St Louis	1	2	1	6	687
1908	London	2	3	4	36	2 035
1912	Stockholm	2	6	11	57	2 574
1920	Antwerp	2	6	13	77	2 607
1924	Paris	3	11	20	136	3 092
1928	Amsterdam	4	14	25	290	3 014
1932	Los Angeles	3	14	18	127	1 408
1936	Berlin	4	15	26	328	4 066
1948	London	5	19	33	385	4 099
1952	Helsinki	6	25	41	518	4 925
1956	Melbourne	6	26	39	384	3 342
1960	Rome	6	29	45	610	5 348
1964	Tokyo	7	33	53	683	5 140
1968	Mexico City	7	39	54	781	5 531
1972	Munich	8	43	65	1 058	7 830
1976	Montréal	11	49	66	1 247	6 189
1980	Moscow	12	50	54	1 125	5 512
1984	Los Angeles	14	62	94	1 567	7 078
1988	Seoul	17	86	117	2 186	9 421
1992	Barcelona	19	98	136	2 708	10 563
1996	Atlanta	21	108	169	3 626	10 744
2000	Sydney	25	132	190	4 069	10 651
2004	Athens	26	135	192	4 306	10 568

Source: IOC Department of International Cooperation, 1998, 2005

6–4, in the final. Cooper was also half of the victorious mixed doubles combination. There were 1318 men and 19 women at these Games. Tennis had been introduced to the Olympics in 1900, largely because it was a sport played by women of the upper classes (Blue, 1988). Females from privileged backgrounds had the necessary access to the money and time needed to facilitate their participation in socially acceptable sports.

The women at these Olympic Games came from five countries and participated in three events in two sports. Since that time women's participation in the Olympics has grown to the extent that 4306 female athletes competed in 135 events in 26 sports at Athens in 2004, representing 41 per cent of athletes at these Games (IOC, 2004b). Yet parity is far less than this in other aspects of the Olympic Movement; for example, in membership of the International Olympic Committee itself, and the total number of sports and events open to women competitors.

Table 9.2. Women's participation in the Winter Olympic Games

| Year | Location | Number of competitors: | | |
		Male	Female	Total
1924	Chamonix, France	247	11	258
1928	St Moritz, Switzerland	438	26	464
1932	Lake Placid, USA	231	21	252
1936	Garmich-Partenkirchen, Germany	566	80	646
1948	St Moritz, Switzerland	592	77	669
1952	Oslo, Norway	585	109	694
1956	Cortina, Italy	657	134	821
1960	Squaw Valley, USA	521	144	665
1964	Innsbruck, Austria	892	199	1 091
1968	Grenoble, France	947	211	1 158
1972	Sapporo, Japan	801	205	1 006
1976	Innsbruck, Austria	892	231	1 123
1980	Lake Placid, USA	840	232	1 072
1984	Sarajevo, Yugoslavia	998	274	1 272
1988	Calgary, Canada	1 122	301	1 423
1992	Albertville, France	1 313	488	1 801
1994	Lillehammer, Norway	1 215	522	1 737
1998	Nagano, Japan	1 389	787	2 176
2002	Salt Lake City, USA	1 513	886	2 399
2006	Torino, Italy	1 548	960	2 508

Sources: Wallechinsky (1992); IOC (2006a); USOC (1999)

Ironically, what little women's participation existed in the early Games was the result of the IOC's laissez-faire attitude to the organisation of the Games. Female athletes participated in 1900 and 1904 without the IOC's official consent. Only eight women participated in the 1904 St Louis Games. All of them were archers from the USA and there have since been doubts expressed as to whether or not their events were even classified as official Olympic competitions (Simri, 1977).

Women's participation in the 1908 Games was more formalised (Hargreaves, 1994). At this point the IOC lacked the necessary organisational skills or infrastructure to control the Games' programmes. This was the responsibility of the Paris and St Louis Games organising committees, which allowed inclusion in their programmes of the socially acceptable sports of tennis in 1900, and archery, classified as an exhibition event, in 1904 (Welsh and Costa, 1994).

Determined to bring order to the chaos caused by conflicting opinions on women's participation, the Olympic Organising Committee for the 1908 London Games admitted the women's events of exhibition gymnastics and aquatics (Welsh and Costa, 1994). These 1908 Olympics were a watershed for a number of reasons, one of which was that the first event open to both sexes, in the sport of sailing, was introduced. In this event Frances Rivett-Carnac and her husband were victorious, making her the first woman to win a gold medal against male competitors at the Olympic Games. Other sports in which there were female competitors at these Olympic Games included tennis, archery and figure-skating (which was later shifted to the winter programme) (Phillips, 1992).

By 1912, the International Federations that had included women's events in the Games were having an observable effect in improving their female constituents' status in achieving recognition in sport. The International Swimming Federation, in particular, provides a clear example of this. At the Stockholm Games 41 of the 55 female competitors were swimmers, the remaining 14 competing in the tennis competition. Fanny Durak of Australia was the first female Olympic swimming champion. She won the 100 metres freestyle in 1 minute 22.2 seconds, a time identical to that of Alfred Hajos of Hungary, the Games' first male winner of the same event at the 1896 Games.

Phillips (1990) notes that the task for women in the Olympic Movement, as in the wider world of sport, was twofold at this time: to avoid exclusion and to create a meaningful presence. For example, in 1920, de Coubertin suggested that the 1924 Games should have no female competitors. The IOC rejected this proposal; however, he was unrepentant and later, in 1925, at the Olympic Congress in Prague, he claimed that female participation in the Games was illegal (Simri, 1977). The most notable outcome of early feminist resistance to this attitude of sporting officials was the creation of the Federation Sportive Feminine Internationale (FSFI), under the leadership of Alice Milliat.

This group organised a separate female sporting contest, the first 'Women's Olympics', held in 1922 in Monte Carlo, with 300 competitors (Blue, 1988). Subsequent to its success, and the IOC's objections to the use of the word 'Olympic' in its title, the event was renamed and the FSFI staged the Women's World Games in 1926, 1930 and 1934, following the four-year cycle of the Olympics, but at the half-way point between them. However, it would be unrealistic and misleading to portray these sporting gains as being universally accepted by all women. There were many women who were against the new sporting patterns of female participants, which now more closely mirrored that of males. These opponents believed that a new model for women's sport should be adopted, based on cooperation, rather than the competitive model that events such as the Olympic Games exemplified.

It was the success and accomplishment of the Women's World Games that forced the hand of the male-dominated IOC into allowing more events for women onto the Olympic programme, yet admittance of female track and field athletes to the Games was still problematic. Indeed, the IOC held a conference in 1925 to examine the 'issue' of sport and women. Hargreaves (1994: 213) notes that its 'medical report was a reaffirmation of the popular nineteenth century theory of constitutional overstrain ... urging caution about the type and amount of exercise ... with a scientific justification limiting women's participation in track and field athletics during the following years'.

In 1928 track and field competitions in the 100 metres, the high jump, discus, 400 metres hurdles and 800 metres were added to the women's schedule at the Olympic Games to placate the FSFI. Unfortunately, several competitors appeared to be distressed at the finish of the 800 metres. This supposed collapse of the women, attributed to tackling a distance in excess of their physiological limits, became a defining point in Olympic history for a number of reasons. Initially, the IOC used it as a justification of its previous stance to severely limit women's participation. As a consequence, women were allowed to compete only at shorter distances in track events for about four decades. Some of the strength-related field events were also deleted from the programme. More recently, feminist scholars have chosen the 1928 800 metres as the exemplar of the oppression of female athletes in the Games.

Count Baillet-Latour had followed de Coubertin as President of the IOC and continued his predecessor's line of philosophical opposition to female Olympians in certain sports. In 1930, he suggested to the Berlin Olympic Congress that women should be allowed to compete only in 'aesthetic events'. His list of acceptable sports included skating, tennis, gymnastics and swimming. This desire to limit female participation was inversely proportional to the plans to increase the number of sports for men, and continued in many forms throughout the twentieth century.

In 1936 attempts to include female competitors in the equestrian events and hockey competitions were rejected (Simri, 1977). In 1984, when Gabrielle Andersen-Schiess' visually disturbing attempts to finish the marathon were broadcast throughout the world, the press was still questioning the endurance ability of females, despite the fact that she had recovered less than two hours later. 'Marty Liquori, the television analyst, was not impressed with her courage, repeatedly saying: "Someone should take charge and stop her. ... Someone should walk out there and take responsibility and grab her"' (Birrell and Theberge, 1994: 354). Despite these problems, there has been a recent change in attitude. The last six Olympic Games have seen the number of sports for women increase more than at any time in Olympic history, as shown in Table 9.1.

Women have taken part in all the Olympic Winter Games since their first celebration in 1924. From the 1998 Nagano Olympic Games (which saw the first female ice hockey and curling competitions), all seven sports on the winter programme have been open to women. However, within the sport of skiing, female athletes do not participate in the discipline of ski jumping.

The notion of the female athlete as a delicate individual dominates the Olympic saga, although the most recent additions to women's events at the Olympic Games have come from sports considered to be 'non-traditional', such as football (1996), weightlifting (2000) and wrestling (2004), as indicated in Table 9.3. The time lag between the introduction of these events for men and for women speaks for past conditions as much as it does for progress.

The twenty-first century

The Sydney 2000 Olympic Games had greater access for female competitors than any previous Olympic Games in terms of events and number of days of competition. This trend continued for the 2004 Athens Games. In the 2000 Sydney Games there were 120 women's events, compared to 97 in Atlanta, an increase of 23. Women were contestants in all but three sports on the Olympic programme (boxing, baseball and wrestling), but at the same time competed exclusively in softball and the disciplines of rhythmic gymnastics and synchronised swimming.

This increase in participation occurred in three ways. First by the introduction of two new Olympic sports (taekwondo and triathlon), both of which had women's events. Second by a sport increasing the number of its events to include women – women's water polo. Last, where sports reduced the number of men's events and concurrently introduced a women's one, for example, modern pentathlon, which included a women's event for the first time and accordingly reduced the number of male athletes competing from 32 to 16, and weightlifting, which included women on the programme for the first time and reduced men's events from ten to eight.

Some of the other statistics relating to female participation in the Sydney 2000 Games should cause us to rethink our perceptions of where and how gender equality at the Olympics is being practised. In Sydney, 53 NOCs had teams that comprised

Table 9.3. Introduction of Women's sports to the Olympic Programme

Year	Sport
1900	Tennis, Golf
1904	Archery
1908	Tennis, Figure Skating
1912	Swimming
1920	Figure skating
1924	Fencing
1928	Athletics, Gymnastics
1936	Skiing, Gymnastics
1948	Canoeing
1952	Equestrian sports
1960	Speed skating
1964	Volleyball, Luge
1972	Archery
1976	Rowing, Basketball, Handball
1980	Field Hockey
1984	Shooting, Cycling
1988	Tennis, Table Tennis, Sailing
1992	Badminton, Judo, Biathlon
1996	Football, Softball
1998	Curling, Ice Hockey
2000	Weightlifting, Pentathlon, Taekwondo, Triathlon
2002	Bobsleigh
2004	Wrestling

Source: IOC, 2004d

at least 50 per cent female athletes. The majority of these came from Africa and Asia. The team from Myanmar, with 85 per cent female athletes, had the highest percentage of female representation of any NOC. There were only seven Western NOC teams where the number of female athletes equalled or exceeded their male athletes (Australian Sports Commission, 2001).

At the Athens 2004 Olympics further records were set for women's participation. Of the 10,864 athletes who competed, 4412, or 41 per cent of the total, were women. This compares well with previous Games (Sydney: 38 per cent, Atlanta: 34 per cent).

Results are less impressive for the accredited media. For the print media, the percentage of accredited females was 17 per cent. The highest relative percentage of these was journalists from Oceania (22 per cent), followed by the Americas (19 per cent) and Europe (18 per cent) (ASC, 2001). Also at these Games, the IOC elected Gunilla Lindberg as its second ever female Vice-President. (IOC, 2004b).

Looking towards the 2008 Beijing Games, Dong Jinxia notes that the Chinese will partly gauge their success by the number of medals won by their team and, significantly, the role of women in achieving this goal has been spelled out:

To ensure Chinese accomplishment in 2008, the 'Plan to Win Glory in the 2008 Olympics' was drafted in 2002. According to the plan Chinese athletes will participate in all 28 sports competitions and obtain more medals in more events than in past games, aiming to be one of the top three powers at least. Specifically, the Chinese wish to capture 180 medals from the 298 events. ... Women will play a major part in achieving this goal. Over 80 per cent of medals are to be won by women. (Jinxia, 2005: 540)

Women in the administration of the Olympics

While it is evident that Olympic female athletes are growing in numbers and in the proportion of athletes competing in the Games, the same cannot be said about their administrative counterparts. It was not until 1981 that the first two women were admitted to membership of the IOC. To date there have been 21 women elected. At present there are 15 female members of the IOC, as shown in Table 9.4.

Table 9.4. Female IOC members (February 2006)

Name	Country
HSH Princess Nora of Liechtenstein	Liechtenstein
Anita L. DeFrantz	USA
HRH the Princess Royal	Great Britain
Gunilla Lindberg (IOC Vice-President)	Sweden
HRH the Infanta Doña Pilar de Borbón	Spain
Nawal el Moutawakel	Morocco
Irena Szewinska	Poland
Manuela di Centa	Italy
Els van Breda Vriesman	Netherlands
Pernilla Wiberg	Sweden
Rania Elwani	Egypt
Barbara Kendall	New Zealand
Nicole Hoevertsz	Aruba
Beatrice Allen	Gambia
Rebecca Scott	Canada
Dame Mary Alison Glen-Haig (honorary member)	Great Britain,
Flor Isava-Fonseca (honorary member)	Venezuela,

Source: IOC website

While there has been a change of mind-set within the IOC, to be more inclusive of women, some critics (e.g. Jennings, 1996; Sheil, 1998) believe that the changes are too slow and are only tokenistic. Be that as it may, the adjustment has lately been in the direction of increasing female representation and is being implemented through a number of initiatives. For example, in December 1995, the then IOC President, Juan Antonio Samaranch, established a Women and Sport Working Group, the purpose of which was to provide advice to the Executive Board and the President on issues related to females and the Olympics. The group had an impact. For example, one of its recommendations was: 'The Olympic Charter be amended to take into account the need to keep equality for men and women' (IOC Department of International Cooperation, 1998: 22). The *Olympic Charter* was duly amended in 1996 to include a statement on women and the 2004 version identifies as one of the roles of the IOC:

> to encourage and support the promotion of women in sport at all levels and in all structures, with a view to the strict application of the principle of equality of men and women. (IOC, 2004: 11)

In July 1996 the IOC adopted the following proposals put forward by the Women and Sport Working Group:

1. The NOCs should immediately establish as a goal to be achieved by 31 December 2000 that at least 10% of all the offices in all their decision-making structures (in particular all legislative or executive agencies) be held by women and that such percentage reach 20% by 31 December 2005.
2. The International Federations, the National Federations and the sports organizations belonging to the Olympic Movement should also immediately establish as a goal to be achieved by 31 December 2000 that at least 10% of all positions in all their decision-making structures ... be held by women and that such percentage reach 20% by 31 December 2005. (IOC Department of International Cooperation, 1998: 22)

While these goals do not require strict equality, and in some cases appear to be modest outcomes, they have not been achieved. Based on information provided by 187 NOCs and 35 Olympic IFs (as of December 2003, rather than the 2000 deadline):

*   61% of NOCs had achieved the objective of 10%.
*   90% of NOCs had at least one woman on their executive body.
*   26% of NOCs had more than 20% of women on their executive body.
*   57% of Olympic IFs had achieved the objective of 10%.
*   91% of Olympic IFs had at least one woman on their executive body.
*   23% of Olympic IFs had more than 20% of women on their executive body.

(IOC, 2004d)

Twenty-nine countries sent female athletes but no female officials to the 2000 Games. Even the country where the Games were held, Australia, had only 27 per cent females as part of its officials contingent (ASC, 2001).

In March 2004 the Women in Sport Working Group became a fully fledged commission, known as the IOC Women and Sport Commission.

Thus, it appears that the Olympic Movement has made some inroads into gender inequality, but what are the penalties for organisations which fail to comply? What are some of the factors that have led to the inequities and the resistance to conform to the proposals? The answer may be clearer if the IOC examined the practices of its own administration in Lausanne. Although the opportunities for some women are encouraging and much progress has been seen in the field of play, much still remains to be done at the leadership level. The IOC acknowledges: 'Of all the sectors of activity, the management and administration of sports organisations is certainly the one in which greater efforts must be made to address the inequalities which still exist' (IOC, n.d.(a)).

The media and women in the Olympic Games

The media are major contributors to the hegemonic discourse which values male sport more highly than female sport. One of the outcomes of this alliance is shown through a number of content analyses investigating relationships between women's sport and the media, which have found a consistency of findings, namely that female sport is grossly under-represented in newspaper, radio and television coverage (Fasting and Tangen, 1983; Australian Sports Commission and Office of the Status of Women, 1985; Wilson, 1990; Theberge, 1991; Ferkins, 1992; Stoddart, 1994; Phillips, 1997). While results of some of these studies indicate that there has been an increase in female coverage in more recent times, it would be difficult to interpret any of the results as truly addressing a situation which is seen by many as discriminatory (Phillips, 1997). Thus, it is manifest that this research has had little, if any, impact on reducing existing inequalities or changing the sentiments of those who determine what is seen, heard, or read in the media.

As a result of the co-dependant relationship between the mass media and sport, which has developed over time, the media have now become one of the key benefactors, and key beneficiaries, of institutionalised sport and, as such, have become a forceful site for constructing gender discourse and fashioning hegemony. As Daddario (1994: 276) notes: 'This is particularly the case for the Olympic Games which offer long-term profitability for the networks, with many hours of potential commercial revenue'. The Olympic Games, as portrayed by the media, may thus provide consensual views of female athletic abilities, views which carry over into other spheres of women's lives.

The increase in the percentage of Olympic athletes who are female has not always been assisted through their media representations. The press have not always willingly helped in seeking equality of coverage for them. In 1928, for example, 'Fed up' in the Australian publication, *The Bulletin* wrote: 'after the 800 metres race at the Olympiad, knocked out and hysterical females were floundering all over the place. Competition in such events can serve no useful or aesthetic purpose in feminine existence' (quoted in Phillips, 1992: 36). This was neither the first nor the last such scathing commentary on women's athletic ability.

The sports media, in particular, have constructed narrative and visual messages, tropes, texts and sub-texts which emphasise physical differences between men and women and consequently have contributed to the construction of a gender hierarchy, based on traditional notions of masculine strength and feminine frailty. While males are often portrayed in a manner that accentuates their athletic abilities, females are presented, more often than not, in terms which define their femininity and/or body image, rather than their athleticism. Consequently, these portrayals often depict women's performances as being inferior to men's. The Olympic Games broadcasts are important in these constructs because of the status of the Olympics as the pinnacle of athletic achievement. They are considered by many people to present and define a consensual view of women's athletic abilities. Yet, from Olympic television broadcasts, Higgs and Weiller (1994: 245) argue: 'there is reason to worry about audience sensemaking about the athletic abilities and limitations of men and women'.

Apart from general principles of equity these results are disturbing because of the pervasiveness of the media in society. One of the most common reason girls have cited as an incentive for becoming active in sport and selecting a particular discipline is the influence of role models (House of Representatives Standing Committee, 1991: 10). Yet girls and women have a paucity of female sports heroes on whom to model themselves, not because females are not participating and succeeding in sport, but rather because their achievements have largely been ignored by the media. Ignoring female sport in turn sends the message to many sections of the community that women's sport is unimportant, trivial and unworthy of attention. This then serves to reinforce and legitimise the patriarchal male sport model (Toohey, 1997).

When asked why they persist in showing mainly male sports and continue to ignore women's sport the media continue to justify their position on the basis of specious logic, for example, that women's sport is dull and lacks excitement, that viewers are uninterested in it and that it is generally not newsworthy (*Ms Muffet*, 1988: 6). However, an Australian case study of the Summer Olympic Games has shown that the public is attracted to televised female sport, if given the opportunity to watch it (Toohey, 1997). A survey conducted during the 1988 Seoul Olympic Games indicated that 90 per cent of respondents watched it on television at least once and 44 per cent daily. Swimming, gymnastics and diving were the three sports which respondents most enjoyed. Television coverage of these three sports provided fairly equal coverage of male and female competition, indicating that viewers enjoy watching female sport, if given the chance (*Australian Olympian*, 1988; Toohey, 1997). Total television coverage of women's events during the 1988 Olympics equalled 33 per cent of sports coverage, significantly higher than during regular programming (Toohey, 1997).

These results are not unique. A similar survey during the 1992 Barcelona Olympics produced comparable results and attitudes. Television coverage of the Games was watched by 98 per cent of respondents. Swimming, gymnastics, rowing and track and field were the most watched sports, with swimming, gymnastics, and track events being rated the three most 'popular' sports (Sweeney and Associates, 1992). These events not only included relatively equal numbers of male and female athletes, but resulted in greater than equal air-time for women's events compared to men's. It is quite realistic to assume that if the women's events were not 'good television', viewers would have changed channels (Toohey, 1997).

While other studies have drawn links between viewers' nationalistic sentiments and their programme preferences, data did not indicate that this was relevant for these broadcasts. Success does however influence television directors' and programmers' selection of which sports to broadcast. For example, in 1988, when the Australian women's hockey team won the gold it received 424 minutes of coverage. The 1992 team was less successful and this resulted in less air time. While the success rate of Australia's female athletes explains their Olympic television exposure in part, it is not the complete answer, for Australian women are also successful in other international sporting events, yet these do not receive air time on commercial television. Thus, while connections can be deduced between nationalism, success and increased coverage of women's sport during the period of the Olympics, this does not always translate into what viewers perceive to be the female sports they most enjoy watching. This implies that arguments for continuing under representation of women's sport, based on lack of the excitement factor and viewers' interest are fallacious (Toohey, 1997).

At the 1988 Seoul Olympic Games 27 per cent of the Australian team members were female but female athletes received only 33 per cent of the Australian airtime given to their male counterparts (*Australian Olympian*, 1988; Toohey, 1997). At the 1992 Barcelona Games 37 per cent of the Australian team were female and they could compete in 38 per cent of the events at the Games, but events for women received only 30 per cent of the total of the Australian television coverage during the time surveyed. While these percentages under-represent female participation in the Games, they far exceed those found in the previous surveys of coverage of female sport in regular programming practices – for example, Stoddard (1994) found that only 4.2 per cent of non-Olympic sports coverage was devoted to women's sport.

As previously noted, during the 1988 broadcasts, viewers indicated that the four most popular sports on Australian television were: swimming, gymnastics, diving and track and field. For the 1992 Barcelona Games the most popular four sports were: swimming, gymnastics, track and field and rowing. Table 9.5 presents data from studies of Australian television coverage of these activities at the two Games. It shows that the proportion of the total coverage which was of female events was on average over 40 per cent, even more than the proportion for all sports, which was 30 per cent.

Table 9.5. Coverage of female events in the Seoul, 1988, and Barcelona, 1992 Games by Australian television networks

	% of coverage devoted to female events
1988, Seoul	
Swimming	49
Gymnastics	46
Diving	36
Track and Field	45
Total	44
1992, Barcelona – Highlights package	
Swimming	45
Gymnastics	38
Track and Field	51
Rowing	43
Total	47
All sports	30

Source: Toohey (1997)

A study investigating Australian newspapers during the 1992 Olympics again indicated that women's sport received much greater coverage than at other times. Embrey *et al.* (1992) analysed three major metropolitan daily newspapers, one in New South Wales, one in Victoria, and one in Western Australia. The *Sun-Herald* allocated 31 per cent of the total Olympic coverage to females, *the Age*, 30 per cent and the *West Australian*, 27 per cent (Embrey, et al., 1992: 11), well above the 4.2 per cent average found by the above-mentioned Stoddard study of non-Olympic coverage.

The findings of these of Olympic broadcasting content analyses indicate that the 'female deficit model', which indicates that women's sport is judged by comparing it to men's and consequently often considered to be lacking speed and strength and thus excitement, is not all-pervasive. This may indicate that the key to breaking existing patterns of sports programming lies through promotion of female sport at major events. While this is not an answer in itself, it could be a legitimate starting point to argue against the inequities in sports broadcasting that currently exist (Toohey, 1997).

Since these studies were conducted there have been many others on the same theme, examining both television and newspaper coverage. For example, Capranica *et al.*, in their a study of newspaper coverage of women's sports in the 2000 Sydney

Olympic Games in Belgium, Denmark, France and Italy, found that: 'the newspaper coverage was similar to the distribution of participating athletes and events. No significant gender differences were found with respect to article size, page placement, accompanying photographs, or photograph size' (Capranica *et al.*, 2005: 212).

Merely increasing the quantity of media coverage does not necessarily guarantee equality in all respects. Some researchers conducting content and semiotic analyses have shown that women's sport reporting can trivialise, marginalise and at times demean females (McKay 1991; Duncan *et al.,*1994). Higgs *et al.* (2003), in their study of the 1996 Olympic television broadcast, found that women's coverage remained stereotyped.

Wensing and Bruce (2003) found that five 'rules' used by the media contributed to the framing of female athletes into their subordinate, culturally prescribed, gender roles. These were:

1. gender marking – referring to an event as a women's event;
2. compulsory heterosexuality – representing the female athlete as a sex object or mother, wife or girlfriend;
3. emphasis on appropriate femininity – where the athlete is shown as fragile, small, beautiful, dependant, etc.;
4. infantisation – when a female athlete is referred to as a girl or young lady, or only her first name is used;
5. non-sport related report – where the focus is on the athlete's appearance or personal life.

To this list they added a newer rule, called 'ambivalence'. By this they mean that 'positive descriptions and images of women are juxtaposed with descriptions and images that undermine and trivialize women's efforts and successes' (Wensing and Bruce, 2003: 388).

An increase in this type of portrayal may indeed be counterproductive in establishing women's sport as an activity worthy of increased exposure, in a manner consistent with that afforded to the male equivalent. As examples of research which illustrate the 'rules', American research examining the media's qualitative portrayal of female athletes in the 1992 Albertville Winter Olympics concluded that, while women were being represented in physically challenging events that advanced women's equality in terms of participation in these sports (e.g., the luge and the biathlon), paradoxically media portrayals did not always emphasise athletic performance traits. An examination of the corresponding Summer Games broadcasts showed that the women's gymnastics was framed by an emotion-charged narrative focusing on athletes' personal lives, their youth, attractiveness and their diminutive stature (Daddario, 1994). Further, different descriptors were used for women engaged in masculine sports and those involved in feminine ones. While the strength of the former was cited, the beauty of the latter was accentuated. There were examples of the press fashioning their own views about female athletes in both these Olympic broadcasts. Examples of marginalising practices included in these Olympic telecasts included: condescending descriptors; the use of compensatory rhetoric; the construction of female athletes according to an adolescent ideal; and the presentation of female athletes as driven by cooperation rather than competition (Daddario, 1994: 275). Daddario's rhetorical analysis concluded that 'the sports media reinforce a masculine sports hegemony through strategies of marginalisation' (1994: 275). Even though women are shown to be competing in sports that require strength, speed and endurance, the narration may give only qualified support or negate the athleticism of the competitors through a media logic, which seeks to appeal to viewers, especially women, by creating human interest story lines, via the narrative approach to Olympic broadcasts.

Wensing and Bruce did find one significant instance when the gender of an athlete was subsumed by a different marker. In their study of mediated representations of Cathy Freeman, the Australian Aboriginal runner who lit the cauldron at the Opening Ceremony of the Sydney 2000 Games and went on to win the 400 metres, they noted that:

> Gender is not always the overriding signifier of identity. It suggests that coverage of international sports events such as the Olympic Games may be less likely to be marked by gendered (or racialized) discourses or narratives than reporting on everyday sports, at least for sportswomen whose success is closely tied to a nation's sense of self. In this instance, the usual rules were significantly bent to accommodate Freeman's presence as a national symbol of recognition... Freeman was marked as female, but this was not a primary framing devise. Instead she was represented as an individual (both Aboriginal and female) who could unite a nation (Wensing and Bruce, 2003: 393–94).

However, as Wensing and Bruce concluded, Freeman is the exception, rather than the rule.

Eleanor Holm Jarrett: a case study of a female Olympic athlete

Despite growing evidence about female physical ability and sporting capabilities, society's collective assumptions of women's frailty have formed part of the ideology in which the Olympic Games are sited. In the past, the Olympic power brokers themselves have helped define and institutionalise this construction which has served to reinforce their power, restricting, confining and subordinating female athletes. Yet, it would also be limiting to assume that all females have conformed to their expected roles. Those women who have contested the stereotypes have had to battle powerful ideologies and resist the logic of male supremacy. Acknowledging that these social barriers exist, and may even be more effectual than beliefs about biological differences, relocates analysis of female participation in sport to be located in the wider context of the power structures in society and how we are socialised by and through them. One such woman who battled the stereotypic image of femininity, compliance and the Olympic power barons was Eleanor Holm Jarrett.

This section of the chapter presents a case study of Eleanor Holm Jarrett, who rejected the narrow confines placed on her behaviour by the press and Olympic authorities alike and paid the price. While time has passed since Jarrett competed, and the story is not new, there are parallels between Jarrett's behaviour and those of other female Olympians who have pushed the femininity envelope, often to their detriment. Later athletes have benefited from the unwillingness of these women to be objectified and subjugated.

Eleanor Holm Jarrett was selected as a member of the 1936 US Olympic team to compete as a backstroke swimmer. Her subsequent dismissal from the team has been suggested by some to have been either the result of an overprotective attitude towards female athletes or a case of double standards, although others suggest that these sentiments are open to question (Leigh, 1974). Regardless of the reason, her lack of traditional training methods was the overt reason for her expulsion from the US team.

This was to be her third Olympics. She had competed in Amsterdam in 1928, winning a bronze medal in the 100 metres backstroke. In 1932, in Los Angeles, she won the gold medal in the same event. She had won the US National Championship in this event twelve times, the first time when she was only 13 years old. Between the 1932 Games and the 1936 Games, she had set records in every backstroke event swum by women. In addition to her swimming prowess she was extremely attractive and by the age of 16 she had been offered a job in the Zigfeld Follies in New York. She refused this offer, but not the one she received from Warner Brothers Studios in Hollywood. This contract guaranteed her US$500 per week and acting lessons from Josephine Dillon, the first wife of Clarke Gable (Mandell, 1971).

Because of these Hollywood connections, the first questioning of her amateur status occurred. A portion of her attraction to the movie studios was obviously her aquatic skills and pressure was applied by the studios to induce her to appear in the water on screen. While she had no qualms about poolside publicity shots, the strict amateur rules of the time would forbid her being filmed while swimming and so Eleanor temporarily abandoned acting.

Figure 9.1. Eleanor Holm Jarrett

Despite this sacrifice she still encountered opposition from the Amateur Athletic Union (AAU) concerning her amateur status and, more importantly, her questionable standing was brought to the attention of the American bastion of amateurism, Avery Brundage, who had acquired an almost monopolistic hold on leadership positions within American amateur sport (Gibson, 1976).

Amateurism had been an integral component since the Olympic revival and Brundage embraced this belief fervently, adopting a more rigid stance than even de Coubertin. Holm Jarrett's amateur 'purity' came under close scrutiny from Avery Brundage. Gibson provides this philosophy as the *raison d'être* for subsequent events. In a letter to John T. Taylor, dated 21 May 1934, Brundage stated:

The advertisement of Eleanor Holm Jarrett in the *Gantes Swimming News* ... in my opinion eliminates her from amateur competition. This is the same sort of offence for which proceedings were instituted against Babe Didrickson. I am surprised to see this advertisement because apparently Miss Holm has been very careful to protect her amateur standing. Her appearance in moving pictures is only allowed so long as she does not appear in any role that has connection with sports or games or athletic events, provided that in the advertisements there is no reference to her athletic prowess. If there have been any violations of this understanding she will be eliminated from amateur competition. (Brundage in Gibson, 1976: 94–95)

During December 1934, when the AAU met in Miami, Florida, the question of Holm Jarrett's amateur status was raised. She competed in amateur swimming under the jurisdiction of the metropolitan association of New York, which had already examined her case and had found no cause for concern. The charges brought against her at the AAU convention were initiated by the central association of Chicago, an interesting development as this was hardly a geographic area in which Holm Jarrett would be likely to have much contact, but more understandable when it is considered that this was the centre of 'Brundage territory'. The focus of the charges was the use of her picture and endorsement in an advertisement for a swimming suit, as alluded to in Brundage's letter above (*New York Times*, 1934: 8 Dec.). Following its investigation the AAU decided that Holm Jarrett had not contravened her amateur status and she was allowed to continue her swimming 'career'.

The trials for the US swimming team for the 1936 Olympic Games were held at Astoria, Long Island, New York. Holm Jarrett won the 100 metres backstroke final in spite of the fact that she had been 'partying' with her husband, the band leader, Art Jarrett, the night before (*New York Times*, 1936: 25 July). This was a typical training regime for her. When she boasted of training on caviar and champagne these claims were not unfounded. According to Holm Jarrett, they had done her no harm in the past and she saw no reason to modify her behaviour when selected for the 1936 team.

As mentioned in Chapter 4, the US participation in the 1936 Games was fraught with problems, principally focusing on the Nazi doctrine of anti-Semitism. These problems did not dissipate once the USA had committed itself to competing. The public, which was the principal source of funding, was reticent to contribute, so that, 10 days before the team was due to depart, it was still some US$150,000 short of its target. A last minute drive raised US$75,000 and, notwithstanding the threat of constant cutbacks, a full contingent of athletes and officials set sail on the SS *Manhattan*, when the team departed for Europe on 15 July.

Each athlete had been issued with the *American Committee Handbook*, containing information pertinent to competitors, a congratulatory note from Avery Brundage and a list of rules and regulations. After reading the handbook, athletes were required to sign a certificate accepting its conditions. Portions of this document are germane to subsequent events because of the sections dealing with training methods and the expected demeanour of athletes. For example, it stated: 'it is understood, of course, that all members of the American Olympic team refrain from smoking and the use of intoxicating drinks and other forms of dissipation while in training', and: 'I agree to maintain strict training during the voyage and until my competition in Berlin is completed' (Rubien, 1936: 53). Holm Jarrett, as did all other members of the team, signed the certificate, thus agreeing to abide by its conditions.

One day out of port, Brundage, on behalf of all officials, lifted the ban on alcohol and cigarettes, leaving the degree of indulgence to the discretion of the individual athlete. In lieu of total abstinence, the athletes were placed on their honour to maintain their fitness. However, by July 18, the first reports of athletes carousing reached the ears of officials. No athletes were singled out for disciplinary action and team managers were given the responsibility for enforcing a stricter ban. Relations between some of the swimming officials and Holm Jarrett had been strained even before the sea voyage: this made the situation worse.

However, the press reports for the next few days gave no more information of behaviour problems. Apparently, even the 10 p.m. curfew was lifted on one occasion. Brundage was quoted as saying:

> The fact that we were dealing with high-strung athletes who had emerged from an extended series of strenuous tryout [sic] contributed to our problem. However, on being placed on their honour, they responded magnificently, maintaining a high standard of conduct and trained conscientiously under obvious shipboard handicaps. (*Los Angeles Times*, 1936: 23 July)

The following day the papers carried a contrary communication: 'Mrs Jarrett has been dropped from the American team for violation of training rules and her entry into the Olympic Games has been cancelled' (*New York Times*, 1936: 24 July). This was the first occasion that an American athlete had been dismissed from a US team *en route* to the Games.

The decision to dismiss Holm Jarrett was made at an American Olympic Committee meeting. Testimony regarding her indiscretions was furnished by: Ada Sackett; Herbert Holm, the manager of the women's swimming team; Herbert Lawson, the team physician; and the ship's doctor. The accused was not invited to attend. Press reports suggested that her discharge was triggered by an on-board party she attended on 17 July, escorted by the writer, Charles MacArthur, husband of the actress Helen Hayes. The straw that broke the camel's back, however, was that, on her way back to her cabin after another party on 24 July, while in a less-than-sober state, she bumped into Mrs Sackett. Immediately after this incident the team's executive called a meeting and voted unanimously to dismiss her (*Los Angeles Times*, 1936: 25 July).

Apart from this indiscretion, Holm Jarrett's general demeanour, while on board, had not endeared her to the Olympic officials. Initially, she had complained to them about inequities in accommodation. They were travelling first class while the athletes were in third-class cabins. Later, she had boasted of impunity from team rules. The *Los Angeles Times* (1936: 25 July) reported that: 'prior to last Saturday's warning Mrs Jarrett had declared she liked to imbibe and enjoy the relaxation of party life and intended to do so regardless of what officials may think. Waving her hand to all listeners she declared: "This is the way I'm accustomed to train and I don't see why I should change now"'. She had also boasted that officials wouldn't dare to put a champion off the team. When she found news to the contrary, her attitude changed. She became contrite, declaring: 'I'm on the spot now, I feel like jumping overboard but will train and not touch another drop if I'm given another chance' (*Los Angeles Times*, 1936: 25 July).

Such declarations were not enough to sway the committee, even when she insisted that she was not a lone transgressor and that other team members were as guilty as she. Meanwhile, many team athletes and coaches rallied to her defence. A petition requesting clemency for her was signed by 220 athletes from a total 333, including all the women's swimming team. Some coaches spoke in favour of her reinstatement. One athlete was quoted as saying: 'she deserves punishment for misbehaviour but many of us feel she's being made the scapegoat for other less conspicuous offenders against disciplinary orders and training rules' (*New York Times*, 1936: 25 July).

In America, too, the incident created much controversy. 'Dink' Templeton, the Stanford University Track coach declared:

> The Olympic Committee, as had been its wont, dared the young lady with threats and Eleanor is not a gal to take a dare. It is unfortunate that a true reflection of the difference between the committee and the athletes, who are looked on as prize livestock and taken to Europe to be exhibited for the benefit of the august American Olympic Committee, had to be brought to light in this manner. ... But it will probably be patched up and should be a means of closer understanding between the two classes of free tourists, one of which earns its way, while the other holds the whip hand. (*New York Times*, 1936: 25 July)

Art Jarrett, Eleanor's husband, thought that it would be a good idea to give all the swimmers champagne, in the hope that they would win some races. However, not everyone was so sympathetic. One of the strongest anti-Holm Jarrett comments came from Lawrence Robertson, the head coach of the Olympic Team. He was quoted in the *New York Times* (1936: 25 July) as saying: 'The Greeks had the right idea over 2,000 years ago when all women were barred'.

Holm Jarrett was given the opportunity to present her case to a subcommittee. This group upheld the previous decision, meaning there was now no further avenue for recourse. The AOC requested the return of her uniform and booked a return passage for her to the US on the 'Brennan'. Eleanor, however, had no intention of being dismissed so easily.

Once her name had been officially withdrawn from the 100 metres backstroke event, Holm Jarrett's attitude reverted to attacking the AOC. She issued a 700 word statement condemning its actions. In this document she insisted that there was no general rule against drinking, the bars in the athletes' section of the ship were open daily and on one occasion did not close until after midnight (*Los Angeles Times*, 1936: 26 July). Brundage's response was brusque. He was so offended by the article that he suggested that the AAU (of which he was President) might consider rescinding Holm Jarrett's amateur status, although he did not specify the ground on which this would be based.

As she could no longer compete, Holm Jarrett accepted the offer of the International News Service to cover the Games as a reporter. Even in this role she attracted attention, especially at the Opening Ceremony as the *New York Times* reported in a style that reinforced the notion of the fragile female:

> She came bravely to this initial pageant, a little figure in a rose costume and a picture hat and she sat in the front row to do her job, She was courageous, in a sense, and for a while she chatted gaily, taking notes meanwhile, and all went well until the flag passed and behind it came the serried ranks of American women competitors. .... That was too much and she was missing. Her colleagues found her sobbing her heart out in a far corner of the press room. (*New York Times*, 1936: 3 Aug.)

Apart from this temporary breakdown, her high spirits and public appearances were not curtailed. The *New York Times*, on 29 July, reports her meeting with former Crown Prince, Frederick Willhelm and being escorted through the Netherlands Palace. True to form, Holm Jarrett was anything but retiring, complimenting the Prince on his handsome features, suggesting that he would be an asset to the movie industry in

Hollywood and that Americans would go crazy over him if he ever graced their shores.

While she was charming Europe, her relations with Brundage were becoming more strained. Brundage utilised his power to disqualify her from amateur competition in Europe, invoking his authority as head of the AAU. In essence, this action was purely of a punitive nature, as Eleanor had no intention of competing in Europe. Its effectiveness lay in demonstrating the lack of power of athletes who questioned authority. Holm Jarrett took this further disqualification in true form, commenting:

> He may have the power to suspend me in Europe ... but this is the first time I knew he could just point a finger at a person and say; 'Now you're a professional'. I call this adding insult to injury. ... I do not see how he can do it without giving my case some kind of hearing. If they start barring everyone who takes a drink, they won't have any amateurs left. (*New York Times*, 1936: 9 Aug.)

Even though her competitive time as a swimmer was now finished, the situation was not entirely detrimental. The brouhaha had created a deluge of publicity, much of it in Holm Jarrett's favour. Publicity is the stuff of life to a celebrity and so it appeared in her case. On her return from Germany she set out on a vaudeville tour throughout the USA, accompanied by her husband. This signalled the beginning of her rise as an entertainer. The following year she discarded both her current career and husband and acquired new ones of each. She married Billy Rose (previously the husband of Fanny Brice) and joined his 'Aquacade'. Not only was she the star of this show but she also returned to Hollywood, playing the role of Jane in a 1938 version of *Tarzan of the Apes* movie, which featured Glen Morris (winner of the 1936 Olympic decathlon) as Tarzan (Mandell, 1971).

The AOC purged Holm Jarrett's name from its 1936 *Official Report*. Even its photograph of the women's swimming team is minus her visage. The only direct mention of her occurs on page 279, when it is noted that Eleanor Holm Jarrett of the Women's Swimming Association of New York won the 100 metres backstroke at the finals of the Women's Swimming Trials. Brundage circuitously mentions her dismissal in the 'Report of the President' (p.33) but does not mention her by name. He insinuated that the whole incident was blown out of all proportion by those who wished to discredit the Olympic Committee because of its decision to attend the Games in spite of the exclusion of Jews from the host nation's team.

What was the prime reason for Eleanor Holm Jarrett's dismissal? Obviously she disobeyed the rules of the AOC, but her instant dismissal, without an opportunity to plead her case, defies the boundaries of due process. Avery Brundage had tried to dismiss Holm Jarrett through the proper channels in 1934 and failed. On the SS *Manhattan* he had a second opportunity and this time he succeeded. Female athletes of this period were far more rigidly bound by what society considered acceptable codes of feminine behaviour than today's woman. Would Holm Jarrett have been dismissed for the same offence had she been male? Whether she should have been dismissed from amateur status by the lone decree of Brundage is another vexed question. She would have automatically forfeited her amateur status when she performed with the Aquacade and, in hindsight, as the next two Olympics were cancelled, this action meant little, except perhaps to Holm Jarrett.

Although 1936 has long passed, a form of poetic justice has been met. Avery Brundage's character has been shown to be less than honourable and in conflict with the ideals he espoused and which he censured others for not adhering to. In a 1980 *Sports Illustrated* article he was described as a lecherous adulterer, while Eleanor

Holm Jarrett received far more positive recognition by being inducted into the Women's Sports Foundation Hall of Fame (Johnson, 1980). These two seemingly unconnected events occurred within two months of each other.

The double standard of moral and social behaviour condoned by the sports establishment of the 1930s, and illustrated by the Holm Jarrett saga illustrates one aspect of the inequities and ordeals that have been experienced by some female Olympic athletes. Another inequity that many female athletes have been subjected to is gender verification.

Gender verification, or sex testing

The idea of binary sexual status and thus the implicit belief in a male's athletic supremacy, has resulted in one of the most controversial tests in sport, namely 'sex testing' or, as it has more recently termed, gender verification. During its implementation, Hargreaves (1994: 222) noted that 'the femininity control test, which is obligatory for all female Olympic competitors ... is the most potent symbol of the concern to prove that there is an absolute distinction between the sexes'.

As part of the Olympic medical procedures for athletes competing in women's events, it lasted from the 1968 Mexico City Games until it was conditionally rescinded before the 2000 Sydney Games. Underlying its introduction was the outward appearance of 'fairness', however there was also another agenda. Politics was also a factor in the introduction of the tests. Iain Ritchie writes that:

> it was at the height of the Cold War that the East Bloc female athletic body emerged as a visible challenge to Western normative ideals regarding what a proper female body should be. Images and perceptions of the sexual body played a vital role in national ideologies and in the inculcation of nationalistic feelings. ... Soviet and East Bloc athletes were regarded as implicit challenges to the Western heterosexual imperative – they were portrayed as unfeminine, 'Amazons', lesbian, or men. (Ritchie, 2003: 85, 86)

Before the introduction of the test to the Olympic Games in 1968, the same Games at which a woman (Enriquetta Basilio) first lit the flame in the Olympic cauldron, only a few men had been caught posing as female Olympic competitors. Not all of these had been deliberate attempts to gain an advantage. Some of those uncovered had gender ambiguities that even they were unaware of.

Adrianne Blue gives examples of some of the most commonly known examples of such athletes who were exposed to the world as having gender irregularities.

> In 1938 a German high jumper was found to be a hermaphrodite, with both male and female organs. Two Frenchwomen on the relay team which won silver at the 1946 European championships were later found to be living as men, but whether they had pretended to be women or were now pretending to be men was not completely certain. A skier who had failed the chromosome test ... had her male sex organs hidden inside her body since birth. In 1980, the elderly Mrs Stella Olsen, a Polish American, who had been the 1932 Olympic 100 metre sprint champion as Stanislawa Waldrewicz, was killed as an innocent bystander in a robbery and it was discovered that she had male sex organs. (Blue, 1988: 160)

In the 1936 Olympics, Waldrewicz, who competed for Poland, but was known in the USA, where she lived, as Stella Walsh, was beaten by Helen Stephens, who represented the USA. Paul Gallico, writing in his usual uncomplimentary manner towards female athletes and sports administrators, described what occurred after the 100 metres women's final.

> Miss Helen Stephens, a big rangy schoolgirl from Mississippi, out-galloped all the best women sprinters ... including Poland's favorite Stella Walsh. The Poles ... immediately accused Miss Stephens of being Mr Stephens. ... The American Athletic Union ... revealed solemnly that before being permitted to board the boat to uphold the honour of the USA as a member of its Olympic team the Olympic Committee had had La Stephens frisked for sex and checked her as being hundred per cent female. With no thought whatsoever for the feelings of the young lady in question these findings were triumphantly if ungallantly aired in the press. (Gallico, 1940: 233)

In a similar invasion of privacy, in 1966, when sex testing was first introduced by the International Amateur Athletic Federation (IAAF) at the European Track and Field Championships in Budapest, all of the 243 female entrants were required to appear nude before a panel of doctors. 'The "nude parades" were humiliating as physicians searched for the absence of a vaginal opening or an enlarged clitoris or testicles' (Canavan, 1997: 16). This practice of physical inspections continued. Later, Mary Peters, the British Gold medallist in the Pentathlon at the 1972 Munich Games, described the procedure as 'the most crude and degrading experience I have ever known in my life' (Jennings, 1996: 214).

Because of the growing resentment against this physical examination it was replaced by a chromosome test, the Buccal Smear Test. The test involved taking a scraping of buccal and mucosa cells from the inside of the woman's mouth. The sample was then subject to microscopic examination for the presence of 'sex chromatin (i.e. inactive X or Barr bodies and fluorescent Y-body chromatin material)' (Dickinson *et al.,* 2002: 1541). This evaluative technique led to a new set of problems, as it provided new criteria to determine eligibility as a female competitor. Not everyone believed that its definition of 'female' was correct. 'At least 13 women were excluded from athletic competition between 1972 and 1990 using sex chromatin testing; many others with abnormal sex chromatin tests "retired" or opted to forgo further assessment to avoid public scrutiny' (Dickinson *et al.*, 2002: 1541).

In 1967, Eva Klobukowska, from Poland, became the first candidate to fail this new test at the European Cup Track and Field Events where the IAAF had introduced it. It was found that Klobukowska possessed a Y chromosome in addition to the XX combination that was determined to be the only standard for being classified as a 'woman'. Subsequently, her world record in the 100 metres and an Olympic Gold medal were revoked and she was banned from further female sporting competition, even though it was thought that her genetic makeup provided her with no physical advantage (Blue, 1988; Ritchie, 2003).

In 1992 at the Barcelona Olympic Games the Buccal Smear Test was replaced by a polymerase chain reaction (PCR) form of testing with DNA analysis for Y chromosome material (Jennings, 1996). PCR is a 'technique that detects the male SRY (sex-determining region of the Y chromosome) gene in a fragment of DNA taken from a buccal smear' (Ritchie, 2003: 91).

These two tests were far less invasive than the earlier measures of physical inspection, however arguments for and against their use continued. On one side were those who believed that they provided the genetic 'level playing field, by only including competitors in female only designated competitions who were genetically 46 XX'. On the other side of the argument were those who argued that there were female athletes now excluded from Olympic competitions for minor genetic irregularities which did not endow them with any additional physical advantage. At the Barcelona Games, 2406 female athletes were tested. Eleven tests were positive for DNA located on the Y chromosome. From these five athletes 'failed' the test (Dickinson *et al.*, 2002).

At the 1996 Atlanta Games a more comprehensive gender verification process, comprising: 'screening, confirmation of testing and counselling of affected individuals' was used (Dickinson *et al.*, 2002: 1541). 'Eight of the 3387 female athletes had positive tests for *SRY*, 7 had partial or complete androgen insensitivity, and the other had undergone gonadectomy ... All of these females were allowed to compete' (Dickinson *et al.*, 2002: 1541).

In 1999 the IOC conditionally rescinded the gender screening of all women entered in female-only events for the 2000 Olympics. Instead 'intervention and evaluation of individual athletes by appropriate medical personnel could be employed if there was any question about gender identity' (Dickinson *et al.*, 2002: 1541). While this move stifled the critics who were questioning the validity of the medical procedures, a new debate emerged in regard to the gendering of athletes. It revolved around the eligibility of competitors who had changed their sex.

The issue first came to the fore in the sport of tennis, when Renee Richards, who had undergone a sex change, competed on the women's circuit in the 1970s. Ian Ritchie (2003: 83) notes that the media 'framed the controversy either in terms of liberal notions of competitive fairness, or in terms of the debate regarding whether Richards was a man or woman. Interestingly, it was his/her inability to dominate woman's tennis that eventually confirmed the media's acceptance of Richards as a woman.' Since that time, there has been continued debate on the issue of intersexed or transsexual athletes, again couched in terms of an unfair advantage.

Yet it was not until May 2004 that the IOC Executive Board approved a proposal by the IOC Medical Commission, stating the conditions in which a person who has changed sex could compete in Olympic sports competitions. This was implemented, beginning at the 2004 Games in Athens. The IOC declared that individuals undergoing sex reassignment of male to female before puberty would be regarded as female. Individuals undergoing female to male reassignment should be regarded as male. Individuals undergoing sex reassignment from male to female after puberty (and vice versa) would be eligible for participation in female or male competitions, respectively, under the following conditions:

- Surgical anatomical changes have been completed, including external genitalia changes and gonadectomy.
- Legal recognition of their assigned sex has been conferred by the appropriate official authorities.
- Hormonal therapy appropriate for the assigned sex has been administered in a verifiable manner and for a sufficient length of time to minimise gender-related advantages in sport competitions.

This eligibility would begin no sooner than two years after gonadectomy (IOC, 2004a).

The IOC proposed a confidential case-by-case evaluation and that, in the event that the gender of a competing athlete being questioned, the medical delegate (or equivalent) of the relevant sporting body should have the authority to take all appropriate measures for the determination of the gender of a competitor (IOC, 2004a).

Like so many other issues relevant to the Olympic Movement, there is no straightforward answer to the question of athletes' gender and eligibility. Whatever the ruling, many of those who are not on the winning side of a decision will feel aggrieved. However, because so many cultures, with different norms, customs and mores, are represented at the Games, this individual basis of evaluation, and the general removal of gender verification testing, is a step forward.

As discussed above, although the IOC has taken this move, the diversity of cultures and values at the Games means that there are still many other gender-related areas that impact on participation. Those who argue that the issue of gender equality should be a universal one, based on a binary approach, may need to rethink this either/or perspective.

As Dickinson *et al.* (2002: 1542) note, gender verification has resulted in: 'invalid screening tests, failure to understand the problems of intersex, the discriminatory singling out of women based only on laboratory results, and the stigmatization and emotional trauma experienced by individuals screened positive'. Ritchie (2003: 92) is even more critical. He wrote: 'sex testing was, in many cases, a misguided policy and a colossal failure. The test never met its purported objective of catching men clandestinely posing as women in athletic events because, for all intents and purposes, this was not occurring in the first place'.

Conclusion

Historically one of the most controlling arguments used to oppose women's participation in sport is that men are physically superior to women in performance measures (Figler and Whitaker, 1995). Yet, 'from an anatomical and physiological standpoint, males and females are more alike than different ... other than the obvious differences in reproductive organs' (Figler and Whitaker, 1995: 301). The differences between women and men in terms of physical performances are relatively minor and the gap is closing. During the twentieth century women's athletic performances improved more than males (Simri, 1977) – some comparisons are shown in Table 9.6.

In recent times, it has been suggested that the undetected use of performance-enhancing drugs in the 1980s accounts for the fact that, since drug testing has become more sophisticated, many male and female results have not improved. There is no reason to believe that the twenty-first century will be any different. It is also arguable that such measurable differences in athletic performance may have social expectations and opportunities as their basis, rather than a biological variance (Figler and Whitaker, 1995). In sport, even today, it appears that norms and standards are still based on male performance, consequently females' sporting achievements are judged in terms of their 'otherness'. As a result they are generally perceived to be inferior to or less than those of their male counterparts. This viewpoint of sex based differentiation has become accepted as biologically natural, rather than socially constructed and culturally reproduced. Yet research has 'raised serious doubts, if not refuted the commonly held and taken-for-granted assumptions concerning physical/ physiological sex differences' (Scraton, 1992: 8).

Table 9.6. Comparison of male and female athletic performances in selected events at recent Olympic Games

Event	Year	Men's Winning Performance	Women's Winning Performance
100 metres	1988	9.92 s	10.54 s
	1992	9.96 s	10.82 s
	1996	9.84 s	10.94 s
	2000	9.87 s	10.75 s
	2004	9.85 s	10.93 s
200 metres	1988	19.75 s	21.34 s
	1992	20.01 s	21.81 s
	1996	19.32 s	22.12 s
	2000	20.09 s	21.84 s
	2004	19.79 s	22.05 s
400 metres	1988	43.87 s	48.65 s
	1992	43.50 s	48.83 s
	1996	43.49 s	48.25 s
	2000	43.84 s	49.11 s
	2004	44.00 s	49.41 s
Long jump	1988	8.72 m	7.40 m
	1992	8.67 m	7.14 m
	1996	8.50 m	7.12 m
	2000	8.55 m	6.99 m
	2004	8.59 m	7.07 m
High jump	1988	2.38 m	2.03 m
	1992	2.34 m	2.02 m
	1996	2.39 m	2.05 m
	2000	2.35 m	2.01 m
	2004	2.36 m	2.06 m
Shot	1988	22.47 m	22.24 m*
	1992	21.70 m	21.06 m
	1996	21.62 m	20.56 m
	2000	21.29 m	20.56 m
	2004	21.62 m	21.06 m
Discus	1988	68.82m	72.30 m*
	1992	65.12m	70.06 m
	1996	69.40m	69.66 m
	2000	69.30m	68.40 m
	2004	69.89m	67.02 m

Source: Smith (2004). * weight of the women's and men's shot and discus differ.

Through sex-role socialisation we learn to behave in ways that are expected of us as either males or females. One aspect of this is that boys are channelled into activities such as sport. Sport, in Western societies, is still considered to be a highly instrumental activity, often inconsistent with notions of feminine behaviour, which is based on the attributes of dependence, passivity and physical and emotional weakness.

In other cultures there are also gender role barriers. One of these was broken in 1984 when the 400 metre hurdler, Nawal El Moutawekel, from Morocco, became the first Islamic woman to win an Olympic medal (ASC, 2001).

Medically-based arguments that female athletes are physically unsuited to intense physical training or sport competition have been shown to be invalid. There is no conclusive evidence that competitive sport is any more dangerous for females than males (Figler and Whitaker, 1995). While some conditions, such as menstrual irregularities (for example amenorrhoea), have been associated with strenuous physical activity for women, these symptoms are considered to be reversible (Figler and Whitaker, 1995).

Women have yet to achieve their Olympic potential. The IOC has now acknowledged that it has to adopt a more active role in redressing the gender-based inequalities in the Olympic Movement that have existed for over a hundred years. As part of this process, the IOC has created performance goals in this area – a role that is relatively recent, still not universally acknowledged as being necessary or advisable, and one where targets are not always being met. As with other aspects of the Games, this historical inequality is not unique to the Olympic Movement. Gendered disparity has been part and parcel of sport throughout its history and has been based on two main assumptions: that women are physically inferior to men and that it is unbecoming for them to indulge in certain activities. Many Olympic sports are still considered to be 'inappropriate pastimes' for girls and women. Some cultures do not allow women to participate in sport in front of males at all. These great cultural differences in acceptance of sport for women at the Games have raised dilemmas for athletes, sports officials and feminists alike, especially when religious grounds are cited as the reason behind the restrictions.

Further reading

IOC statements on women	IOC (2004a, 2004b, 2004d)
Loughborough University study	Loughborough University (2004)
Gender verification	Ritchie (2003)
Women's Sports Foundation website	www.womenssportsfoundation.org

Questions

1. Should the IOC require quotas for women's participation from NOCs and IFs? Why or why not?
2. Do you think that women's sport is less interesting to watch on TV than men's sport? Why or why not?
3. Who do you think are some of the outstanding female Olympians of all time? Why have you chosen them for your list? Are the criteria the same as you would have chosen for a list of outstanding male Olympians? Why or why not?

Chapter 10

Case Studies of the Summer Olympic Games

The Olympic Games requires a tremendous investment of human, financial and physical resources from the communities which stage them. They challenge (or distract) the best talents available for the better part of a decade and well beyond the terms of most governments. They play a decisive role in the character and progress of a region's economic development. ... At the level of ideology they illuminate competitive notions of public good. Not surprisingly bidding for and staging a public festival on this scale can be a highly charged political exercise, requiring the consummate skills of negotiation and consensus building from those in leadership. Bruce Kidd (1992a: 154)

Introduction

Every Olympic Games can be seen as a learning experience, for host cities and nations, for the Olympic Movement and for sport at large. The Games are such a large-scale event that they also have repercussions beyond sport, contributing to the development of contemporary world culture and even affecting international politics. What then can be learned from the experience of individual Olympic Games? In the earlier chapters of the book the focus has been on particular dimensions of the Olympic phenomenon, such as politics, economics, media, drugs and gender. Here we examine individual Games in the round.

Each Olympiad tends to generate more research and commentary than its predecessors. Consequently there is generally more written material available on later Games – more data, more evaluation, more comment and analysis – than on earlier Games. The main case studies presented here therefore focus on the last four Summer Games – Barcelona (1992), Atlanta (1996), Sydney (2000) and Athens (2004) – and look forward to Beijing (2008) and London (2012). Appendix 10.1 provides a brief overview of the Games of the modern era, with guides to the literature on individual Games. For each case study, one of the types of information presented is financial. Sums have been converted to US dollars to provide a certain point of comparison, but it should be noted that different host cities and governments use different accounting practices and therefore the sums shown are not strictly comparable. This issue is discussed in Chapter 6.

Barcelona 1992

Introduction

What was unique about the Games of the 25th Modern Olympiad, held in Barcelona in the region of Catalonia, Spain in July 1992? The initial notable feature is the choice of Barcelona at all. Why? Because Catalonia was the home of the then President of the IOC, Juan Antonio Samaranch – and the city where he spent much of his professional administrative life, prior to taking up the IOC presidency in 1980. It was in Barcelona and Catalonia that Samaranch served in various administrative roles under Spain's Franco régime, although precisely how close he was to the régime and just how prominent, is a matter of some dispute (Jennings, 1996: 28–33). The City of Barcelona bid for the 1992 Games in competition with, among others, Paris. The latter was seen by many as the front runner and Jennings (1996: 127) suggests that Barcelona would not have been awarded the Games if Albertville, France, had not, somewhat surprisingly, won the Winter Olympics for 1992, thus making a second French venue in 1992 impossible (it was only from 1994 that the Winter Games were switched to run two years after the Summer Olympics). As can be seen from Table 10.1, Paris still commanded considerable support among IOC members, but Barcelona won majority support in the third round of voting.

Table 10.1. IOC voting for the 1992 Games

Candidates	Round 1	Round 2	Round 3
Barcelona	29	37	47
Paris	19	20	23
Belgrade	13	11	10
Brisbane	11	9	8
Birmingham	8	8	-
Amsterdam	5	-	-

Source: Cuyàs (1992: 316).

   This examination of the 1992 Barcelona Games considers in turn: the philosophy of the Games, their organisation and their economic dimensions. To understand the significance of the Olympic Games to Barcelona and the surrounding region of Catalonia, it is appropriate to consider the historical background, which we do first, drawing on Brunet (1993).

History

Barcelona is an industrial Mediterranean port in north-eastern Spain, with a population of 1.6 million, in an urban area with a population of some 3.0 million. It is the capital of Catalonia, a region which has its own language and national identity and ethnic links with people over the border in France, similar to the situation of the Basque region in northern Spain. Following rapid industrialisation in the nineteenth century, Barcelona found a place on the world stage when it hosted international 'universal exhibitions' in 1888 and 1929. During the Civil War of 1936–39, the

Barcelona area saw some of the most bitter resistance to the Fascist forces of General Franco, whose régime subsequently ruled Spain from 1939 to 1975. During much of the Franco era Barcelona and the surrounding region experienced economic depression and physical neglect by the central government.

An interesting footnote in political history is that, in 1936, Barcelona was to be have been host to an alternative 'Popular Olympic Games' organised by socialists and communists in opposition to the 'Hitler Games' in Berlin, and one of a series of Workers' Olympics held in the first half of the century (see Chapter 4). The day before the games were due to start a military uprising, inspired by Franco, took place in Barcelona and the Spanish Civil War had begun. The 6000 athletes and estimated 20,000 visitors were forced to return home (Riordan, 1984; Pujadas and Santacana, 1992).

With the return of democracy in 1977, Catalonia, along with other regions of Spain, acquired an autonomous regional government, dominated by right-wing nationalistic parties, while the city of Barcelona was governed by left-wing coalitions. The 1980s was a period in which Spain sought to 're-enter' Europe, politically and economically, after the years of relative isolation under Franco. The year 1992 was an important watershed in this process:

> For the central government, the Barcelona Olympic Games were a piece within the overall group of events of the '1992 project'. They were not only in coincidence with the Seville Universal Exposition and the Madrid European Cultural Capital, but in a wider sense, the will of the central government was to show the world how Spanish society had modernized and transformed, and aspired to play an important role in the heart of the European Community. (Botella, 1995: 141)

Organisation

As is required by the IOC for all Olympic Games, the organisation of the Barcelona Games was vested in an Organising Committee, the 1992 Barcelona Olympic Organising Committee (COOB'92), with involvement of the Barcelona City Council, the Government of Catalonia, the Government of Spain and the Spanish Olympic Committee. The Mayor of Barcelona was President of COOB'92. Public works were carried out by a specially established public corporation, Barcelona Holding Olympic, S.A. (HOLSA), owned jointly by the Spanish Government and Barcelona City Council.

Philosophy

A number of contributors to the volume of essays published after the Barcelona Games, and entitled *The Keys to Success* (de Moragas and Botella, 1995), agree that the most significant feature of the Barcelona Games was the role they played in the economic, physical and political regeneration of the city. As one of the contributors put it:

> The Barcelona Games will only with difficulty be known as a technological event, in spite of having outdone the levels of quality and complexity of all previous editions. Nor will they be recalled as a commercial success, in spite of the fact

that the economic management was considerably more brilliant than in Los Angeles. Nor will they take on a significant political meaning, even though they coincided with historical changes in Eastern Europe, making them the most universal Games in history. ... everyone would agree ... that the true success of the Barcelona Games lay in the transformation the city underwent. (Millet i Serra, 1995: 189)

What was the nature of this transformation? Following the neglect of the Franco years, hosting the Olympic Games was seen as much more than a sporting event for the city: it was a stimulus to catch up on decades of lost economic opportunity.

The mobilization of energy generated by hosting the games was to serve the development of the city. In this way, the Olympic Games would act as a catalyst and provide an excuse to bring about *urban change* that would improve the *quality of life* and the *attractiveness* of Barcelona. (Brunet, 1993: 11)

This 'urban project' involved a number of major tasks, namely to 'open the city to the sea, supply it with basic transportation infrastructures, turn the old port into a place for public use, modernise the commercial port and the airport' (Abad, 1995: 13). The project was conceived in a unique way. Rather than seeking to concentrate Olympic facilities as much as possible, as has been done in other host cities, the decision was made to distribute the facilities in four 'Olympic Parks' around the city, one of which involved the redevelopment and opening up of the ocean frontage to create the athletes' village. In addition some facilities were decentralised to other cities in the region. The urban project also involved the construction of a system of ring-roads to link the Olympic Parks (Millet i Serra, 1995: 193). Thus the Olympics provided the impetus for a massive change to the urban infrastructure of the city.

This 'catalyst syndrome', which involves host cities using the occasion of the Olympic Games as a catalyst for developing, or redeveloping, urban infrastructure way beyond the immediate needs of the Games, is not unusual, although in Barcelona it was seen in extreme form. The syndrome particularly relates to transport developments, such as the building of freeways, rail systems and airports. Such developments cannot be economically justified on the basis of a single two week or month-long event, even an event as large as the Olympic Games, but, since the developments would undoubtedly facilitate the smooth running of the Games, the latter provides the deadline for their completion. Often these are projects which have been 'on the drawing board' for many years but, because of lack of funds or political or technical disagreements, they have not been proceeded with. The hosting of the Games focuses the attention of politicians and things get done which would otherwise not get done, or would be delayed. As one member of COOB'92 put it, in referring to the planning task for the Games, 'what mattered eleven years ahead of time was to determine the dominating idea that would allow us to do in five or six years what had not been done in fifty, with the risk of taking another fifty if the opportunity was not taken' (Abad, 1995: 12).

While the syndrome is largely a public sector phenomenon, driven by politicians, it can also be seen in the private sector – for example in the timing of the building of hotels. However, while sentiment may play a part in such commercial decisions, more hard-nosed, rational factors are also likely to come into play – for example the

Figure 10.1. Barcelona, 1992: Opening ceremony

calculation that a period of high occupancy for a hotel during the few weeks before, during and after the Games, would be a good start to the business, which would also benefit from the enhanced image of the host city, resulting in increased tourism and business traffic after the Games.

In smaller cities and smaller countries the scale of the undertaking to host the Olympic Games is daunting, and is viewed as a public test of the organisational capabilities of the city or country in the eyes of the world. Abad (1995: 12) recalled three years after the Barcelona Games that 'little more than five years ago few people thought that success was possible'. In the lead-up to the Games, 'the question of our image before the world was still pending: to 'come across well', to overcome the fear of universal ridicule'. In the event, the success of the Games, according to Abad (1995: 12), left a 'moral legacy, the affirmation that we as a country could and knew how to do things well'.

This qualitative dimension is related to an issue raised in Chapter 4, namely the question of political and community support for the Games. Abad, as a member of COOB'92, is of course not impartial, but he expressed the political imperative as follows:

> Citizens, being undoubtedly those most directly affected, could not, did not want to, nor had to remain ignorant or distant. They had to be informed, of course. Yet beyond this, they could not remain passive but had to be active partners, giving support to the organization with their participative attitude, both demanding and impatient. This great challenge, that of confidence – laid over skepticism if you wish – won out in the end. Only when the citizens had made the project fully their own did it acquire the category of 'untouchable', so that nobody, neither political parties nor administrations nor people in general could allow it to be denaturalized or pushed to one side. (Abad, 1995: 16)

Economic aspects

The gross cost to COOB'92 of running the Barcelona Games was some US$1.3 billion, made up as shown in Table 10.2 and Figure 10.2. After the cost of facilities, it can be seen that the second largest item is 'Services to the Olympic Family' – consisting primarily of provision of accommodation, subsistence and transportation for athletes (10,200), members of National Olympic Committees, International Federations, and trainers (3400), judges and umpires (2400), accredited media personnel (5800), guests of the Organising Committee (2700) and sponsors and their guests (9200).

Table 10.2. Barcelona Games: Organising Committee budget

		US$ millions*
Expenditure	Facilities and surroundings	305.8
	Services to the Olympic Family	246.8
	Technology	165.3
	Support/administration	152.8
	Media services	121.7
	Sport event organisation	93.6
	Commercial management/ticketing	71.2
	Ceremonies and cultural events	60.3
	Publicity/promotion	52.9
	Security	31.3
	Total	1301.6
Income	Sponsors	387.7
	Television rights	361.1
	Lotteries	134.3
	Services	99.9
	Government grants etc.	86.3
	Tickets	63
	Accommodation	59.1
	Stamps/coins	50.2
	Other	38.1
	Sale of assets	14
	Licenses	10.2
	Total	1303.9

* Converted from pesetas at 150 to US$. Data source: Brunet, 1993: 24, 37.

The costs were approximately balanced by income generated, as shown in Table 10.2 and Figure 10.3. This shows the dominance of sponsorship and television rights, as discussed in Chapter 6. But in the case of Barcelona the significance of lottery income and the comparatively small contribution of government grants are also notable. The latter is explained by the existence of the lottery, but also by the fact that government expenditure was largely on infrastructure investments.

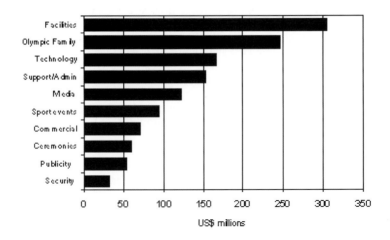

Figure 10.2. Barcelona Games: Organising Committee expenditure
Source: based on Brunet, 1993: 37

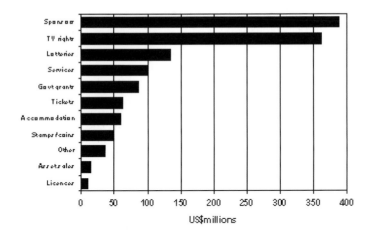

Figure 10.3. Barcelona Games: Organising Committee income
Source; based on Brunet, 1993: 24

As shown in Table 10.3, these investments amounted to some US$6.3 billion, or almost five times the running costs of the Games. Approximately 40 per cent of this expenditure was for transport schemes and 36 per cent for development of the Olympic facility precincts. Private sector investment, particularly on hotels, accounted for one third of the total.

Is this pattern of expenditure typical of the Olympic Games? Brunet (1993: 69) compares investment expenditure in Barcelona with that in the previous four Olympic

Games and shows that, while expenditure in Barcelona was considerably higher than in Seoul, Los Angeles and Montréal, it was lower than in Tokyo in 1964. As discussed in Chapter 6, the extent to which investment should be counted as 'Olympic Games costs' is debatable.

Table 10.3. Barcelona Games: investments 1986–1993

	US$ millions
Roads/airport	2521.7
Olympic areas (Poblenou, Montjuïc, Vall d'Hebron, Diagonal area, Port Vell)	2250.3
Cultural, health etc. facilities	141.5
Improvement of hotel facilities	799.2
Olympic satellite villages	466.1
Other sporting infrastructure	198.7
Total	6377.5

* Converted from pesetas at 150 to US$ (1999 exchange rate)
Source: based on Brunet, 1993: 43

Brunet (1993) conducted a detailed assessment of the economic impact of the Games on Barcelona. Total expenditure on the Games, including all investment expenditure, the expenditure of COOB'92 and expenditure by visitors, was US$7.8 billion. After multiplier analysis (see Chapter 6), this produces an estimated 'global economic impact' of US$20.7 billion, which results in an additional annual average of 59,000 full-time equivalent jobs over the period 1986 to 1992 (Brunet, 1993: 119). However, to treat this as a net effect of the Games assumes that none of the investment expenditure would have taken place but for the Games. While, as discussed above, the 'catalyst' effect may cause public bodies to undertake investment which would not otherwise have been undertaken, it is likely that at least *some* of the Barcelona infrastructure investments – for example on some roads or hotels – would have taken place without the Games, so the economic impact of this portion of the expenditure should not be attributed to the Games. Thus the size of the economic impact of the Games would seem to have been exaggerated in this case (see also Table 6.10).

A further issue in assessing the economic impact of the Games is the question of just how the investments are funded. Some of the funding came from international sources (television rights, sponsors, visitor expenditure) and some from the national and regional governments and can therefore be considered a net gain for the city.

Investment by the city government, if funded by loans, eventually has to be repaid; if funded from current taxes, then the money represents taxpayers' funds which, if not used for these investments, would have been spent on something else. Thus, while it is true to say that the levels of expenditure and jobs indicated are attributable to the Games, it should not be assumed that they represent, in total, a net gain for the city.

In the case of Barcelona, however, the 'catalyst' effect is considered highly significant. Brunet summarises the effect as follows:

This legacy is summarized in the urban transformation of Barcelona and the changes in the economic structure (greater capitalization, greater tertiary activity, greater internationalization, greater attractiveness, greater central focus, greater productivity, and greater competitiveness). The permanent additional employment that was a product of the greater collective capital and the private investments prompted by the Olympic Games and, in short, the greater capacity of the economic fabric, was calculated in this study to be 20,000 individuals. (Brunet, 1993: 119)

Economic impact studies of 'hallmark' events generally refer to the stimulus which the event is expected to give to tourism, not just during the Games, but for a number of years after. This appears to have been borne out in the case of Barcelona, with the number of visitors to the city increasing from less than two million in 1990 to more than three million in 1996, and the number of participants in congresses increasing from around 100,000 to over 200,000 in the same period (De Lange, 1998: 132–133), although it must always be borne in mind that such increases might possibly have come about even without the Games.

Sporting impact

As noted in Chapter 4, one of the aims of the Olympic Movement is the promotion of sport participation by the community in general. Truñó (1995), a member of COOB'92 and a member of Barcelona City Council, provides some evidence on the impact of the Games on sport participation in Barcelona. Initially, he points out that new sporting facilities provided for the Olympics were a lasting legacy for sport in the city. But of course facilities can become 'white elephants' if not appropriately managed. A new system, referred to as 'concerned management', was introduced to operate many of the new facilities, involving contracting of management to local private organisations.

> One of the keys to the successful functioning of the city's new sports facilities was precisely this management model, which made it possible for local administration to close the gap between itself and the average citizen by means of sport organisations which were in touch with the day-to-day reality of sporting activity and which were well-known in their respective neighbourhoods. (Truñó, 1995: 51)

The large 'flagship' facilities were managed by a new body, *Barcelona Promoció* (Barcelona Promotion). This and the private contract organisations provided a total of 450 new jobs in facility and event management and maintenance.

Truñó quotes survey evidence indicating that the proportion of the population participating in sporting activity at least once a week rose from 36 per cent in 1983, to 47 per cent in 1989 and 51 per cent in 1995 and he notes that 300,000 people belong to the city's 1200 sports clubs. A school programme, 'Campus Olympia', involving school use of the Olympic facilities, was launched in 1993, attracting 1750 participants, rising to 6500 participants in 1995 (Truñó, 1995: 56).

Conclusion – Barcelona

There is a wide consensus that the 1992 Olympic Games were a success. The success was not related particularly to events in the sporting arenas, although the Games produced their fair share of sporting drama and new records. Rather, the success appears to have been related to the interaction of city, culture, event and people. John MacAloon expresses it as follows:

> A preliminary review of Olympic media coverage ... shows a striking agreement that the city of Barcelona itself was the star of the Games. ... In a sense, Barcelona upstaged the Olympics, though in another sense the Olympic created the 'Barcelona'. ... The nightly flows of people on the Ramblas, and the fact that the sociability of evening extended so quickly and deeply in to the wee morning hours, attracted participation and special social rapport from persons in whose home environments pleasures are taken indoors and 'the streets are rolled up' at midnight. ... For many visitors, this code of seeing and being seen brought the people and the material city of Barcelona into a common expression of spectacle logic. ... This public meeting of guest and host populations ... was unprecedented in my experience of summer Olympic games. I believe it is what will be remembered about Barcelona for those who were there, long after the outcomes of this or that competition or the grandiose entertainments of the opening ceremonies have been forgotten. (MacAloon, 1995: 182–183)

Other aspects of the success story were the stimulus given to the economic regeneration of Barcelona, as discussed above, and the boost to Catalan nationalism, a feature which MacAloon asserts, was, to outsiders, a private 'conversation' between Catalonia, Spain and the rest of Europe.

Atlanta 1996

Introduction

Atlanta, Georgia, in the southern USA, has a population of 400,000, with a further 2.5 million in the surrounding urban area. Famous around the world as the headquarters of the Coca Cola corporation, it was one of 14 American cities which, in 1987, sought the United States Olympic Committee's endorsement as the US candidate city for the 1996 Olympic Games. When it entered the international bidding competition in 1988, it faced five other cities: Athens, Belgrade, Manchester, Melbourne and Toronto. Being the centenary Olympic Games of the modern era, Athens was the popular favourite. Further, many believed that just 12 years after the Los Angeles Games was too soon for another American city to host the Games. However, as shown in Table 10.4, in the five-round sequence of IOC votes at its January 1990 meeting in Tokyo, Belgrade and Manchester were eliminated in the early rounds, and in the last two rounds Melbourne's and Toronto's votes swung behind Atlanta, giving it a decisive win over Athens. While it is always claimed that cities win on the basis of their bid and the facilities they offer for the athletes and spectators, the fact that the city hosts the headquarters of Coca Cola, the Olympics' most consistent and generous sponsor, is thought by some to have been influential in the choice of Atlanta (Jennings, 1996: 133–134).

The Atlanta bid was initiated by Atlanta lawyer Billy Payne, who established the Georgia Amateur Athletic Foundation for the purpose, and later became the high profile President and Chief Executive Officer of the Atlanta Committee for the Olympic Games (ACOG). In the enthusiastic words of the official report of the Games:

Table 10.4. IOC voting for the 1996 Games.

Candidates	Round 1	Round 2	Round 3	Round 4	Round 5
Atlanta	19	20	26	34	51
Athens	23	23	26	30	35
Toronto	14	17	18	22	-
Melbourne	12	21	16	-	-
Manchester	11	5	-	-	-
Belgrade	7	-	-	-	-

Source: Watkins, 1997: 14.

One man's vision to bring the Olympic Games to his city inspired thousands to participate in something beyond themselves, to demonstrate their human grace and offer their innate kindness to the world. Buoyed by their tenacity and their faith, this man's dream grew and the power of his dream united a community, a city, a state, a nation, and ultimately a world in sharing an experience so uplifting to the human spirit that for a span of time all peoples were united. (Watkins, 1997: 6)

Philosophy

The Atlanta Games were an entirely private-sector phenomenon, without the usual financial underwriting by government. In fact, the constitution of the state of Georgia precluded it from taking on a number of the obligations normally required by the IOC and neither did the Atlanta City Council take on these obligations, although it was supportive and involved. The obligations were taken on by a specially created body, the Metropolitan Atlanta Olympic Games Authority (MAOGA), which in turn passed them on to the OCOG itself (Watkins, 1997: 18). Continuing the practice initiated in Los Angeles, the 'spirit' of the Games was seen by many observers as highly commercial, with the activities of sponsors very much to the fore.

The substantial urban infrastructure programme seen in Barcelona and other Olympic cities in the past was not a feature of Atlanta, a modern city with a modern, albeit road-based, transport system and one of the world's busiest airports. While major new facilities were built for the Games, use was made of the local university campus, so that Olympic facilities, including the athletes' village, had post-Games university usage.

Economic aspects

Because of differences in accounting practices, it is difficult to compare the finances of different Olympic Games in any precise way without considerable research (see Preuss, 2004 and the discussion in Chapter 6). Nevertheless, broad patterns are apparent. As shown in Table 10.5 and Figure 10.4, while total expenditure of the Atlanta Committee for the Olympic Games (ACOG) was, at US$1720 million, some US$400 million higher than that of COOB'92, there was no additional infrastructure budget.

As with Barcelona, broadcasting rights and sponsorship (here referred to as 'joint ventures' and TOP III) provide two thirds of all ACOG income (see Figure 10.5 and Table 10.5). But there is a major difference in the remaining third, with Atlanta generating over US$400 million in ticket sales, compared with Barcelona's mere US$60 million. Atlanta did not have Barcelona's access to lotteries or government grants to make up the balance.

Humphreys and Plummer (1993, 1995) estimated that the net economic impact of the Games on the economy of the State of Georgia would be over US$5 billion, generating some 77,000 jobs, over the period 1991–1997. They also note the legacy of almost US$600 million worth of sporting and other facilities, largely paid for from Olympic revenues.

Table 10.5. Atlanta Committee for the Olympic Games: budget

		US$ million
Expenditure	Administration	218
	Olympic programmes and physical legacy	68
	Marketing/PR	44
	Ceremonies	27
	Transportation/logistics	133
	Security/accreditation	35
	Technology	219
	Sport event management	91
	Other services	57
	Ticketing	35
	Merchandising	18
	Host broadcasting	141
	Olympic village	110
	Facilities	494
	Reserves	32
	Total	1721
Income	Broadcast rights	568
	Joint venture	427
	TOP III	81
	Ticket sales	425
	Merchandising	32
	Other	188
	Total	1721

Source: Watkins, 1997: 222.

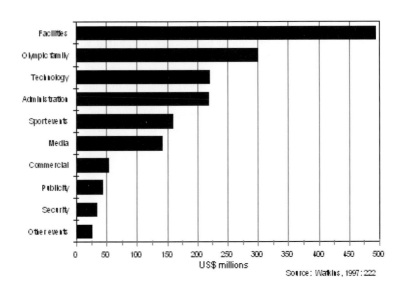

Figure 10.4. Atlanta Committee for the Olympic Games: expenditure [1]

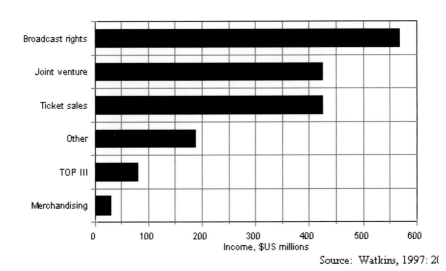

Figure 10.5. Atlanta Committee for the Olympic Games: income

---

[1] Using same categories as in Figure 10.2.

Events

In addition to the high level of commercialisation, Atlanta will also be remembered for three unfortunate phenomena: the bomb in Olympic Park, the problems with the computerised results system and the alleged transport chaos.

The bomb in Olympic Park

Reports suggested at the time that coordination of security might be a problem at the Atlanta Games because of the large number of agencies involved, including municipal, state and federal bodies. In the middle of the Games period a bomb was detonated in Olympic Park, a down-town area created as the focus of activity for Olympic spectators and residents. Two people were killed and many injured. As noted in Chapter 5, a suspect, Eric Rudolph, was eventually arrested five years later and sentenced to life imprisonment. The case became quite celebrated in the USA and at least three books have been written on the man-hunt and the motivations of Rudolph (Walls, 2003; Schuster & Stone, 2005; Vollers, 2006).

Transport

Despite having one of the busiest and most sophisticated airports in the world (De Lange, 1998: 141) Atlanta received a great deal of negative media coverage because of defects in its transport system. Such complaints are not uncommon at Olympic Games, when taxi and bus drivers who are not familiar with the local area are drafted in to cope with the burst of demand, but the problems seemed to be greater than usual in Atlanta, with complaints of long delays and poor coordination.

The Atlanta Games received further bad publicity when the computerised results system provided by IBM as part of its sponsorship commitment, malfunctioned in the early days of the Games.

Media

The organisers' problems were exacerbated by inadequate facilities provided for the media (Gratton, 1999), who broadcast stories not only on the sporting events but also on their own experiences. Up to 10,000 accredited media representatives attend an Olympic Games, and extensive services must be provided for them, including accommodation, transport and appropriate communication technology. When something goes wrong, the story has worldwide coverage. In addition, as many as 5000 non-accredited journalists just 'turn up'; they are provided with few services and must generally make do with the facilities provided for the public. Without privileged access to the events and the athletes, they can be on the look out for any extraneous story which will produce headlines back home.

Legacy

The legacy of the Atlanta Olympic Games was examined by French and Disher (1997), a year after the event. They note just two items which arose directly from Olympic funding, namely:

- the newly constructed and refurbished sports facilities, which provided a significant addition to Atlanta's sporting infrastructure;
- new Georgia State University student housing provided by the athletes' village, 17 per cent funded from the Olympic budget.

The Olympic Games were a catalyst for a number of urban improvement projects, with varying success:

- the nine hectare Centennial Olympic Park, designed as a meeting place during the games, remains as a legacy for the community;
- the Olympic Games were used as a catalyst to bring about neighbourhood redevelopment, but only 2–3 of the 16 neighbourhoods identified for redevelopment had received significant funding by the time of the Games;
- nine times as much money was spent on a series of urban design projects, such as pedestrian plazas, tree-planting and provision of street furniture
- while the Olympic Games provided an impetus to issue bonds to finance the repair of the city's water and sewerage systems, the works were not completed in time for the Games.

French and Disher also note that increased business investment following the Olympic Games has been attributed to the media exposure of Atlanta received during the games.

Conclusion – Atlanta

The result of the various 'glitches' in the organisation of the games was that, in his speech at the closing ceremony, the IOC President, Juan Antonio Samaranch, failed to make the traditional declaration, that the Atlanta Games had been the 'best ever'; they were merely 'most exceptional' (Attwood, 1996). Typical of some journalists' comments were those of Michael Cockerill, one of the *Sydney Morning Herald*'s Olympic correspondents:

> Whatever the Atlanta Olympics were, they were not Barcelona. Arguably the greatest Games of the modern era were followed by arguably the worst Games of the modern era – the only argument being just how bad Atlanta was. The sincerity and hospitality of the Georgians notwithstanding, these Games were fundamentally flawed from the outset. No amount of effort could disguise the obvious fact that Atlanta is not a particularly nice city. Nice people, yes. Nice place, no. .... The Atlanta Olympics have been the ultimate hard-sell. The International Olympic Committee, to its eternal discredit, sold out for money. And it got burnt. It is true the sporting competition has been memorable, and the crowds have been the largest in Olympic history. But only in America is bigger always viewed as better. Many others prefer a more human scale. And the scale applied most in Atlanta was the one that measured profit and loss, television ratings, and advertising income. These were the Private Enterprise Games. But they cost. (Cockerill, 1996)

Sydney 2000

Introduction

Sydney, with a population of four million, and renowned for its spectacular harbour and Opera House, is the largest city in Australia and the capital of the State of New South Wales. The British founded the city in 1788 as a colonial convict settlement, displacing the indigenous population, whose descendants now form only a small proportion of the population. The city has grown rapidly, particularly in the twentieth century, being host to waves of immigration, first from Britain, then from southern Europe and, more recently, Asia. It is a 'new world' city with a high-rise central business district surrounded by seemingly endless single-storeyed residential suburbs stretching inland for 50 kilometres. Sydney has a long-standing tradition of, mostly friendly, rivalry with Melbourne, the capital of the State of Victoria and Australia's second largest city. Melbourne and is arguably the sporting heart of the nation and was host to the 1956 Olympic Games but, having beaten Sydney to become the Australian candidate, had been an unsuccessful bidder for the 1996 Games (see Table 10.4).

On September 24, 1993, amid much euphoria, the City of Sydney was awarded the right to host the Games of the 27th Modern Olympiad to be held in the year 2000. Sydney won the bid by a narrow margin in competition with Beijing, Manchester, Berlin and Istanbul. Table 10.6 shows the results of the four rounds of IOC voting which resulted in Sydney's selection.

Table 10.6. IOC voting for the 2000 Games

Candidates	Round 1	Round 2	Round 3	Round 4
Sydney	30	30	37	45
Beijing	32	37	40	43
Manchester	11	13	11	-
Berlin	9	9	-	-
Istanbul	7	-	-	-

Source: IOC website

The strengths of Sydney's bid for the year 2000 Games were, reportedly, its claim to be the 'athletes' Games', reflected in the concentration of most of the sports in two locations (Homebush and Darling Harbour), and the housing of all the athletes in one village adjacent to the main site. Other influential factors were believed to have been: the fact that many of the needed sports facilities were already in existence; the apparent strong support from the community; Australia's long and consistent record of participation in the modern Olympic Games (Australia claims to be one of only two countries, the other being Greece, to have been represented at every one of the modern Olympic Games); and the environmental components of the bid.

Figure 10.6. Sydney Olympic Park at Homebush Bay, showing the Olympic stadium, aquatic centre and venues

The bid was organised by the Sydney Olympic 2000 Bid Ltd (SOBL), technically a private company, but with a number of high profile public figures among its board membership. SOBL had raised its US$12 million budget largely from private sector sponsors and a US$4 million federal government grant. The bid was nevertheless underwritten by the New South Wales state government, which would be responsible for building many of the facilities. The bid document (SOBL, 1993a, b) included a budget for the running of the Games which showed a total cost of US$1.4 billion, off-set by income primarily from television rights, sponsorship and ticket sales, to produce a small surplus of US$12 million.

Such is the scale of the modern Olympic Games that even the bid process is a major undertaking. In Sydney's case, the story of the bid is available in book form in *The Bid: How Australia Won the 2000 Games*, written by Rod McGeoch, the CEO of SOBL, and journalist Glenda Korporaal (McGeoch and Korporaal, 1994). The notable feature of the saga is the assiduous lobbying of IOC members to gain their votes, a long-standing practice which has been subject to much criticism (e.g. Booth and Tatz, 1994b) and led to the scandal faced by the IOC over the Salt Lake City bidding process in 1998–99, as discussed in Chapter 5.

Critics

During the period up to the announcement of its success there were few local critics of Sydney's bid, although this itself led to some questioning of the independence of the media, especially given that leading media executives were members of the bid committee (Bacon, 1993). The most high profile and consistent critic was Max Walsh of the *Sydney Morning Herald*, as discussed below. It is claimed that critical articles by freelance journalist Mikael Kjaerbye, published in September 1993 in *Reportage*, the newsletter of the Australian Centre for Independent Journalism (Hendy and

Kjaerbye, 1993; Kjaerbye, 1993; Salleh and Kjaerbye, 1993a, b), had been rejected by a number of newspapers. Whether this lack of criticism was as a result of an organised media/government conspiracy or a spontaneous and uncoordinated desire on all sides not to jeopardise the bid by providing competing cities with critical ammunition, criticism of the idea of holding the Games in Sydney was muted (Lenskyj, 2002: 13–42).

Following the success of the bid, however, criticisms and concerns emerged on three fronts: financial, social and environmental.

Financial critics

Financial criticism of the Sydney proposals had been put forward by journalist Max Walsh from as early as 1992 and continued throughout 1993 (Walsh, 1992, 1993a–c). In October 1993 he was joined by Bob Walker (1993), Professor of Accounting in the University of New South Wales and a consistent critic of government financial practices. The main focus of the criticisms was that there appeared to be, in effect, *two* Olympic budgets rather than one. The first was the official 'Games' budget, while the second involved a number of major infrastructure items, which together would cost state taxpayers some US$1.2 billion and it was claimed that the New South Wales state government was being less than open about this burden.

The government claimed that these items were quite properly separated from the main Olympic budget because they would have been incurred regardless of the success or failure of the bid: the effect of the Olympic bid was merely to bring them forward in time. In fairness to the government, the *Homebush Bay Strategy* had been promulgated as early as August 1989, and included mention of a number of the disputed items (Sydney Olympic Games Review Committee, 1990: 9–10). An information sheet produced in October 1992 by the responsible government agency, the Homebush Bay Development Corporation, stated:

> The development of Homebush Bay is proposed over a 15–20 year period and will cost the NSW Government an estimated net $667 million in today's dollars. The *Masterplan* for Homebush Bay is primarily a non-Olympic plan, however it could be expanded to accommodate facilities necessary for the Olympics. The costs for the development are therefore purely non-Olympic based and will be required over an extended development period up to 2010. Overall, the development costs will be $807 million and will be offset against an expected $140 million income derived through property asset sales. Government has already committed $300 million for the construction of the Sydney Aquatic and Athletics Centre and associated infrastructure which are due for completion in 1994. (Homebush Bay Dev. Corp., 1992: 1; A$ amounts)

One criticism of the bid budget was the lack of financial provision for the media and athlete villages, but the government asserted that their funding would be undertaken by private developers, for subsequent sale as private dwellings. Critics questioned whether the Sydney housing market would be able to absorb the several thousand units involved, and therefore whether the villages would be attractive to private developers. In the event, private developers took on the project and decided to solve the potential market glut problem by providing many of the housing units in temporary, demountable form. This turned out to be a successful ploy: there were no complaints about the quality of the athletes' accommodation and, after the Olympic

Games, the temporary buildings, which could be transported on the back of a truck, were snapped up by buyers such as holiday resort operators.

Other financial criticisms put forward by Walsh and Walker included the following:

- the Games budget erroneously counted the sale of a public asset (the city-centre Royal Agricultural Society showground site) and government grants as income – the critics were vindicated here;
- the possibility that the facilities inherited from the Games could become a financial liability rather than an asset had not been considered – this is discussed more fully below but, since certain of the major facilities were developed by the private sector, this was not directly the government's or Games organisers' problem – the developers and operators of the main stadium eventually sustained major losses (see below);
- because of its high profile, it was claimed, political rather than economic factors would govern the planning of the event, resulting in an inevitable cost blow-out – here the critics were only partially vindicated (see below);
- interest payments on capital were ignored – this is a matter of opinion, since state government expenditure for the Games was funded from current income rather than borrowing;
- additional capital spending by the New South Wales government on the scale envisaged would need to be financed by savings or deferral of expenditure from elsewhere, such as education and health – here the critics have been largely vindicated (see Audit Office of New South Wales, 1998: 60–61; Searle, 2002, 2003);
- the anticipated size of television fee income and corporate sponsorship indicated in the Games budget were questioned – here the critics were proved wrong: actual broadcasting fee income was higher than anticipated, although the eventual flow of sponsorship income was thought to have been affected by the 1998/99 IOC bribery scandal;
- the economic benefits from the Games were being promoted as some sort of panacea for Australia's economic problems when, in fact, when related to GDP and overseas earnings, the impact was quite small – critics were vindicated in this regard, as indicated below, although it must be said that the amount of unrealistic promotion of the benefits of the Games by government was limited, even if media coverage sometimes gives a contrary impression.

Social/communitarian critics

In addition to purely financial considerations, there were concerns that the Games could have adverse social impacts on the community, through disruption to such services as housing and transport and the diversion of resources from existing social programmes (Hall and Hodges, 1996, 1998). A two-part social impact report was produced by the state Office on Social Policy setting out a framework for the conduct of such a study (Johnston, 1993) and making proposals for the establishment of a process for dealing with potentially adverse social impacts before, during and after the Games (Deakin, 1993). The factors considered in the report were: housing and accommodation; transport; employment and training; economic and pricing issues; health and the environment; social and community services; security and human rights; recreational issues; cultural issues; population change; and sub-population issues. The proposals of the report were not followed up by the state government, although other agencies considered some of the topics.

The social issue taken most seriously was housing, with fears that demand for short-term rentals before and during the Games would raise rents and tempt landlords to evict long-term, low-rent tenants. An early report prepared for the housing charity, Shelter, confirmed this danger (Cox *et al.*, 1994), and Lenskyj (2002: 99) refers to press reports of instances of substantial rent increases. However, a later report suggested that, while Seoul and Barcelona had experienced substantial increases in house prices and rents in the lead-up to their respective Olympic Games, 'Atlanta and Sydney experienced little or no Olympic related boost' in house prices or rents (McKay and Plumb, 2001: 12).

In Chapter 1 we noted that within the 'critical' paradigm of social research is a strand which might be termed 'communitarian', being concerned with issues such as the negative impacts of the Games on disadvantaged groups and the cost to the public purse. Helen Lenskyj epitomises this strand of research and commentary in her book *The Best Olympics Ever? Social Impacts of Sydney 2000* (Lenskyj, 2002). Her targets are wide-ranging:

> My goal is to disclose what the Sydney 2000 Olympic industry suppressed: the real Olympic costs and impacts, the forgotten victims of Olympic-related housing and homelessness crises, the unrecognized and undermined efforts of community organizations, the Olympic industry's co-option of universities, Sydney 2000's 'symbolic reconciliation' efforts in light of over two hundred years of Indigenous people's suffering, and other key social issues related to Sydney's Olympic preparations. (Lenskyj, 2002: 1)

Some of Lenskyj's criticisms are as follows.

*   *Print media* – the two major Australian newspaper chains were seen to be compromised in any critical coverage of the Games by the fact that they both became sponsors of the Games and were heavily involved in development of Olympic information products.
*   *Security measures*, including special legislation, introduced for the Olympics were seen to be excessive and a threat to human rights, especially of would-be protesters, including homeless people, street people and Indigenous groups.
*   *Indigenous* dimensions were exploited by the organisers as a positive feature of the Games, despite continued neglect of Aboriginal people in Australia generally and official attempts to block Aboriginal protest action during the Games (see also Morgan, 2003).
*   *Housing rents* rose in the years leading up to the Olympics, although, as discussed above, other commentators have offered differing views, and it is not clear whether 'the Olympics constituted the major cause or one of many causes' (see also Cox *et al.*, 1994; Hall and Hodges, 1996).
*   *Paid employment* generated by the Sydney 2000 Games was mostly temporary (as might be expected), low-skilled service work and did not offer opportunities to the long-term unemployed.
*   *Universities* and a number of academics are seen to have been co-opted by the 'Olympic industry', thus failing to maintain their critical independence (see Cashman and Toohey (2002) for an account of the contribution of the higher education sector to the Sydney 2000 Games).
*   *Resistance* against the Sydney 2000 Olympics was offered by numerous

community and political activist groups and some official and unofficial consultative and reference groups, but many instances of lack of cooperation and excessive secrecy on the part of official Olympic organisations are recorded. It is argued that the oppositional stance of some of the protest and consultative groups was compromised as they succumbed to the 'Olympic Spirit', reflected in the term: 'We're not against the Olympics, but ...' (Lenskyj, 2002: 182 - see also: Neilson, 2002; Morgan, 2003).

As Lenskyj says, her book is not intended to be 'comprehensive or balanced' and does not employ 'a traditional scholarly approach' (p. 1) and, indeed, evidence for many assertions is not presented or sources are difficult, even impossible, to check. The value of Lenskyj's compilation is to demonstrate that the Olympic Games are not a separate, cocooned entity, but can be, and are, seen by a variety of groups from a variety of viewpoints as an example of the problem or issue around which they campaign. Thus Lenskyj links the Sydney 2000 Olympics to: Indigenous human rights campaigns; the 'S11' protests against the World Economic Forum (one session of which was held in Melbourne during the week before the Sydney Olympics); campaigns for the homeless; the green movement; and campaigns against specific multinationals, such as Nike Corporation.

'Green' critics

In the context of the IOC's emerging concern for the environment (see Chapter 4) the environmental, 'Green Games', emphasis of the Sydney bid was seen as an important ingredient in its success. The environmental organisation Greenpeace was directly involved in the bid, which included an environmentally innovative design for the athletes' village and an explicit set of *Environmental Guidelines* (SOBL, 1993c). The Homebush site itself was faced with severe environmental problems, due to decades of use by industry and as a dumping ground for domestic and industrial waste. It had never been a secret that the Homebush site required massive expenditure for decontamination, although the bid budget underestimated the cost by a substantial margin.

Apart from the issue of costs, questions arose over a number of environmental issues. Doubts were expressed as to whether the site could be adequately decontaminated at all and whether the best procedures were being used (Beder, 1993). The feasibility of ferry access to the site was queried, since the bay would require dredging, and would cause disturbance to toxic wastes in the river bed (Salleh and Kjaerbye, 1993b; Whittaker, 1993) – in fact, although funds were set aside for the task, at the time of writing, the bay has still not been decontaminated, although, in reality, ferry access was never considered a realistic proposition for the bulk of visitors to the Olympic site. Doubts were expressed as to whether the 'green' features of the athletes' village would survive seven years of government, developer and architects' inputs (Whittaker, 1993) and whether the green guidelines for the whole event had enough 'teeth' (Salleh and Kjaerbye, 1993a).

The environmental performance of the 'Green Games' has been subject to considerable public scrutiny. In 1995, a coalition of Australian environmental groups, with government funding support, formed Green Games Watch 2000 Inc. to monitor the environmental performance of Sydney 2000 developments. The organisation produced a series of reports and newsletters drawing attention to Olympic agencies' environmental failings (Green Games Watch 2000 Inc., 1999, 2000). A 1998 conference on the subject aired a number of criticisms of the 'Green Games' efforts (Cashman and Hughes, 1998b) and, while a number of environmental 'firsts' were achieved, the conclusion as to whether the overall performance of the Sydney 2000 Olympics fully merits the accolade 'Green Games' are mixed (Kearins and Pavlovich, 2002). The final declaration of 'Green Games Watch 2000' on its website was:

> Sydney could be called the 'half green' or 'light green' games, in that many environmental initiatives were adopted, but much more could have been achieved. The main green wins include public transport access, solar power applications, good building material selection, recycling of construction waste, progressive tendering policies, energy and water conservation and wetland restoration. The main green losses include the failure of most sponsors to go green, poor quality Olympic merchandising, environmentally destructive refrigerant selection, loss of biodiversity in some projects, failure to clean up contaminated Homebush Bay sediments in time for the Games and the lack of transparency and effective public consultation by OCA (Olympic Coordination Authority) and SOCOG (Sydney Organising Committee for the Olympic Games). (Green Games Watch 2000, 2000)

Organisation

In accordance with IOC rules, the organising of the Games was entrusted to the Sydney Organising Committee for the Olympic Games (SOCOG), a body constituted by Act of the New South Wales Parliament, with membership appointed by the New South Wales government, the City of Sydney and the Australian Olympic Committee. In its early days SOCOG experienced a number of changes in the Chair and Chief Executive Officer. While the constant changes at the helm were not accompanied by scandal or bad blood, they were certainly unsettling for the organisation. Eventually the state government minister with responsibility for the Olympic Games, Michael Knight, took over the chair – a move criticised by many as politicising the Games, but one which at least ensured a largely trouble-free relationship with the government. A career public servant, Sandy Hollway, was eventually appointed as CEO and saw the Games through to completion, although his authority was later reduced by the appointment by the minister of an overall Director-General of Sydney 2000.

Within SOCOG, a separate organisation, the Sydney Olympic Broadcasting Organisation (SOBO) was established to coordinate broadcasting arrangements. Much of the facility development was initially in the hands of a number of government bodies, causing a certain amount of confusion and over-lapping of responsibilities. Eventually a single body was created – the Olympic Coordination Authority (OCA) – which took over responsibility for the main site at Homebush and a number of other sites, and coordinated the state's direct involvement and the tendering process for private sector involvement. An additional body, the Olympic Roads and Traffic Authority (ORTA), was created to oversee transport arrangements. To complete the organisational arrangements, the Sydney Paralympic Organising Committee (SPOC) was established, with close links with SOCOG. The result was that the employed staff running the Paralympic Games and the Olympic Games were much the same.

Opinion polls suggest that public support for the Sydney 2000 Games was generally strong, but commentators have drawn attention to the 'short cuts' in planning procedures arising from the significant powers vested in the OCA and the Minister for the Olympics, which raised questions as to the extent to which the public were consulted, involved and made aware of developments (Beder, 1993: 17; Lenskyj, 1994; Dunn and McGuirk, 1999). While other bidding cities and host cities have seen significant opposition, in Sydney criticism was muted. The major public opposition was to the location of the beach volleyball facilities on Bondi Beach, as discussed below.

Economic dimensions

Finance

The financing of the Games followed the pattern set in other host cities with, as the critics implied, two budgets. The first is the budget of SOCOG, concerned with the direct organisation of the Games and largely funded from television revenues, sponsorship and ticket sales, as shown in Figure 10.7 and Table 10.7.

While the original bid budget, as indicated above, was of the order of US$1.6 billion and showed a small surplus, Table 10.7 shows that the version produced by the state Audit Office in 1998 revealed that even the original budget had been under-estimated by some US$400 million.

The second budget, that of the OCA, was concerned with facilities and other infrastructure and is shown in Table 10.8. Again it can be seen that costs in the original bid budget had been substantially underestimated, in this case by some US$720 million, and the revised budget was US$1200 million higher, at US$1.9 billion. While five years had elapsed between the original bid and the new sets of estimates, very little could be put down to inflation. The major changes were due to the inclusion of items in the budget which had previously been deliberately or fortuitously excluded.

The fact that these budget changes were later made so clearly and unequivocally can be seen to be due to two factors. First, between the bid and the new estimates, there had been a change of state government, from Liberal to Labor, and the new government had no hesitation in claiming that the previous government had been hiding the true cost of the Olympics from the public. Second, the review was carried out by the New South Wales Audit Office, an organisation specifically charged with taking an independent and, if necessary, critical view of government expenditure. While the publication of the Audit Office report in late 1998 caused a flurry of headlines about the 'Olympic Budget blowout', the political fallout of these revelations was minor. The Labor government was returned with a much increased majority in the March 1999 elections.

Economic Impact

As part of the bid process consultants KPMG Peat Marwick (1993) produced, free of charge, an economic impact study in which they estimated that the economic impact of the Games on the Australian economy would be some US$5.8 billion, resulting in the creation of 156,000 one-year full-time equivalent jobs, as summarised in Table 10.9 (KPMG Peat Marwick (1993). The benefits included generated tax revenues of some US$1.5 billion, a factor largely ignored in subsequent debates on the cost of the Games, although the NSW Premier, John Fahey, drew attention to the item in a press

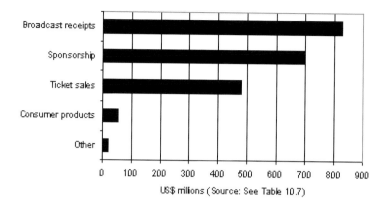

Figure 10.7. Sydney 2000: Organising Committee income

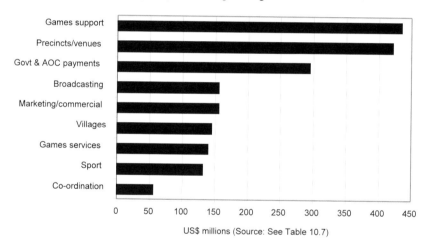

Figure 10.8. Sydney 2000: Organising Committee expenditure

interview (O'Neill, 1995: 30). It should, however, be borne in mind that the impacts of US$5.6 billion and 165,000 jobs are spread over 13 years and, since the annual GDP of Australia around 2000 was some US$550 billion and the labour force was more than 10 million, the impacts amount to only about 0.1 per cent of GDP and 0.16 per cent of the labour force per annum.

Two subsequent studies were commissioned by the NSW Treasury in the late 1990s (NSW Treasury, 1997; Madden, 2002). These were able to use more up-to-date data and more sophisticated computable general equilibrium (CGE) modelling, as discussed in Chapter 6. An existing model of the Australian economy was modified to take account of the Olympic Games. Economic flows between twelve industries, the federal government and eight state and territory governments and the rest of the

Table 10.7. Sydney Organising Committee for the Olympic Games: budget

		1993 Bid Budget US$m*	1998 Revision US$m*
Expenditure	Games support	178.2	434.6
	Precincts and venues	314.1	421.4
	Sport	122.1	132.0
	Villages	126.4	144.5
	Games Services	168.9	140.0
	Broadcasting	168.9	156.5
	Commercial	28.8	89.3
	Marketing and image	67.2	66.2
	Co-ordination	-	55.8
	Ceremonies	40.2	31.4
	Government & ATSI	-	6.2
	Command/control/communication	-	4.9
	Australian Olympic Committee	48.0	60.0
	Paralympics	16.2	13.4
	Payments to government	218.4	228.0
	IOC payments	-	8.9
	Contingencies	96.6	60.6
	Total	1 593.9	2 053.6
Income	Sponsorship	497.7	699.0
	Ticket sales	213.4	480.7
	Broadcast receipts	758.4	825.8
	Consumer products	77.3	52.2
	Other	-	20.0
	Total	1 546.7	2 063.2
Surplus (-Deficit)		-47.2	2063.2

Source: Audit Office of New South Wales, 1999. * at A$1 = US$0.8

world were represented by over 27,000 equations and 50,000 variables (NSW Treasury, 1997: Section 2.2). The total effect of the Games on the Australian Gross Domestic Product over a 12–year period was estimated at US$6.04 billion, an average of just over US$500 million a year, or 0.1% of GDP. This was very close to the earlier KPMG estimate of US$5.86 billion. Madden's (2002) study represented an update of this study, producing only a minor change in the estimated impact.

A significant proportion of the anticipated economic impact arose from the predicted boost to international tourism which the Games would provide, not just during the games year but for a number of years subsequently. Did the boost to tourism eventuate? It is almost impossible to say because, despite the establishment of research projects to assess tourism outcomes (Faulkner *et al.*, 2003), events in the years following the games so disrupted international tourism trends that any 'Olympic boost' is difficult to disentangle. The events were the '9/11' terrorist attacks of 2001,

Table 10.8. Sydney 2000: Olympic Coordination Authority budget

		Bid budget	Adjusted bid budget	OCA budget 1998
		US$m*	US$m*	US$m*
Expenditure	Media village	-	-	102.2
	Athletes' village	-	-	58.2
	Athletes' village site remediation	-	-	79.7
	Other venue costs	62.2	87.8	181.7
	Olympic stadium	288.3	288.3	101
	Transport	-	213.8	337.8
	Sydney Superdome	67.9	67.9	125.2
	Showground development	0	261.6	310.6
	Sports hall	95.8	95.8	-
	Contingency items	86.8	86.8	54.8
	Services infrastructure	-	75.7	92.1
	Site infrastructure	22.2	87.4	93.4
	Athletic/aquatic centres	173.4	173.4	173.4
	Site remediation	-	62.3	38.3
	Operating costs	-	15.0	188.7
	Total	796.7	1 515.8	1937.2
Income	Race days	24.6	24.6	-
	Showground sale	69.1	69.1	-
	Site sale	-	-	28.0
	SOCOG rental fee	47.1	47.1	61.6
	Federal govt contribution	125.9	125.9	140
	State govt contribution	25.2	25.2	-
	SOCOG construction fee	167.8	167.8	175.0
	Recurrent income	-	-	58.5
	Other	-	-	7.0
	Interest	45.6	45.6	24.3
	Total	505.4	505.4	494.4
Net OCA cost (met by NSW govt)		291.4	1 010.4	1 442.8
Private sector capital expenditure		948.5	948.5	867.8

Source: Audit Office of NSW, 1999: 73. * at A$1 - US$0.8

the Bali terrorist bombings of 2002 and the SARS (Severe Acute Respiratory Syndrome) outbreak of 2003, all three of which affected people's willingness to travel. Figure 10.9 shows the trends in international tourist arrivals and official forecasts of arrival numbers in Australia around this time. Actual arrivals peaked in 2000 and had been predicted to go on rising, but instead they went into decline for three years, with a recovery beginning in 2004. Current predictions of international tourist arrivals are therefore almost two million a year less than predictions made in

Table 10.9. Sydney 2000: economic impact 1991–2004*

	US$m**
Increase in GDP by area:	
Australia	5 869
New South Wales	3 670
Sydney	2 848
Increase in GDP by industry sector	
Manufacturing	920
Retail trade	990
Personal services	906
Finance	794
Construction	298
Other	2 062
Total	5 869
Increase in taxation revenue 1991– 004	
Commonwealth	1 547
New South Wales	301
Local Government	58
Increase in annual jobs	No.
Australia	156 198
New South Wales	89 504
Sydney	73 089

Source: KPMG Peat Marwick, 1993   * 'Most Likely' scenario   ** A$1 = US$0.80 (2007)

2000. An additional 500,000 international visitors had been predicted by the KPMG Peat Marwick (1993: 13) study in the period 2001–2004 as a result of the Sydney 2000 Olympics. Whether the Olympic 'boost' was still present in the reduced figures, such that the downturn would have been even more severe without the Olympics, it is difficult, if not impossible to say.

It should also be noted that the three studies mentioned above (KPMG Peat Marwick, NSW Treasury and Madden) were *economic impact* studies and not cost-benefit analyses. The KPMG report outlines the range of issues which would need to be taken into account in a full-scale cost-benefit study, as shown in Appendix 10.1. These would include environmental and social factors as well as financial items and would provide a good starting point for such a study if combined with the social impact report outlined by the Office of Social Policy (1993), but never implemented. Since the necessary data collection processes were not put in place at the time, it is not now possible for a full cost-benefit study to be undertaken for the Sydney Games.

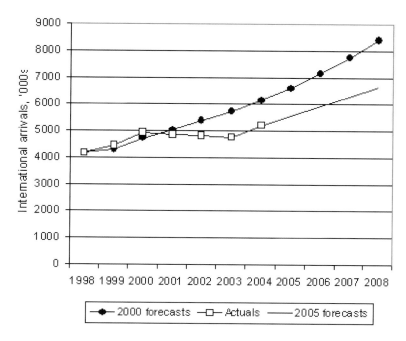

Figure 10.9. Australian inbound tourism trends, 1998–2008
Source: Tourism Forecasting Council, via: Lynch and
Veal (2001: 325); Lynch and Veal (2006: 306)

Events

The lead-up to the Sydney 2000 Olympics was not without its problems. In any project lasting seven years and involving thousands of people, there are bound to be problems along the way, and the Sydney 2000 Olympics were no exception. The public problems of the Sydney 2000 Games, as discussed below, were relatively minor and were largely overshadowed by the highly publicised problems faced by the IOC in 1998/99.

The IOC bribery scandal

The IOC bribery and corruption scandals which arose towards the end of 1998 are discussed in more detail in Chapter 5. Here, it is appropriate to draw attention to the effect of these events on the Sydney Games. While the accusations of improper behaviour mainly involved the Salt Lake City 2002 Winter Games, the impact on Sydney was notable because of the numerous accusations made against Australian IOC member and SOCOG Board member, Phil Coles. At the time the accusations were made public, SOCOG was still short of some US$160 million in sponsorship money. It is widely believed that the bad publicity hampered SOCOG's effort at raising this money. Consequently, in May 1999, SOCOG announced cuts of some US$60 million in expenditure.

Floating the stadium

The main Olympic stadium, with 110,000 seats the largest ever, was built by a private sector consortium. Some government subsidy was involved, but the consortium planned to finance at least half the US$480 million cost by selling membership shares in the stadium. For US$8,000 investors would have shares in the company and a seat at the stadium for all events for the first 30 years of its life, including the Olympic Games. Unfortunately, the public were less than enthusiastic and fewer than half the 30,000 memberships were sold, leaving the underwriters to make up the US$160 million shortfall. Failure to secure sufficient events in the period after the Games resulted in a large write-down of the stadium's value, so that the stock market valuation of the Stadium Australia Group in 2005 was only US$8 million (Masters, 2005). Ownership was eventually taken over by the company's bankers in lieu of debts of US$112 million (Askew, 2006).

The marching bands fiasco

The marching band problem resulted from the decision of the organiser of the opening ceremony, Ric Birch, to deploy, as part of the entertainment, a 2000-person marching band made up primarily of experienced American and Japanese marchers, with only a small representation of Australians. When this fact emerged, the marching band fraternity of Australia was outraged and was supported by talk-back radio hosts and their callers and by politicians. As a result of the adverse publicity, SOCOG decided to cancel the contract with World Projects Corporation (WPC), an American company contracted to provide the marchers. Hundreds of young marching band players, who had been fund-raising in order to pay their way to Sydney, were reportedly disappointed and WPC took SOCOG to court. Eventually SOCOG reversed its decision and reinstated the contract, but with the proviso that more countries were to be represented in the band and more Australians were to be included (Moore, 1999). The story was represented in the media as an example of inept bungling, just at the time when the Olympic tickets were going on sale.

The beach volleyball saga

The beach volleyball saga problem arose from the decision of the organisers to hold the Olympic beach volleyball competition in a specially constructed temporary stadium located on the world-famous Bondi Beach. When the plans for the stadium were submitted for consideration by the local council, various local residents' groups raised objections to the scale of the structure, the amount of beach that would be commandeered and the length of time (six months) for which the area of beach would be required. For a while it appeared that the local council would oppose the facility and various alternatives, such as artificial beaches in football stadiums, were mooted. However, with some minor changes, the plans were approved and went ahead, but some local residents were still threatening to 'lie down in front of the bulldozers' rather than allow the facility to go ahead. Again, the media attention was intense, this time the Olympic organisers being portrayed as undemocratic and riding roughshod over community interests. As it happened, the temporary stadium was one of the most successful venues of the Games. The public outcry did, however, secure increased expenditure by the Olympic Coordination Authority on the existing Bondi Pavilion, thus providing some sort of lasting legacy for Bondi residents and visitors (Owen, 2001: 28), although Lenskyj (2002: 183–202) suggests that the facilities provided were needed for VIP use during the Games and that the saga 'provides a classic example of the worst abuses of power on the part of the Olympic industry'.

The tickets embarrassment

In October 1999, widespread disappointment among those who had been unsuccessful in the ballot for Games tickets turned to outrage when it emerged that tickets to 'sold out' prime events were still available, at several times face value, to corporate and other organisations that could afford them and that, after overseas visitors, media, sponsors and the Olympic Family had been catered for, less than a third of the tickets overall, and in some prime events as few as 10 per cent, were available for sale to the Australian public. SOCOG was investigated by the Australian Competition and Consumer Commission for misleading advertising, but eventually managed to 'find' some thousands of additional tickets which partly mollified the public.

Legacy

It was noted in Chapter 4 that there is increasing interest in the *legacy* of the Olympic Games in host cities and countries. The rhetoric of city bids concerning what is expected to be left behind after the Games is being increasingly examined against the reality – by media and academic commentators and, in future, by the IOC's OGGI (Olympic Games Global Impact) programme, as discussed in Chapter 4. The most comprehensive examination of the legacy of a single Olympic Games has been provided by Richard Cashman (2006) in regard to the Sydney Games. The Sydney Games' legacy of sporting facilities and economic impacts have been discussed above. Cashman considers a much wider range of issues, including:

* *The memory* – the Sydney public took great pleasure in the month-long 'party' that was the Olympics and the Paralympics and retain fond memories of the 'once-in-a-lifetime' event.
* *Enhanced sporting participation* – is invariably invoked in bid documents, but in the case of Sydney, the evidence for an 'Olympic boost' to grass roots sport participation is weak (see Veal, 2003).
* *Expertise* – numerous Australians gained substantial experience and know-how as a result of working on the Olympics – the 'Olympic caravan' of architects, designers, engineers, marketers, promoters and managers is in high demand around the world at Olympic Games and other major sports events.
* *Academic* – an Olympic studies centre, started in the University of New South Wales, continues in the University of Technology, Sydney (see Appendix I).

Cashman concludes:

there is a greater need to plan for the post-Games environment and to establish institutions to develop appropriate post-Games policies. The challenge for post-Games organisers is not simply to wind down the Olympic infrastructure and to avoid additional costs, but also to access new Olympic investment opportunities. (Cashman, 2006: 275)

Conclusion – Sydney

During Juan Antonio Samaranch's period as IOC President, the sign of a successful Olympic Games was the president's statement during the closing ceremony, that it had been 'the best Olympic Games ever'. Samaranch did not give this imprimatur to the Atlanta Games, but he did to the Sydney Games.

Athens 2004

Athens, the capital of Greece, with a population of four million, was not host to the Ancient Olympic Games, which took place on the other side of Greece, at Olympia, but was host to the first modern Games of 1896. Many thought that it was unfortunate that Athens was not chosen to host the 1996 Olympic Games, which marked the centenary of the first modern Olympic Games. However, in 1997, it won the right to host the 2004 Games, after five rounds of voting, as shown in Table 10.10.

Table 10.10. 2004 Summer Olympics voting results

Candidates	Round 1	Round 2 tie-breaker	Round 3	Round 4	Round 5
Athens	32	-	38	52	66
Rome	23	-	28	35	41
Cape Town	16	62	22	20	-
Stockholm	20	-	19	-	-
Buenos Aires	16	44	-	-	-

Although the IOC President did not pronounce the Athens Games the 'best ever', but the 'unforgettable dream games', there was a broad consensus among commentators, worldwide, that the event was a success (see, for example: Baum, 2004; BBC Sport, 2004; Huxley, 2004). The following are comments from an editorial in the *New York Times*:

> Hats off to Greece for running a Summer Olympics that defied all dire predictions. The facilities were completed on time, no terrorists showed up to wreak havoc, the anticipated traffic jams failed to materialize, and the main glitches, such as judging disputes in several sports, were hardly the fault of the host country. Greece showed that a small country could indeed play host to this massive quadrennial extravaganza. The achievement raises anew the question of whether Greece, where the games originated, should be made the permanent site of the Summer Olympics, thus ending the road show that moves the Olympics to whatever city submits the most compelling bid for the next go-round.
> *(New York Times, 2004)*

In an exit poll of over 5000 Greek and foreign spectators, 79 per cent indicated that they were 'completely' satisfied with their experience at the Games and 16 per cent 'quite' satisfied (ATHOC, 2004).

At the time of writing (March 2007), the official report of the Athens Games has not been published and the Athens Organising Committee's official website has been terminated, so up-to-date evaluative information on the Athens Games is scarce. Academic commentary on the Games in English is also very limited at this stage.

Events

As far as the rest of the world was concerned, the most notable feature of the build-up to the Athens 2004 Games was the delay in the preparations, which raised concerns with the IOC and rumoured threats, in 2000, that the Games might be taken away from Athens. Considerable investment was made in new sporting facilities and urban infrastructure, including new transport systems and hotels. Delays in many projects were caused by archaeological constraints when excavating. The IOC's concerns about the lack of progress had, however, been allayed by early 2001 (Knight, 2001).

During the Games themselves, the single event which attracted the most attention was the doping scandal involving two Greek athletes, who eventually withdrew from the Games (see Chapter 8). Barnard *et al.* (2006) give some idea of the significance of this event in terms of media coverage.

Economic aspects

In the absence of an official report, a final budget for the Athens 2004 Games is not available, but the budget for the organising committee (OCOG) as set out in the bid document, comprised expenditure of US$1.57 million and revenue of US$1.61 billion, resulting in a small predicted surplus, as shown in Table 10.11. This is similar to other recent Olympic Games. The cost of 'non-OCOG' infrastructure investments, as indicated in the bid document, was, at US$1.4 billion, clearly a gross underestimate, since it was increased to US$8.3 billion in later estimates (Greek Embassy, n.d.). This investment was funded at least in part by loans, which are seen as a significant burden on the national budget of a relatively small economy seeking to conform to the European Union's guidelines on fiscal discipline (Wood, 2005).

A notable feature of the early broadcasts of the Games events was the scene of mostly empty stadiums. While crowds appeared for the later stages of events, it seems likely that income from ticket sales will have been below expectations.

No study of the economic impact of the Athens 2004 Games has been published in English, but Kasimati (2003) refers to two studies in Greek, which produced estimates of impacts of between US$11 billion and US$15 billion and the creation of between 300,000 and 450,000 jobs over a 10–12 year period, based largely on an increase of some 15 million in tourist visits.

Environment

Athens 2004 was the second Summer Olympic Games to be subject to the IOC's environmental guidelines (see Chapter 4). The Greek branch of the World Wildlife Fund (WWF) monitored the 'environmental progress' of the Athens Games and, a month before the start of the Games, issued a quite damming report on the Games (WWF, 2004), giving the organisers a 'score' of only 0.8 out of a possible maximum of 4.0. The 'scorecard' is shown in Table 10.12 and shows that, for 10 of the 17 items assessed, the WWF awarded a score of zero. Positive achievements were recorded

Table 10.11. Athens 2004 bid budget

OCOG Expenditure	US$, m.	OCOG Revenue	US$, m.
Capital investments		Television rights (via IOC)	597
Sports facilities	75	TOP sponsorship (via IOC)	111
Olympic village	40	Local sponsorship	200
Media centre	27	Licensing	40
Operations		Official suppliers	85
Sports events	250	Coins/stamps	37
Olympic village	75	Lotteries	235
Media centre	100	Ticket sales	200
Ceremonies/programmes	120	Donations	20
Medical	20	Other	82
Catering	75	Total OCOG Revenue	1 607
Transport	50	OCOG Surplus	37
Security	75	*Non-OCOG Investments*	
Paralympics	50	Roads, railways	520
Advertising/promotion	150	Sports venues	257
Administration	142	Olympic accommodation	290
Pre-Olympic events	40	Other	345
Other	281	Total non-OCOG	1 412
Total OCOG expenditure	1 570		

Source: Evaluation Commission (1997: 334–38)

Table 10.12. Athens 2004 environmental scorecard

Issue	Items	Score out of 4*
Overall planning	Environmental planning	0
Natural environment	Protection of natural habitats	0
Urban environment	Protection of open spaces	0
	Increase of urban green	0
	Improvement of the built environment	3
Transport	Public transport	3
Construction	Siting of Olympic venues	0
	Use of existing infrastructure	1
	Use of green technologies	0
Energy	Green energy	0
Water	Water saving scheme	0
Waste	Integrated waste management/recycling	0
Public participation	Social consultation	1
	Transparency	1
	Public information	1
General issues	Respect for environmental legislation	0
	Public awareness	4
Total (average) score		0.77

Source: WWF (2004: 15). * 4 = Very positive; 3 = Positive; 2 = Fair; 1 = Disappointing; 0 = Very disappointing.

for only three items: public awareness; improvement of the built environment; and public transport.

Throughout the report the authors use the Sydney 2000 experience as a benchmark against which to assess the Athens performance – generally unfavourably.

Beijing 2008

Following one unsuccessful bid, for the 2000 Games, Beijing won the right to host the 2008 Olympic Games after just two rounds of voting at the IOC session in Moscow in 2001, as shown in Table 10.13.

Table 10.13. 2008 Summer Olympics voting results

Candidates	Round 1	Round 2
Beijing	44	56
Istanbul	17	9
Osaka	6	-
Paris	15	18
Toronto	20	22

As the most populous nation on earth, and one of the most successful Olympic participants, in terms of medals won, it was inevitable that China would, sooner or later, host the Games. But it required the country's political and economic transformation of the last 20 years for this to be realised. While China continues to be controlled by the Communist Party, the economy is being rapidly privatised – even the Olympic Stadium in Beijing is being funded by private investors (Magnay, 2007).

China's involvement with the Olympic Games goes back to 1912, under the Nationalist government, with the establishment of the Far East Sport Association and the inauguration of the Far East Games and Chinese National Games modelled on the Olympic Games and endorsed by the IOC (Hong, 1998). These games tended to displace traditional Eastern sports, such as martial arts, and were somewhat in conflict with traditional communal cultural values (Hong, 1998). However, when the Communist Party took control and founded the People's Republic of China (PRC) in 1949, the IOC continued to recognise the surviving Nationalist regime in Taiwan as the representatives of China and it was not until 1979 that the PRC joined the IOC. At the 1984 Los Angeles Games the PRC competed alongside Taiwan/Chinese Taipei for the first time, and the Soviet boycott enabled China to be placed fourth in the medal rankings. It was then placed 11th in Seoul 1988, rising back to fourth in Barcelona 1992 and Atlanta 1996, and third in Sydney 2000 and Athens 2004. This went some way towards satisfying the Chinese 'medal fever' and indicated that China had emerged as an undoubted 'Olympic superpower' (Hong *et al.*, 2005). Hosting the summer Olympic Games will reinforce that status. The Summer Games of the 29th Olympiad will open at the eighth hour of the eighth day of the eighth year of the millennium (the lucky number eight indicating prosperity and development).

But to many commentators, China's hosting of the Games is not just about its status as a sporting power, but about its emergence as a political and economic power. Xu and Ping state that the Games are coming to Beijing:

at a critical juncture of the world history of globalization and the Chinese history of grand socioeconomic transformation. Following in the footsteps of its two East Asian neighbours, Japan and South Korea, ... the People's Republic of China is determined to turn this sporting mega-event into a celebration of a Chinese renaissance and the harmonization of world civilizations under the theme slogan 'One World, One Dream'. In the making is a new history – as the low politics of sport is conspicuously connected with the high politics of national identities and international relations in the spotlight of the upcoming Beijing Olympics in 2008. (Xu *et al.*, 2006: 90)

Economic aspects

Table 10.14 shows the bid budget for the Beijing Games. The projected revenue of US$1.62 billion, expenditure of US$1.57 billion and surplus of US$16 billion is almost routine, but the 'non-OCOG' expenditure of $14.2 billion is much higher than any previous Olympic Games. Particularly unusual is that, of this, US$8 billion is for 'environmental protection', a large proportion of which is being devoted to reducing air pollution in Beijing.

Table 10.14. Beijing 2008 bid budget

OCOG Expenditure	US$, millions	OCOG Revenue	US$, millions
Capital investments		Television rights (via IOC)	709
Sports facilities	102	TOP sponsorship (via IOC)	130
Olympic village	40	Local sponsorship	130
Media centres	48	Licensing	50
Operations		Official suppliers	30
Sports events	275	Coins/stamps	20
Olympic village	65	Lotteries	180
Media centres	370	Ticket sales	140
Ceremonies/programmes	100	Donations	20
Medical	30	Government subsidies	100
Catering	51	Other	46
Transport	70	Total OCOG Revenue	1 625
Security	50	OCOG Surplus	16
Paralympics	82	*Non-OCOG Investments*	
Advertising/promotion	60	Environmental protection	8 627
Administration	125	Airport	85
Pre-Olympic events	40	Roads, railways	3 673
Other	101	Olympic village	442
Total OCOG expenditure	1 570	Sports venues	1 429
		Total non-OCOG	14 257

Source: Beijing Bid Committee (2001a: 73)

Human rights

One aspect of the Beijing Games which is of concern to some observers is the question of human rights in China. Susan Brownell states:

> People in the developed Western countries seem fixated on the question of whether the Olympic Games will change China. Will they improve China's human rights record? Will they open China to the outside world? Will they bring democracy to China? (Brownell, 2006: 53)

In the presentation of the Beijing bid to the IOC, Mr Liu Qi, Mayor of Beijing, stated of the Games:

> They will help promote our economic and social progress and will also benefit the further development of our human rights cause. (Beijing Bid Committee, 2001b)

What precisely are the concerns of the Western critics? Essentially the critics are referring to the high ideals enshrined in the *Olympic Charter* and arguing that certain of China's practices are incompatible with such ideals. In particular, reference is made to the fifth of the 'fundamental principles' of Olympism as set out in the charter:

> Any form of discrimination with regard to a country or a person on grounds of race, religion, politics, gender or otherwise is incompatible with belonging to the Olympic Movement. (IOC, 2004: 9)

Amnesty International, the international organisation devoted to the protection of human rights, has monitored China's human rights-related activities in the lead-up to the Beijing Games and, in its April 2007 report, refers to:

- the excessive use of the death penalty, related judicial procedures and claims of use of death penalty prisoners for organ transplants – a Swedish representative at the UN Council on Human Rights is quoted as saying: 'More than 80% of the total number of executions in the world today take place in China where a shockingly high number of crimes can lead to the death penalty. This is certainly not in the Olympic spirit' – a statement rejected by the Chinese representative;
- police powers to impose 'enforced rehabilitation' on drug users;
- repression of human rights defenders and their families, including practitioners of the religious movement, Falun Gong;
- double standards for foreign vs. domestic journalists – with freedom of movement increased for foreign journalists accredited for the Games, but not necessarily for domestic journalists. (Amnesty International, 2007)

Amnesty International themselves note a number of instances where practices have changed in recent years, suggesting that the advent of the Olympics, and the associated global spotlight, may be having an effect, and changing China, but they also quote official Chinese sources who deny that changes are being made just because of the Olympics.

Brownell sums up the scale of the impact on a country where there has been a long tradition of state control of the media:

In sum, there could be 40,000 members of the world's media swarming around all the nooks and crannies in Beijing. Journalists being what they are, we can be sure that they will not all be looking for whitewashed stories. There will be no way for the Chinese government to control what they see and do. Dissidents and critics will gain more media attention than they would otherwise have had, and will have a platform from which to make their voices heard. (Brownell, 2004: 60)

Legacy

Susan Brownell (2004: 53) raises not only the question, 'Will Olympism change China?' but also, 'Will China change Olympism?' Based on the experience of Japan and Korea in hosting the games, it is posited that Beijing 2008 may at least push the IOC in the direction of a more appropriate geographical distribution of membership, away from the current situation where Europe, for historical reasons, accounts for 45 per cent of IOC Members.

London 2012

London's successful bid to host the 2012 Summer Olympic Games was announced in Singapore in July 2005. In contrast to Athens 2004, it seems likely that the London summer Olympics of 2012 will be the most analysed and written-about modern Olympic Games to date. Already, at the time of writing (early 2007), a number of publications on the Games has appeared, including two books on the bid itself (Davé, 2006; Lee, 2006), at least one academic article (Kennedy *et al.*, 2006), an impact study (Blake, 2005; PriceWaterhouseCoopers, 2005) and a significant collection of papers looking forward to the anticipated legacy of the London Games (Vigor *et al.*, 2004).

London competed against Madrid, Moscow, New York and Paris to win the bid and the four-round voting sequence is shown in Table 10.15.

Table 10.15. IOC voting for the 2012 Games

City	Round 1	Round 2	Round 3	Round 4
London	22	27	39	54
Madrid	20	32	31	-
Moscow	15	-	-	-
New York	19	16	-	-
Paris	21	25	33	50

Source: IOC website

Economic aspects

Table 10.16 shows the bid budget for the London 2012 Games. Revenue and expenditure are exactly the same, at almost US$2.5 billion. This is higher than the corresponding figure for Athens and Beijing, but Greece and Beijing are both countries with lower wages and prices than the UK. The London 2012 sum is roughly in line with the Atlanta 1996 and Sydney 2000 figures if adjusted for inflation. The non-OCOG expenditure of US15.8 million is surprisingly high for a large city in a developed country, but reflects the strategy to use the Olympics to trigger extensive infrastructure development in east London.

The bid budget was published in 2005, but revisions were announced by the responsible minister in relation to the non-OCOG element in March 2007, as shown in Table 10.17. Some of the non-OCOG items are now the responsibility of the newly created Olympic Delivery Authority. Since the minister's statement does not use similar headings to the bid budget and does not compare the bid budget directly with the ODA budget, it is difficult to compare like with like. One item illustrates the key issue discussed in Chapter 6, namely: what to include as 'costs of the Olympics' and what to exclude. The bid budget included US$11.5 billion for 'Roads and railways', but this large item was not mentioned in the minister's statement. The newly announced US$1.2 billion for 'wider security costs' no doubt covers additional security which must be provided by the authorities at airports and throughout London, particularly in the transport system, but it is curious that this was not included in the bid budget. Finally, while an addition of a contingency item of almost US$1 billion for 'programme cost increases' is probably more realistic than the US$105 million in the bid budget, it is difficult to understand the huge sum of US$4.4 billion, which is set aside for 'potential additional programme contingency held by Government' (DCMS, 2007).

Table 10.16. London 2012 bid budget

OCOG Expenditure	US$, millions	OCOG Revenue	US$, millions
Operations		Television rights (via IOC)	600
Sports venues	417	TOP sponsorship (via IOC)	300
Olympic village	218	Local sponsorship	435
Media centres	46	Licensing merchandise	90
Games workforce	187	Official suppliers	290
Information systems	327	Coins	2
Telecommunications	101	Ticket sales	496
Internet	20	Government subsidies	72
Ceremonies & culture	92	Other	177
Medical	19	Total OCOG Revenue	2 462
Catering	21	OCOG Surplus	-
Transport	198		
Security	37	*Non-OCOG Investments*	
Paralympics	144	Roads, railways	11 522
Advertising/promotion	92	Sports venues	917
Administration	255	Olympic Park infrastructure	2 100
Pre-Olympic events	20	Media centres	215
Contingency	105	Olympic village	1 040
Other	163	Total non-OCOG	15 794
Total OCOG expenditure	2 462		

Source: London 2012 Ltd (2005: 103, 105)

Table 10.17. London 2012: revised non-OCOG budget

	Bid	Revised
	US$, millions	US$, millions
Roads, railways	11 522	*
Media centres**	215	*
Olympic village**	1 040	*
Olympic venues (ODA)	917	6 169
Infrastructure and regeneration (ODA)	2 100	3 383
Contingency (re. programme cost increases) (ODA)	0	995
Sports, Paralympics and other costs	0	776
Wider security costs	0	1 194
Tax (VAT, to be refunded by government)	0	1 672
Contingency (additional programme)	0	4 378
Total	15 794	18 567

Source: DCMS (2007). * not mentioned in minister's statement. ** possibly included in the revised 'Olympic venues' item. ODA = Olympic Development Authority budget).

At the time of writing, a revised budget for the organising committee (LOCOG) does not appear to be available on the London 2012 website, but Nathan and Kornblatt (2007) indicate that it is US$3.98 billion, an increase of 60 per cent over the bid budget, although some of the change in the US dollar figure is accounted for by the change in the exchange rate.

As part of the bidding process, an 'Olympic Games Impact Study' was commissioned from consultants by the Department of Culture, Media and Sport on behalf of a 'multi-agency stakeholder group' comprising a number of private sector and public sector organisations (PriceWaterhouseCoopers, 2005: 1). The report covers anticipated economic, social and environmental impacts for the UK, London and areas adjacent to the main Olympic sites. Research on the economic impact was subcontracted to Adam Blake of Nottingham University and a full report of this was published separately (Blake, 2005). As noted in Chapter 6 (Table 6.10), the economic impact is estimated at US$3.8 billion.

Legacy

The *Olympic Games Impact Study* commissioned by the government as part of the bid process notes, in the 'social impacts' section, that one of the legacies of the games is expected to be increased participation in sport leading to 'knock-on social and physical impacts, for example in terms of health and well-being' (PriceWaterhouse Coopers, 2005: 11). But, while a substantial research report was commissioned to assess the *economic* impact of the games (Blake, 2005), less attention had been paid to the social impact: in particular, the report goes on to state: 'No substantive work has, however, been done to quantify the potential legacy impacts on sporting participation' (p. 12).

This is perhaps surprising, given the importance attached to this dimension in various public pronouncements about the Games. In a speech in January 2007,

Sebastian Coe, Chairman of the London 2012 Games Organising Committee, said it was:

> vital that more efforts [be] made to make sport more accessible to millions of children around the world who live in desperate poverty or in war zones and have neither the resources nor physical energy to play sport.Using the force of the Olympic movement in combination with other international and national bodies and organisations, we can also try to build up a coalition of government and sports organisations, and businesses to create more opportunities for more young people and their communities to experience the benefits of sport and exercise. (London 2012, 2007)

Tessa Jowell, the minister responsible for the 2012 Olympics stated:

> Across the country, the games will inspire a whole generation of young people to play sport, volunteer in their communities and be proud of what their country has achieved. (DCMS, 2007)

Post-Games, the east London Olympic facilities are to be managed under the auspices of the 'London Olympic Institute' which can be expected to benefit élite athletes and non-élite participants living in a part of east London, but there is nothing in the candidature file which indicates how the 'mounting excitement' and the inspiration of the Games will be translated into practical support for increased participation levels across the country.

Further reading

Barcelona
    Economic impact   Brunet (1993)
    Legacy   De Moragas and Botella (1995)
Atlanta
    General   Maloney (1996b); Rutheiser (1996); Watkins (1997); Yarborough (2000)
    Media   Billings *et al.* (1998)
    Politics   Andranovich *et al.* (2000)
    Opposition   Burbank *et al.* (2000)
    Bombing   CNN (1996); Cooper (2005); Vollers (2006)
    Economic impact   Humphreys & Plummer (1995); Glisson (1996); Baade & Matheson (2002);
    Legacy   Bragg (1997); French and Disher (1997)
Sydney
    General   Cashman & Hughes (1999)
    Finances   Walsh (1993a-c); O'Neill (1995)
    Economic impact   KPMG Peat Marwick (1993); NSW Treasury/Centre for Regional Economic Analysis (1997); Madden (2002)
    Critical   Lenskyj (2002)
    Protest   Lenskyj (2002); Neilson (2002)
    Legacy   Adair *et al.* (2005); Cashman (2006)
    Green Games   Lenskyj (1998a, b); Chalkley and Essex (1999b); Kearns and Pavlovich (2002)

Athens

It is regrettable that, at the time of writing, there is a dearth of English-language scholarly writing on Athens 2004. English is the main language of international research communication, but the process of refereeing and publication in scholarly journals can take some time. The major retrospective collection of papers on the previous most recent example of a Summer Olympic Games being held in a non-English-speaking country, Barcelona 1992, was published in 1995 (De Moragas and Botella, 1995). Information on any major English-language publications on Athens 2004 will be listed in the online bibliography (Veal and Toohey, 2007) and the book website as they become available. A few specialist academic analyses have been identified, as follows:

Media	Linardopoulos (2005); Barnard *et al.* (2006)
Health and safety	Hadjichristodoulou *et al.* (2005)
Spectators/travel	Kaplanidou (2007)
Volunteers &	
national identity	Karkatsoulis *et al.* (2005)

Beijing

Human rights	Amnesty International (2007)
Olympics/Olympism	Hong (1998); Hong *et al.* (2005)

London

General	MacDonald (2006)
The bid	Lee (2006)
Economic impact	Blake (2005); PriceWaterhouseCoopers (2005)
Legacy	Vigor *et al.* (2004); Arblutt (2005); Kornblatt (2006)
Finance	Nathan and Kornblatt (2007)

Questions

1. What constitutes a 'successful' Olympic Games from the point of view of the host community?
2. Contrast the experience of Sydney, Athens and Beijing with regard to the impact of the Games on the environment.
3. Contrast two of the Games discussed in this chapter with regard to the level of investment in infrastructure.

Appendix 10.1. The Games of the modern era

This Appendix draws on a number of sources which provide accounts of the modern Olympic Games, including Findling and Pelle (1996), Cuyàs (1992), De Lange (1998), Gordon (1994), Guttman (1992), Jennings (1996) and the irreverent Sheil (1998). The IOC website also provides information on each of the modern Games.

References to literature dealing with individual Games are given separately in each entry below – being confined to English-language material, the information therefore tends to be more extensive for Games hosted in English-speaking countries.

I: 1896, Athens, Greece

The organisational aspects of these first Games of the modern era are discussed in Chapter 3. See also: Holmes (1979); Lucas (1980); Davenport (1996); and Mallon and Widlund (1998b).

II: 1900, Paris, France

The Paris Games, which lasted from May to October, were appended to the Universal Paris Exposition – at de Coubertin's urging, but against the wishes of the exposition organisers. While 19 nations were represented by over 1000 competitors, by all accounts, the event did not enhance the prestige of the Olympic idea. Gordon reports:

> the festival set new, heroic standards of confusion. It was spread over five months and most of Paris and the surrounding countryside, and it turned out to be the kind of carnival that might well have been scripted by the Marx Brothers. Competitors waged fierce fishing contests in the Seine, indulged in ballooning and fire-fighting matches, raced underwater and through water-obstacle courses, and took rifle pot-shots at live pigeons. ... The athletic events were held in the Bois de Boulogne, where shady elm trees often got in the way of the discus and hammer, and also tended to block the timekeepers' view of the starter. (Gordon, 1994: 29)

There were disputes between competitors, accusations of cheating and confusion as to whether the event was the official Olympic Games at all, or just a sport programme of the exposition – which was perhaps not surprising since the programme was referred to as the *Concours Internationaux d'Exercises Physiques et de Sports*. Mallon (1998) refers to these and the 1904 St Louis Games as the 'Farcical Games'. See also Howell and Howell (1996).

III: 1904, St Louis, USA

Despite the lessons of 1900, the 1904 Games, originally awarded to Chicago, were again incorporated into an international exposition – the St. Louis World Fair. Only 12 countries were represented, by a shrunken field of under 700 competitors, of whom some 70 per cent were from the USA. 'Even Baron de Coubertin did not attend. Neither France nor England sent a single competitor' (Gordon, 1994: 40).

The commonly accepted view was that the St Louis Games were less than impressive. It was reported that the initial winner of the marathon being disqualified for having hitched a lift in a car for 11 miles, the eventual winner later admitting to having been dosed on strychnine sulphate, eggs and brandy, and the final events of the Games being little more than exotic sideshows of the fair (Gordon, 1994: 42). Against the wishes of the IOC, 'Anthropology days' were held, in which only non-white competitors were allowed, and which consisted of a number of traditional activities, such as spear throwing, participated in by competitors representing various indigenous groups from around the world. A number of these accounts are, however, disputed by Matthews (2005), who concludes:

> Resurrected from neglect and denigration, the St. Louis Olympics deserve to be recognized for their significant conribution to enhancing and promoting the establishment of the infant Olympic games and for their immensely successful presentation to the American public as part of the greatest World's Fair of all time. (Matthews, 2005: 211)

See also Crawford (1991) and Barnett (1996).

IV: 1908, London, England

Originally planned for Rome, the 1908 Games were staged in the purpose-built White City stadium, seating 68,000. The Games lasted six months, from April to October, and were generally considered to be well-organised, with over 2000 competitors for the first time. Metric measures were used as standard for the first time. Some 21 sports were involved, including ice skating, and specially written rule-books were introduced for the first time and more women's events were included. But there was reportedly considerable antagonism between the British organisers and judges and some of the teams, particularly the USA.

The distance for the marathon was set at this Games event, being the distance from Windsor Castle, the royal residence, west of London, to White City – 26 miles, 385 yards (42.2 km) – and has remained at that distance ever since. The actual race was, however, controversial, with the collapsing initial winner being helped over the final yards by officials, resulting in his disqualification. See also Matthews (1980) and Coates (1996).

V: 1912, Stockholm, Sweden

The 1912 Stockholm Games were well organised and notable for officially involving women's events for the first time. Electronic time-keeping and the photo-finish were used for the first time. There were 2500 competitors, including 57 women, from 26 countries. At de Coubertin's behest, competitions in music, painting and poetry, inspired by sport, were held (Ueberhorst, 1996).

VI: 1916, Cancelled

Originally planned for Berlin, these games were cancelled, due to the World War (see Durick, 1996).

VII: 1920, Antwerp, Belgium

The 1920 Games were held in Antwerp in Belgium, the country most affected by the ravages of the Great War. They were held without the support of the Belgian government, in quite spartan conditions. The defeated countries – Germany, Austria, Bulgaria, Hungary and Turkey – were excluded. The Olympic Flag was first displayed at these Games (Lucas, 1983) and the athletes' Olympic Oath was introduced (Renson, 1996a, b).

Renson (1996b) indicates that the official report of the Games is inaccurate and that Mallon (1992) provides a corrected version of the athletic results. See also Lucas (1983) and Renson (1985).

VIII: 1924, Paris, France, and I: Chamonix, France

The Paris Games of 1924 saw the first use of the Olympic motto 'Citius, Altius, Fortius'. The Games were broadcast via radio for the first time, and 1000 journalists were in attendance. Spectator numbers, at 625,000, were much higher than for previous Games (Welch, 1996a). The question of the definition of 'amateur' arose, and it is these Games that form the background to the film *Chariots of Fire* (see also Beck, 1980 and Dyreson, 1996).

Welch (1996b) provides an account of the first Winter Games, held at Chamonix, France. This event was only recognised by the IOC retrospectively, in 1926 (Gordon, 1994: 414).

IX: 1928, Amsterdam, Netherlands, and II: St Moritz, Switzerland

The Amsterdam Games of 1928 saw the introduction of women's track and field events (Morrow, 1992). The Olympic Flame was introduced for the first time, the flame having been brought from Olympia, but not by relay. Almost 300 women competitors (10 per cent of the total) took part (Goldstein, 1996). Simmons (1996a) provides an account of the St Moritz Winter Games.

X: 1932, Los Angeles, USA, and III: Lake Placid, USA

The 1932 Games were held at a time of world-wide economic depression, with unemployment rates as high as 30 per cent in some countries. Nevertheless, the American organisers were determined to 'put on a show' for the 'first Olympics held outside Europe since the farce of St Louis in 1904' (Gordon, 1994: 134). The Coliseum, seating 100,000, and a swimming pool with 17,000 spectator seats, were constructed for the event, resulting in over a million spectators (Pieroth, 1996b). The Coliseum was used again for the 1984 Games. Innovations at these Games included the first specially constructed athletes' village (for men competitors only), teletype communications for the press, electric photo-finish timing, and individual medal ceremonies incorporating a podium as well as flags and national anthems. Foreshadowing the 1984 Games, the organisers returned a profit of US$1 million (Gordon, 1994: 135). See also Lucas (1982), Stump (1988), Pieroth (1996a) and Barney (1998). Fea (1996a) provides an account of the Lake Placid Winter Games.

XI: 1936, Berlin, Germany, and IV: Garmich-Partenkirchen, Germany

Because of the controversy arising from their links with the German Nazi regime, the Berlin Games of 1936 have been written about more than any other Olympic Games (e.g. Snider, 1936; Spencer, 1966; Holmes, 1971; Mandell, 1971, 1987; Gotlieb, 1972; Kass, 1976; Kidd, 1980; Marvin, 1982; Guttman, 1988b; Hart-Davis, 1988; Gray and Knight-Barney, 1990; Wenn, 1991, 1996; Murray, 1992a, b; Masumoto, 1993, 1994; Dyreson, 1994; Herz and Altman, 1996; Krüger, 1996; Rosenzweig, 1997; Rippon, 2006; Walters, 2006). The political aspects of the Berlin Games have already discussed in some detail in Chapter 5 and it is not proposed to elaborate on that discussion here.

Again, held in a massive, specially built stadium, which still stands, Berlin was the first Games to feature the torch relay from Olympia. It was also the first to be celebrated in an official film, in this case two films, shot by the controversial Leni Riefenstahl (Masumoto, 1993, 1994). The Games were televised for the first time at Berlin, albeit to a very small domestic audience. With almost 4000 competitors, it has been suggested that the Berlin Games marked a turning point from Olympic sport as a mere personal pastime for élite performers, to an activity which was taken seriously by governments and which required serious devotion and commitment to training on the part of athletes, raising again the issue of professionalism (Gordon, 1994: 156, 161). Pierre de Coubertin did not attend the Berlin Games, and died just a few weeks after their conclusion.

Stauff (1996) provides an account of the Garmisch-Partenkirchen Winter Games.

XII: 1940 and XIII: 1944, Cancelled

The 1940 Games were originally planned for Tokyo but, following the Japanese invasion of China, were later awarded to Helsinki, only to be cancelled with the outbreak of the Second World War (see Pattengale, 1996). The 1944 Games, also cancelled, had been awarded to London in 1939 (Manning, 1996). Scharenberg (1996) and Engelbrecht (1996) provide accounts of the events surrounding the cancelled Winter Games.

XIV: 1948, London, England, and V: St Moritz, Switzerland

As with the 1920 Antwerp Games, the 1948 Games took place in a city still affected by the disruption and shortages of war (Martueci, 1988; Baker, 1994a, b). Nevertheless, the event attracted over 4000 competitors from 59 countries and, by using mostly existing facilities and being successful in selling tickets to a British public starved of international sporting events during the war years, the organisers managed to return a profit (de Lange, 1998: 61). The London Games were the first to enjoy a multi-million worldwide audience, with the BBC broadcasting commentaries in 43 languages (de Lange, 1998: 61). Thus the new Olympic stars, such as Fanny Blankers-Koen of the Netherlands, who won four gold medals, and Emil Zatopek of Czechoslovakia, who won the 10,000 metres, became household names around the world. See also Voeltz (1996).

Simmons (1996b) provides an account of the St Moritz Winter Games and MacDonald (1998) provides an account of US involvement with ice hockey at those Games.

XV: 1952, Helsinki, Finland, and VI: Oslo, Norway

Originally planned for 1940, the Helsinki Games of 1952 attracted over 5000 competitors. They were notable for the first appearance of the Soviet Union (Jokl *et al.*, 1956; Maxwell and Howell, 1976; Hornbuckle, 1996), inaugurating the 30 year Cold War sporting rivalry between the two great powers. Germany and Japan re-entered the Games. The hero of the Games was Emil Zatopek, who won three gold medals. MacDonald and Brown (1996) provide an account of the Oslo Winter Games.

XVI: 1956, Melbourne, Australia/Stockholm, Sweden, and VII: Cortina, Italy

The Games of the XVIth Olympiad were awarded to Melbourne by the IOC in 1949, but years of wrangling followed, resulting in protracted delays in building facilities, and incurring the wrath of IOC president Avery Brundage over the delays (Gordon, 1994: 200). The 1956 Melbourne Olympics, the first to be staged in the southern hemisphere, were, however, widely viewed as a great success. Referred to as the 'Friendly Games', Gordon says of them:

> When the Olympic Games moved into Melbourne ... it was as if the city had been touched by a certain magic. Nothing before or since ... has ever evoked such sheer emotional involvement from the whole community. ... there was ... a dimension that seemed almost transcendental. Certainly there was about those Games, at a time of fierce international tension, a reassuring innocence. (Gordon, 1994: 203)

Consistent with the 'friendly' theme, and prompted by a letter from an Australian schoolboy, in the closing ceremony the athletes mingled, rather than parading in separate teams, a tradition which has been maintained ever since.

Because of Australia's strict quarantine regulations, the equestrian events were held in Stockholm, Sweden. Political boycotts arose for the first time, with a number of countries withdrawing as a result of the Suez crisis. And for the first time the Soviet Union gained more medals than the USA.

Mainly as a result of the distance to Australia from the main northern hemisphere population centres (and bearing in mind that travel was by ship), the number of competitors fell to 3000.

The Melbourne Games have been the subject of numerous studies and commentaries from academics and others (e.g. Donald and Selth, 1957; Soldatow, 1980; Kent and Merritt, 1986; Mazitelli, 1988; Woodhead, 1988; Cahill, 1989; Wenn, 1993; Gordon, 1994; Jobling, 1994, 1996; Cashman, 1995; Davison, 1997).

Allan Hall (1996) provides an account of the Cortina Winter Games.

XVII: 1960, Rome, Italy, and VIII: Squaw Valley, USA

Originally promised the Games of 1908, Rome had waited more than 50 years to host the Games, which were presented as a mixture of the ancient, with classical backdrops for a number of events, and modern, with a spectacular new 100,000-seat stadium and other modern venues (Davies, 1996). The costly facilities were partly funded by a government-run soccer lottery, but revenue from television rights were also a source of income for the first time. The IOC became concerned about the scale of the Games, and placed a limit of 7000 on the number of athletes and of 1800 on officials (de

Lange, 1998: 71); in the event the number of athletes was just 5300. Despite underlying international tensions (for example, over South Africa and recognition of China) the Games took place without political disruption.

The first Paralympic Games were held in Rome following the 1960 Games. Ashwell (1996) gives an account of the Squaw Valley Winter Games.

XVIII: 1964, Tokyo, Japan, and IX: Innsbruck, Austria

Originally promised the 1940 Games, it was 24 years later that the Olympics came to Asia for the first time. Although the Games were generally free from political incident, Indonesia and North Korea were excluded over events related to the recognition of China (Alam, 1996). The Japanese invested huge sums of money in transport infrastructure and sporting facilities, raising the issue, as discussed in Chapter 6, of just what categories of expenditure should be deemed 'Olympic' expenditure and which categories charged to local development.

Sporting highlights included Australian swimmer Dawn Fraser and Russian rower Vyacheslav Ivanov defending their Olympic titles for a record third time. See also Shigeru (1988).

Kennedy (1996a) gives an account of the Innsbruck Winter Games.

XIX: 1968, Mexico City, Mexico, and X: Grenoble, France

Mexico City is 2500 metres above sea level, making it the highest altitude location at which the Olympic Games have been held. Together with the infamous air pollution of the city, this presented problems for many athletes, but also resulted in a larger than usual number of broken records. Politically the Games were notable for two separate German teams, East and West, being involved for the first time, and for the banning of South Africa, in face of threatened boycotts by African teams over its apartheid policies. Wendl (1998) points out other unique features of these Games; they were the first:

- to be held in a 'developing country';
- to be held in Latin America;
- in which the running events took place on a synthetic surface;
- in which a female athlete lit the Olympic Flame at the opening ceremony;
- at which athletes from African countries came to the fore.

Sporting highlights included Bob Beaman's long-jump record, which remained unbroken until the 1990s, and the introduction of the 'Fosbury Flop' by American high-jumper Dick Fosbury. The Games are, however, remembered particularly for the political events which surrounded them, namely the student riots and their suppression before the Games, which reportedly resulted in the death of over 100 protesters, and the 'black power' salute of American black athletes, as discussed in Chapter 5 (see Aguilar-Darriba, 1988; Arbena, 1991, 1996).

Brown and MacDonald (1996) provide an account of the Winter Games at Grenoble. Brohm (1978: 123) outlines a critical thesis that promotion of the Olympic Games at Grenoble was linked to the French government's perceived need to promote ski resorts in the French Alps.

XX: 1972, Munich, Germany, and XI: Sapporo, Japan

The Olympic Games returned to Germany after a period of 36 years. The Games were notable for their costly and architecturally dramatic sporting facilities, for the seven-medal haul of American swimmer Mark Spitz and the instant fame of Russian gymnast Olga Korbut; but mostly they will be remembered for the terrorist attack on and subsequent death of Israeli athletes, as outlined in Chapter 5 (see Groussard, 1975; Lenk, 1976; Czula, 1978; Guttman, 1984; Mandell, 1991; Brichford, 1996).

Brohm (1978: 126–134) uses the examples of both the Munich Olympics and the Sapporo Winter Olympics to outline the idea of a 'capitalist state-sports bloc' or a 'state monopoly capitalist bloc' – that is a close relationship between sporting organisations, government and business interests designed to promote the interests of business – in the case of Munich a wide range of business interests are involved, including those concerned with the construction of venues and infrastructure, while in Sapporo the focus is on ski equipment manufacturers. See also: Addkison-Simmons (1996) for an account of the Sapporo Games.

XXI: 1976, Montréal, Canada, and XII: Innsbruck, Austria

The 1976 Olympics were experienced and have been remembered as a kaleido-scope of contradictory narratives and outcomes. Promised as a 'modest', 'self-financing' Games, they ended up with such monumental facilities, constructed with little regard for their cost, that the Montréal Games have become a byword for gargantuan extravaganzas. (Kidd, 1996: 153)

Despite this reputation, Kidd points out that, with revenue of $430 million (including $235 millions from a special lottery) and running costs of $207 millions, the Games actually produced a surplus of $223 million. Preuss (2004) also draws tis conclusion, as noted in Chapter 6.The $1.20 billion deficit arose from the extensive expenditure on city infrastructure, including transport. (See Auf der Maur, 1976; Baka, 1976; Ludwig; 1976; Takac, 1976; Commision Royale Enquête, 1977; Iton, 1978, 1988; Wright, 1978; Franks, 1988; Kidd, 1992a; Marsan, 1988).

With the growing importance of the media in paying for and bringing the Games to the world, Montréal marked the point at which researchers began turning their attention to the pattern of media coverage of the Games – see, for example, Chorbajian and Mosco (1981), McCollum and McCollum (1981), MacAloon (1989), Rabkin and Franklin (1989) and Wenn (1996).

Kennedy (1996b) provides an account of the Winter Games at Innsbruck.

XXII: 1980, Moscow, USSR, and XIII: Lake Placid, USA

The 1980 Moscow Olympics, held in the Soviet Union when the Cold War was still a feature of international relations, were notable for the Western boycott, led by the USA, in protest at the Soviet invasion of Afghanistan. The boycott included the USA and Canada and Israel and some Moslem nations, but not all Western nations joined the boycott – in the case of Britain, the bulk of the Olympic team attended despite the government's call to join the boycott. Only 80 countries took part in the Games. Such overt political disruption so soon after the Munich events and the financial problems of Montréal, raised doubts about the survival of the Olympics, and Riordan (1996:

153) suggest that those in the West who resented the sporting success of Eastern bloc countries saw this as an opportunity to recast the Games as a Western event. See also, Barret (1980), Maître (1980), Booker (1981), Hazan (1982), Barton (1983), Deane (1985), Duncan (1986, 1990), Hulme (1988, 1990), Real *et al.* (1989) and Crossman and Lappage (1992); and see Fea (1996a) on the Lake Placid Winter Games.

XXIII: 1984, Los Angeles, USA, and XIV: Sarajevo, Yugoslavia

In response to the USA-led boycott of the 1980 Games, the Soviet Union led a 'tit-for-tat' boycott by most of the Eastern bloc countries, claiming that anti-Soviet sentiment in the USA posed a security threat to its athletes.

Following the excesses of Montréal few cities were prepared to take on the financial risks now associated with the Olympics, so Los Angeles was awarded the 1984 Games with no opposition. It was the first 'private enterprise' Games, with the contract to undertake the Games being struck with a private company, rather than a city council. True to their word, the Americans, with $290 million of television revenue and extensive commercial sponsorship, produced a financial surplus of $225 million. This regenerated worldwide interest in hosting the Games and ushered in the commercialisation of the Games, as discussed in Chapter 6. Economics Research Associates (1984) estimated that the economic impact of the Games on California was some $2.5 billion.

For analysis and comment on the Los Angeles Games, see: Biles (1984), Edwards (1984), Henry (1984), Network 10 (1984), Perelman (1985), Duncan (1986, 1990), Lawrence (1986), Reich (1986, 1989), Ueberroth (1986), DeFrantz (1988), Haag and Riesinger (1988), Nixon (1988), Shanklin (1988), Simon (1988), Farrell (1989), Real *et al.* (1989), Levitt (1990), MacAloon (1991), Chalip and Chalip (1992), Wilson (1993, 1994, 1996) and De Lange (1998: 105–114).

Dunkelberger (1996) provides and account of the Sarajevo Winter Games.

XXIV: 1988, Seoul, Korea, and XV: Calgary, Canada

Seoul was an unlikely choice for the Games, given that South Korea lacked any great Olympic tradition, and given the political uncertainty of a divided country (Guttman, 1992: 165; Palenski, 1996). In the first Games for 12 years to be unaffected by boycotts, and the last Games of the Cold War era, the Soviet Union and East Germany emerged in first and second place in the medal table. The Seoul Games were most notable for the drug scandal involving 100 metre winner Ben Johnson of Canada, who, having tested positive for anabolic steroids, was stripped of his medal, in favour of Carl Lewis of the USA (see Chapter 8).

For further commentary on and analysis of the Seoul Games see Herr (1988), Kang (1988), Kim (1988, 1990), Joynt *et al.* (1989), Lee (1989), Mohsen and Alexandraki (1989), Switzer *et al.* (1989), Chalip (1990), Hyup (1990), Jeung *et al.* (1990), Kidd (1990a, b), Boutilier and San Giovanni (1991), Park and Samaranch (1993); Tewnion (1993), Whitson and Macintosh (1993), Mount and Leroux (1994), Pound (1994), Wamsley and Heine (1994) and De Lange (1998: 115–124).

The Calgary Winter Games were notable for the major research project on public participation and awareness of the Games (Ritchie, 1990; Ritchie and Lyons, 1990; Ritchie and Smith, 1991; Haxton, 1993). See also Canadian Ministry for Fitness and

Benefits	Costs
Technology	
• Knowledge gained from rejuvenating Homebush Bay site could be applied to other degraded sites • Increased communication infra-structure and know-how • Systems development leading to inter-nationally marketable service • More rapid deployment of new media technologies, e.g. high density TV	• None mentioned
Human capital	
• Large scale employment associated with Games • Reduced unemployment leading to reduced social problems associated with unemployment • Technology transfer from visiting Olympic support staff, e.g. production, event staging, computing, etc. • Improved sporting prowess through increased exposure to international standard competition	• Post-Games demobilisation
Economic	
• Business development; Sydney's profile as a place to do business enhanced by Olympic exposure (overseas business people attending the Games identifying investment opportunities)	• Inflationary impact of increased tourism • Investment in Olympics 'crowd out' investment in other product-ive enterprises
National Identity	
• Increased national pride through increased international exposure • More awareness of Australian culture following from Olympics Cultural Programme	• None mentioned

Source: KPMG Peat Marwick, 1993.

Chapter 11

The Future of the Olympic Games

The Olympic Games are not what Pierre de Coubertin intended them to be. They will never be simply an occasion for athletes to compete in friendly rivalry, for spectators to admire extraordinary physical performances, and for everyone involved to feel himself or herself a part of the family of man. But the Olympic Games are not the opposite either. They are not simply occasions for sexism, racism, religious fanaticism, ideological display, nationalism, commercialism and the instrumentalization of the body. Every four years, as the Olympics more nearly approach or more tragically disappoint our ideals, they provide us with a dramatic indication of who we are. Perhaps that is the best argument for their continuation. Allen Guttman (1988a: 443)

Introduction

The modern Olympic Games have survived for over a hundred years, but during that period their future has not always been assured. Will the Games survive for a second century, and if so, in what form? These are the questions addressed in this chapter.

When we began writing the first edition of this book, in early 1997, the idea that the future of the Olympic Games might be questioned was, at least in the popular mind, unthinkable. The Games appeared to be going from strength to strength. However, the 1998/99 corruption scandals, as discussed in Chapter 5, gave rise to speculation on the continued existence of the Games. But it is worth bearing in mind that this was not the first time that doubts about the Games' long-term viability had been raised.

In the early years of the twentieth century the Olympic Games barely enjoyed a separate existence at all: they were mere appendages to international trade expositions (for example, in Paris, 1900, and St Louis, 1904). Of the Paris Games, even Pierre de Coubertin himself is quoted as declaring: 'It's a miracle that the Olympic movement survived that celebration' (quoted in Gordon, 1994: 29).

Financial problems threatened the continuation of the Games in the 1970s, when it was widely believed that the 1976 Montréal Olympics had virtually bankrupted the host city, although, as noted in Chapter 6, these claims have since been questioned. Nevertheless, the result was that only one city, Los Angeles, was interested in bidding to host the 1984 Games. But money has not been the only threat to the Games. War caused their cancellation in 1916, 1940 and 1944 and, as we have seen in Chapter 5,

274

political disputes intervened in the disagreements over South Africa's involvement in the 1970s and 1980s and the Cold War boycotts in 1980 and 1984. In 1980 Lord Killanin, in handing over the presidency of the IOC to Juan Antonio Samaranch, is quoted as having said: 'Good luck. I don't think the Games will survive your presidency' (quoted in Pound and Johnson, 1999). Since 1988 in particular, highly publicised drug scandals have also raised questions about the Games' future.

The various crises faced by the Olympic Games, and the IOC's responses to them, have attracted criticism, even from the most ardent proponents of the Games. In 1988, one of the most consistent academic champions of the Olympic Movement, wrote:

> among scholars of the Olympic Movement, an unmistakable malaise pervades its future. The universality of the play instinct, humankind's passion for competing in and watching games, plus the special attraction of the Olympic Games combine to make the immediate demise of the games unlikely. But all human institutions are inherently imperfect, and if loving care and sensible revisions are not at work, the Olympic Movement and the Olympic Games will die prematurely. (Lucas, 1988b: 427)

Numerous commentators have predicted or called for the end of the Olympic Games. For example, Marxist Jean-Marie Brohm and his colleagues wrote a number of anti-Olympic tracts in the 1970s, seeing the Games as: 'the most extreme example of the moronic sports spectacle, the purpose of which is to hammer obedience to the bourgeois order into the heads of young people and the oppressed masses generally', and calling on 'all workers the world over to condemn the masquerade of the Olympics' (Brohm, 1978: 168).

Also writing in the 1970s, McMurty (1973) outlined 'A case for killing the Olympics'. In the 1980s Edwards (1981) wrote of the 'Crisis in the Olympic Movement', Hoberman published *The Olympic Crisis* (1986) and Rose (1988) asked the question: 'Should the Olympic Games be abolished?' The latter discussion considered the proposition that the Games should be abolished because they were too big, too professional, too commercial and too political, but concluded that the main reason why they deserved to be abolished was that they failed to live up to their own declared ideals in promoting peace and human rights. The Olympic Movement stood accused of paying only 'obsequious respect to human dignity and to an honest yearning for the survival of the planet' (Rose, 1988: 404). As we have seen, Helen Lenskyj (2000, 2002, 2004) has been assiduous in documenting local anti-Olympic movements, particularly in cities bidding for, or hosting, the Games and, while she stops short of advocating the abolition of the Olympics, she calls for the 'dismantling of the Olympic industry as presently constituted' (Lenskyj, 2000: 194). Essays in a recently published volume, entitled *Post-Olympism?* (Bale and Christensen, 2004), mostly advocate reform or transformation of the Olympic phenomenon, but the final sentence in the book states:

> the best indication on the world's cultural landscape that we are prepared for peace and equality, that Olympism and those often quoted values have finally triumphed, is that the Olympic Games will be gone. (Wamsley, 2004: 242)

The question of the Games' survival can be discussed in terms of two related but distinct dimensions: the external environment and internal organisational and cultural issues. The external environment includes the political, social, cultural, technological and economic conditions within which the Games operate; they may not necessarily affect the Games themselves directly, but have an influence through changing relation-ships and economic pressures and changing values, lifestyles and patterns of consumer behaviour. Internal organisational issues relate to the nature of the Games themselves and their governance and organisation. These broad issues are discussed in turn below.

The environment of the Games

A number of external conditions are discussed in turn here, namely: the question of war and peace; the growth of leisure; the commercialisation of sport; globalisation and communication technology; the issue of the use of performance-enhancing drugs; and competition from other sporting events.

War and peace

With the end of the Cold War, the threat of worldwide conflict, which forced the cancellation of the Olympic Games on three occasions in the last century, was lifted. While numerous conflicts continue around the world and the 'war on terrorism' raises security concerns, major world-wide divisions threatening nuclear conflagration, which would end civilisation as we know it, now seem less likely.

In the post-World War II era, the world was divided into the West, or 'first world', led by the USA, and the Eastern bloc (or 'second world'), led by the Soviet Union. The developing countries (or 'third world') were either aligned with one or other of the two sides or sought to maintain some sort of neutrality. In many ways it was a tribute to the political acumen of the leaders of the Olympic Movement that these worldwide divisions did not result in more frequent disruption of the Games than the mutual boycotts of 1980 and 1984, as described in Chapter 5. One perspective on the era between 1952 (when athletes from the Soviet Union took part in the Games for the first time) and 1988 (when the last Games took place under Cold War conditions) is that the intense east-west rivalry which was a feature of the Cold War, resulted in far more political importance being attached to international sporting contests than might otherwise have been the case (Torres and Dyreson, 2005). As one commentary on official views of sport in communist China puts it: 'China's sporting success demonstrated the fact that socialism was superior to capitalism' (Hong *et al.*, 2005: 518). But whether the Olympic Games actually played a role in preventing the *Cold War* from becoming *hot* – that is in promoting and maintaining world peace, as the *Olympic Charter* claims – is debatable.

The idea of international sporting events being a substitute for war – in George Orwells's phrase: 'war minus the shooting' (quoted in Torres and Dyreson, 2005: 61) – is an intriguing one. The term 'bread and circuses' has been used to describe the practice of the Ancient Roman state of supposedly pacifying the masses by providing them with free food and quasi-sporting entertainment to keep them occupied and unconcerned about serious political issues and, indeed, was adopted by a local Toronto-based anti-Olympic pressure group. The long-standing existence of ritualised forms of combat within and between communities, as described by anthropologists (e.g. Cherfas and Lewin, 1980), suggests that aggression, particularly among young males, may be endemic and in need of some form of outlet. One thesis is that events such as the Olympic Games therefore contribute to the maintenance of peace by absorbing these aggressive tendencies, as a number of science fiction films, such as

Rollerblade, seek to illustrate. A complementary thesis is that the survival of the Olympic Games, and of other international sporting events, is dependent on the continuation of international peace, since their role as outlets for aggression and competition is necessary *only* in the absence of war. A third thesis is that events such as the Olympic Games make war *more* likely by celebrating and stimulating nationalism and aggression.

It is not possible to test any of these theses empirically since, despite the rhetoric, the role or influence of the Olympic Games, if any, in these matters is likely to be minor and swamped by much more significant causes of war and peace, such as the play of national and ethnic political and economic interests. Nevertheless, the promotion of peace is a prime goal of the Olympic Movement, and is enshrined in the *Olympic Charter* and in the revived notion of the 'Olympic Truce' (see Chapter 4). While a number of minor concessions among hostile nations has been claimed in the name of the latter (Lambrinidis, 2003), there is no evidence to suggest that, in reality, the Olympic Games have any significant or lasting effect on modern armed conflicts. Nevertheless, the idea that people should join together in sporting contests rather than fight each other in wars is a noble one and perhaps has an educational, if not practical, value.

The growth of leisure

The traditional view of the growth of leisure is that, at certain stages in economic development, leisure time increases for the individual and leisure industries expand to serve the leisure needs of an increasingly affluent and increasingly 'leisured' population. Sport and sporting contests can be seen as part of the growing leisure industries and can therefore be expected to become increasingly important as economies develop. This is predicated on a world which enjoys increasing prosperity and which continues to develop through *industrial* stages into *post-industrial* and possibly *postmodern* phases. In these conditions, activities previously seen as 'unproductive' become increasingly significant, in an economy where production of material goods becomes ever more automated and in a culture where ephemeral, electronically communicated events and images hold centre stage. Thus we have seen, in recent years, that the Olympic Games and other 'hallmark' events have become one of the most potent tools of 'city boosterism', which sees cities competing to host sporting events in order to achieve or maintain 'world class' status and thus secure jobs, prosperity and economic security (Syme *et al.*, 1989; Roche, 1992; Whitson & Macintosh, 1993; Hall, 1994; Andranovich *et al.* 2000; Waitt, 2001).

As the pan-Hellenic Games of Ancient Greece and the games and circuses of Ancient Rome testify, major spectator events can take place only when certain conditions prevail, including the existence of wealth (even if not equally shared) and a leisured citizenry, a peaceful environment and facilities for travel. All these conditions – together with modern communication technology – have come together in much of the world in the contemporary era. They cannot, however, be taken for granted. The inevitability of the scenario of increasing industrial productivity continuing to deliver wealth and leisure to the mass of the population in the Western world has recently been questioned. The smooth growth path which had come to be expected for Western economies was interrupted by: the oil crises of the 1970s; the subsequent high inflation and high unemployment rates; the rise of the competitive Asian 'tiger' economies of the east; the disruptions cause by the adjustments of Russia and Eastern Europe following the collapse of the Berlin Wall; the Asian financial crisis of the late 1990s; the September 11 events; and the advent of global warming. More specifically, it has been suggested that, after many decades of declining working hours and increased leisure time, those with jobs in the West, at least in the USA, are working longer rather than shorter hours and are faced with a 'time squeeze' (Schor, 2006). Countries around the world are at different stages of economic development and are following different trajectories in that process. In countries in the process of industrialisation, working hours tend to be high. Thus increasing leisure time cannot be taken for granted as a driving force delivering ever-increasing numbers of sports participants, spectators and consumption as was expected by Western-based commentators in the past.

Given the commoditised form in which the majority of people enjoy modern sporting events, however, large amounts of leisure time are not required to engage in the act of consumption. The average individual in the Western world currently spends around two hours a day watching television (Eurostat, 2004). If, during the fortnight of the Olympic Games, half of those viewers were to devote an hour to watching Olympic coverage, the television networks broadcasting the signal would more than recoup their cost in advertising revenue. Thus, while further increases in leisure time would no doubt assist the television networks in selling the 'consumption' of sporting events via television, this is not a necessary condition for continued success. Sport merely competes, generally very successfully, with other television 'product' for the viewer's time and, within sport, the Olympic Games, as arguably the leading 'brand', generally has no difficulty in attracting a high market share. The continued success of the Olympic Games as a leisure product is therefore not necessarily dependent on increasing leisure time.

Commercialisation of sport

The modern era has seen the commoditisation and commercialisation of numerous activities, including sport. Sport has been transformed from an amateur activity undertaken by small, self-help groups, into a global business, bolstered by the advertising power of television and the companies which spend money on advertising and sponsorship. Along with this goes the development of sport as a popular cultural phenomenon, which celebrates sporting heroes alongside film stars and rock stars. This nexus between the sport event and its many related stakeholders is illustrated in Figure 6.1 in Chapter 6.

The Olympic Games, as the most significant of world sporting events, are therefore at the vortex of this dynamic economic and cultural phenomenon. Thus it is no longer just athletes and sport enthusiasts who have an interest in the survival of the Games: they are joined by mass media organisations, local and global corporate advertisers and sponsors and venue owners and a host of professionals, such as managers, marketers, agents, trainers, coaches, physiotherapists and psychologists (and even academics and authors of books!) who derive their livelihood, wholly or in part, from the resources flowing into what is now, as Helen Lenskyj (2000) has termed it, the 'Olympic industry'.

Of course this level of involvement on the part of non-sporting, and non-Olympic, interests could contain the seeds of destruction of the Games. The 'spirit' of Olympism is ostensibly non-materialist: the alliance between Olympism and commerce is therefore potentially a fragile one. The question might be asked: how can all these organisations and 'hangers on' be making money out of the Games when the whole ethos of the Games is about something other than making money? As we have seen, the Olympic Games are unique in being associated with a 'movement' and a philosophy, 'Olympism', with almost religious connotations. Olympism enshrines certain ideals which, as with a religion, its custodians are sworn to uphold. Many see commercialisation as undermining these ideals (see Gruneau and Cantelon, 1988; Wamsley, 2004; Tomlinson, 2005). How can the Games be about the 'spirit of friendly competition' and 'participation for its own sake', when such enormous rewards are available to those involved, both as athletes and as associated marketers and sponsors? The Olympics, in such circumstances, it is argued, become a vehicle for the pursuit of personal, material gain, rather than for the celebration of sport.

Looked at another way, in a capitalist world in which commerce operates on a global scale, a phenomenon as well-known as the Olympic Games clearly has market potential. The question is: who should benefit from this? The IOC has taken the view that the Olympic Movement should share in the material rewards that flow from the commercial exploitation of the Olympic 'brand'. International market research shows that, among the general public, the Olympic rings are the most widely recognised symbol in the world, beating those of Shell, McDonald's and Mercedes, and the public generally associate the Games and their symbols with positive moral values, while not objecting to commercial sponsorship (Meenaghan, 1997). This translates into billions of dollars-worth of marketing potential, which the IOC has chosen to exploit rather than ignore.

The Los Angeles Games of 1984, termed the 'Hamburger Games', were the first to bring the commercial dimension to the fore and also saw the first signs of a backlash against commercialisation of the Games. Similar sentiments were expressed in relation to the highly commercialised Atlanta Games of 1996. Thus the very source of financial salvation for the Games is at the same time seen by some as a source of danger. However, while traditionalists bewail the loss of 'innocence' or 'purity' in the modern, commercial Games (Barney *et al.*, 2002: 282), while at the same time often arguing that such innocence never really existed (Gruneau, 1984), the evidence suggests that, for the time being at least, the general public are prepared to take their sport with increasing helpings of commercialism, in the form of advertising and sponsorship. Nevertheless, there remains a chance that the public will one day cry 'enough!' or simply lose interest, and turn away from the commercialised sporting 'product'. Sponsors and advertisers who provide the funds would simply switch their resources to whatever new phenomenon the public turned to. The ease with which this can happen was demonstrated by the withdrawal and threats of withdrawal of corporate sponsors during the bribery scandals of 1998/99 (Booth, 1999).

A particular feature of the commercialisation of sport is the professionalisation of the athletes themselves, brought about by the increased flow of money into sport and the consequently enhanced market value of individual athletes. The degree of professionalisation varies from sport to sport and from country to country. Nevertheless, the value of an Olympic gold medal, in terms of official rewards from the athlete's own country, subsequent appearance money and endorsement income, can amount to millions of dollars for some athletes. The principles of the Olympic Creed concerning the importance of *taking part* as opposed to *winning* (see Chapter 4) are placed under considerable strain when the direct and indirect financial rewards for winners are so great. In particular it is often suggested that it is the prospect of large financial rewards which tempts athletes to take proscribed performance-enhancing drugs. As discussed in Chapter 8, the pressures on athletes from this source are likely to increase in future rather than decrease. The potential responses of the Olympic Movement to these pressures and their likely impact on the future of the Games are discussed further below.

Finally, in considering external commercial and economic factors, it should be noted that the scale of the Games, and with it their cost, increased markedly in the post-World War II era, partly as a result of more countries taking part. Initially the process of decolonisation and, more recently, the break-up of the Soviet Union and the growth, and in some cases success, of nationalist movements in many parts of the world, have resulted in an increase in the number of countries eligible to take part in the Olympic Games. All member countries have the right to enter a team in the Games, however small. The cost of mounting the Games has therefore increased substantially and with this has come an increased risk that they will become unwieldy and therefore be unable to pay their way commercially or, if publicly funded, place unacceptable financial burdens on host city, provincial and national governments. The perceived threat of bankruptcy dissuaded cities from offering to host the Games in the 1980s. While recent Games, particularly those which have taken place in the USA, have been run profitably, this is not guaranteed. Again, the response to the pressures to increase the scale and consequent costs of the Games is an organisational challenge for the Olympic Movement and the IOC in particular, and is discussed further below.

In the early period of the modern Olympic Games' existence, lack of money was their major problem and the main threat to their survival. In an era of commercialisation and commoditisation, the quantity of money flowing into sport, and the 'strings attached' to it, present equally significant challenges.

Communication technology and globalisation

It can be argued that the current scale and status of the Olympic Games, as with other major international sporting events, is owed entirely to the developments in communication technology over the last 30–40 years – in particular the development of satellite television broadcasting. The ability to broadcast pictures of the event instantly, or, in edited and packaged form, within a few hours, to anywhere in the world became possible only in the last third of the twentieth century. This coincided with the emergence of trans-national companies, such as McDonald's, Coca-Cola, Toyota and Nike, with products and services targeted at global markets. And the communications systems which facilitate television and the Internet also facilitate the development of international commerce and 'global capital'. Global communications and global commerce, then, constitute the key components of the phenomenon of globalisation. In the second half of the twentieth century, as the number of participating countries approached 200, the Summer Olympic Games became a truly global phenomenon in a political sense, but it was its 'fit' with communication technology and the marketing needs of global commerce which generated the resources to transform it into the preeminent global cultural event we see today.

Hoberman (2004) argues that, in the second half of the nineteenth century, steamship lines, railways, free trade and the telegraph created what he terms the 'first era' of globalisation. Numerous international organisations came into being at this time – including the International Olympic Committee. Thus the modern Olympic Games can be said to have been born out of the first era of globalisation, but reached their current scope and scale in the second era of globalisation.

As we have seen, this state of affairs has been welcomed by some but not by others. But what of the future? It seems unlikely that the Olympic Movement will turn its back on the media and commercial nexus which currently sustains it. And, as discussed in the previous section, the global public seems largely content with the mix of sport and commerce which this entails. But what changes can be expected in these supporting mechanisms?

Further developments in television technology are likely to continue to generate advertising and sponsorship income. Television picture quality is improving with the advent of digital technology, further enhancing the ability of the broadcasters to deliver a 'being there' sensation for the viewer. Further enhancement of satellite capacity will facilitate the transmission of more images, complemented by high-capacity fibre-optic cable which will deliver multiple channels to subscribers' homes. Thus, in addition to the *broad*casting of the Games to mass audiences using free-to-air signals, advertiser-sponsored media, we will see *narrow*casting to subscribers who are interested in specific aspects of the Games (Lynch *et al.*, 1996). It is possible to envisage coverage of all 28 or so of the Olympic sports being transmitted simultaneously to the home by satellite and cable. This is what the technology will offer. Whether it will actually develop into a significant feature of sport broadcasting in future depends not just on technological possibilities but also on financial and economic realities and consumer taste and willingness and ability to pay.

The Internet is likely to play an increasing role, as discussed in Chapter 7. Although it was treated cautiously by Olympic organisations initially, because of the possible threat to the revenues from traditional media, the Internet is now a key component of Olympic Games communication. However, as Garry Whannel (2005: 174–75) points out, television companies, particularly NBC, would not buy television broadcasting rights for several Olympiads in advance if they were not confident that television would retain its preeminence in bringing the Games to the global audience.

With the collapse of the Soviet Union and with the remaining major communist power, China, rapidly embracing the market, the only notable opposition to global capitalism today is certain fundamentalist Islamic movements. While such movements may succeed in diminishing the influence of the West in a number of Islamic countries, few would expect them to have a significant impact on globalisation trends. Existing transnational companies continue to extend their reach and new ones are continually emerging.

Thus global commerce and global communications which sustain the modern Olympic Games look set to continue to flourish. The tensions between 'Olympic values' and the materialist values of global capitalism therefore look set to continue.

This Western scenario must be balanced by consideration of possible trends in the developing world. One scenario sees parts of the developing world slipping deeper into crisis and further poverty. Alternative scenarios see massive growth in consumer markets – including sporting consumers – as economic growth takes hold. The rapid rates of growth of the Asian 'tiger' economies during the 1970s, 1980s and early 1990s and the ability of China and India to maintain high economic growth rates over a decade or more, demonstrates that such a scenario is possible.

Performance-enhancing drugs

As outlined in Chapter 8, the Olympic Movement has assumed a leadership role in relation to the control of performance-enhancing drugs in sport. The very ethos of 'Olympism' is antithetical to the use of performance-enhancing drugs. Three alternative future scenarios are outlined in Chapter 8, namely: (i) continuation of the status quo, in which performance-enhancing drugs are banned, but their use is known to be widespread as chemists and athletes keep 'one step ahead' of the enforcement system; (ii) a considerable enhancement of the enforcement régime, resulting in effective elimination of proscribed drugs from the Games; and (iii) abandonment of prohibition, resulting in a 'competition between chemists' rather than between athletes.

Few see the first option as viable; to make strong statements about drugs, but not to devote the necessary resources to ensure their elimination raises questions as to the integrity of the Olympic Movement, and of the IOC in particular. Any such questioning poses a threat to the continued viability of the Games from both commercial sponsors and traditional enthusiasts for the 'purity' of sport. Since the third, 'open slather', option is unthinkable given the stance of the Olympic Movement to date, the IOC has no choice, if its integrity is to be preserved, but to expand considerably the resources and measures devoted to research on drugs and testing of athletes.

Competition from other sporting events

In addition to the effects of commercialisation, one reason why the public might fail to continue be drawn to the Olympic Games is that they might find other sporting events more attractive. The preeminence of the Olympic Games may be threatened by the rise in popularity of other international sporting events. It is already claimed that the soccer World Cup commands a larger television audience than the Olympics (FIFA, 2006). For a number of sports, such as tennis, basketball and soccer, the Olympic Games do not represent the pinnacle of competition. Even in some 'classic' Olympic sports, such as swimming and athletics, their world championships can be seen as at least as important as the Olympics to athletes. In some cases the Olympics retain a distinctive role by placing restrictions on the nature of competitors, for example the age restrictions on soccer players and the amateur status of boxers. Thus, increasingly, the Olympic Games retain their status as a result of tradition, their overall 'aura' and their multi-sport nature. It is possible that these features could lose their 'edge' in terms of public attraction and therefore attraction to advertisers and broadcasters.

The organisation of the Games

The modern Olympic Games, while rooted in history, have nevertheless changed dramatically in the 110 years of their existence. For some observers, however, change has not been fast enough or radical enough. Numerous suggestions have been made for change over the years. A number of these are reviewed and evaluated here, including: the question of a permanent site for the Games; whether the Games should be limited in scale, particularly by limiting the sporting programme; whether criteria for admission of athletes to the Games should be modified. Finally, the question of the reform of the International Olympic Committee and the overall structure of the Olympic Movement is addressed.

A permanent site?

It has often been suggested that the Olympic Games should be staged at a permanent site rather then being moved to a new city in every Olympiad (Loder, 1997; *New York Times*, 2004). What would be the advantages and disadvantages of such a move? Advantages and disadvantages are discussed in turn below.

Advantages

Having a permanent site for the Olympic Games could produce a number of advantages, including: the end of the 'bid circus'; cost savings; the provision of ideal facilities; and management benefits.

1. *The end of the 'bid circus'.* Elsewhere in this final chapter the question of bribery and corruption within the IOC is discussed. Most of these problems have arisen in relation to the process of deciding on the awarding of the Games to bidding cities. The use of a permanent site would remove this source of temptation. The 'bid circus' is expensive: even without the wining and dining and 'junketing' of IOC members, the development of a bid can be an expensive process, involving planning, feasibility studies and even the building of facilities to demonstrate a city's commitment. A permanent site would save this time, money and effort.

2. *Cost savings.* A permanent site would produce further long-term cost-savings to the Olympic Movement in not having to subsidise the building of new facilities every four years, bearing in mind that a large proportion of the cost of mounting the Games is met from the broadcasting rights and worldwide sponsorship funds which accrue initially to the IOC. The resources which are devoted to the building of facilities could, it is argued, be devoted to the promotion of sport in other ways.

3. *The provision of ideal facilities.* At a permanent site it might be expected that ideal, 'state-of-the-art', facilities could be built. It could be claimed that the current system already provides ideal, state-of-the-art facilities, but this is not true for all facilities at all Games. The need to constantly upgrade facilities at a permanent site could of course negate at least part of the savings noted in 2. above. It might also be countered that, whereas each new host city tends to build new state-of-the-art facilities for each Games, with a permanent site, the temptation might be to 'make do', and not to upgrade facilities in every Olympiad.

4. *Management benefits.* With the current system, each host city must learn how to run the Games from scratch – some host cities have more experience than others in managing 'mega-events'. But the Olympic Movement takes a risk, every time it awards the Games to a new host city, that the organisation will malfunction. The most recent example of such risk becoming reality was the transport problems claimed to have been experienced at the 1996 Atlanta Games. At a permanent site there would be at least a core of permanent staff, with accumulated experience on how to run the Games. Equally, of course, such a permanent team could become complacent and staid, and deliver a less well managed event than those provided under current arrangements.

Disadvantages

Disadvantages of a permanent site include: the loss of 'reach' likely to result from not spreading the benefits of the event around the world; the problems caused by constant environmental conditions of a single site; the risk presented by host country politics; and the problem of actually choosing a permanent site.

1. *Not spreading the benefits.* Not holding the event in different parts of the world would have a number of negative consequences. First, certain regions of the world might come to feel alienated from the Games. This might well be the case if the permanent site were to be located in the 'first world' – Greece has often been mentioned as a potential location for a permanent Summer Games site. Second, the legacy of superior sporting facilities which the Games leave behind in host cities around the world would be lost. Third, the 'party' which cities enjoy when they play host to the Games, and which reportedly leaves behind a legacy of goodwill for the Olympics, would be lost. While residents in the permanent host city would have a 'party' every four years, the role of the Games as a world-wide 'goodwill ambassador for sport and the Olympics' would be lost. Fourth, the learning experience which goes with hosting the Games, which can be said to benefit sport management worldwide, would no longer be spread around – the Games would be run by a permanent, albeit highly skilled and experienced, bureaucracy. Fifth, the economic stimulus which the Games bring, through construction as well as from visitors to the event, would again not be spread around but, in a more limited form, would be enjoyed only by the permanent host city. Sixth, a permanent site would fix the Games in one time-zone, with implications for television coverage and revenues. This issue is further complicated by the fact that the bulk of such funding currently comes from US media and sponsoring companies – an investment which produces maximum returns when the Games are held in the USA.

2. *Environmental conditions.* Sites vary in terms of such things as average humidity, temperature and altitude. A permanent site would result in just one set of environ-mental conditions, which would therefore always tend to favour one type of athlete. Moving the event around prevents the development of such built-in environmental discrimination.

3. *Host country politics.* There would always be the possibility that the host country would be politically unacceptable to some participating countries. For example, for a period during the 1960s Greece was ruled by a military junta ('the colonels') which was not acceptable to much of the rest of the world. Of course such issues arise with the current system, but at least such issues as political stability and human rights records of bidding countries can be taken account of in the assessment process.

4. *Choosing the permanent site.* Just where would the permanent site be located? Greece is a sentimental favourite for the Summer Games; within Greece the two options would be Olympia and Athens. However, Olympia does not have the necessary infrastructure (such as an international airport and the required hotels) so its provision would add considerably to the cost of establishing the permanent site. The success of Athens in hosting the Games in 2004 is clearly relevant to this discussion. There has been little discussion of possible permanent sites for the Winter Games.

Considering all of these issues, it would seem that, as a global phenomenon, and despite the difficulties presented by the bidding system, the Olympic Movement will continue to see the disadvantages of a permanent site as outweighing the advantages.

The scale of the Games

We have already noted that the increasing number of member countries has resulted in increases in the scale of the Games. There are also pressures to increase the number of events for sports already included, to add sports not currently included and to increase the number of women's events, which currently constitute less than half of the total.

The sheer size of the Games has, as noted above, increased the cost and financial risk involved in hosting them, but it has also increased the planning and logistical challenges – and the risk of organisational failure. For example, in the case of the Atlanta Games of 1996, negative press reports of transport problems at times threatened to undermine the goodwill which any host city expects to gain from hosting the Games. If the Games were to become so big that the logistical and financial problems of running them outweighed the benefits generated for host cities, their future would be in doubt.

Any reduction in the scale of the Games runs the risk of reducing their attraction to advertisers and sponsors: it is, after all, the sheer scale of the Games which is a large part of their attraction. However, as a result of the deliberations of the 1997 Centennial Olympic Congress (Mbaye, 1996) the IOC decided to limit the number of athletes in the Summer Games to 10,000 and the number of officials to 5000. This limitation is somewhat arbitrary – why not 11,000 or 12,000 athletes? – and the limitation itself presents problems, since any additional event can only be introduced at the expense of an existing one or by reducing the number of participants in existing events.

In Chapter 4 it was noted that, in the 2002–05 period, the IOC took two initiatives to address the problems presented by the growing scale of the Games: the Programme Commission conducted a substantial review of the sporting programme of the Games and the Olympic Games Study Commission reviewed the overall management of the hosting of the Games, resulting in the publication of the 'Pound Report' (Olympic Games Study Commission, 2003). It is not proposed to discuss the latter here, but to give some consideration to the future of the programme.

The sporting programme

Lucas (1992: 212) suggested, without being specific, that some sports currently included in the Olympic programme are incompatible with its ideals. Some might argue that sports which are violent in nature (for example, boxing, shooting) are incompatible with the Olympic Movement's goal of promoting peace. The irony of this argument is that the origin of the Games, in classical Greece, lie in the training of young men for combat in war.

A second type of event which might be considered for exclusion are those activities which do not involve 'citius, altius, fortius', that is, activities which must be judged on the basis of aesthetics rather than measurable speed, height or weight. The problem with this principle is that, while it would exclude certain controversial activities such as synchronised swimming and ice dancing, it would also be in danger of excluding other, more traditional activities, such as gymnastics and diving.

A third type of activity which might be considered for exclusion are those which, because of their cost, involve only a small number of élite, wealthy, participants. This applies particularly in the area of equestrian events. The latter attract those with the wealth to maintain horses or those with access to horses professionally, such as landowners or the military. Cycling might also come into this category since the cost of modern 'high tech' bicycles can only be afforded by teams sponsored by cycle manufacturers, which are based in the wealthier countries. Thus cycling has moved closer in nature to motor sports, which have always been excluded partly because of their exclusive and commercial nature.

The programme review conducted in 2000 by the Programme Commission, as outlined in Chapter 4, resulted in a reduction of the Summer Games programme from 28 sports to 26. While a large amount of data was collected on each sport to inform this decision, it is not clear how these data were assessed by the IOC members.

Criteria for participation

How should participants in the Olympic Games be selected? Present selection procedures do not ensure that the 'best in the world' compete, because of the need for widespread involvement by member countries. Thus, for example, if any one country is limited to, say, three entrants in a particular event, but that country has the top six performers in that event, then the fourth, fifth and sixth best performers in the world will be excluded. Meanwhile, since any country that can meet certain minimum standards is entitled to send a team, numerous quite mediocre performers get to compete at the Olympics, while many top performers are excluded. Thus the Olympic principle of widespread participation is promoted at the expense of excellence. This is one of the reasons why, for some sports, as discussed above, their own world championships, which may operate using different parameters, are seen as representing a higher standard of competition.

Reform of the IOC

In Chapter 4 we noted the undemocratic and anachronistic nature of the International Olympic Committee, and the fact that it had been subject to criticism for many years for its lack of accountability and questionable *modus operandi*. In 1998/99 these issues were brought sharply into focus and were subject to unprecedented public scrutiny and debate, as outlined in Chapter 5.

In Chapter 4 we noted that, in response to the 1998/99 crisis, an Ethics Commission was established to monitor IOC activity in general. As regards the phenomenon which has given rise to most of the bribery and corruption activity, the bidding process, there is little talk of the permanent site solution discussed above. Rather, once a city's candidature is official, visits to bid cities are restricted and promotional activity to IOC members is severely controlled (see Chapter 4 discussion of the Ethics Committee).

While the recent reforms also included a widening of IOC membership, longer term reform would involve a reconstitution of the IOC to bring it in line with other modern international organisations. This would involve some sort of democratic, representational membership, to replace the current somewhat *ad hoc* and self-perpetuating membership system. Such a structure would inevitably involve formal representation of the 40 or so International Federations and the 200 National Olympic Committees. The Special Bid Oversight Committee established by the United States Olympic Committee as a result of the scandals surrounding the Salt Lake City bid, included among its recommendations:

The IOC must make fundamental structural changes to increase its accountability to the Olympic Movement and to the public:

    a.   A substantial majority of its members should be elected by the National Olympic Committees for the country of which they are citizens, by the International Federations, and by other constituent organizations. The athlete members should be chosen by athletes. There should be members from the public sector who best represent the interests of the public.

    b.   Its members and leaders should be subject to periodic re-election with appropriate term limits. (Special Bid Oversight Committee, 1999)

The effect of such reforms would be to make the IOC more clearly accountable to the Olympic Movement and the sporting community as a whole. It might also assist in correcting the Eurocentric constitution of the IOC, with 45 per cent of the current membership being from Europe.

The past, present and future of the Olympic Games

In this book we have attempted to provide a broad overview of the Olympic Games phenomenon, from their ancient beginnings, via their nineteenth century revival to the modern multi-billion dollar, global phenomenon which the Games have now become. In particular, we have sought to illustrate the multi-faceted nature of the Games – while they remain primarily a sporting event, they are also undoubtedly a major media event, a tourism event, an event with significant political dimensions and a major economic enterprise. We are sure that the future of the Games, in all their dimensions, is assured. But the nature of that future remains to be seen – offering endless opportunities for future research and speculation.

Further reading

Cold War and the Olympics	Torres and Dyreson (2005)
Post-Olympism	Bale and Christensen (2004)
Commercialisation	Barney *et al.* (2002); Tomlinson (2005)
Globalisation	Hoberman (2004); Roche (2000)
Reform of the IOC	Special Bid Oversight Committee (1999)
Communication technology	Whannel (2005)

Questions

1.   What are the main threats to continued existence of the Olympic Games?
2.   What aspects of globalisation affect the Olympic Games?
3.   Does the idea of Olympism have a future?

Appendix I

Websites, Films, Videos, CDs, DVDs

Websites

Olympic organisations

- International Olympic Committee: www.olympic.org
- LA84 Foundation (official reports): www.aafla.org/5va/reports_frmst.htm
- British Olympic Association: www.olympics.org.uk
- International Paralympic Committee: www.paralympic.org

Recent and future Olympic Games Organising Committees

- Salt Lake City, 2002: www.slc2002.org/
- Athens 2004: site no longer operational
- Torino, 2006: www.torino2006.org
- Beijing, 2008: http://en.beijing2008.cn
- Vancouver, 2010: www.vancouver2010.com/en
- London, 2012: http://main.london2012.com/en

Academic

- Australian Centre for Olympic Studies: www.olympic.uts.edu.au
- Centre for Olympic Studies, Barcelona:
  http://olympicstudies.uab.es/eng/index.asp
- Centre for Olympic Studies and Research, UK:
  www.lboro.ac.uk/departments/sses/institutes/cos/
- International Centre for Olympic Studies, Canada: www.uwo.ca/olympic/
- International Society of Olympic Historians: www.isoh.org
- The Olympic Games: A Social Science Perspective:
  www.business.uts.edu.au/lst/books
- Tufts University: www.olympics.tufts.edu/index.html
- UTS Olympic Bibliography:
  www.business.uts.edu.au/lst/research/bibliographies.html

Other international games

- Commonwealth Games Federation: www.thecgf.com
- Goodwill Games: www.goodwillgames.com/html/hm_index.html
- SInternational masters games association: www.imga.ch/
- Special Olympics: www.specialolympics.org
- World Games: www.worldgames-iwga.org

Other sites

- Games Bids: www.gamesbids.com
- CNN (Atlanta Olympic Park Bombing): www.cnn.com/US/9607/27/olympic.bomb.main/index.html

Films, videos and CDs

The Ancient Games

- *Olympia: 2,800 Years of Athletic Games*, Finatec Multimedia (CD ROM)
- *The Ancient Olympics: Athletes, Games and Heroes*, The Institute for Mediterranean Studies, Ohio (video)
- *'Perseus Project' Olympic Exhibit*, Tufts University, 1997, http://olympics.tufts.edu/index.html
- *The First Olympics - Blood, Honor, and Glory* (History Channel), 2004, A & E Home Video, (DVD).
- *First Olympians*, BBC Horizon Special, 2004, available via www.bbcactive.com.

The Revival

- *Modern Olympic Movement,* British Olympic Association, *www.olympics.org.uk/*
- *The Golden Flame: the Story of the Olympic Revival,* G. Murray, 1996, Athens: Efstathiadis Group (CD)
- *Olympia: 2,800 Years of Athletic Games,* Finatec Multimedia (CD)
- *Olympic Gold: A Hundred Year History of the Summer Olympic Games*, Discovery Channel, Multimedia (CD)
- *Olympic Century #2, Myths and Legends*, IOC, Lausanne (Video)

General

- *Olympia*, 1938, Director: Leni Reifenstahl (Germany)
- *Olympic Games in White*, 1948, Director: Torgny Wickman (Switzerland)
- *The Bob Mathias Story*, 1954, Director: Francis Lyon (USA)
- *Wee Geordie*, 1955, Director: Frank Launder
- *Dawn,* 1979, Director: Ken Hannam (Australia)
- *Goldengirl*, 1979, Director: Joseph Sargeant (USA)

- *Tokyo Olympiad,* 1965, Director: Kon Ichikawa (Japan)
- *Walk, Don't Run*, 1966, Director: Charles Walkers (USA)
- *The Games*, 1970, Director: Michael Winner (USA)
- *Visions of Eight*, 1973, Directors: various (USA)
- *Great Moments at the Winter Games*, 1979, Director: Bud Greenspan (USA)
- *Dawn,* 1979, Director: Ken Hannam (Australia)
- *Goldengirl*, 1979, Director: Joseph Sargeant (USA)
- *Ice Castles*, 1979, Director: Donald Wrye (Australia)
- *Dawn,* 1979, Director: Ken Hannam (Australia)
- *Chariots of Fire*, 1981, Director: Hugh Hudson (Great Britain)
- *Personal Best*, 1982, Director: Robert Towne (USA)
- *16 Days of Glory*, 1986, Director: Bud Greenspan (USA)
- *16 Days of Glory*: *Seoul' 88*, 1989: Director: Bud Greenspan (USA)
- *Barcelona '92 Olympic Games,* 1992: NBC Sports (USA)
- *16 Days of Glory*: *Barcelona '92,* 1993, Director: Bud Greenspan (USA)
- *Cool Runnings*, 1993, Director: Jon Turtletaub (USA)
- *16 Days of Glory: Lillehammer '94,* 1994, Director: Bud Greenspan (USA)
- *16 Days in September: Games Highlights of the XXVII Olympiad*, 2000, Warner Vision Australia, 2000 (video) (Australia)
- *Following the Flame: the Olympic Torch Relay*, 2000, Director: Philippe Meylan, Lausanne: Olympic Museum, International Olympic Committee (Video).
- *The Real Olympics. A History of the Ancient and Modern Olympic Games*, 2004 PBS Direct (VHS), PBS paramount (DVD).

References

Abad, J. M. (1995) Introduction: a summary of the activities of the COOB '92. In De Moragas and Botella, *op. cit.*, pp. 11–17.

Adair, D., Coe, B., and Guoth, N. (eds) (2005) *Beyond the Torch: Olympics and Australian Culture.* Australian Society for Sports History Studies No. 17. Melbourne: ASSH, (www.sporthistory.org).

Addkison-Simmons, D. (1996) Sapporo, 1972. In J. Findling and K. D. Pelle (eds) *Historical Dictionary of the Modern Olympic Movement.* Westport, CN: Greenwood Publishing, pp. 284-288.

Advertiser (Adelaide) (1998) Send them home. 16 January, p. 19.

Africa News (1996a) Two medal winners thrown out of Olympics for drug violations. *Africa News*, 29 July, available at: www.afnews.org/ newsroom/sports/ol (no longer current).

Africa News (1996b) Drug cheats stay ahead of the game. *Africa News*, 2 August, Accessed via: www.afnews.org (no longer current).

Age (2004) Greek sprinters quit Games. *The Age* (Melbourne), 18 August.

Aguilar-Darriba, A. (1988) The Olympic Games in Mexico - 1968: a long-term investment strategy. In EAAPP, *op. cit.*, pp. 265-280.

Alam, M. B. (1996) Tokyo, 1964: the Games of the XVIIIth Olympiad. In J. Findling and K. D. Pelle (eds) *Historical Dictionary of the Modern Olympic Movement.* Westport, CN: Greenwood Publishing, pp. 135-138.

Alexandrakis, A., and Krotee, M. L. (1988) The dialectics of the IOC. *International Review for the Sociology of Sport*, 23(4): 325-344.

Allens Arthur Robinson (2000) Ambush at Homebush - Ambush marketing at the 2000 Olympics. *IP & IT Bulletin*, No 7, December, available at: www.aar.com. au/pubs/ ip/ipit7.htm

Amateur Athletic Foundation of Los Angeles (2005) *Gender in Televised Sports:. News and Highlights Shows - 1989-2004.* Los Angeles: AAFLA, available at: www.aafla.com/9arr/ResearchReports/tv2004.pdf (accessed April 2007).

Amnesty International (2007) *People's Republic of China: the Olympics Countdown – Repression of Activists Overshadows Death Penalty and Media Reforms.* London: Amnesty International, available at: http://web.amnesty.org/library/ index/ ENGASA 170152007 (accessed May 2007).

Andranovich, G., Burbank, M. J. and Heying, C. H. (2000) Olympic cities: lessons learned from mega-event politics. *Journal of Urban Affairs*, 23(2): 113-131

Arbena, J. L. (1991) Sport, development and Mexican nationalism, 1920-1970. *Journal of Sport History*, 18(3): 350-364.

Arbena, J. L. (1996) Mexico City, 1968: the Games of the XIXth Olympiad. In J. Findling and K. D. Pelle (eds) *Historical Dictionary of the Modern Olympic Movement*. Westport, CN: Greenwood Publishing, pp. 139-147.

Arblutt, D. (2005) The Olympic legacy. *Leisure Management* (UK), 25(6), 66-67.

Armstrong, K. (2005) *A Short History of Myth*. Edinburgh: Canongate

Ashwell, T. (1996) Squaw Valley, 1960. In J. Findling and K. D. Pelle (eds) *Historical Dictionary of the Modern Olympic Movement*. Westport, CN: Greenwood Publishing, pp. 263-269.

Askew, K. (2006) Debt sinks Stadium Australia: ANZ to take control for $10m. *Sydney Morning Herald*, 16 November, p. 23.

Aso, N. (2002) Sumptuous repast: the 1964 Tokyo Olympics Arts Festival. *Positions: East Asia Cultures Critique*, 10(1): 7-38.

Athens 2004 Organising Committee (ATHOC) (2004) *Visitor Satisfaction Poll Results: What spectators thought of the Athens Olympics*. Media release, accessed via: www.mediainfo2004.gr (accessed March 2007).

Athens Olympic Committee (ATHOG) (2004) *Olympic Prizes*. Available at: www.athens2004. com/en/Olympic Prizes (site no longer available).

Atkinson, M. & Young, K. (2002) Terror games: media treatment of security issues at the 2002 Winter Olympic Games. *Olympika*, 11: 53-78.

Atkinson, M., and Young, K. (2005) Political violence, terrorism, and security at the Olympic Games. In K. B. Wamsley and K. Young (eds) *Global Olympics: Historical and Sociological Studies of the Modern Games*. Amsterdam: Elsevier, pp. 269-294.

Atlanta Committee for the Olympic Games (ACOG) (1998) *The Official Report of the Games of the XXVI Olympiad,* Atlanta, GA: Peachtree Publishers.

Attwood, A. (1996) Now, let the fun and Games begin. *The Age*, August 6, (available at: www.smh.com.au/atlanta/ - accessed 8.6.99).

Audit Office of New South Wales (1999) *Performance Audit Report: The Sydney 2000 Olympic and Paralympic Games: Review of Estimates*. Sydney: Audit Office of New South Wales.

Audit Office of New South Wales (2002) *Auditor-General's Report to Parliament, 2002, Volume 2*. Sydney: Audit Office of New South Wales, (available at: www.audit.nsw.gov.au, accessed June 2006).

Auf der Maur, N. (1976) *The Billion-Dollar Game: Jean Drapeau and the 1976 Olympics*. Toronto: James Lorimer.

Australian Centre for Independent Journalism (1993) *Reportage: Newsletter of the Australian Centre for Independent Journalism*, (UTS, Sydney), September.

Australian Olympian (1988) Task of sending the news home was quite a story. December, p. 9.

Australian Olympic Committee. (2005) *Montgomery Ruling A 'Reminder' About Doping Charges, CAS*. Media release, 16 December, available at: http://olympics. com.au/ news.cfm?ArticleID=6122.

Australian Parliament (1980) *Parliamentary Debates (House of Representatives), Hansard 117, 20 February*. Canberra: Commonwealth Government Printer.

Australian Sports Commission (ASC) (2001) *Women's Participation – 2000 Sydney Olympics*. Canberra: Australian Sports Commission, available at: www.ausport. gov.au/fulltext/2001/ascpub/women_olym.asp.

Australian Sports Commission (ASC) (2006) *Australian Sports Commission: Ethics in Sport: Anti-doping in Sport, World Anti-Doping Code*. Canberra: Australian Sports Commission, available at: www.ausport.gov.au/ethics/adwadacode.asp (accessed August, 2007).

Australian Sports Commission and the Office of the Status of Women (1985) *Women, Sport and the Media, Report to the Federal Government from the Working Group on Women in Sport.* Canberra: AGPS.

Baade, R. A., and Matheson, R. A. (2002) Bidding for the Olympics: fool's gold? In C. P. Barros, M. Ibrahimo and S. Szymanski (eds) *Transatlantic Sport: the Comparative Economics of North American and European Sports.* Cheltenham, UK: Edward Elgar, pp 127-151.

Bacon, W. (1993) Watchdog's bark muffled. *Reportage: Newsletter of the Australian Centre for Independent Journalism* (UTS, Sydney), September: 3-5.

Baka, R. (1976) Canadian federal government policy and the 1976 summer Olympics. *Canadian Association for Health, Physical Education and Recreation Journal*, 42(1): 52-60.

Baker, N. (1994a) The Games that almost weren't: London 1948. In Barney and Meier, *op. cit.*, pp. 107-116.

Baker, N. (1994b) Olympics or Tests: the disposition of the British sporting public, 1948. *Sporting Traditions*, 11(1): 57-74.

Baldwin, D. A. (1998) Exchange theory and international relations. *International Negotiation*, 3(2): 139-149.

Bale, J., and Christensen, M. K. (eds) (2004) *Post-Olympism? Questioning Sport in the Twenty-first Century.* Oxford: Berg.

Bandy, S. J. (1988) The Olympic celebration of the arts. In Segrave and Chu *op. cit.*, pp. 163-169.

Bannister, R. (1988) The Olympic Games: past, present and future. In Segrave and Chu, *op. cit.*, pp. 419-426.

Barnard, S., Butler, K., Golding, P., and Maguire, J. (2006) 'Making the news': the 2004 Athens Olympic Games and competing ideologies? *Olympika*, 15, 35-58.

Barnes, M. (1997) *Observance or Repudiation? Australia's Role in the Modern Olympic Movement as it Relates to the Olympic Charter.* MA thesis, School of Leisure, Sport and Tourism, University of Technology, Sydney.

Barnett, C. R. (1996) St. Louis, 1904: the Games of the IInd Olympiad. In J. Findling and K. D. Pelle (eds) *Historical Dictionary of the Modern Olympic Movement.* Westport, CN: Greenwood Publishing, pp. 18-24.

Barney, R. K. (1998) The great transformation: Olympic victory ceremonies and the medal podium. *Olympika*, 7: 89-112.

Barney, R. K., and Meier, K. V. (eds) (1992) *Proceedings of the First Inter-national Symposium for Olympic Research.* London, Ontario: Centre for Olympic Studies, University of Western Ontario.

Barney, R. K., and Meier, K. V. (eds) (1994) *Critical Reflections on Olympic Ideology, Second International Symposium for Olympic Research.* London, Ontario: Centre for Olympic Studies, University of Western Ontario.

Barney, R. K., Wamsley, K. B., Martyne, S. G., and MacDonald, G. H. (eds) (1998) *Global and Cultural Critique: Problematizing the Olympic Games.* London, Ontario: International Centre for Olympic Studies, University of Western Ontario.

Barney, R. K., Wenn, S. R., and Martyn, S. G. (2002) *Selling the Five Rings: The International Olympic Committee and the Rise of Olympic Commercialism.* Salt Lake City, UT: University of Utah Press.

Barrett, N. (1980) *Olympics 1980.* London: Piper Books.

Barthes, R. (1983) *Mythologies.* London: Paladin.

Barton, L. (1983) *The American Olympic Boycott of 1980: the Amalgam of Diplomacy and Propaganda in Influencing Public Opinion.* PhD dissertation, Boston University.

Baum, G. (2004) Doubters are losers as Games wind up. *Sydney Morning Herald*, 30 August, available at: www.smh.com.au/olympics, accessed Feb. 2007.

BBCSport (2004) Greece bids Games farewell. London: British Broadcasting Corporation, 29 August, available at http://newsvote.bbc.co.uk (accessed March, 2007).

Beck, P. J. (1980) Politics and the Olympics: the lessons of 1924. *History Today*, 20, July: 7-9.

Beder, S. (1993) Sydney's toxic green Olympics. *Current Affairs Bulletin*, 70(6): 12-18.

Beijing Bid Committee (2001a) *Beijing 2008 Candidature File*. Beijing: Beijing Bid Committee. Available at Beijing 2008 website: http://en.beijing2008.cn under: Archives > Beijing Olympic Database > Candidature Files (accessed May 2007).

Beijing Bid Committee (2001b) *Presentation in Moscow*. Beijing: Beijing Bid Committee. Available at Beijing 2008 website: http://en.beijing2008.cn under: Archives > Beijing Olympic Database > Presentation in Moscow (accessed May 2007).

Berman, G., Brooks, R., and Da Vidson, S. (2000) The Sydney Olympic Games announcement and Australian stock market reaction. *Applied Economics Letters*, 7(12): 781–784.

Bernstein, A. and Blain, N. (eds) (2003) *Sport, Media, Culture: Global and Local Dimensions*. London: Frank Cass.

Bilder, R. (n. d.) Drug testing in sport. www.gemini.co.uk/biopages/, accessed 2000, no longer available.

Biles, F. R. (1984) Women and the 1984 Olympics. *Journal of Physical Education, Recreation and Dance*, 55(1): 64-65, 72.

Billings, A. C., Eastman, S. T. and Newton, G. D. (1998) Atlanta revisited: prime time promotion in the 1996 Summer Olympics. *Journal of Sport and Social Issues*, 22(1): 65-78.

Birrell, S., and Cole, C. (1994) *Women, Sport and Culture*. Champaign, IL: Human Kinetics.

Birrell, S., and Theberge, N. (1994) Biological control of women in sport. In Costa, D. M. and Guthrie, S. R. (eds) *Women and Sport: Interdisciplinary Perspectives*. Champaign, IL: Human Kinetics, pp. 341–360.

Black, D. R., and Van Der Westhuizen, J. (2004) The allure of global games for 'semi-peripheral' polities and spaces: a research agenda. *Third World Quarterly*, 25(7): 1195-1214.

Blair, T. (1998) An athletic about face. *Time Australia,* 10 August, p. 63.

Blake, A. (2005) *The Economic Impact of the London 2012 Olympics*. Nottingham: Christel DeHaan Tourism and Travel Research Institute, Nottingham University (Available via: www.nottingham.ac.uk/ttri/).

Blue, A. (1988) *Faster, Higher, Further: Women's Triumphs and Disasters at the Olympics*. London: Virago Press.

Board of Ethics of the Salt Lake Organizing Committee (1999) *Report to the Board of Trustees*. Salt Lake City, UT: Salt Lake Organizing Committee for the Olympic Winter Games of 2002, SLOC website: www.slc2002.org/news/ html/report.html.

Booker, C. (1981) *The Games War: A Moscow Journal*. London: Faber and Faber.

Booth, D. (1999) Gifts of corruption? Ambiguities of obligation in the Olympic movement. *Olympika*, 8, 43-68

Booth, D. (2004) Post-olympism? Questioning olympic historiography. In J. Bale and M. K. Christensen (eds) *Post-Olympism? Questioning Sport in the Twenty-first Century*. Oxford: BERG, pp. 13-32.

Booth, D. (2005a) *The Field: Truth and Fiction in Sport History*. London: Routledge.

Booth, D. (2005b) Lobbying orgies: Olympic city bids in the post-Los Angeles era. In K. B. Wamsley and K. Young (eds) *Global Olympics: Historical and Sociological Studies of the Modern Games*. Amsterdam: Elsevier, pp. 201–226.

Booth, D., and Tatz, C. (1994a) Sydney 2000: the games people play. *Current Affairs Bulletin*, 70(7): 4-11.

Booth, D., and Tatz, C. (1994b) 'Swimming with the big boys'? The politics of Sydney's Olympic bid. *Sporting Traditions*, 11(1): 3-23.

Borgers, W. (1996) *Olympic Torch Relays 1936-1994*. Kassel: Agon Sportverlag.

Borrie, S. (1999) Being visible: Gay Games and Festival, Sydney 2000. In Taylor, T. (ed) *How You Play the Game: the Contribution of Sport to the Protection of Human Rights - First International Conference on Sports and Human Rights, September 13, 1999*, Sydney, Australia, Sydney: Faculty of Business, University of Technology, Sydney, pp. 116-20.

Botella, M. (1995) The political games: agents and strategies in the 1992 Barcelona Olympic Games. In De Moragas and Botella, *op. cit.*, pp. 139-148.

Boutilier, M. A., and San-Giovanni, L. F. (1991) Ideology, public policy and female Olympic achievement: a cross-national analysis of the Seoul Olympic Games. In Landry *et al., op. cit.*, pp. 396-409.

Bragg, R. (1997) A year later, some Atlantans are asking: what Olympic legacy? *New York Times*, July 20.

Brain, P., and Manolakos, J. (1991) The 1996 Melbourne Olympics: an economic evaluation. *National Economic Review*, 14(1): 14-21.

Brasher, C. (1972) *Munich '72*. London: Stanley Paul.

Bread not Circuses (n.d.) Bread, not Circuses: a coalition of groups concerned about Toronto's 2008 Olympic bid. Toronto: Bread, not Circuses Coalition, accessed, 2002, via www.breadnotcircuses.org - website no longer available.

Brichford, M. (1996) Munich, 1972: the Games of the XXth Olympiad. In J. Findling and K. D. Pelle (eds) *Historical Dictionary of the Modern Olympic Movement*. Westport, CN: Greenwood Publishing, pp. 148-152.

British Olympic Association (n.d.) *The Modern Olympics. Olympic Fact Sheet. London: BOA*, available at: www.olympics.org.uk/

British Olympic Association (1998) *Official Website*, at: www.olympics.org.uk/.

British Olympic Council (BOC) (1908) *The Olympic Games of 1908 in London: A Reply to Certain Criticisms*. London: BOC.

Brohm, J.-M. (1978) The Olympic opiate. The Olympic Games and the imperialist accumulation of capital. The anti-Olympic appeal of the Ecole Emancipé; and Draft appeal for the setting up of an Anti-Olympic Committee. In *Sport: A Prison of Measured Time*, (Tr. Ian Fraser), London: Ink Links, pp.102-174.

Brown, D. (2004) Post-Olympism: Olympic legacies, sport spaces and the practices of everyday life. In J. Bale and M. K. Christensen (eds) *Post-Olympism? Questioning Sport in the Twenty-first Century*. Oxford: Berg, pp. 99-118.

Brown, D., and MacDonald, G. (1996) Grenoble, 1968. In J. Findling and K. D. Pelle (eds) *Historical Dictionary of the Modern Olympic Movement*. Westport, CN: Greenwood Publishing, pp. 276-283.

Brownell, S. (2004) China and Olympism. In J. Bale and M. K. Christensen (eds) *Post-Olympism? Questioning Sport in the Twenty-first Century*. Oxford: Berg, pp. 52–64.

Brownell, S. (2006) The Beijing effect. *Olympic Review*, June-Sept, 52-55.

Brunet, F. (1993) *Economy of the 1992 Barcelona Olympic Games* (Trans. Adapta Traductions). Lausanne: International Olympic Committee/Centre d'Estudis Olímpics.

Brunet, F. (1995) An economic analysis of the Barcelona '92 Olympic Games: resources, financing and impact. In De Moragas and Botella *op. cit.*, pp. 203-237.

Bryson, L. (1987) Sport and the maintenance of masculine hegemony, *Women's Studies International Forum,* 10: 349-360.

Bryson, L. (1990) Challenges to male hegemony in sport. In M. A. Messner and D. F. Sabo (eds), *Sport, Men and the Gender Order: Critical Feminist Perspectives*, Champaign, IL: Human Kinetics, pp. 173-184.

Burbank, M. J., Heying, C. H., and Adranovich, G. (2000) Antigrowth politics or piecemeal resistance? Citizen opposition to Olympic-related economic growth. *Urban Affairs Review*, 35(3): 334-357.

Burns, J. P. A., Hatch, J. H., and Mules, T. J. (eds) (1986) *The Adelaide Grand Prix: The Impact of a Special Event.* Adelaide: Centre for South Australian Economic Studies.

Burroughs, A. (1999) Winning the bid. In Cashman, R., and Hughes, A. (eds) *Staging the Olympics: The Event and its Impact.* Sydney: University of New South Wales Press, pp. 18-34.

Buschman, J., and Lennartz, K. L. (1996) From Los Angeles (1932) to Melbourne (1956): the Olympic Torch's protagonism in ceremonies. In De Moragas, M., MacAloon, J. and Llines, M. (eds) *Olympic Ceremonies: Historical Continuity and Cultural Exchange.* Lausanne: International Olympic Committee, pp. 111-30.

Butler, B. S. (1992) Muscular Marxism and the Chicago Counter-Olympics of 1932. *International Journal of the History of Sport*, 9(3): 397-410.

Byong-Ik, K. (ed.) (1990) *Toward One World Beyond All Barriers: Seoul Olympiad Anniversary Conference.* Seoul: Seoul Olympic Sports Promotion Foundation.

Cahill, J. (1998) The Olympic flame and torch: running towards Sydney 2000. In Barney *et al.*, *op. cit.*: 181–190.

Cahill, J. (1999a) Political influence and the Olympic flame. *Journal of Olympic History*, 7(1): 29-32.

Cahill, J. (1999b) *Running Towards Sydney 2000: The Olympic Flame and Torch.* Sydney: Walla Walla Press.

Cahill, S. (1986) *Olympic Spirit.* Melbourne: Australian Gallery of Sport.

Cahill, S. (1989*) Friendly Games'? The Melbourne Olympic Games in Australian Culture (1946-1956).* MA thesis, University of Melbourne.

Cameron, J. (1995) Blazer and black tie dinners: some aspects of the marginal-isation of women in New Zealand sport. *ANZALS Leisure Research Series*, 2: 26-42.

Canadian Ministry for Fitness and Amateur Sport (1986) *Economic Impact of the 1988 Winter Olympic Games.* Ottawa: Ministry of Fitness and Amateur Sport.

Canavan, J. (1997) Sex frauds vs doping cheats. *Sport Health*, 15, Dec. 4: 16-17.

Canton, D. (2006) Olympics embrace Internet - but not in Canada. *CNews*, 4 February, available at: http://cnews.canoe.ca/.

Capranica, L., Minganti, C., Billat, V., Hanghoj, S. Piacentini, M., Cumps, E., and Meeusen, R. (2005) Newspaper coverage of women's sports during the 2000 Sydney Olympic Games: Belgium, Denmark, France and Italy. *Research Quarterly for Exercise and Sport*, 76(2): 212-23.

Carter, T. (2002) On the need for an anthropological approach to sport. *Identities: Global Studies in Culture and Power.* 9(3): 405-22.

Cashman, R. (1995) When the bid party's over: Sydney's problem of delivering the Games. *Australian Quarterly*, 67(1): 49-54.

Cashman, R. (1999a) The greatest peacetime event. In R. Cashman and A. Hughes (eds) *Staging the Olympics: The Event and its Impact*. Sydney: University of New South Wales Press, pp. 3-17.

Cashman, R. (1999b) Legacy. In R. Cashman and A. Hughes (eds) *Staging the Olympics: The Event and its Impact*. Sydney: University of New South Wales Press, pp. 183-194.

Cashman, R. (2006) *The Bitter-Sweet Awakening: The Legacy of the Sydney 2000 Olympic Games*. Petersham, NSW: Walla Walla Press in Association with the Australian Centre for Olympic Studies, University of Technology, Sydney.

Cashman, R., and Hughes, A. (1998a) Sydney 2000: cargo cult of Australian sport? In Rowe and Lawrence, *op. cit.* pp. 216-225.

Cashman, R., and Hughes, A. (eds) (1998b) *The Green Games: A Golden Opportunity*. Sydney: Centre for Olympic Studies, University of New South Wales.

Cashman, R., and Hughes, A. (eds) (1999) *Staging the Olympics: The Event and its Impact*. Sydney: University of New South Wales Press.

Cashman, R., and Toohey, K. (2002) *The Contribution of the Higher Education Sector to the Sydney 2000 Olympic Games*. Sydney: Centre for Olympic Studies, University of New South Wales (Now available from Australian Centre for Olympic Studies, University of Technology, Sydney).

Cashman, R., Toohey, K., Darcy, S., Symons C., and Stewart, B. (2002) When the carnival is over: evaluating the outcomes of mega-sporting events in Australia. *Sporting Traditions*, 21(1): 1–32.

Catlin, G. (1927) *The Science and Methods of Politics*. London: Keegan Paul.

Chalip, L. (1990) The politics of Olympic theatre: New Zealand and Korean cross-national relations. In Byong-Ik, *op. cit.*, pp. 408-433.

Chalip, L. and Chalip, P. (1992) Gatekeeper categories: meanings of government types in a Los Angeles Olympic press kits. *Olympika*, 1, 136-153.

Chalkley, B., and Essex, S. (1999a) Urban development through hosting international events: a history of the Olympic Games. *Planning Perspectives*, 14(4): 369-394.

Chalkley, B., and Essex, S. (1999b) Sydney 2000: the 'green games'? *Geography*, 84(4), 299-307.

Chappelet, J.-L. (2003) The legacy of the Winter Olympic Games - an overview. In M. De Moragas, C. Kennett and N. Puig (eds) *The Legacy of the Olympic Games, 1984-2000*. Lausanne: International Olympic Committee, pp. 54-66.

Cheek, N., and Burch, W. (1976) *The Social Organisation of Leisure in Human Society*. New York: Harper and Rowe.

Cherfas, J., and Lewin, R. (eds) (1980) *Not Work Alone: A Cross-cultural View of Activities Superfluous to Survival*. London: Temple Smith.

Chorbajian, L., and Mosco, V. (1981) 1976 and 1980 Olympic boycott coverage. *Arena Review*, 5(3): 3-28.

City of Calgary and Alberta Tourism and Small Business (1985) *Economic Impacts of the XV Olympic Winter Games*. Calgary: City of Calgary and Alberta Tourism and Small Business.

Clarke, A., and Clarke, J. (1982) Highlights and action replays – ideology, sport and the media. In J. Hargreaves (ed.) *Sport, Culture and Ideology*. London: Routledge and Kegan Paul, pp. 62-87.

Clarke, S. (1997) Olympus in the Cotswolds: The Cotswold Games and continuity in popular culture, 1612-1800. *International Journal of the History of Sport*, 14(2): 40-66.

Clegg, S. (1989) *Frameworks of Power*. London: Sage.

CNN (1996) Olympic Park bombing special section, CNN Interactive, available at: www.cnn.com/US/9607/27/olympic.bomb.main/index.html (accessed April 2007).

Coakley, J. J. (1992) *Sport in Society: Issues and Controversies*. St. Louis, Missouri: Mosby.

Coates, J. R. (1996) London, 1908: the Games of the IIIrd Olympiad. In J. Findling and K. D. Pelle (eds) *Historical Dictionary of the Modern Olympic Movement*. Westport, CN: Greenwood Publishing, pp. 26-40.

Cockerill, M. (1996) Barcelona beats Atlanta by a bull's roar. *Sydney Morning Herald*, August 6, available at: www.smh. com.au/atlanta/ (accessed June 1999).

Commission Royale Enquête (1977) *The Report of the Inquiry into the Cost of the 21st Olympiad*. Monreal: Commission Royal Enquête.

Commonwealth Games Federation (1997) Website: www.thecgf.com.

Connell, R. W. (1995) *Masculinities*. Berkely, CA: University of California Press.

Consoli, J. (2006) Games don't help NBC win sweeps. *MediaWeek* 27 February, available at: www.mediaweek.com.

Cooper, M. (2005) Atlanta Olympic bomber gets life sentence. *Voice of America*, 22 Aug. - accessed at www.globalsecurity.org.

Coubertin, P. de (1988) Why I revived the Olympic Games. In Segrave and Chu, *op. cit.*, pp. 101–106 (originally published 1908).

Cox, G., Darcy, M., and Bounds, M. (1994) *The Olympic Games and Housing: A Study of Six International Events and Analysis of Potential Impacts of the Sydney 2000 Olympics*, Campbelltown, NSW: Housing and Urban Studies Research Group, University of Western Sydney and Shelter NSW.

Crawford, S. A. G. M. (1991) The 1904 Olympics: a study of contemporary news sources. *Journal of Sports Philately*, 29(4): 3-7.

Crawford, S. A. G. M. (1996) Olympic feature films. In J. Findling and K. D. Pelle (eds) *Historical Dictionary of the Modern Olympic Movement*. Westport, CN: Greenwood Publishing, pp. 415-420.

Crompton, J. L. (1996) The potential contributions of sports sponsorship in impacting the product adoption process. *Managing Leisure*, 1(4): 199-212.

Cronau, P. (1993a) Social impact of Games under wraps. *Reportage: Newsletter of the Australian Centre for Independent Journalism*, (UTS, Sydney), September: 16-19.

Cronau, P. (1993b) City's poor left behind in race for Olympic gold. *The Australian*, 21 Oct.

Crowther, N. (2002) The Salt Lake City scandals and the ancient Olympic Games. *International Journal of the History of Sport*, 19(4): 169-178.

Crossman, J., and Lappage, R. (1992) Canadian athletes' perceptions of the 1980 Olympic boycott. *Sociology of Sport Journal*, Vol.9, No.4): 354-371.

Curry, R. L. and Wade, L. L. (1968) *A Logic of Public Policy: Aspects of Political Economy*. Englewood Cliffs, NJ: Prentice-Hall.

Cuyàs, R. (ed.) (1992) *Official Report of the Games of the XXV Olympiad, Barcelona 1992*, (4 Vols.) Barcelona: COOB'92 (Barcelona Olympic Organising Committee).

Czula, R. (1978) The Munich Olympics assassinations: a second look. *Journal of Sport and Social Issues*, 2(1): 19-23.

Da Costa, L. (1998) Olympism and the equilibrium of man. In Müller, N. (ed.) *Coubertin and Olympism: Questions for the Future, Report of the Congress, 17-20 September, 1997, Le Havre.* Lausanne: Comité International Pierre de Coubertin: 188-199.

Daddario, G. (1994) Chilly scenes of the 1992 Winter Games: the mass media and the marginalisation of female athletes. *Sociology of Sport Journal*, 11(3): 275-288.

Dahl, R. (1984) *Modern Political Analysis 4th edn.* Englewood Cliffs, N. J. : Prentice-Hall

Dahl, R. and Lindblom, C. (1953) *Politics, Economics and Welfare.* New York: Harper & Brothers.

Dantzig, P. (2002) Architecture and design of high volume websites. Accessed from : www.portal.acm.org/ (Accessed: 15.12.04 - no longer available).

Darcy, S. (2001) A games for everyone? Planning for disability and access at the Sydney 2000 Games. *Disability Studies Quarterly*, 21(1): 70–84.

Darcy, S. (2003) The politics of disability and access: the Sydney 2000 Games experience. *Disability & Society*, 18(6): 737–757.

Davé, C. (2006) *The 2012 Bid: Five Cities Chasing the Summer Games.* Bloomington, IN: Authorhouse.

Davenport, J. (1996) Athens, 1896: the Games of the Ist Olympiad. In J. Findling and K. D. Pelle (eds) *Historical Dictionary of the Modern Olympic Movement.* Westport, CN: Greenwood Publishing , pp. 3-11.

Davies, E. L. (1996) Rome, 1960: the Games of the XVIIth Olympiad. In J. Findling and K. D. Pelle (eds) *Historical Dictionary of the Modern Olympic Movement.* Westport, CN: Greenwood Publishing , pp. 128-134.

Davison, G. (1997) Welcoming the world: the 1956 Olympic Games and the re-presentation of Melbourne. In J. Murphy and J. Smart (eds) *The Forgotten Fifties: Aspects of Australian Society and Culture in the 1950s. Australian Historical Studies No. 109*, Melbourne: Melbourne University Press, pp. 64-76.

Dawn: the Internet Edition (2005) Kim Un-yong resigns from top IOC post. 21 May, 2005, Available at: www.dawn.com/2005/05/21/spt9.htm. Accessed March 2007.

De Coubertin, P. (1997) *Olympic Memoirs.* Lausanne: International Olympic Committee (Originally published by the Bureau International de Pédagogie Sportive, 1931).

De Coubertin, P. (2000) *Olympism. Selected Writings.* Lausanne: International Olympic Committee.

De Lange, P. (1998) *The Games Cities Play.* Monument Park, South Africa: C.P. de Lange Inc.

De Moragas Spa, M. (2001) *Internet and the Olympic Movement.* Centre for Olympic Studies, Universitat Autonoma de Barcelona, Available at http://olympicstudies.uab.es/pdf/od012_eng.pdf [Accessed: 15.12.04]

De Moragas, M., and Botella, M. (eds) (1995) *The Keys to Success: The Social, Sporting, Economic and Communications Impact of Barcelona '92.* Barcelona: Centre d'Estudis Olimpics i del Esport, Universitat Autonoma de Barcelona.

De Moragas, M., Kennett, C., and Puig, N. (eds) (2003) *The Legacy of the Olympic Games, 1984-2000: International Symposium, Lausanne, 2002.* Lausanne: International Olympic Committee.

De Moragas, M., Llines, M., and Kidd, B. (eds) (1997) *Olympic Villages: Hundred Years of Urban Planning and Shared Experiences.* Lausanne: Olympic Museum, International Olympic Committee.

De Moragas, M., MacAloon, J., and Llines, M. (eds) (1996) *Olympic Ceremonies: Historical Continuity and Cultural Exchange*. Lausanne: International Olympic Committee.

De Moragas, M., Kennett, C., and Puig, N. (eds) (2003) *The Legacy of the Olympic Games, 1984-2000: International Symposium, Lausanne, 14-16 November, 2002*. Lausanne: International Olympic Committee.

De Moragas, M., Rivenburgh, N., and Larson, J. (1995) *Television in the Olympics*. London: John Libbey.

Deakin, E. (1993) Sydney Olympics 2000: Issues for social impact assessment and management. In Office on Social Policy, *op. cit.*, pp. B1-B53.

Deane, J. (1985) The Melbourne press and the Moscow Olympics. *Sporting Traditions*, 1(2): 27-42.

DeFrantz, A. (1988) The long-term impact of the Los Angeles Olympics. In EAAPP, *op. cit.*, pp. 55-62.

DeFrantz, A. (2005) Introduction. In W. Wilson (Ed.) *Gender in Televised Sports: News and Highlights Shows 1989– 2004*, Los Angeles, CA: Amateur Athletic Foundation of Los Angeles , p. 3, available at: www.aafla.com/9arr/Research Reports/tv2004.pdf (accessed August 2007).

Department for Culture, Media and Sport (DCMS) (2007) *Jowell tells Parliament: Full Steam Ahead for 2012 – The Legacy Games*. Press Notice 042/07, 15 March, available at: www.culture.gov.uk under 2012 Olympic Games and Paralympic Games > Find out more > Press Notices.

Diaz, G. (2001) Olympics stress safety: Salt Lake City officials will re-evaluate the safety measures of the 2002 Olympic Games. *Orlando Sentinel*, 12 Nov.: 1.

Dickinson, B., Genel, M., Robinowitz, C., Turner, P., and Woods, G. (2002) Gender verification of female Olympic athletes. *Medicine and Science in Sports and Exercise*, 34(10):1539-42.

Dickson, G, and Schofield, G. (2005) Globalisation and globesity: the impact of the 2008 Beijing Olympics on China. *International Journal of Sport Management and Marketing*, 1(1–2): 169-179.

Donald, K., and Selth, D. (1957) *Olympic Saga: The Track and Field Story, Melbourne 1956*. Sydney: Futurian Press.

Duncan, M. C. (1986) A hermeneutic of spectator sport: the 1976 and 1984 Olympic Games. *Quest*, 38(1): 50-77.

Duncan, M. C. (1990) Sports photographs and sexual differences: images of women and men in the 1984 and 1988 Olympic Games. *Sociology of Sport Journal*, 7(1): 22-43.

Duncan, M., Messner, M., Williams, L., Jensen, K., and Wilson, W. (1994) Gender stereotyping in televised sports. In S Birrell and C. Cole (eds) *Women, Sport and Culture*. Champaign, IL: Human Kinetics, pp 249-272.

Dunkelberger, R. (1996) Sarajevo, 1984. In J. Findling and K. D. Pelle (eds) *Historical Dictionary of the Modern Olympic Movement*. Westport, CN: Greenwood Publishing, pp. 302-309.

Dunn, K. M., and McGuirk, P. M. (1999) Hallmark events. In Cashman and Hughes, *op. cit.* pp. 18-34.

Durantez, C. (1988) *The Olympic Flame: The Great Olympic Symbol*. Lausanne: International Olympic Committee.

Durántez Corral, C. (1994) *Pierre de Coubertin: the Olympic Humanist*. Lausanne: International Olympic Committee.

Durick, W. (1996) Berlin, 1916: the Games of the VIIth Olympiad. In J. Findling and K. D. Pelle (eds) *Historical Dictionary of the Modern Olympic Movement.* Westport, CN: Greenwood Publishing , pp. 47-53.

Dyreson, M. (1994) From civil rights to scientific racism: the variety of American responses to the Berlin Olympics, the legend of Jesse Owens and the 'Race Question'. In Barney and Meier, op. *cit.*, pp. 46-54.

Dyreson, M. L. (1996) Scripting the American Olympic story-telling formula: the 1924 Paris Olympic Games and the American media. *Olympika*, 5(1): 45-80.

East Asian Architecture and Planning Program (EAAPP) (1988) *Hosting the Olympics: the Long-Term Impact, Conference Report*, Seoul: East Asian Architecture and Planning Program, MIT and Graduate School of Environmental Studies, Seoul National University.

Economics Research Associates (1984) *Community Economic Impact of the 1984 Olympic Games in Los Angeles and Southern California, (report to the Los Angeles Olympic Organizing Committee).* Los Angeles: Economics Research Associates.

Edwards, H. (1981) Crisis in the modern Olympic movement. In Segrave and Chu, *op. cit.*, pp. 227-241.

Edwards, H. (1984) The free enterprise Olympics. *Journal of Sport and Social Issues*, 8: i-iv.

Embrey, L., Hall, A., and Gunter, A. (1992) Olympians facing the media. *Refractory Girl*, 43, Winter: 10-13.

Engelbrecht, A. (1996) Cortina d'Ampezzo, 1944. In J. Findling and K. D. Pelle (eds) *Historical Dictionary of the Modern Olympic Movement.* Westport, CN: Greenwood Publishing , pp. 246-247.

Espy, R. (1979) *The Politics of the Olympic Games.* Berkeley, CA: University of California Press.

Essex, S. and Chalkley, B. (2003) The infrastructural legacy of the Summer and Winter Olympic Games: a comparative analysis. In M. De Moragas, C. Kennett and N. Puig (eds) *The Legacy of the Olympic Games, 1984-2000.* Lausanne: International Olympic Committee, pp. 94-101.

Eurostat (2004) *How Europeans Spend Their Time: Everyday Life of Women and Men.* Luxembourg: Office for Official Publications of the European Communities.

Evaluation Commission (1997) *Report of the Evaluation Commission for the Games of the XXVIII Olympiad in 2004.* Lausanne: International Olympic Committee.

Evans, L. (1998) Get that sport into the Games! *The Olympic Club Magazine: The Official Club of the Sydney 2000 Olympic Games*, Issue 3: 16-18.

Evans, L. (1999) Tainted IOC must draw the line to save itself. *Sydney Morning Herald*, 29 January, p. 28.

Farrell, T. B. (1989) The 1984 Winter Olympics as an American media event: an 'official' rhetorical criticism. In Jackson and McPhail, *op. cit.*, pp. 6.3-6.6.

Fasting, K., and Tangen, J. (1983) Gender and sport in Norwegian mass media, *International Review of Sport Sociology*, 18(1): 61–70.

Faulkner, B., Chalip, L., Brown, G., Jago, L. March, R., and Woodside, A. (2003) Monitoring the tourism impacts of the Sydney 2000 Olympics. *Event Management*, 6(4): 231–246.

Fea, J. (1996a) Lake Placid, 1932. In J. Findling and K. D. Pelle (eds) *Historical Dictionary of the Modern Olympic Movement.* Westport, CN: Greenwood Publishing, pp. 232-236.

Fea, J. (1996b) Lake Placid, 1980. In J. Findling and K. D. Pelle (eds) *Historical Dictionary of the Modern Olympic Movement.* Westport, CN: Greenwood Publishing, pp. 295-301.

Federation of Gay Games (1996) *A Brief History of the Gay Games*, San Francisco, CA., Federation of Gay Games, available at: www.gaygames.org/purpose.htm.

Federation of Gay Games (nd) *Gay Games Legacy.* San Francisco, CA., Federation of Gay Games, available at: www.gaygames.com (accessed March 2007).

Ferkins, L. (1992) *New Zealand Women in Sport: An Untapped Media Resource.* Masters Thesis, Victoria University of Wellington, New Zealand.

FIFA (2006) More people, more countries tune in than ever before. Media release, 3 July, Available on FIFA World Cup 2006 website: www.fifaworldcup.yahoo.com (accessed March 2007).

Figler, S., and Whitaker, G. (1995) *Sport and Play in American Life.* Madison, Wisconsin: Brown and Benchmark

Findling, J. (1996) Nagano. 1998. In J. Findling and K. D. Pelle (eds) Historical Dictionary of the Modern Olympic Movement., Westport, CN: Greenwood Publishing , pp. 335-336.

Findling, J., and Pelle, K. D. (eds) (1996) *Historical Dictionary of the Modern Olympic Movement.* Westport, CN: Greenwood Publishing.

Fletcher, J. E. (1989) Input-output analysis and tourism impact studies. *Annals of Tourism Research*, 16(2): 514-29.

Fordyce, T. (2003) Human growth hormone explained. *BBC Sport,* 27 July, Accessed via: http://news.bbc.co.uk/sport1/hi/front_page/3101343.stm

Franks, C. E. S. (1988) Sport and Canadian diplomacy. *International Journal*, 43(4): 665-682.

Freedman, L. (ed.) (2003) *Superterrorism.* Malden, MA: Blackwell Publishing.

French, S. P., and Disher, M. E. (1997) Atlanta and the Olympics: a one-year retrospective. *Journal of the American Planning Institute,* 63(3): 379-92.

Frisby, W. (2005) The good, the bad, and the ugly: critical sport management research. *Journal of Sport Management,* 19(1):1-12.

Fuller, L. K. (1996) Olympic documentary films. In J. Findling and K. D. Pelle (eds) *Historical Dictionary of the Modern Olympic Movement.* Westport, CN: Greenwood Publishing, pp. 405-414.

Furbank, M., Cromarty, H., and McDonald, G. (1996) *William Penny Brooks and the Olympic Connection.* Much Wenlock, Shropshire: Wenlock Olympian Society.

Gallico, P. (1940) *A Farewell to Sport.* New York: Alfred A. Knopf.

Ganor, B. (2003) *Terrorism: No Prohibition Without Definition.* Herzliyya, Israel: International Policy Institute for Counter-Terrorism, available at: www.ict.org.il (accessed 14 April 2003).

Gardiner, E. N. (1930) *Athletics in the Ancient World.* Oxford: Clarendon Press.

Geitner, P. (1997) The price of East German gold fever. *Sydney Morning Herald*, 7 October, p. 40.

Georgiadis, K. (1992) International Olympic Academy: the history of its establishment, aims and activities. In IOA, *op. cit.*, pp. 57-61.

Gesterland, P. H., Gardner, R. M., Tsui, F. C., Espino, J. U., Rolfs, R. T., and James, B. C. (2003). Automated syndromic surveillance for the 2002 Winter Olympics. *Journal of America Medical Information Association*, 10(6), 547-554.

Gibbs, J. (1898) *A Cotswold Village*, London: John Murray.

Gibson, R. (1976) *Avery Brundage: Professional Amateur, PhD.* dissertation, Kent State University, Kent, Ohio.

Glasser, E. (1978) *Amateurism and Athletics.* West Point, New York: Leisure Press.

Glisson, P. C. (1996) Economic impact on the State of Georgia of hosting the 1996 Olympic Games. *Government Finance Review*, 12(3): June 1; 19-21.

Goggin, G. and Newell, C. (2000) Crippling Paralympics? Media, disability and Olympism. *Media International Australia*, 97, 71-84.

Goksøyr, M., Lippe, G. von der, and Mo, K. (eds) (1996) *Winter Games, Warm Traditions*. Norwegian Society of Sports History, Sankt Augustin, Norway: Academia Verlag.

Golden, M. (1998) *Sport and Society in Ancient Greece*. Cambridge: Cambridge University Press

Goldlust, J. (1987) *Playing for Keeps: Sport, Media and Society*. Melbourne: Longman Cheshire.

Goldman, B., and Klatz, R. (1992) *Death in the Locker Room: Drugs and Sport*. Chicago, IL: Elite Sports Medicine Publications.

Goldstein, E. S. (1996) Amsterdam, 1928: the Games of the Xth Olympiad. In J. Findling and K. D. Pelle (eds) *Historical Dictionary of the Modern Olympic Movement*. Westport, CN: Greenwood Publishing, pp. 68-74.

Good, D. (1999) The Cultural Olympiad. In Cashman and Hughes *op. cit.*, pp. 159-169.

Gordon, H. (1994) *Australia and the Olympic Games*. St. Lucia, Queensland: Queensland University Press.

Gordon, S., and Sibson, R. (1998) Global television: the Atlanta Olympics opening ceremony. In Rowe and Lawrence, *op. cit.*, pp. 204-215.

Gotlieb, M. (1972) The American controversy over the Olympic Games. *American Jewish Historical Quarterly*, 61: 181-213.

Graham, C. (1986) *Leni Riefenstahl and Olympia*. Meutchen, New Jersey: Scarecrow Press.

Graham, C. (1989) Leni Riefenstahl's film coverage of the 1936 Olympics. In Jackson and McPhail, *op. cit.*, pp. 2.3-2.6.

Graham, P.J., and Ueberhorst, H. (eds) (1976) *The Modern Olympics*. West Point, New York: Leisure Press.

Gratton, R. (1999) The media. In R. Cashman and A. Hughes (eds) *Staging the Olympics: The Event and its Impact*. Sydney: University of New South Wales Press, pp. 121-131.

Gray, W., and Knight-Barney, R. (1990) Devotion to whom? German-American loyalty on the issue of participation in the 1936 Olympic Games. *Journal of Sport History*, 17(2): 214-231.

Greek Embassy, Netherlands (nd) *Athens 2004 Olympics – Summary Fact Sheet*. The Hague, Netherlands: Embassy of Greece, accessed, March 2007, via: www.greekembassy.nl/press.article15.htm.

Greek Ministry of Culture (1996) *Mind and Body: The Revival of the Olympic Idea 19th-20th Century*. Athens: Greek Ministry of Culture.

Greek sprinters quit Games (2004) *The Age* (Melbourne)/Reuters, 18 August. Available at: http://theage.com.au/olympics/articles/2004/08/18/1092764947158.html.

Green Games Watch 2000 (1999) *Second Environmental Performance Review of the Green Games*. Sydney: Green Games Watch 2000 Inc.

Green Games Watch 2000 (2000) *How Green Are the Sydney 2000 'Green Olympic Games'? What Have Been the Main Wins and Losses?* Sydney: Green Games Watch 2000, available at: http://pandora.nla.gov.au/tep/13438.

Groussard, S. (1975) *The Blood of Israel: The Massacre of the Israeli Athletes, The Olympics , 1972*, (Tran. H. J. Salemson). New York: William Morrow.

Gruneau, R. (1983) *Class, Sports and Social Development.* Amherst, MA: University of Massachusetts Press.

Gruneau, R. (1984) Commercialism and the modern Olympics. In Tomlinson and Whannel, *op. cit.*, pp. 1-15.

Gruneau, R. (1989) Television, the Olympics, and the question of ideology. In Jackson and McPhail, *op. cit.*, pp. 7.23-7.34.

Gruneau, R. (1999) *Class, Sports and Social Development*, 2nd edn. Champaign, IL: Human Kinetics.

Gruneau, R., and Cantelon, H. (1988) Capitalism, commercialism and the Olympics. In Segrave and Chu, *op. cit.*, pp. 345-364.

Guba, E. G. (ed.) (1990) *The Paradigm Dialog.* Newbury Park, CA.: Sage.

Guegold, W. K. (1996) *One Hundred Years of Olympic Music: Music and Musicians of the Modern Olympic Games, 1896-1996.* Mantua, Ohio: Golden Clef.

Guttman, A. (1984) *The Games Must Go On: Avery Brundage and the Olympic Movement.* New York: Columbia University Press.

Guttman, A. (1988a) The modern Olympics: a sociopsychological interpretation. In J. O. Segrave and D. Chu (eds) *The Olympic Games in Transition.* Champaign, Ill.: Human Kinetics, pp. 433-443.

Guttman, A. (1988b) The Nazi Olympics. In Segrave and Chu, *op. cit.*, pp. 201-220.

Guttman, A. (1992) *The Olympics: A History of the Modern Games.* Urbana, IL: University of Illinois Press.

Haag, H. (1994) Alternate ways of assessing performance – a new look at the results from the 1992 Albertville Olympic Games. In Barney and Meier, *op. cit.*, pp. 159-174.

Haag, H., and Riesinger, G. (1988) Comparative analysis of the results of the 1984 Los Angeles Summer Olympic Games. In E. F. Broom, *et al.* (eds) *Comparative Physical Education and Sport, Vol.5*, Champaign, IL: Human Kinetics, pp. 83-89.

Hadjichristodoulou, C., Mouchtouri, V., and Soteriades, E. S. (2005) Mass gathering preparedness: the experience of the Athens 2004 Olympic and Para-Olympic Games. *Journal of Environmental Health*, 67(9): 52-57

Halbwirth, S., Johanson, J., and Toohey, K. (2005) Sporting event websites: friend or foe? *12th International Association for Sport Information Conference Proceedings*, Beijing, pp. 54-62.

Hall, Allan W. (1996) Cortina d'Ampezzo. In J. Findling and K. D. Pelle (eds) *Historical Dictionary of the Modern Olympic Movement.* Westport, CN: Greenwood Publishing , pp. 258-262.

Hall, Anne (1996) *Feminism and Sporting Bodies- Essays on Theory and Practice.* Champaign, IL: Human Kinetics.

Hall, Anne, Cullen, D., and Slack, T. (1990) *The Gender Structure of National Sports Organisations.* Occasional Paper No.1, Sport Canada: Ottawa.

Hall, C. M. (1994) *Hallmark Tourist Events: Impacts, Management and Planning.* London: Belhaven.

Hall, C. M., and Hodges, J. (1996) The party's great, but what about the hangover? The housing and social impacts of mega-events with special reference to the 2000 Sydney Olympics. *Festival Management and Event Tourism*, 4(1): 13-20.

Hall, C. M., and Hodges, J. (1998) The politics of place and identity in the Sydney 2000 Olympics: 'Sharing the spirit of corporatism'. In M. J. Roche (ed.) *Sport, Popular Culture and Identity*, Aachen, Germany: Meyer and Meyer): 95-112.

Harding, A. (1994) Urban regimes and growth machines: toward a cross-national research agenda. *Urban Affairs Quarterly*, 29(3): 356-82.

Hargreaves, J. (1994) *Sporting Females: Critical Issues in the History and Sociology of Women's Sports*, London: Routledge.

Hart-Davis, D. (1988) *Hitler's Olympics: the 1936 Games*. Sevenoaks, Kent: Coronet.

Haugaard, M. (2003) Reflections on seven ways of creating power. *European Journal of Social Theory*, 6(1): 87-113.

Haxton, P. (1993) *A Post-Event Evaluation of the Social Impacts and Community Perceptions of Mega-Events*. Honours Thesis, Townsville, Queensland: James Cook University.

Hazan, B. (1982) *Olympic Sports and Propaganda Games: Moscow 1980*. New Brunswick, New Jersey: Transaction Books.

Hegel, G. W. F. (1953) *Reason in History* (Trans. R. S. Hartman). New York: Liberal Arts Press.

Henderson, K. (1994) Broadening an understanding of women, gender and leisure. *Journal of Leisure Research*, 26(1): 1-7.

Henderson, P. (1989) Toronto's 1996 bid. In Jackson and McPhail, *op cit.*, pp. 10.9-10.11.

Hendy, P., and Kjaerbye, M. (1993) Olympic waters: algae threat to canoeing lakes. *Reportage: Newsletter of the Australian Centre for Independent Journalism*, (UTS, Sydney), September: 15.

Henry, W. M. (1984) *An Approved History of the Olympic Games*. Los Angeles: Southern California Committee of the Olympic Games.

Herman, D., and Chomsky, N. (1988) Manufacturing Consent: The Political Economy of the Mass Media., Pantheon: New York.

Herodotus (1962) *The Histories of Herodotus of Halicarnassus*. Translated by Harry Carter, London: Oxford Press.

Herr, P. B. (1988) *Hosting the Olympics: the Long-Term Impact, Summary Report of the Conference*. Seoul: East Asian Architecture and Planning Program, MIT and Graduate School of Environmental Studies, Seoul National University (see also, EAAPP).

Herz, D., and Altman, A. (1996) Berlin, 1936: the Games of the XIIth Olympiad. In J. Findling and K. D. Pelle (eds) *Historical Dictionary of the Modern Olympic Movement*. Westport, CN: Greenwood Publishing , pp. 84-94.

Hewitt, J. (1996) A grim challenge to world summit on terrorism. *Sydney Morning Herald*, July, 29, p. 11.

Higgs, C., and Weiller, K. (1994) Gender bias and the 1992 Summer Olympic Games: an analysis of television coverage. *Journal of Sport and Social Issues*, 18(3):234-246.

Higgs, C., Weiller, K., and Martin, S. (2003) Gender bias in the 1996 Olympic Games: a comparative analysis. *Journal of Sport and Social Issues*, 27(1): 52-64.

Hill, C. R. (1996) *Olympic Politics, 2nd edn*. Manchester: Manchester University Press.

Hiller, H. (1990) The urban transformation of a landmark event: the Calgary Winter Olympics. *Urban Affairs Quarterly*, 16(1): 118-137.

Hinds, R. (1996) Second when a city lost its soul. *Sydney Morning Herald*, July 29, p. 8.

Hoberman, J. (1986) *The Olympic Crisis: Sport, Politics, and the Moral Order*. New Rochelle, New York: Ariste D. Carataz.

Hoberman, J. (2001) How drug testing fails: the politics of doping control. In W. Wilson and E. Derse (eds) *Doping in Elite Sport; the Politics of Drugs in the Olympic Movement*. Champaign, Illinois: Human Kinetics, pp 241-274.

Hoberman, J. (2004) Sportive nationalism and globalization. In J. Bale and M. K. Christensen (eds) *Post-Olympism? Questioning Sport in the Twenty-first Century.* Oxford: Berg, pp. 177-188.

Hoberman, J. (2005) Olympic drug testing: an interpretive history. In K. B. Wamsley and K. Young (eds) *Global Olympics: Historical and Sociological Studies of the Modern Games.* Amsterdam: Elsevier, pp. 249-268.

Hogan, K. and Norton, K. (2000) The 'price' of Olympic gold. *Journal of Science and Medicine in Sport,* 3(2): 203-218.

Holmes, B. (1984) *The Olympian Games in Athens, 1896: the First Modern Olympics.* New York: Grove Press.

Holmes, J. (1971) *Olympiad 1936: Blaze of Glory for Hitler's Reich.* New York: Ballantine.

Holmes, P. (1979) *The Olympic Games in Athens 1896: The First Modern Olympics.* New York: Grove Press.

Homebush Bay Development Corporation (1992) *The Cost of Developing Homebush Bay, Homebush Bay Information Sheet 16.* East Sydney, NSW: NSW Government Property Services Group.

Hong, F. (1998) The Olympic Movement in China: ideals, realities and ambitions. *Culture, Sport, Society* (now *Sport in Society*), 1(1), 149-68.

Hong, F., Wu, P., and Xion, H. (2005) Beijing ambitions: an analysis of the Chinese elite sports system and its Olympic strategy for the 2008 Olympic Games. *International Journal of the History of Sport,* 22(4), 510-29

Hooker Research (1993a) *The Olympic Corridor: Residential Development at the Starting Block.* Sydney: Hooker Research.

Hooker Research (1993b) *Sydney: Olympics 2000 - Impact on Property.* Sydney: Hooker Research.

Hope, K. (2001) Greece focuses on Olympic security. *Europe,* January 10, 46.

Hopkins, J. (1966) *The Marathon.* London: Stanley Paul.

Hornbuckle, A. R. (1996) Helsinki, 1952: the Games of the XVIth Olympiad. In J. Findling and K. D. Pelle (eds) *Historical Dictionary of the Modern Olympic Movement.* Westport, CN: Greenwood Publishing , pp. 109-118.

Horner, S., and Swarbrooke, J. (2005) *Leisure Marketing: A Global Perspective,* Oxford: Elsevier.

Horton, P.A. (1994) The modern Olympic Games and the cause of black nationalism. In Barney and Meier, *op. cit.,* pp. 55-60.

Hotchkiss, J. L., Moore, R. E., and Zobay, S. M. (2003) Impact of the 1996 Summer Olympic Games on Employment and Wages in Georgia. *Southern Economic Journal,* 69(3): 691-704.

Houlihan, B. (1994) *Sport and International Politics.* Hemel Hempstead, UK: Harvester.

Houlihan, B. (1997) *Sport, Policy and Politics.* London: Routledge.

Houlihan, B. (2005) International politics and Olympic governance. In K. B. Wamsley and K. Young (eds) *Global Olympics: Historical and Sociological Studies of the Modern Games.* Amsterdam: Elsevier, pp. 127-42.

House of Representatives Standing Committee on Legal and Constitutional Affairs and Australian Sports Commission (1991) *A Chance to Have a Say: Equity for Women in Sport. Hansard Report.* Canberra: Parliament House.

Howard, J. (2000) We must build on Sydney spirit. *The Australian,* 25 October, p. 1.

Howell, R. A., and Howell, M. L. (1996) Paris, 1900: the Games of the IInd Olympiad. In J. Findling and K. D. Pelle (eds) *Historical Dictionary of the Modern Olympic Movement.* Westport, CN: Greenwood Publishing, pp. 12-17.

Hruska, B. (1996) High tech and high drama. *TV Guide*, 44(29): July 20-26, pp 8-10.

Hughes, A. (1999) The Paralympics. In Cashman, R. and Hughes, A. (eds) *Staging the Olympics: The Event and its Impact*, Sydney: University of New South Wales Press, pp. 170-182.

Hulme, D. L. (1988) *The Viability of International Sport as a Political Weapon: the 1980 US Olympic Boycott.* PhD dissertation, Fletcher School of Law and Diplomacy, Tufts University, MA.

Hulme, D. L. (1990) *The Political Olympics: Moscow, Afghanistan, and the 1980 US Boycott.* New York: Praeger.

Humphreys, J. M., and Plummer, M. K. (1993) The 1996 Olympic Games - a $5.1 billion prize. *Urban Land*, 52, May: 10-12.

Humphreys, J.M., and Plummer, M.K. (1995) *The Economic Impact of Hosting the 1996 Summer Olympic.* Atlanta, GA: Selig Center for Economic Growth, University of Georgia, available at: www.selig.uga.edu/forecast/olympics/olym text.htm (accessed June 2006).

Huxley, J. (2004) The unforgettable dream Games. *Sydney Morning Herald*, 31 August, available at: www.smh.com.au/olympics, accessed Feb., 2007.

Hyup, C. (1990) The Seoul Olympiad and the Olympic ideals: a critical evaluation. In Byong-Ik, *op. cit.*, pp. 345-356.

IBM (2000) IBM delivers gold medal performance for Olympic Games technology: official website sets records for Internet traffic. *Business Wire*, October 1. (Online service at; http://home.businesswire.com).

International Olympic Academy (1992) *International Olympic Academy: Thirty-Second Session, 17th June - 2nd July 1992.* Lausanne: International Olympic Committee.

International Olympic Committee (IOC) (1995) *The Olympic Charter.* (1995 edition), Lausanne: IOC.

International Olympic Committee (IOC) (1996a) The IOC Medical Commission and the fight against doping. *IOC Medical Code.* Lausanne: IOC.

International Olympic Committee (IOC) (1996b) *The IOC Companion.* Lausanne: IOC*.

International Olympic Committee (IOC) (1997) *Manual on Sport and the Environment.* Lausanne: IOC*.

International Olympic Committee (IOC) (1998a) *The IOC Directory.* Lausanne: IOC

International Olympic Committee (IOC) (1998b) *Olympic Marketing Matters.* Lausanne: IOC*.

International Olympic Committee (IOC) (1998c) *Olympic Media Fact File, Winter 1998.* Lausanne: IOC*.

International Olympic Committee (IOC) (1999a) *Highlights of the Week's Olympic News.* 353, 5 February, Lausanne: IOC*.

International Olympic Committee (IOC) (1999b) *Report of the IOC ad hoc Commission to Investigate the Conduct of Certain IOC Members and to Consider Possible Changes in the Procedures for the Allocation of the Games of the Olympiad and the Olympic Winter Games, (Presented to the Executive Board, January 24).* Lausanne: IOC*.

International Olympic Committee (IOC) (1999c) *Second Report of the IOC ad hoc Commission to Investigate the Conduct of Certain IOC Members and to Consider Possible Changes in the Procedures for the Allocation of the Games of the Olympiad and the Olympic Winter Games, Presented to the Executive Board, March 11.* Lausanne: IOC*.

International Olympic Committee (IOC) (2004) *The Olympic Charter*. Lausanne: IOC*.

International Olympic Committee (IOC) (2004a) *IOC Approves Consensus with Regard to Athletes who have Changed Sex. Media Release 17 May*, and *Explanatory Note to the Recommendation on Sex Reassignment and Sports.* Lausanne: IOC*.

International Olympic Committee (IOC) (2004b) *Women and Sport Commission*. Lausanne: IOC*.

International Olympic Committee (IOC) (2004c) *Athens 2004 Marketing Report*. Lausanne: IOC*.

International Olympic Committee (2004d) *Women in the Olympic Movement Fact Sheet*. Lausanne: IOC.

International Olympic Committee (IOC) (2005a) *2014 Candidature Acceptance Procedure*. Lausanne: IOC*.

International Olympic Committee (IOC) (2005b) *Rules of Conduct Applicable to all Cities Wishing to Organise the Olympic Games*. Lausanne: IOC*.

International Olympic Committee (IOC) (2005c) *Women [sic] Participation in the Games of the XXVIII Athens 2004*. Lausanne: Dept of International Cooperation and Development, IOC* .

International Olympic Committee (IOC) (2005d) *Anti-doping Rules Applicable to the XX Olympic Winter Games in Turin, 2006*. Lausanne: IOC*. Available at: http://multimedia.olympic.org/pdf/en_report_1018.pdf.

International Olympic Committee (IOC)(2005e) *Singapore 2005: IOC President Reflects on a Successful 117th Session*. Media Release 9 July, Lausanne: IOC*.

International Olympic Committee (IOC) (2006a) *2006 Marketing Fact File*. Lausanne: IOC*.

Internationa International Olympic Committee (IOC) (2006b) *Olympic Movement Medical Code*. Lausanne: IOC*.

International Olympic Committee (IOC) (2007a) *The Fight Against Doping and Promotion of Athletes' Health Update*. Lausanne: IOC* February, http://multi media.olympic.org/ pdf/en_report_838.pdf

International Olympic Committee (IOC) (2007b) *IOC Teams up with United for Global Promotional Campaign*. Media statement, Lausanne: IOC Marketing Commission, available at: www.olympic.org under: The Movement > Comm-issions > Marketing (accessed April, 2007).

International Olympic Committee (IOC) (2007c) The Fight Against Doping and Promotion of Athletes' Health (update - February 2007). Lausanne: IOC*, available at: www.olympic.org under: Olympic Game> Torino> Anti-doping Centre.

International Olympic Committee (IOC) (n.d.) *Official Web-site,* at: www.olympic. org, Lausanne: IOC. * NB most of the IOC documents cited above can be found on the IOC website.

International Olympic Committee (IOC) (n.d.(a)) *Missions: Promotion of Women in Sport.* Lausanne: IOC*.

International Olympic Committee, City of Sydney, Australian Olympic Committee (IOC) (1993) *Host City Contract for the Games of the XXVII Olympiad in the Year 2000*. Monte Carlo, Monaco: IOC, City of Sydney, AOC (typescript).

International Olympic Committee, Department of International Cooperation (1998) *Women in the Olympic Movement*. Unpublished document, May, Lausanne: IOC.

International Paralympic Committee (n.d.) *Official Web-site*, at: www. aralympic.org.

International Skating Union (2006) *ISU Judging System for Figure Skating and Ice*

Dancing 2004/5. Lausanne: International Skating Union, available at: www.isu.org (Accessed March 2006).

InterVISTAS (2002) *2010 Olympic and Paralympic Games: Economic Impact Update*. Vancouver: InterVISTAS, available via: www.intervistas.com (accessed March 2007).

Iton, J. (1978) *The Economic Impact of the 1976 Olympic Games, Report to the Organising Committee of the 1976 Games*. Montreal: Office of Industrial Research, McGill University.

Iton, J. (1988) The longer-term impact of Montreal's 1976 Olympic Games. In EAAPP, *op. cit.*, pp. 195-224.

Jackson, R., and McPhail, T. (eds) (1989) *The Olympic Movement and the Mass Media: Past, Present and Future Issues, International Conference Proceedings*. University of Calgary, Feb. 15-19, Calgary: Hurford Enterprises.

Jeffrey, N. (1997) The scandal we had to have. *Weekend Australian*, 17 January, p. 21.

Jennings, A. (1996) *The New Lords of the Rings*. London: Pocket Books.

Jennings, A.(and Sambrook, C.) (2000) *The Great Olympic Swindle: When the World Wanted its Games Back*. London: Simon and Schuster.

Jennings, A. (2006) *Foul! The Secret World of FIFA: Bribes, Vote Rigging and Ticket Scandals*. London: Harper Sport.

Jeung, G. H., Jafari, J., and Gartner, W.C. (1990) Expectations of the 1988 Seoul Olympics: a Korean perspective. *Tourism Recreation Research*, 15(1): 26-33.

Jinxia, D. (2005) Women, nationalism and the Beijing Olympics: preparing for glory. *The International Journal of the History of Sport*, 22(4): 530-44.

Jobling, I. (1994) Olympic proposals and bids by Australian cities. *Sporting Traditions*, 11(1): 37-56.

Jobling, I. (1996) Melbourne, 1956: the Games of the XVIth Olympiad. In J. Findling and K. D. Pelle (eds) *Historical Dictionary of the Modern Olympic Movement*. Westport, CN: Greenwood Publishing , pp. 119-127.

Johnson, C. (2005) *A Brief overview of Technical and Organisational Security at Olympic Events*. Glasgow; Dept of Computing Science, Glasgow University, available at: www.dcs. gla.ac.uk/~johnson/ (accessed April 2007).

Johnson, W. (1980) Avery Brundage, the man behind the mask. *Sports Illustrated*, 4 August: 48-63.

Johnston, C. (1993) Sydney Olympics 2000: approach to assessment and management of social impacts. In Office on Social Policy, *op. cit.*, pp. A1-A44.

Jokl, E., Karvonen, M., Kihilberg, J., Koskela, A., and Noro, L. (1956) *Sports in the Cultural Pattern of the World: A Study of the Olympic Games 1952 at Helsinki*. Helsinki: Institute of Occupational Health.

Joynt, J., Sten, O., and Steward, T. (1989) The XV Winter Olympics Games Organizing Committee (OCO '88) communications plans. In Jackson and McPhail, *op cit.*, pp. 15.3-15.7.

Kammerer, R. (2001) What is doping and how is it detected? In Wilson and Derse, *op cit.*pp3-28.

Kane, M., and Parks, J. (1992) The social construction of gender difference and hierarchy in sports journalism- few new twists on very old themes. *Women's Sport and Physical Activity Journal*, 1(1): 49-83.

Kang, H. (1988) Accelerating the future-state: urban impact of hosting the 1988 Seoul Olympic Games. In EAAPP, op. *cit.*, pp. 17-32.

Kanin, D.B. (1981) *A Political History of the Olympic Games*. Boulder, CO: Westview Press.

Kaplanidou, K. (2007) Affective event and destination image: their influence on Olympic travelers' behavioral intentions. *Event Management*, 10(2), 159–173.

Karam, Z. (2006) Olympics snub that led to Munich bloodbath. *Sydney Morning Herald*, 25-26 February, p.19.

Karkatsoulis, P., Michalopoulos, N., and Moustakatou, V. (2005) The national identity as a motivational factor for better performance in the public sector: the case of the volunteers of the Athens 2004 Olympic Games. *International Journal of Productivity & Performance Management*, 54(7): 579-594.

Kasimati, E. (2003) Economic aspects and the Summer Olympics: a review of related research. *International Journal of Tourism Research*, 5(6): 433-444. [Economic impact]

Kass, D.A. (1976) The issue of racism at the 1936 Olympics. *Journal of Sport History*, 3(2): 223-235.

Kearins, K., and Pavlovich, K. (2002) The role of stakeholders in Sydney's green games. *Corporate Responsibility and Environmental Management*, 9(3): 157-69.

Kennedy, E., Pussard, H., and Thornton, A. (2006) 'Leap for London'? Investigating the affective power of the sport spectacle. *World Leisure Journal*, 48(3): 6-21.

Kennedy, J. J. Jr. (1996a) Innsbruck, 1964. In J. Findling and K. D. Pelle (eds) *Historical Dictionary of the Modern Olympic Movement*. Westport, CN: Greenwood Publishing, pp. 270-275.

Kennedy, J. J. Jr. (1996b) Innsbruck, 1976. In J. Findling and K. D. Pelle (eds) *Historical Dictionary of the Modern Olympic Movement*. Westport, CN: Greenwood Publishing, pp. 289-294.

Kennelly, M. (2005) *Business as Usual: Elite Australian Athletes' Viewpoints of Terrorism Post 9/11*. BA Honours thesis, School of Leisure, Sport and Tourism, University of Technology, Sydney.

Kent, H., and Merritt, J. (1986) The Cold War and the Melbourne Olympic Games. In A. Curthoys and J. Merritt (eds) *Australia's First Cold War: 2, Better Red than Dead*. Sydney: Allen and Unwin, pp. 170-185, 207-210.

Kew, F. (1997) *Sport: Social Problems and Issues*. Oxford: Butterworth-Heinemann.

Kidd, B. (1980) The Popular Front and the 1936 Olympics. *Canadian Journal of History of Sport and Physical Education*, 11(1): 1–18.

Kidd, B. (1990a) ... and Ben Johnson: Canada at the 1988 Olympics. In Byong-Ik, *op. cit.*, pp. 442-454

Kidd, B. (1990b) Seoul to the world, the world to Seoul. In Byong-Ik, *op. cit.*, pp. 434-441.

Kidd, B. (1992a) Culture wars of the Montreal Olympics. *International Review for the Sociology of Sport*, 27(2): 151–164.

Kidd, B. (1992b) The Toronto Olympic commitment: towards a social contract for the Olympic Games. *Olympika*, 1: 154-167.

Kidd, B. (1996) Montreal, 1976: the Games of the XXIInd Olympiad. In J. Findling and K. D. Pelle (eds) *Historical Dictionary of the Modern Olympic Movement*. Westport, CN: Greenwood Publishing , pp. 153-160.

Kidd, B. (2005) 'Another world is possible': Recapturing alternative Olympic histories, imagining different Games. In K. B. Wamsley and K. Young (eds) *Global Olympics: Historical and Sociological Studies of the Modern Games*. Amsterdam: Elsevier, pp. 143-160.

Killanin, L., and Rodda, J. (eds) (1976) *The Olympic Games*, New York: Collier.

Kim, J.-G. (1988) The potential impact of the Seoul Olympics on national development. In EAAPP, *op. cit.*, pp. 319-326.

Kim, U. (1990) *The Greatest Olympics: from Baden-Baden to Seoul*. Seoul: Si-sa-yong-o-sa.

Kirshenbaum, J. (1972) A sanctuary violated. *Sports Illustrated*, 15 September: 24-26.

Kirsty, D. (1995) *Coubertin's Olympics: How the Games Began*. Minneapolis: Lerner Publications.

Kittell, S. (1997a) The Olympic village of Atlanta '96. In De Moragas, M., Llines, M. and Kidd, B. (eds) (1997) *Olympic Villages: Hundred Years of Urban Planning and Shared Experiences*, Lausanne: Olympic Museum, International Olympic Committee, pp. 101–104.

Kittell, S. (1997b) The Olympic village of Sydney 2000. In De Moragas, M., Llines, M. and Kidd, B. (eds) (1997) *Olympic Villages: Hundred Years of Urban Planning and Shared Experiences*. Lausanne: Olympic Museum, International Olympic Committee, pp. 111–120.

Kjaerbye, M. (1993) More than simply 'Sharing the Spirit'. *Reportage: Newsletter of the Australian Centre for Independent Journalism* (UTS, Sydney), September: 8-11.

Klausen, A. M. (ed.) (1999) *Olympic Games as Performance and Public Event: the Case of the XVII Winter Olympic Games in Norway*. New York: Berghahn Books.

Knight, T. (2001) Olympic Games: Athens 2002 'is back on track'. *The Telegraph* (London), 4 May, via: www.telegraph.co.uk – accessed, March 2007.

Knightly, P. (2000) The wizards of Oz. *Sydney Morning Herald*, 13 October.

Kok, C. N. (2002/03) *An Analysis of the Olympic venues and their post-Games use: case studies of the Albertville 1992, Lillehammer 1994, Nagano 1998 and Salt Lake City 2002 Olympic Winter Games*. Master of Arts in European Tourism Management Thesis, Högskolan Dalarna, Borlänge, Sweden, and Université de Savoie, Chambéry, France. Available at: www.du.se/upload/3648/ETM%20Thesis%20KOK.pdf (accessed April 2007)

Kornblatt, T. (2006) *Setting the Bar: Preparing for London's Olympic Legacy*. Discussion Paper No. 8, London: Centre for Cities/Institute for Public Policy Research (available via www.ippr.org.uk – accessed Dec. 2006).

Korporaal, G., and Evans, M. (1999) Games people play. *Sydney Morning Herald*, 11 February, p. 2.

Kok, C. N. (2002/03) *An Analysis of the Olympic Venues and their post-Games use: Case Studies of the Albertville 1992, Lillehammer 1994, Nagano 1998 and Salt Lake City 2002 Olympic Winter Games*. Master of Arts in European Tourism Management Thesis, Högskolan Dalarna, Borlänge, Sweden, and Université de Savoie, Chambéry, France. Available at: www.du.se/ upload/3648/ETM%20 Thesis%20KOK.pdf (accessed April 2007).

KPMG Peat Marwick (1993) *Sydney Olympic 2000: Economic Impact Study, Two Volumes, Report to Sydney Olympics 2000 Bid Ltd*. Sydney: KPMG Peat Marwick..

Krane, V., and Waldron, J. (2000) The Gay Games: creating our own sports culture. In K. Schaffer and S. Smith (eds) *The Olympics at the Millennium: Power, Politics, and the Games*. New Brunswick, N.J.: Rutgers University Press, pp. 147-164.

Krotee, M. L. (1981) Sociological perspectives on the Olympic Games. In J. O. Segrave and D. Chu (eds) *Olympism*, Champaign, Ill.: Human Kinetics, pp. 207-226

Krotee, M.L. (1988) An organizational analysis of the International Olympic Committee. In Segrave and Chu, *op. cit.*, pp. 113-148.

Krüger, A. (1996) The history of the Olympic Winter Games: the invention of a tradition. In M. Goksøyr, G. Lippe and K. von der Mo (eds) *Winter Games, Warm Traditions.* Sankt Augustin, Norway: Norwegian Society of Sports History/Academia Verlag: 101–122.

Krüger, A. (1998) The Ministry of Popular Enlightenment and Propaganda and the Nazi Olympics of 1936. In Barney *et. al., op. cit.*, pp. 33-48.

Kumar, K. (1995) *From Post-industrial to Post-modern Society*, Oxford: Blackwell.

Lambrinidis, S. (2003) The Olympic Truce: an ancient concept for the new millennium. In M. De Moragas, C. Kennett and N. Puig (eds) *The Legacy of the Olympic Games, 1984-2000.* Lausanne: International Olympic Committee, pp. 262-265.

Landry, F. (1995) Paralympic Games and social integration. In M. De Moragas and M. Botella (eds) *The Keys to Success: The Social, Sporting, Economic and Communications Impact of Barcelona '92*, Barcelona: Centre d'Estudis Olímpics i de l'Esport, Universitat Autònoma de Barcelona, pp. 124-138.

Landry, F., Landry, M., and Yerlès, M. (eds) (1991) *Sport .. The Third Millenium: Proceedings of the International Symposium, Quebec City, May 21–25 1990.* Sainte-Foy, Quebec: Presses de l'Université Laval.

Landry, F., and Yerlès, M. (1994-1997) The presidencies of Lord Killanin and Juan Antonio Samaranch. In R. Gafner and N. Müller (eds) *The International Olympic Committee One Hundred Years: the Idea, the Presidents, the Achievements Vol. 3.* Lausanne: IOC.

Lapchick, R. E. (1975) *The Politics of Race and International Sport: The Case of South Africa.* Westport, CN: Greenwood.

Larson, J. F. (1989) Seoul Olympics television concerns: 'Seoul to the world, the world to Seoul' - television as the essence of the 1988 Summer Olympics. In Jackson and McPhail, *op. cit.*, pp. 12.3-12.4.

Larson, J. F., and Rivenburgh, N. K. (1991) A comparative analysis of Australian, US and British telecasts of the Seoul Olympic opening ceremony. *Journal of Broadcasting and Electronic Media*, 35(1): 75-94.

Lasswell, H. D., and Kaplan, A. (1950) *Power and Society: A Framework for Critical Inquiry.* New Haven, CN: Yale University Press

Laura, R., and White, S. (1991) *Drug Controversy in Sport: the Socio-Ethical and Medical Issues.* Sydney: Allen and Unwin.

Lawrence, G. (1986) The race for profit: commercialism and the Los Angeles Olympics. In Lawrence and Rowe, *op. cit.*, pp. 204-214.

Lawrence, G., and Rowe, D. (eds) (1986) *Power Play: Essays in the Sociology of Australian Sport.* Sydney: Hale and Iremonger.

Lee, J.-S. (1989) Seoul Olympics - television concerns. In Jackson and McPhail, *op. cit.*, pp. 12.5-12.9.

Lee, M. (2006) *The Race for the 2012 Olympics: the Inside Story of How London Won the Bid.* London: Virgin Books.

Leigh, M. (1974) *The Evolution of Women's Participation in the Summer Olympic Games: 1900-1948.* PhD dissertation, Ohio State University.

Leiper, J. M. (1976) *the International Olympic Committee: its Structure and Function, Past and Present Problems, and Future Challenges.* PhD Dissertation, University of Alberta.

Leiper, J. M. (1981) Political problems in the Olympic Games. In Segrave and Chu, *op. cit.*, pp. 104-117.

Lellouche, M. (1996) Albertville and Savoie, 1992. In J. Findling and K. D. Pelle (eds) *Historical Dictionary of the Modern Olympic Movement.* Westport, CN: Greenwood Publishing , pp. 318-325.

Lennartz, K. (1994-1997a) The presidency of Henri de Baillet-Latour. In R. Gafner and N. Müller (eds) *The International Olympic Committee One Hundred Years: the Idea, the Presidents, the Achievements, Vol. 1.* Lausanne: IOC.

Lennartz, K. (1994-1997b) The presidency of Sigfrid Edström. In R. Gafner and N. Müller (eds) *The International Olympic Committee One Hundred Years: the Idea, the Presidents, the Achievements, Vol. 2.* Lausanne: IOC.

Lenk, H. (1976) The 1972 Munich Olympic Games: a dilemma? In Graham and Ueberhorst, *op. cit.*, pp. 199-208.

Lenskyj, H. J. (1992) More than games: community involvement in Toronto's bid for the 1996 Summer Olympics. In Barney and Meier, *op. cit.*, pp. 78-87.

Lenskyj, H. J. (1994) Buying and selling the Olympic Games: citizen participation in the Sydney and Toronto bids. In Barney and Meier, *op. cit.*, pp. 70-77.

Lenskyj, H. (1997) Sydney 2000, Olympic sport and the Australian media. Paper presented to *Everyday Wonders Conference on Popular Culture.* June, Brisbane.

Lenskyj, H. (1998a) Green Games or empty promises? Environmental issues and Sydney 2000. In Barney *et al., op. cit.*, pp. 173-179.

Lenskyj, H. (1998b) Sport and corporate environmentalism: the case of the Sydney 2000 Olympics. *Review for the Sociology of Sport*, 33(4): 341–354.

Lenskyj, H. J. (2000) *Inside the Olympic Industry: Power, Politics and Activism.* Albany, NY: State University of New York Press.

Lenskyj, H. J. (2002) *The Best Olympics Ever? Social Impacts of Sydney 2000.* Albany, NY: State University of New York Press.

Lenskyj, H. J.. (2004) Making the world safe for global capital: the Sydney 2000 Olympics and beyond. In J. Bale and M. K. Christensen (eds) *Post-Olympism? Questioning Sport in the Twenty-first Century.* Oxford: BERG, pp. 135-146.

Leonard, J (2001) Doping in elite swimming: a case study of the modern era from 1970 onwards. In Wilson and Derse, *op cit.* pp 241–274.

Levitt, S. (1990) *1984 Olympic Arts Festival: Theatre.* PhD dissertation, University of California, Davis.

Lin, X. (2003) The economic analysis of Beijing 2008 Olympic Games. In M. de Moragas, C. Kennett and N. Puig (eds) *The Legacy of the Olympic Games: 1984-2000: International Symposium, Lausanne, 14-16 November, 2002.* Lausanne: Olympic Museum and Studies Centre, 227-8.

Linardopoulos, N. (2005) Commentary: the use of press releases; A case study of the Athens 2004 Olympic Games. *Prism*, 3, online journal, Dept of Communication and Journalism, Massey University, NZ, available at: http://praxis.massey.ac.nz/prism_on-line_journ.html.

Loder, C. (1997) *Politics and the Olympic Games: Beyond Athletic Endeavours*, BA in Human Movement Studies, Honours thesis, University of Technology, Sydney.

Loland, S. (1994) Pierre de Coubertin's ideology of Olympism from the perspective of the history of ideas. In Barney and Meier, *op. cit.*, pp. 26-45.

London 2012 Ltd (2005) *London 2012 Candidate File.* London: London 2012 Ltd. Available at London 2012 website: www.london2012.org/en/news/publications, accessed March 2007.

London 2012 (2007) *Sport - A hidden social worker to help young people and society, Coe tells international legacy conference.* Media Release, 31 Jan.,

London: London 2012, available at: www.london2012.org under News > News archive > 2007 > January (accessed may 2007).

London 2012 (nd) London Organising Committee for the Olympic Games website: www.london2012.org.

Los Angeles Times (1936) Various news reports, 23 July: 7; 25 July: 13, 17, 25; 26 July: 1.

Loughborough University (2004) *Women, Leadership and the Olympic Movement: Final Report*. Report to the International Olympic Committee Loughborough, UK: Institute of Sport and Leisure Policy, Loughborough Univ., available at: http://multimedia.olympic.org/pdf/en_report_994.pdf.

Lucas, J. A. (1980) American involvement in the Athens Olympic Games. *Stadion*, 6(2): 217-228.

Lucas, J. A. (1982) Prelude to the Games of the Tenth Olympiad in Los Angeles, 1932. *Southern California Quarterly*, 64(4): 313-317.

Lucas, J. A. (1983) American preparations for the first post World War Olympic Games, 1919-1920. *Journal of Sport History*, 10(2): 30-44.

Lucas, J. A. (1988a) The genesis of the modern Olympic Games. In Segrave and Chu *op. cit.*, pp. 89-99.

Lucas, J. A. (1988b) A decalogue of Olympic Games reform. In Segrave and Chu, *op. cit.*, pp. 427-432.

Lucas, J. A. (1992) *The Future of the Olympic Games*. Champaign, IL: Human Kinetics.

Lucian (1905) *The Works of Lucian of Samosata*. (trans. W. H. Fowler and F. G. Fowler), Oxford: Clarendon Press.

Ludwig, J. (1976) *Five Ring Circus: The Montréal Olympics*. Toronto: Doubleday.

Lui, M., Vlahou, T., and Robert, M. (2004) Olympic insecurity. *Newsweek International*, 8 March, p. 22

Lusetich, R. (1999) The buying Games. *Weekend Australian*, 16-17 January, p. 22.

Lyberg W. (1996) *Fabulous 100 Years of the IOC: Facts, Figures and Much More*. Lausanne: International Olympic Committee.

Lynch, R., and Veal, A. J. (2006) *Australian Leisure, 3rd edn*. Frenchs Forest, NSW: Pearson Longman.

Lynch, R., McDonnell, I., Thompson, S., and Toohey, K. (eds) (1996) *Sport and Pay TV - Strategies for Success*. Sydney: School of Leisure and Tourism Studies, University of Technology, Sydney.

MacAloon, J. J. (1981) *This Great Symbol: Pierre de Coubertin and the Origins of the Modern Olympic Games,* Chicago: Chicago Univ. Press.

MacAloon, J. J. (1989) Festival, ritual and television. In Jackson and McPhail, *op. cit.*, pp. 6.21–6.40.

MacAloon, J. J. (1991) Comparative analysis of the Olympic ceremonies, with special reference to Los Angeles. In Commision Interministerial de Ciencia y Tecnologia, *International Syposium on Olympic Games, Media and Cultural Exchanges*, Barcelona: Commision Interministerial de Ciencia y Tecnologia. pp. 35-54.

MacAloon, J.J. (1995) Barcelona '92: the perspective of cultural anthropology. In De Moragas and Botella (eds) *op. cit.*, pp. 181–187.

MacAloon, J. J. (1999) Anthropology at the Olympic Games: an overview. In A. M. Klausen, (ed.) *Olympic Games as Performance and Public Event: the Case of the XVII Winter Olympic Games in Norway*. New York: Berghahn Books, pp. 9-26.

MacDonald, G. (1998) A colossal embroglio: control of amateur ice hockey in the United States and the 1948 Olympic Winter Games. *Olympika*, 7: 43-60.

MacDonald, G., and Brown, D. (1996) Oslo, 1952. In J. Findling and K. D. Pelle (eds) *Historical Dictionary of the Modern Olympic Movement.* Westport, CN: Greenwood Publishing , pp. 252-257.

MacDonald, S. (2006) London 2012: the story so far. *CLES Bulletin* (Manchester: Centre for Local Economic Strategies) (Available at www.cles.org.uk – accessed Dec. 2006)

Madden, J. R. (2002) The economic consequences of the Sydney Olympics: the CREA/Arthur Anderson study. *Current Issues in Tourism*, 5(1): 7-21.

Magdalinski, T. (1998) Recapturing Australia's glorious sporting past: drugs and Australian identity. *Bulletin of Sport and Culture*, 14 March: 1, 6-8.

Magnay, J. (2004) Drug agency ups the ante on dirty stars to take their medicine. *Sydney Morning Herald*, 15 June, p. 1

Magnay, J. (2006) Athletes do a runner amid jail fears as coach runs into bind. *Sydney Morning Herald*, 21 February.

Magnay, J. (2007) Faster, higher and on target. *Sydney Morning Herald*, Feb. 3-4, p. 26.

Magnay J., and Hinds, R. (1996) Terror: bomb blast hits Atlanta Games. *Sydney Morning Herald*, July 28 pp. 1, 7.

Magnay, J., and Korporaal, G. (1999) Rich sports nobble Olympic drugs fight. *Sydney Morning Herald*, 5 February, p. 1.

Maguire, J., Jarvie, G., Mansfield, L., and Bradley, J. (eds) (2002) *Sport Worlds: A Sociological Perspective.* Champaign, IL: Human Kinetics.

Mâitre, H. J. (1980) *The 1980 Moscow Olympics: Politics and Polity.* Palo Alto, CA: Hoover Institution on War, Revolution and Peace, Stanford University.

Mallon, B. (1992) *The Unofficial Report of the 1920 Olympics.* Durham, NC: Most Publications.

Mallon, B. (1998) *The 1900 Olympic Games: Results for all Competitors in All Events.* Jefferson, NC: McFarland.

Mallon, B., *and* Widlund, T. (1998) *The 1896 Olympic Games: Results for all Competitors in All Events.* Jefferson, NC: McFarland.

Maloney, L. (1996) Barcelona, 1992: the Games of the XXVth Olympiad. In J. Findling and K. D. Pelle (eds) *Historical Dictionary of the Modern Olympic Movement.* Westport, CN: Greenwood Publishing, pp. 185-193.

Maloney, L. (1996a) Lillehammer, 1994. In J. Findling and K. D. Pelle (eds) *Historical Dictionary of the Modern Olympic Movement.* Westport, CN: Greenwood Publishing , pp. 326-334.

Maloney, L. (1996b) Atlanta, 1996: the Games of the XXVIth Olympiad. In J. Findling and K. D. Pelle (eds) *Historical Dictionary of the Modern Olympic Movement.* Westport, CN: Greenwood Publishing, pp. 194-200.

Mandell, R. (1971) *The Nazi Olympics.* New York: MacMillan.

Mandell, R. (1976a) *The First Modern Olympics.* Berkeley, California: University of California Press.

Mandell, R. D. (1976b) The modern Olympic Games: a bibliographic essay. *Sportwissenschaft*, 6(1): 89-98.

Mandell, R. D. (1978) Sportsmanship and Nazi Olympism. In B. Lowe, D. B. Kanin and A. Strenk (eds) *Sport and International Relations*, Champaign Il.: Stipes): 135-152.

Mandell, R. (1987) *The Nazi Olympics.* Urbana, IL: University of Illinois Press.

Mandell, R. D. (1991) *The Olympics of 1972, A Munich Diary.* Chapel Hill, NC: University of North Carolina Press.

Manning, M. J. (1996) London, 1944: the Games of the XIVth Olympiad. In J. Findling and K. D. Pelle (eds) *Historical Dictionary of the Modern Olympic Movement.* Westport, CN: Greenwood Publishing , pp. 101–102.

Marsan, J.-C. (1988) Expo '67, The 1976 Olympic Games and Montreal urban design. In EAAPP, *op. cit.*, pp. 225-244.

Martin, D., and Gynn, R. (1979) *The Marathon Footrace.* Springfield, IL: Charles C Thomas.

Martueci, D. (1988) The London Olympics 40 years on. *Olympic Review* (253): 653-656.

Marvin, C. (1982) Avery Brundage and American participation in the 1936 Olympic Games. *Journal of American Studies*, 16(1): 81–105.

Mascagni, K. (2003) The Olympic Games and sport as an opportunity for peace and development. In M. De Moragas, C. Kennett and N. Puig (eds) *The Legacy of the Olympic Games, 1984-2000.* Lausanne: International Olympic Committee, pp. 265-267.

Masters, R. (2005) Telstra Stadium: losing ground. *Sydney Morning Herald*, 30 April.

Masumoto, N. (1993) Revival of 'Olympia': reflections of body by Leni Riefenstahl. *Journal of Philosophy and Principles of Physical Education*, 23(1): 1–15.

Masumoto, N. (1994) Interpretation of the filmed body: an analysis of the Japanese version of Leni Riefenstahl's 'Olympia'. In Barney and Meier, *op. cit.*, pp. 146-158.

Matthews, G. R. (1980) The controversial Olympic Games of 1908 as viewed by the *New York Times* and the *Times* of London. *Journal of Sport History*, 7(2): 40-53.

Matthews, G. R. (2005) *America's First Olympics: The St Louis Games of 1904.* Columbia, MO, University of Missouri Press.

Maxwell, L., *and* Howell, R. (1976) The 1952 Helsinki Olympic Games: another turning point? In Graham and Ueberhorst, *op. cit.*, pp. 187-198.

May, V. (1995) Environmental implications of the 1992 Winter Olympic Games. *Journal of Tourism Management*, 16(4): 269-276.

Mazitelli, D. (1988) Melbourne's Olympic inheritance: subsequent impacts. In EAAPP, *op. cit.*, pp. 171–194.

Mbaye, K. (ed.) (1996) *Centennial Olympic Congress, Congress of Unity, Study Commission: Final Report, Atlanta, July 1996.* Lausanne: IOC.

McCollum, R. H., *and* McCollum, D. F. (1981) Analysis of the ABC-TV coverage of the 21st Olympiad Games. In Segrave and Chu, *op. cit.*, pp. 127-139.

McCoy, J. (1997) Radio sports broadcasting in the United States, Britain and Australia (1920-1956) and its influence on the Olympic Games. *Journal of Olympic History*, 5(1): 20-25.

McGeoch, R. with Korporaal, G. (1994) *The Bid: How Australia Won the 2000 Games*, Melbourne: William Heinemann.

McIntosh, M. (1984) *Security Measures at the Summer Olympics.* Unpublished paper, University of Toronto, Toronto.

McIntyre, N. (1995) The legacy of Lillehammer. In C. Simpson and B. Gidlow (eds) *Australian and New Zealand Association for Leisure Studies: Second Conference: Leisure Connections*, Canterbury, NZ: Lincoln University: 391–394.

McKay, J. (1991) *No Pain, No Gain? Sport and Australian Culture*, Sydney: Prentice-Hall.

McKay, J. (1992) *Why so few? Women Executives in Australian Sport.* Report to the Applied Sports Research Program of the Australian Sport Commission, Canberra.

McKay, M., and Plumb, C. (2001) Reaching beyond gold: the impact of the Olympic Games on real estate markets. *Global Insights, Issue 1*, Chicago: Jones Lang Lasalle (Available from: www.joneslanglasalle.com, accessed March 2007).

McMurty, J. (1973) A case for killing the Olympics. *Maclean's*, January: 34, 57-57, 60.

Meadow, R. G. (1989) The architecture of Olympic broadcasting. In Jackson and McPhail, *op cit.*, pp. 6.7-6.20.

Meenaghan, T. (1997) *Olympic Market Research: Analysis Report.* Lausanne: International Olympic Committee.

Messinesi, X. L. (1976) *History of the Olympics.* New York: Drake Publications.

Messner, M., *and* Sabo, D. (eds) (1990) *Sport, Men and the Gender Order: Critical Feminist Perspectives.* Champaign, IL: Human Kinetics.

Miller, D. (1996) *The Olympic Revolution.* London: Pavilion.

Miller, D. (2003) *Athens to Athens: the Official History of the Olympic Games and the IOC, 1894-2004.* Edinburgh: Mainstream Publishing.

Müller, N. 1994, *One Hundred Years of Olympic Congresses 1894-1994.* (Translated by Ingrid Sonnleiterner-Hauber). Lausanne: International Olympic Committee.

Millet i Serra, L. (1995) The games of the city. In De Moragas and Botella (eds) *op. cit.*, pp. 188-202.

Ministry of Competition, Science and Enterprise (2002) *The Economic Impact of the Winter Olympic and Paralympic Games: Initial Estimates.* Edmonton, BC: Ministry of Competition, Science and Enterprise, available at: www.ecdev.gov.bc.ca/2010Secretariat/2010/ecimpact.pdf. (accessed March 2007).

Miyazaki, A.D., and Morgan, A.G. (2001) Assessing market value of event sponsoring: corporate Olympic sponsorships. *Journal of Advertising Research*, 41(1): 9-15.

Mohsen, S., *and* Alexandraki, A. (1989) Organisation of the 1988 Calgary Winter Olympic Games. In Jackson and McPhail, *op. cit.*, pp. 11.55-11.60.

Moore, M. (1998) Games sponsor blasts delay in hotel room allocations. *Sydney Morning Herald*, 2 February, p. 3.

Moore, M. (1999) How SOCOG learned the score. *Sydney Morning Herald*, 14 August, p. 47.

Moore, M., and Magnay, J. (1998) In hot water. *Sydney Morning Herald*, 17 January, p. 35.

Morgan, G. (2003) Aboriginal protest and the Sydney Olympic Games. *Olympika*, 12, 23-38.

Morrow, D. (1992) Grace without pressure: Canadian scintillation and the media in the Amsterdam Olympic Games. In Barney & Meier, *op. cit.*, pp. 125-134.

Mottram, D. (2003) Drugs in Sport, 3rd edition. London: Routledge

Mount, J., and Leroux, C. (1994) Assessing the effects of a mega-event: a retrospective study of the impact of the Olympic Games on the Calgary business sector. *Festival Management and Event Tourism*, 2(1): 15-23.

Mouratidis, J. (1984) Heracles at Olympia and the exclusion of women from the Ancient Olympic games. *Journal of Sport History*, 11(3), 56-78.

Ms Muffet (1988) Women, sport and the media. 35, May: 6-8.

Murray, W. J. (1992a) Berlin in 1936: old and new work on the Nazi Olympics. *International Journal of the History of Sport*, 9(1): 29-49.

Murray, W. J. (1992b) France, Coubertin and the Nazi Olympics: the response. *Olympika*, Vol.1): 46-69.

Nathan, M., and Kornblatt, T. (2007) *Paying for 2012: the Olympics Budget and Legacy.* London: Centre for Cities/Institute for Public Policy Research (available via www.ippr.org.uk – accessed March 2007).

Naul, R. (ed.) (1997) *Contemporary Studies in the National Olympic Games Movements, Sport Sciences International,* 2, Frankfurt: Peter Lang.

Nauright, J., and Schimmel, K. S. (eds) (2005) *The Political Economy of Sport.* Basingstoke, UK: Palgrave Macmillan.

Neilson, B. (2002) Bodies of protest: performing citizenship at the 2000 Olympic Games. *Continuum: Journal of Media and Cultural Studies,* 16(1): 13-25.

Nello, O. (1997) The Olympic village of Barcelona '92. In M. De Moragas, M. Llines and B. Kidd (eds) (1997) *Olympic Villages: Hundred Years of Urban Planning and Shared Experiences.* Lausanne: Olympic Museum, Inter-national Olympic Committee, pp. 9–96.

Network 10 (1984) *XXIII Olympic Games: The Official Pictorial History, Los Angeles.* Sydney: Australian Olympic Federation.

New York Times (1934) News report, 8 December, p. 20.

New York Times (1936) Various news reports. 15 July, p.15; 24 July, p. 21; 25 July, p. 7; 3 August, p. 19; 9 August, p. V2.

New York Times (1972) Wrestling star hits at politics. 27 April.

New York Times (2004) Olympic disasters are no-shows. (Editorial), 31 August.

New Zealand Herald (2000) Operation Olympics: Sydney is ready for terrorists. August 28. Available at: www.nzherald.co.nz (accessed October, 2004).

Nii , J. (2002) Olympic skating scandal broadens. *Deseret News* (Salt lake City), August 1, (KSL TV & radio), accessed via: http://deseretnews.com/oly/view/ 0,3949,900000 24,00.html

Nixon, H. (1988) The background, nature and implications of the organization of the 'Capitalist Olympics'. In Segrave and Chu, *op. cit.,* pp. 237-252.

North, R. (1963) *Content Analysis: A Handbook with Applications for the Study of International Crises.* Evanston, IL: Northwestern University Press.

NSW Treasury and the Centre for Regional Economic Analysis (1997) *The Economic Impact of the Sydney Olympic Games.* Treasury Research and Information Paper TRP 97-10, Sydney: New South Wales Treasury, available from the Office of Financial Management, under 'Publications', at: www.treasury.nsw.gov.au (accessed May 2007).

Office of National Drug Control Policy (ONDCP) (2005) *Steroids.* Washington, DC: ONDCP, available at: www.whitehousedrugpolicy.gov/drugfact/steroids/index. html.

Office on Social Policy (1993) *Sydney Olympics 2000: Approaches and Issues for Management of Social Impacts.* Sydney: NSW Government Office on Social Policy.

Olympic Coordination Authority (OCA) (1996) *State of Play: A Report on Sydney 2000 Olympics Planning and Construction.* Sydney: OCA.

Olympic Games Study Commission (2003) *Olympic Games Study Commission: Report to the 115th IOC Session Prague, July,* (Pound Report). Lausanne: International Olympic Committee, (available on IOC website).

Olympic Programme Commission (2005) *Olympic Programme Commission Report to the 117th IOC Session.* Lausanne: IOC, available at: http://multimedia.olympic.org/pdf/en_report_953.pdf (accessed April, 2007).

Onigman, M. (1976) Discontent in the Olympic Winter Games, 1908-1980. In Graham and Ueberhorst, *op. cit.,* pp. 226-244.

O'Neill, J. (1995) How the Olympics will slug taxpayers. *Independent Monthly*

(Sydney), September: 28-30.

Owen, K. A. (2001) *The Local Impacts of the Sydney 2000 Olympic Games: Processes and Politics of Venue Preparation*. Sydney: Centre for Olympic Studies, University of New South Wales.

Palenski, R. (1996) Seoul, 1988: the Games of the XXIVth Olympiad. In J. Findling and K. D. Pelle (eds) *Historical Dictionary of the Modern Olympic Movement*. Westport, CN: Greenwood Publishing , pp. 178-184.

Parisotto, R. (2006) *Blood Sports: the Inside Dope on Drugs in Sport*. Prahran, Victoria: Hardie Grant Books.

Park, S-J., and Samaranch, J. A. (1993) *The Seoul Olympics: the Inside Story*. London: Bellew Publishing.

Pattengale, J. A. (1996) Tokyo/Helsinki, 1940: the Games of the XXIIth Olympiad. In J. Findling and K. D. Pelle (eds) *Historical Dictionary of the Modern Olympic Movement*. Westport, CN: Greenwood Publishing , pp. 95-100.

Pausanias (1962) *Guide to Greece*. Translated by W. Jones, Cambridge, Massachusetts: Harvard University Press

Perelman, R. (ed.) (1985) *Olympic Retrospective: the Games of Los Angeles*. Los Angeles: Los Angeles Olympic Organising Committee.

Perrottet, T. (2004) *The Naked Olympics: the True Story of the Ancient Games*. New York: Random House.

Persson, C. (2002) The International Olympic Committee and site decisions: the case of the 2002 Winter Olympics. *Event Management*, 6(2), 143-47.

Phillips, D. (1990) Australian women at the Olympics: achievement and alienation. *Sporting Traditions*, 6(2): 18−200.

Phillips, D. H. (1992) *Australian Women at the Olympic Games: 1912-92*. Kenthurst, NSW: Kangaroo Press.

Phillips, M. G. (1997) *An Illusory Image: a Report on the Media Coverage and Portrayal of Women's Sport in Australia (1996)*, Canberra: Women's Sport Unit, Australian Institute of Sport.

Phillips, D*., and* Pritchard, D. (eds) (2003) *Sport and Festival in the Ancient Greek World*. Swansea: Classical Press of Wales.

Philostratis (1987) On athletics. In W. Sweet (ed.) *Sport and Recreation in Ancient Greece: A Sourcebook with Translations*. New York: Oxford University Press, p. 125.

Pieroth, D. H. (1996a) *Their Day in the Sun: Women of the 1932 Olympics*. Seattle: University of Washington Press.

Pieroth, D. (1996b) Los Angeles, 1932: the Games Xth Olympiad. In J. Findling and K. D. Pelle (eds) *Hist-orical Dictionary of the Modern Olympic Movement*. Westport, CN: Greenwood Publishing, pp. 75-83.

Poliakoff, M. (1987) *Combat Sports in the Ancient World: Competition, Violence, and Culture*. New Haven, CN: Yale University Press.

Pound, R. W. (1994) *Five Rings Over Korea: the Secret Negotiations Behind the 1988 Olympic Games in Seoul*. Boston: Little, Brown.

Pound, R. W. (2004) *Inside the Olympics*. Toronto: John Wiley & Sons.

Pound, E. T., and Johnson, K. (1999) Pricey project sheds light on courting of Samaranch. *USA Today*, 17 March: 1A-2A.

Powell, J. T. (1994) *Origins and Aspects of Olympism*. Champaign, IL: Stipes.

Preuss, H. (2000) *Economics of the Olympic Games: Hosting the Games 1972-2000*. Petersham, NSW: Walla Walla Press

Preuss, H. (2004) *Economics of Staging the Olympic Games: A Comparison of the Games 1972-2008*. Cheltenham, UK: Edward Elgar.

PriceWaterhouseCoopers (2005) *Olympic Games Impact Study Final Report.* Report to Department of Culture, Media and Sport, London: DCMS (Available via www.culture.gov.uk).

Pujadas, X., *and* Santacana, C. (1992) The popular Olympic Games: Barcelona 1936: Olympians and anti-fascists. *International Review for the Sociology of Sport*, 27(2): 139-150.

Rabkin, Y. M., *and* Franklin, D. (1989) Soviet/Canadian press perspectives on the Montréal Olympics. In Jackson and McPhail, *op. cit.*, pp. 4.29-4.38.

Rasmussen,K. (2005) The quest for the imaginary evil: a critique of anti-doping. *Sport in History*, 25(3): 515-535.

Real, M., Mechikoff, R., and Goldstein, D. (1989) Mirror images: the Olympic Games in Cold War rhetoric: US and Soviet press coverage of the 1980 and 1984 Summer Olympics. In Jackson and McPhail, *op. cit.*, pp. 4.39-4.46.

Redmond, G. (1981) Prologue and transition: the 'pseudo-Olympics' of the nineteenth century. In Segrave and Chu, *op. cit.*, pp. 7-21.

Redmond, G. (1988) Towards modern revival of the Olympic Games: the various 'pseudo-Olympics' of the 19th century. In Segrave and Chu, *op. cit.*, pp. 7–87.

Reich, K. (1986) *Making it Happen: Peter Ueberroth and the 1984 Olympics.* Santa Barbara, CA: Capra Press.

Reich, K. (1989) L. A. Organising Committee and press relations. In Jackson and McPhail, *op. cit.*, pp. 4.3-4.6.

Reiterer, W. (2000) *Positive: an Australian Olympian Reveals the Inside Story of Drugs and Sport.* Sydney: Pan Macmillan.

Renson, R. (1985) From the trenches to the track: the 1920 Antwerp Olympic Games. In N. Müller and J. K. Rül (eds) *Olympic Scientific Congress, 1984 Official Report: Sport History*, Niederhausen, Germany): 234-244.

Renson, R. (1996a) Antwerp, 1920: the Games of the VIIth Olympiad. In J. Findling and K. D. Pelle (eds) *Historical Dictionary of the Modern Olympic Movement.* Westport, CN: Greenwood Publishing , pp. 47-60.

Renson, R. (1996b) The Games Reborn: the VIIth Olympiad - Antwerp 1920., Ghent: Pandora.

Renson, R. M., Lämmer, M., Riordan, J., and Chassiotis, D. (eds) (1991) The Olympic Games through the ages: Greek antiquity and its impact on modern sport. *Proceedings of the 13th International HISPA Congress*, HISPA (Hellenic Sports Research Institute), Olympia, Greece, May 22-28, 1989.

Rich, F.C. (1982) The legal regime for a permanent Olympic site. *The New York University Journal of International Law and Politics*, 155): −53.

Riley, M. (1999) Atlanta bid files to be scrutinised. *Sydney Morning Herald*, 11 May, p. 5.

Riordan, J. (1984) The workers' Olympics. In Tomlinson and Whannel, *op. cit.*, pp. 98-112.

Riordan, J. (1993) Soviet-style sport in Eastern Europe: the end of an era. In L. Allison (ed.) The Changing Politics of Sport., Manchester: Manchester University Press: 37-57.

Riordan, J. (1996) Moscow, 1980: the Games of the XXIInd Olympiad. In J. Findling and K. D. Pelle (eds) *Historical Dictionary of the Modern Olympic Movement.* Westport, CN: Greenwood Publishing, pp. 16–168.

Rippon, A. (2006) *Hitler's Olympics: The Story of the 1936 Nazi Games.* Barnsley, UK: Pen and Sword Books.

Ritchie, I. (2003) Sex tested, gender verified: controlling female sexuality in the age of containment. *Sport History Review,* 34(1): 80-98.

Ritchie, J. R. B. (1990) Promoting Calgary through the Olympics: the mega-event as a strategy for community development. In S. H. Fine (ed.) *Social Marketing: Promoting the Causes of Public and Non-profit Agencies.* Boston: Allyn and Bacon: 258-274.

Ritchie, J. R. B. (2000) Turning 16 days into 16 years through Olympic legacies. *Event Management,* 6(2): 155-65.

Ritchie, J. R. B., and Lyons, M. (1990) Olympulse VI: a post-event assessment of resident reaction to the XV Olympic Winter Games. *Journal of Travel Research,* 28(3): 14-23.

Ritchie, J. R. B., and Smith, B. (1991) The impact of a mega-event on host-region awareness: a longitudinal study. *Journal of Travel Research,* 30(1): 3-10.

Rivenburgh, N. (1991) Learning about Korea - or did we? A multi-national comparison of televised cultural coverage of the Seoul Olympic opening ceremony. In Landry *et al., op. cit.,* pp. 95-97.

Rivenburgh, N. (2004) The Olympic Games, media, and the challenges of global image making. *University Lectures on the Olympics,* Centre d'Estudis Olímpics UAB, http://olympicstudies.uab.es/lectures (Accessed June, 2006).

Roberts, A. J., and McLeod, P. B. (1989) The economics of a hallmark event. In Syme *et al., op. cit.,* pp. 242-9.

Roche, M. (1992) Mega-events and micro-modernization: on the sociology of the new urban tourism. *British Journal of Sociology,* 43(4): 563-600.

Roche, M. (2000) *Mega-events and Modernity: Olympics and Expos in the Growth of Global Culture.* Routledge, London.

Rofe, S., and Ordway, C. (1998) *Anti-Doping Policies.* Unpublished paper, Sydney: College of Law.

Rogge, J. (2006) *IOC President's Speech At the Closing Ceremony of the XX Olympic Winter Games.* Press Release, 26 February, Lausanne: International Olympic Committee.

Rose, D. (1988) Should the Olympic Games be abolished? In Segrave and Chu, *op. cit.,* pp. 393-406.

Rosenberg, D. and Lockwood, K. L. (2005) Will the new figure skating judging system improve fairness at the Winter Olympics? *Olympika,* 14: 69-84.

Rosenzweig, R. (1997) The Nazi Olympics: Berlin 1936. *Journal of Sport History,* 24(1): 77-80.

Rowe, D. and Lawrence, G. (eds) (1998) *Tourism, Leisure, Sport: Critical Perspectives.* Rydalmere, NSW: Hodder

Rowe, D., Markwell, K., and Stevenson, D. (2006) Exploring participants' experiences of the Gay Games: intersections of sport, gender and sexuality. *International Journal of Media and Cultural Politics,* 2(2): 149-65.

Rubien, F. (ed.) (1936) *Report of the American Olympic Committee for the Games of the Xith Olympiad: Berlin, Germany, August 1 to 16, 1936.* New York: American Olympic Committee.

Rühl, J. K., and Keuser, A. (1997) Olympic Games in 19th century England with special consideration of the Liverpool Olympics. In Naul, *op. cit.,* pp. 55-70.

Rutheiser, C. (1996) How Atlanta lost the Olympics. *New Statesman,* (125), 19 July, pp. 28-29.

Salleh, A., and Kjaerbye, M. (1993a) Putting on the Green Glitz. *Reportage: Newsletter of the Australian Centre for Independent Journalism,* (UTS, Sydney), September: 12-13.

Salleh, A., and Kjaerbye, M. (1993b) Olympic waters: ferries stir up toxic fears. *Reportage: Newsletter of the Australian Centre for Independent Journalism*, (UTS, Sydney), September, p. 14.

Salt Lake Organizing Committee for the Olympic Winter Games of 2002 (1999) *Board of Ethics Report to the Board of Trustees*. Salt Lake City, Utah: SLOC (available at: www.slc2002.or/news/).

Salt Lake City Olympic Committee (2002) *Official Report of the XIX Winter Olympic Games*. Salt Lake City, Utah: SLOC.

Samaranch, J. A. (n. d.) *The IOC Medical Commission and the Fight Against Doping*. International Olympic Committee, Accessed via: www.olympic.org/medical/eddop.htm.

Sandler, D. M., and Shani, D. (1989) Olympic sponsorship vs 'Ambush' marketing: who gets the gold? *Journal of Advertising Research*, 29(4): 9-14.

Sandler, D. M., and Shani, D. (1993) Sponsorship and the Olympic Games: the consumer perspective. *Sport Marketing Quarterly*, 2(3): 38-43.

Savulescu, J., Foddy, B., and Clayton, M. (2004) Why we should allow performance enhancing drugs in sport. *British Journal of Sports Medicine*, 38(4): 666-670

Scharenberg, S. (1996) Sapporo/St. Moritz/Garmisch-Partenkirchen, 1940. In J. Findling and K. D. Pelle (eds) *Historical Dictionary of the Modern Olympic Movement*. Westport, CN: Greenwood Publishing , pp. 242-245.

Schneider, A., and Butcher, R. (2001) An ethical analysis of drug testing. In Wilson and Derse, *op cit.*, pp.129-152.

Schor, J. (2006) Overturning the modernist predictions: recent trends in work and leisure in the OECD. In C. Rojek, S. Shaw and A. J. Veal (eds) *A Handbook of Leisure Studies*, Basingstoke, UK: Palgrave Macmillan, pp. 203-215.

Schuster, H., and Stone, C. (2005) Hunting Eric Rudolph. Berkley, CA: Berkley Hardcover. [Atlanta] [Security]

Scraton, S. (1992) *Shaping up to Womanhood*. Buckingham: Open University Press.

Searle, G. (2002) Uncertain legacy: Sydney's Olympic stadiums. *European Planning Studies*, 10(7), 845-60.

Searle, G. (2003) The urban legacy of the Sydney Olympic Games. In M. de Moragas, C. Kennett and N. Puig (eds) *The Legacy of the Olympic Games: 1984-2000: International Symposium, Lausanne, 14-16 November, 2002*. Lausanne: Olympic Museum and Studies Centre, 118-26.

Segrave, J. O., and Chu, D. (eds) (1981) *Olympism*. Champaign, IL: Human Kinetics.

Segrave, J. O., and Chu, D. (eds) (1988) *The Olympic Games in Transition*. Champaign, IL: Human Kinetics.

Selth, A. (1988) *Against Every Human Law*. Canberra: Australian National University Press.

Senn, A. E. (1999) *Power, Politics and the Olympic Games: A History of the Power Brokers, Events, and Controversies that Shaped the Games*. Champaign, IL: Human Kinetics.

Shani, D., and Sandler, D. M. (1998) Ambush marketing: is confusion to blame for the flickering of the flame? *Psychology and Marketing*, 15(4): 367-383

Shanklin, B. (1988) *Sport and Politics: the Olympics and the Los Angeles Games*. New York: Praeger.

Sheil, P. (1998) *Olympic Babylon*. Sydney: MacMillan.

Shigeru, I. (1988) Urban planning evaluation of the Tokyo Olympics. In EAAPP, *op. cit.*, pp. 9–124.

Simmons, D. C. (1996) St. Moritz, 1928. In J. Findling and K. D. Pelle (eds) *Historical Dictionary of the Modern Olympic Movement.* Westport, CN: Greenwood Publishing , pp. 228-231.

Simmons, D. C. (1996) St. Moritz, 1948. In J. Findling and K. D. Pelle (eds) *Historical Dictionary of the Modern Olympic Movement.* Westport, CN: Greenwood Publishing , pp. 248-251.

Simon, D. (1988) Long-term impact of the Olympic Games on Los Angeles. In EAAPP, *op. cit.*, pp. 4–54.

Simri, U. (1977) *A Historical Analysis of the Role of Women in the Modern Olympic Games.* Netanya, Israel: Wingate Institute for Physical Education and Sport.

Simson, V., and Jennings, A. (1992) *The Lords of the Rings: Power, Money and Drugs in the Modern Olympics.* London: Simon and Schuster.

Slater, J. (1998) Changing partners: the relationship between the mass media and the Olympic Games. In Barney *et al., op. cit.*, pp. 49-68.

Slot, O. (2006) Gene therapy a death threat. *The Australian,* 15 February, p. 28.

Slowinowski, S. (1991a) Ancient sport symbols and postmodern tradition. In Renson *et al., op. cit.*, pp. 400-411.

Slowinowski, S. (1991b) Burning desire: festival flame ceremony. *Sociology of Sport Journal,* 8(3): 239-259.

Smith, C. (2004) Women closing in on men? *Athletics*, 4, Dec.

Smith, R. J., and Gibbs, M. (1993) *Navigating the Internet.* Carmel, IN: Sams Publishing.

Snider, C. D. (1936) The real winners in the 1936 Olympic Games. *Scientific Monthly*, 43, October: 372-374.

Soldatow, S. (1980) *Politics of the Olympics.* North Ryde, NSW: Cassell.

Special Bid Oversight Commission (1999) *Report of the Special Bid Oversight Commission.* Irvine, CA: United States Olympic Committee, available at: http://commerce.senate.gov/hearings/0414ioc.pdf (Accessed April, 2007).

Spencer, B. (1966) *High Above the Olympians.* Los Altos, CA: Tafnews Press.

Sports Illustrated (1956a) In full view of the world. 15, 3 December: 22-23.

Sports Illustrated (1956b) The Battle of Melbourne. December 17, p. 23.

Stanton, R. (2000) *The Forgotten Olympic Art Competitions: the Story of the Olympic Art Competitions of the 20th Century.* Victoria, BC: Trafford.

Stauff, J. W. (1996) Garmisch-Partenkirchen, 1936. In J. Findling and K. D. Pelle (eds) *Historical Dictionary of the Modern Olympic Movement.* Westport, CN: Greenwood Publishing, pp. 237-241.

Steadward, R. D. (1996) Integration and sport in the paralympic movement. *Sport Science Review*, 5(1): 26-41.

Steven, C. (2002) Outrage over Olympic skating vote. *The Scotsman*, 6 August.

Stevens, M. (1999) Prince of the Past shames the Games. *Weekend Australian*, 6-7 February, p. 19.

Stevens, M., and Stewart, C. (1999) IOC bribe inquiry claims new scalp. *Weekend Australian*, 23-24 January, p. 6.

Stevenson, D. (1998) The art of the Games: leisure, tourism and the Cultural Olympiad. In Rowe, D. and Lawrence, G. (eds) *Tourism, Leisure, Sport: Critical Perspectives*, Rydalmere, New South Wales: Hodder): 124-134.

Stevenson, D, Rowe, D., and Markwell, K. (2005) Explorations in 'event ecology': the case of the International Gay Games. *Social Identities*, 11(5): 447-65.

Stipp, H., and Schiavone, N. (1996) Modelling the impact of Olympic sponsorship on corporate image. *Journal of Advertising Research*, July/August, 22-28.

Stoddart, B. (1994) *Invisible Games. A Report on the Media Coverage of Women's Sport, 1992.* Canberra: Sport and Recreation Ministers' Council.

Strenk, A. (1970) Back to the very first day: eighty years of politics in the Olympic Games. *Journal of Sport and Social Issues*, 2(1): 24-36.

Strenk, A. (1979) What price victory? The world of international sports and politics. *Annals of the American Academy of Political and Social Science*, 445: 128-140.

Stringer, H. (1995) China's Great Wall of lies. *Inside Sport*, 37, January: 16-27.

Stump, A. J. (1988) The Games that almost weren't. In Segrave and Chu, *op. cit.*, pp. 19–200.

Sutcliffe, K. (1995) Insight into the media in sport. *NSW Session of the Australian Olympic Academy, 13-14 April.* North Ryde, NSW: Macquarie University.

Swaddling, J. (1999) *The Ancient Olympic Games, 2nd edn.* Austin, Texas: University of Texas Press.

Sweeney, Brian, and Associates (1992) *The Olympic Reality: A Survey into Australians' Views on the Barcelona Olympics.* South Melbourne: Brian Sweeney and Associates.

Sweet, W. (1987) *Sport and Recreation in Ancient Greece.* Oxford: Oxford University Press.

Switzer, P. *et al.* (1989) Calgary Olympics: CTV host broadcaster concerns. In Jackson and McPhail, *op. cit.*, pp. 14.3-14.9.

Sydney Morning Herald (1988) Plan to set up 'super' website for Sydney. 15 May, p. 14.

Sydney Morning Herald (1998) Early alerts on Beijing blooms were ignored. 16 January.

Sydney Olympic Games Review Committee (1990) *Report to the Premier of New South Wales.* Sydney: Premier's Department.

Sydney Olympic Broadcasting Organisation (SOBO) (1998) *Infosheet.* Sydney: SOBO.

Sydney Olympics 2000 Bid Ltd (SOBL) (1993a) *The Bid by the City of Sydney to Host the Games of the XXVII Olympiad in the Year 2000.* Sydney: SOBL.

Sydney Olympics 2000 Bid Ltd (SOBL) (1993b) *Fact Sheets: A Summary of the Bid by the City of Sydney to Host the Games of the XXVII Olympiad in the Year 2000.* Sydney: SOBL.

Sydney Olympics 2000 Bid Ltd (SOBL) (1993c) *Environmental Guidelines for the Summer Olympic Games.* Sydney: SOBL.

Syme, G. J., Shaw, B. J., Fenton, M. D., and Mueller, W. S. (eds) (1989) *The Planning and Evaluation of Hallmark Events.* Aldershot, UK: Avebury.

Symons, C. (2002) The Gay games and community. In D. Hemphill and C. Symons (eds) *Gender, Sexuality and Sport: A Dangerous Mix*, Sydney: Walla Walla Press, 100-114.

Takac, A. (1976) Forty years for fourteen days. *The Gazette* (Montréal), July 17, p. 2.

Terrorism Research Centre (2000) *Terrorism Threat to the Australian Olympics.* N. Virginia: Terrorism Research Center, available at: www.terrorism.com/ analysis-olympics.html (accessed March 2006).

Tewnion, T. (1993) *The University of Calgary and the XV Olympic Winter Games.* Calgary, Alberta: University of Calgary.

Theberge, N. (1988) Making a career in a man's world: the experience and orientations of women in coaching. *Arena Review*, 12(2): 116-127.

Theberge, N. (1991) A content analysis of print media coverage of gender, women and physical activity. *Journal of Applied Sports Psychology,* 3(1): 36-50.

Tomlinson, A. (1984) De Coubertin and the modern Olympics. In Tomlinson and Whannel, *op. cit.*, pp. 84-97.

Tomlinson, A. (2005) The commercialisation of the Olympics: cities, corporations, and the Olympic commodity. In K. B. Wamsley and K. Young (eds) *Global Olympics: Historical and Sociological Studies of the Modern Games.* Amsterdam: Elsevier, pp. 179-200.

Tomlinson, A. and Whannel, G. (eds) (1984) *Five Ring Circus: Money, Power and the Politics in the Olympic Games.* London: Pluto.

Toohey, K. (1990a) *The Politics of Australian Élite Sport: 1949-1982.* PhD thesis, Pennsylvania State University

Toohey, K. (1990b) A content analysis of the Australian television coverage of the 1988 Seoul Olympics. Paper presented to the *Ninth Commonwealth and International Conference of Physical Education, Sport, Health, Dance, Recreation and Leisure.* January, Auckland.

Toohey, K. (1997) Australian television, gender and the Olympic Games. *International Review for the Sociology of Sport*, 31(1): 19-29.

Toohey, K. (ed.) (2001) *Official Report of the Games of the XXVII Olympiad: Preparing for the Games (Vol.1),* Sydney: Sydney Organising Committee for the Olympic Games.

Toohey, K. (2005) The 1980 and 1984 Olympic Games Boycotts. In D. A. Kluka, G. Schilling and W. F. Stier (eds) *Sport Governance.* Oxford: Meyer & Meyer Sports, pp. 79-92.

Toohey, K. (2006) *Public Policy: the Olympic Games and Terrorism.* Paper presented to the Otago School of Public Policy, Otago, New Zealand, June.

Toohey, K., and Taylor T. (2005) The Olympics and terrorism. Paper presented to the *Australian Society for Sports History Conference, Sporting Traditions XV.* July, Melbourne.

Toohey, K., and Taylor, T. (2006) Here be savages, here be dragons, here be bad plumbing: Australian media representations of sport and terrorism. *Sport in Society*, 9(1): 7–94.

Toohey, K., Taylor, T., and Lee, C. (2003) The FIFA World Cup 2002: the effects of terrorism on sports tourists. *Journal of Sports Tourism,* 8(3): 186-196.

Toohey, K., and Warning, P. (1998) Olympic flames: analysis of an Olympic internet newsgroup In Barney *et al., op. cit.*, pp. 14–154.

Torres, C. R., and Dyreson, M. (2005) The Cold War games. In K. B. Wamsley and K. Young (eds) *Global Olympics: Historical and Sociological Studies of the Modern Games.* Amsterdam: Elsevier, pp. 59-82.

Trott, D., and Jenkins, G. (2003). How FIFA sold terrorist risk to the capital markets. *International Financial Law Review*, 22(12): 49-52.

Truñó, E. (1995) Barcelona: city of sport. In De Moragas and Botella (eds) *op. cit.*, pp. 43-56.

Tsui, F., Espino, J., Dato, V., Gesteland, P., Hutman, J., and Wagner, M. (2003) Data, network, and application: technical description of the Utah RODS Winter Olympic biosurveillance system. *Journal of the American Medical Informatics Association*, 10(5): 399–408.

Tufts University (1997a) Did politics ever affect the ancient games? Available at: www.olympics.tufts.edu/pol.html

Tufts University (1997b) Spectators at the Games. Available at: www.olympics. tufts.edu/ specs.html

Ueberhorst, H. (1976a) The International Olympic Academy: idea and reality. In Graham and Ueberhorst, *op. cit.*, pp. 50-52.

Ueberhorst, H. (1976b) Conclusion. In Graham and Ueberhorst, *op. cit.*, pp. 245-254.

Ueberhorst, H. (1996) Stockholm, 1912: the Games of the IVth Olympiad. In J. Findling and K. D. Pelle (eds) *Historical Dictionary of the Modern Olympic Movement*. Westport, CN: Greenwood Publishing, pp. 4–46.

Ueberroth, P. (1986) *Made in America*. New York: William Morrow.

Ungerleider, S. (2001) *Faust's Gold: Inside the East German Doping Machine*. New York: Thomas Dunne Books.

United Nations General Assembly (1968) *Official Records of the General Assembly, 34th Session 2 December, Supplement No. 22 (A/34/22)*. New York: UN, pp. 114-131.

United States Olympic Committee (1999) *Official website*, at: www.olympic-usa.org/games/

Vamakaris, F. (1997) Blood sports. *Inside Sport*, June, pp. 26-39.

Van Wynsberghe, R., and Ritchie, I. (1994) (Ir)Relevant rings: the symbolic consumption of the Olympic logo in postmodern media culture. In Barney and Meier, *op. cit.*, pp. 124-135.

Veal, A. J. (2002) *Leisure and Tourism Policy and Planning*. Wallingford, UK: CABI Publishing.

Veal, A. J. (2003) Tracking change: leisure participation and policy in Australia, 1985-2002. *Annals of Leisure Research*, 6(3): 246-78.

Veal, A. J., and Lynch, R. (2001) *Australian Leisure*. Sydney: Pearson Education.

Veal, A. J., and Toohey, K. (2007) *The Olympic Games: A Bibliography*. Online bibliography No. 2, School of Leisure, Sport and Tourism, University of Technology, Sydney, available at: www.business.uts.edu.au/lst/research/biblio graphies. html.

Veraros, N., Kasimati, N., & Dawson, P. (2004) The 2004 Olympic Games announcement and its effect on the Athens and Milan stock exchanges. *Applied Economic Letters*, 11(12): 749-753.

Verbruggen, H. (2003) The IOC, the Olympic Movement and host cities: a common legacy. In M. De Moragas, C. Kennett and N. Puig (eds) *The Legacy of the Olympic Games, 1984-2000*. Lausanne: International Olympic Committee, pp. 2–28.

Vignette Content Management Corporation (2004) *Athens 2004 Customer Story*. Austin, TX: Vignette Corporation, available at: www.vignette.com/us, under 'Customer Stories' (accessed April 2007).

Vigor, A., Mean, M., and Tims, C. (eds) (2004) *After the Gold Rush: A Sustainable Olympics for London*. London: Demos and Institute for Public Policy Research (available via www.demos.co.uk – accessed March 2007)

Vinokur, M. (1988) *More Than a Game: Sports and Politics (2ⁿᵈ edn)*. Westport, CN: Greenwood.

Voeltz, R. A. (1996) London, 1948: the Games of the XVth Olympiad. In J. Findling and K. D. Pelle (eds) *Historical Dictionary of the Modern Olympic Movement*. Westport, CN : Greenwood Publishing, pp. 103-108.

Vollers, M. (2006) *Lone Wolf: Eric Rudolph: Murder, Myth, and the Pursuit of an American Outlaw*. New York: Harper Collins.

Waitt, G. (2001) The Olympic spirit and civic boosterism: the Sydney 2000 Olympics. *Tourism Geographies*, 3(3): 249-78.

Walker, B. (1993) Olympics: $6m surplus or $3bn headache? *New Accountant*, Oct. 14, p.11.

Wallechinsky, D. (1992) *The Complete Book of the Olympics*. London: Aurum Press.

Walls, K. (2003) *Man Hunt – the Eric Rudolph Story*. New York: Global Authors Publications.

Walsh, M. (1992) Risible arithmetic on Olympics bid. *Sydney Morning* Herald, 23 Dec. p. 27.

Walsh, M. (1993a) Olympic backers fail to count the cost. *Sydney Morning Herald*, April 9, p. 25.

Walsh, M. (1993b) Olympic figures just do not add up. *Sydney Morning Herald*, June 25, p. 21.

Walsh, M. (1993c) First gold goes to cost concealment. *Sydney Morning Herald*, September 28, pp. 29, 32.

Walters, G. (2006) *Berlin Games: How Hitler Stole the Olympic Dream*. London: John Murray.

Wamsley, K. B. (1996) Calgary, 1988. In J. Findling and K. D. Pelle (eds) *Historical Dictionary of the Modern Olympic Movement*. Westport, CN: Greenwood Publishing , pp. 310-317.

Wamsley, K. B. (2004) Laying Olympism to rest. In J. Bale and M. K. Christensen (eds) *Post-Olympism? Questioning Sport in the Twenty-first Century*. Oxford: Berg, pp. 23–242.

Wamsley, K. B., and Heine, M. (1994) 'Calgary is not a cowboy town' - ideology, the Olympics and the politics of identity. In Barney and Meier, *op. cit.*, pp. 78-83.

Warning, K. (1980) *A Political History of the Modern Summer Olympic Games*. Masters thesis, California State University, Long Beach, CA.

Warning P., Toohey, K., and Ching, R. (2001) Mapping the discipline of the Olympic Games: an author co-citation analysis. In *Sports Information in the Third Millennium: 11th IASI World Conference*, Lausanne, Switzerland: IOC, pp. 339-345.

Watkins, G. T. (1997) *The Official Report of the Centennial Olympic Games, (3 Volumes)*. Atlanta, GA: Atlanta Committee for the Olympic Games/ Peachtree Publishers (available at: www.aafla.org/5va/reports_frmst.htm).

Welch, P. D. (1996a) Paris, 1924: the Games of the VIIIth Olympiad. In J. Findling and K. D. Pelle (eds) *Historical Dictionary of the Modern Olympic Movement*. Westport, CN: Greenwood Publishing, pp. 6–67.

Welch, P. D. (1996b) Chamonix, 1924. In J. Findling and K. D. Pelle (eds) *Historical Dictionary of the Modern Olympic Movement*. Westport, CN: Greenwood Publishing, pp. 223-227.

Welsh, P., and Costa M. (1994) A century of Olympic competition. In M. Costa and S. Guthrie (eds) *Women and Sport: Interdisciplinary Perspectives*. Champaign, IL: Human Kinetics, pp. 123-138.

Wendl, K. (1998) The route of friendship: a cultural/artistics event of the Games of the XIX Olympiad,in Mexico City, 1968. *Olympika*, 7: 113-134.

Wenn, S. R. (1991) A suitable policy of neutrality? FDR and the question of American participation in the 1936 Olympics. *International Journal of the History of Sport*, 8(3): 319-335.

Wenn, S. R. (1993) Lights! Camera! Little action: television, Avery Brundage and the 1956 Melbourne Olympics. *Sporting Traditions*, 10(1): 38-53.

Wenn, S. R. (1995) Growing pains: the Olympic Movement and television, 1996-1972. *Olympika*, 4: –22.

Wenn, S. R. (1996) Television rights negotiations and the 1976 Montreal Olympics. *Sport History Review*, 27(2): 11–138.

Wensing, E., and Bruce, T. (2003) Bending the rules. media representations off gender during an international sporting event. *International Review for the Sociology of Sport*, 38(4): 387-96.

Whannel, G. (1984) The television spectacular. In Tomlinson and Whannel, *op. cit.*, pp. 30-43.

Whannel, G. (1998) Individual stars and collective identities in media sport. In M. Roche (ed.) *Sport, Popular Culture and Identity*. Aachen: Meyer & Meyer: pp. 23-36.

Whannel, G. (2005) The five rings and the small screen: television, sponsorship, and the new media in the Olympic Movement. In K. B. Wamsley and K. Young (eds) *Global Olympics: Historical and Sociological Studies of the Modern Games*. Amsterdam: Elsevier, pp. 16–178.

Whisenant, W. A. (2003) Using biometrics for sport venue management in a post 9-11 era. *Facilities*, 21(5/6): 134-41.

Whitaker, B. (2001) The definition of terrorism. *The Guardian* (London), 7 May.

White House (2002) *Preparing for the World: Homeland Security and Winter Olympics*. Washington, DC: White House.

Whitson, D. (1998) Olympic sport, global media and cultural diversity. In Barney *et al.*, *op. cit.*, pp. –10.

Whitson, D., and Macintosh, D. (1993) Becoming a world-class city: hallmark events and sport franchises in the growth strategies of Western Canadian cities. *Sociology of Sport Journal*, 10(3): 22–40.

Whittaker, M. (1993) How green the Games?. *The Australian Magazine*, Dec. 1–12): 28-36.

Wilson, H. R. (1993) *The Golden Opportunity: A Study of the Romanian Manipulation of the Olympic Movement During the Boycott of the 1984 Los Angeles Olympic Games*. PhD dissertation, Ohio State University.

Wilson, H. R. (1994) The golden opportunity: Romania's political manipulation of the 1984 Los Angeles Olympic Games. *Olympika*, 3: 83-98.

Wilson, S. (2004) Athens Olympics draw record TV audiences. *USA Today*, 12 September.

Wilson, W. (ed.) (1990) *Gender Stereotyping in Televised Sport*. Los Angeles: Amateur Athletics Foundation of Los Angeles.

Wilson, W. (1996) Los Angeles, 1984: the Games of the XXIIIrd Olympiad. In J. Findling and K. D. Pelle (eds) *Historical Dictionary of the Modern Olympic Movement*. Westport, CN: Greenwood Publishing , pp. 69-177.

Wilson, W., and Derse, E. (eds) (2001) *Doping in Elite Sport: the Politics of Drugs in the Olympic Movement*. Champaign, IL: Human Kinetics.

Wood, C. (2005) Costly sporting. *Harvard International Review*,. 27(1): 1–12.

Woodhead, W. R. (1988) The legacy of the 1956 Melbourne Olympics. In EAAPP, *op. cit.*, pp. 133-170.

World Anti-Doping Agency (WADA) (2003) *World Anti-Doping Code*. Montréal: WADA, available at: www.wada-ama.org (accessed May 2007).

World Anti-Doping Agency (WADA) (nd) *World Anti-Doping Code: Standards: Prohibited List*. Montréal: WADA, available at: www.wada-ama.org (accessed May 2007).

World Wildlife Fund for Nature (2004) *Environmental Assessment of the Athens 2004 Olympic Games*. Gland, Switzerland: WWF. Available at: http://assets.panda.org (accessed March 2007).

Wright, G. (1978) The political economy of the Montreal Olympic Games. *Journal of Sport and Social Issues*, 2(1): 13-18.

Xu, D., He, C. and Ping, X. (2003) Beijing 2008: planning and organising the Olympic legacy. In M. De Moragas, C. Kennett and N. Puig (eds) *The Legacy of the Olympic Games, 1984-2000: International Symposium, Lausanne, 2002.* Lausanne: International Olympic Committee, 422-425.

Yarborough, C. R. (2000) *And They Call Them Games: An Inside View of the 1996 Olympics.* Macon, GA.: Mercer University Press.

Young, D. (1994) On the source of the Olympic Credo. *Olympika,* 3: 17-25.

Young, D. C. (1996) *The Modern Olympics: A Struggle for Revival.* Baltimore: Johns Hopkins University Press.

Zakus, D. (2005) The Olympic charter: a historical analysis of a hegemonic document for global sport. In D. Adair, B. Coe and N. Guoth (eds) *Beyond the Torch: Olympics and Australian Culture.* Australian Society for Sports History Studies No. 17. Melbourne: ASSH, (www.sporthistory.org), pp. 5-14.

Zilberman, V. (1994) 1994 Winter Olympics: major issues and trends. In F. I. Bell and G. H. Van Gyn (eds.), *Proceedings for the 10th Commonwealth and International Scientific Congress: Access to Active Living, 10-14 August 1994.* University of Victoria, Victoria, BC, pp. 538-542.

* Most IOC documents listed above can be found on the IOC website: www.olympic.org.

Index